Oracle 19c AutoUpgrade Best Practices

A Step-by-step Expert-led Database Upgrade Guide to Oracle 19c Using AutoUpgrade Utility

Sambaiah Sammeta

Sukumar Chillakuru

www.bpbonline.com

FIRST EDITION 2022

Copyright © BPB Publications, India

ISBN: 978-93-91030-902

LIMITS OF LIABILITY AND DISCLAIMER OF WARRANTY

To View Complete
BPB Publications Catalogue
Scan the QR Code:

Foreword

This book, written by Sambaiah Sammeta and Sukumar Chillakuru, and technically reviewed by Venkata Ravi Kumar Yenugula will cover most of the scenarios for upgrading the Oracle database from versions 11g, 12c, and 18c databases to Oracle version 19c. This book describes the best methods that can be used to upgrade the Oracle databases, and mainly deals with how to use the Oracle's 'AutoUpgrade' utility to upgrade the databases from the lower versions to Oracle 19c with minimal manual intervention. This book covers the various scenarios tested against the Real Application Clusters databases with Physical Standby databases, and also covers the test cases for both the non-container databases and the multitenant databases. This book also contains the various downgrade scenarios tested and explains both the benefits and pitfalls with each of the downgrade processes. The book is releasing at the right time as Oracle is strongly recommending to use the 'AutoUpgrade' tool to upgrade the Oracle databases. This book covers most of the scenarios that a DBA can find in a real time environment, and most importantly, each chapter is well tested and has hands-on steps, making this book an extremely helpful guide for the Oracle Database upgrade process.

I would like to congratulate Sambaiah Sammeta and Sukumar Chillakuru for this excellent book. It is a must have book for every DBA working on the Oracle Database upgrades.

—Sandesh Rao
Vice President
AIOPS and Machine Learning
– Autonomous Database
ORACLE Corporation

Dedicated to

My beloved Parents,
Sammeta Narayanamma
Sammeta Uma Maheshwar Rao

&

My wife Sujitha and daughter Sarayu

Thanks
— Sambaiah Sammeta

My beloved Parents,
Chillakuru Ramadevi
Chillakuru Rajagopal Reddy
&
My wife Anitha and daughter Akshara Reddy
&
My boss Satyendra Pasalapudi

Thanks
— Sukumar Chillakuru

About the Authors

Sambaiah Sammeta is an Oracle Certified Professional with 15+ years of experience, working as an Oracle Database administrator consultant. He provided the DBA support for various clients including the clients in the Banking sector, Retail, Health care services, automobile sector, and the Financial service verticals. He is an Oracle Cloud certified Architect professional (2020 and 2019), Oracle Autonomous database cloud certified, and Oracle database cloud certified specialist (2020). He planned and performed all the 11g to 19c and 12c to 19c database upgrades in a few of the major banking and Health care clients.

Sukumar Chillakuru is a DBA by profession with 14+ years of experience, currently working as a Database Architect at Infolob Solutions India Pvt Ltd. in Chennai. He has previously worked in reputed IT firms like Oracle, CTS, Apps Associates, and Megasoft. He is an expert in performing the Oracle Database Upgrades and Migrations. He is an Oracle certified Professional in Oracle database, Autonomous database, Oracle Cloud Infrastructure Architect Professional, and Oracle Goldengate Certified Specialist.

He developed his passion in technical writing and grabbed the opportunity to work with the **Oracle University** as an Author and Co-Author of five different courses on Oracle Cloud Infrastructure and Oracle Autonomous Database.

About the Reviewers

 **Yenugula Venkata Ravi Kumar (YVR)** is an Oracle ACE Director and Oracle Certified Master (OCM) with 24 years of experience in the banking, financial services, and insurance (BFSI) verticals. He has worked as a Vice President (DBA), Senior Database Architect, Senior Specialist Production DBA, and Oracle Engineered Systems Architect.

He is an Oracle Certified Professional (OCP) from Oracle 8i to Oracle 19c and also the Oracle Certified in Oracle Golden Gate, RAC, Performance Tuning, Oracle Cloud Infrastructure, Terraform, and Oracle Engineered Systems (Exadata, ZDLRA, and ODA), Certified in Oracle Security and Maximum Availability Architecture (MAA) Certified.

He has published 100+ articles, which includes Oracle Technology Network (OTN), OraWorld Magazine, UKOUG, OTech Magazine, and Redgate. Twice he has been an Oracle Speaker at Oracle Open World (OOW), IOUG 18, NYOUG, AIOUG, and Sangam. He has designed, architected, and implemented the core banking system (CBS) database for the central banks of two countries – India and Mahe, Seychelles.

Oracle Corporation USA has published his profile in their Oracle ACE Program as "Oracle ACE Director (ACED)". They have also published his profile in their Oracle's Certified Master (OCM) list and Spotlight on Success stories.

He has also co-authored a couple of books and for BPB Publications, he has co-authored the book, **Oracle Golden Gate with Microservices**.

 **K M Krishnakumar** is an Oracle OCI certified Architect, Autonomous Database Expert, Exadata specialist, Speaker (Oracle Open World), and Author. He has 16+ years of experience in Information Technology, where he has played various roles like Software Engineer, Senior Consultant, Principal DBA, Solution Engineer, and Cloud Architect. He holds a Master's degree in Business Administration from Anna University. He started working with the Oracle Technologies from 2004 as a DBA and has been with the Oracle Corporation for 11 years.

He has an extensive experience in Oracle Cloud database Infrastructure Design, setup, sizing and BoM preparation, deployment, administration, Migration, DR site creation, Backup/Recovery, and security. He travels with the customers from the PreBid phase till Migration. He is familiar with the EBS Lift and Shift migration to the Cloud environment. He has also been involved in the Beta testings of the Database upgrade, migrate, and patching, and has written quite a few Oracle knowledge articles. He has extensive knowledge in Database Upgrade/Migrate, Installation, patching, Migration, and DB upgrade using various methods including ZDM (zero Data Loss), Data Guard, RMAN, RAC, and Golden gate.

He has delivered presentations to customers through various channels including Oracle Open World SFO in 2018 and 2019, and also AIOUG Sangam. He is an active contributor for the MOS communities and other public forums.

He has co-authored "Oracle Database Upgrade and Migration Methods" and "Oracle High Availability, Disaster Recovery, and Cloud Services".

Acknowledgements

I never imagined that I would be writing a book with the help of a few wonderful people around me, but it did happen, and I got a chance to write this book. I strongly believe in the quote, "It's never too late to learn a new thing" and for me, writing this book is a new and wonderful thing which I loved to its core. This is my first book as a co-author and I want to thank each person mentioned below, without whom this would not have been possible.

I want to thank my parents (**Sammeta Uma Maheshwar Rao & Narayanamma**) for their numerous sacrifices without which I wouldn't be in this position. I want to thank my brother, **Shiva Shankar** and my sister, **Seshavati** who helped and encouraged me in taking the right decisions in my tough times and those decisions have helped me immensely.

A very special thanks to my wife, **Sujitha Chalamalasetty** and my daughter, **Sarayu Sammeta** for being very patient and supportive during my all the extra hours that I had to spend in writing this book. I owe you both princesses a very big time.

I would like to thank **Yenugula Venkata Ravi Kumar** for not only encouraging me to write this book but also for accepting our request to conduct a technical review of this book. I would also like to thank **K M Krishnakumar** for accepting technical review of this book. I want to thank my co-Author, **Sukumar Chillakuru** and publisher, BPB for giving me an opportunity to write my book. Special thanks to all the readers for selecting this book. We have included the most typical scenarios that we would see in the prod environments and tried to explain them in a simple and straightforward way. I hope that this document will help you in performing the Oracle database upgrades to 19c in your environments.

Lastly, I want to cherish this moment with my childhood friend, **Srinivas Kolipaka**. We both have a similar journey from our childhood to working as software engineers. We always feel great and happy about what we have achieved so far in our life. 'From repeating the 8th grade in school to writing the book' – this is a very special achievement for both of us and we enjoy it.

—*Sambaiah Sammeta*

Writing a book is harder than I thought and more worthwhile than I could have ever dreamed. None of this would have been possible without my boss **Satyendra Pasalapudi**. He inscribed my career as an Oracle DBA, He stood by me during every struggle and all my successes. That is true leadership in my opinion. He taught me discipline, tough love, manners, respect, and so much more that has helped me succeed in life.

I'm eternally grateful to **Yenugula Venkata Ravi Kumar**, who took extra care in motivating me, and introducing me as an AUTHOR to this world. Thank you for introducing me to this writing culture.

I also thank my parents (**Chillakuru Ramadevi and RajaGopal Reddy**) for their efforts and for fulfilling my needs at an early age and sustaining me in ways that I never knew was needed. I thank my darling daughter **Akshara** and my lovely wife **Anitha** for bearing the family responsibilities and giving me enough time to complete the book. So thankful to have you back in my life.

I would also like to thank **K M Krishnakumar** for doing technical review for this book.

My special thanks goes to my siblings, friends and all my well-wishers for their support and encouragement in my tough times.

Finally, a very special thanks to all those who have been a part of my journey: my co-Author Sammeta Sambaiah, Technical Reviewers Yenugula Venkata Ravi Kumar and K M Krishnakumar, Editors, Publishers, and the complete BPB team for achieving this success together.

— Sukumar Chillakuru

Preface

This book is for the Oracle Database Administrators (DBAs) and anyone who is interested in performing the upgrades on the older versions of Oracle database to Oracle 19c.

For a better understanding of this book, you must be aware of the following information:

- Oracle database concepts
- Your current Oracle database release
- Your operating system environment
- Database Multi-Tenant architecture
- Methods of the upgrade process
- Suitable upgrade process for your environment

This book covers the concepts of the Oracle's latest upgrade tool known as AutoUpgrade. This book discusses the various benefits of using the AutoUpgrade tool to upgrade the Oracle databases to 19c when compared to the other methods including DBUA and database parallel upgrade utility (dbupgrade). This book takes a practical approach and covers the most typical scenarios that are seen in the real time environments.

This book is divided into 7 chapters. Chapter 1 deals with the introduction to the Oracle database upgrades, whereas the rest of the six chapters deals with specific database upgrade scenarios, and each chapter has all the required steps for upgrading an Oracle database to 19c using AutoUpgrade covering a specific scenario. All the steps in each of the chapters are tested and presented with the output. This book also discusses the various database downgrade methods and has the steps for downgrading the database from 19c back to its source version. Lastly, this book also discusses the various issues (with solutions) that might occur during the Oracle database upgrade.

Chapter 1 covers the introduction to the Oracle database upgrade techniques. This chapter also includes the Oracle database certification matrix, databases upgrade methods, and a brief overview of the AutoUpgrade tool and the various stages that the tool processes through during the database upgrade.

Chapter 2 covers the Oracle database upgrade steps for upgrading a 11.2.0.4 non-container RAC database to 19C non-container RAC database using the Manual Upgrade method (dbupgrade) and also includes the steps to upgrade the physical standby database to 19c. This chapter also covers the steps to downgrade a 19c database back to its source version using the Oracle provided scripts.

Chapter 3 covers the Oracle database upgrade steps for upgrading a 11.2.0.4 non-container RAC database to 19c non-container RAC database using AutoUpgrade. This chapter also includes the steps to upgrade the 11.2.0.4 Physical standby database to 19c. This chapter also covers the steps for downgrading both the 19c Primary and the Physical standby databases to 11.2.0.4 using Flashback to a Guaranteed Restore point.

Chapter 4 covers the Oracle database upgrade steps from 12.1.0.2 non-CDB database to 19c as a pluggable database using AutoUpgrade and Database downgrade using Oracle provided scripts. This chapter also covers the steps to test the downgrade using the RMAN preupgrade backup.

Chapter 5 covers the steps to upgrade an Oracle 12c container RAC database along with all its pluggable database to 19c. This chapter also covers the steps to upgrade a single 18c pluggable database to 19c.

Chapter 6 covers the steps for upgrading and converting a 12.1.0.2 non-container RAC database to 19c using a single AutoUpgrade command. This chapter also discusses the possible option to downgrade a 19c converted pluggable database back to 12.1.0.2.

Chapter 7 covers the steps for upgrading multiple databases running from multiple Oracle versions to 19c using a **single AutoUpgrade command**. It basically has the steps to upgrade 11g, 12c, and 18c RAC databases to 19c database in a single operation.

Downloading the coloured images:

Please follow the link to download the
Coloured Images of the book:

https://rebrand.ly/06974e

Errata

We take immense pride in our work at BPB Publications and follow best practices to ensure the accuracy of our content to provide with an indulging reading experience to our subscribers. Our readers are our mirrors, and we use their inputs to reflect and improve upon human errors, if any, that may have occurred during the publishing processes involved. To let us maintain the quality and help us reach out to any readers who might be having difficulties due to any unforeseen errors, please write to us at :

errata@bpbonline.com

Your support, suggestions and feedbacks are highly appreciated by the BPB Publications' Family.

Did you know that BPB offers eBook versions of every book published, with PDF and ePub files available? You can upgrade to the eBook version at www.bpbonline.com and as a print book customer, you are entitled to a discount on the eBook copy. Get in touch with us at :

business@bpbonline.com for more details.

At **www.bpbonline.com**, you can also read a collection of free technical articles, sign up for a range of free newsletters, and receive exclusive discounts and offers on BPB books and eBooks.

BPB is searching for authors like you

If you're interested in becoming an author for BPB, please visit **www.bpbonline.com** and apply today. We have worked with thousands of developers and tech professionals, just like you, to help them share their insight with the global tech community. You can make a general application, apply for a specific hot topic that we are recruiting an author for, or submit your own idea.

The code bundle for the book is also hosted on GitHub at **https://github.com/bpbpublications/Oracle-19c-AutoUpgrade-Best-Practices**. In case there's an update to the code, it will be updated on the existing GitHub repository.

We also have other code bundles from our rich catalog of books and videos available at **https://github.com/bpbpublications**. Check them out!

PIRACY

If you come across any illegal copies of our works in any form on the internet, we would be grateful if you would provide us with the location address or website name. Please contact us at **business@bpbonline.com** with a link to the material.

If you are interested in becoming an author

If there is a topic that you have expertise in, and you are interested in either writing or contributing to a book, please visit **www.bpbonline.com**.

REVIEWS

Please leave a review. Once you have read and used this book, why not leave a review on the site that you purchased it from? Potential readers can then see and use your unbiased opinion to make purchase decisions, we at BPB can understand what you think about our products, and our authors can see your feedback on their book. Thank you!

For more information about BPB, please visit **www.bpbonline.com**.

Table of Contents

CHAPTER 1
Introduction to Database Upgrades

As the lower versions of the databases are getting expired in terms of extended support, Oracle recommends their customers to upgrade their databases to Oracle 19c to run their environments by keeping the database support with the world class database technical experts (Oracle Support).

With Oracle Support, we will know for how long your Oracle database products are being supported. The lifetime support policy gives you the access to get the technical experts' assistance whenever required, for as long as you have a valid license of your Oracle products. The Oracle Support consists of three support stages – premier support, extended support, and sustaining support. It provides you extreme value with rights to major product releases, so that you can take full advantage of the technology and product enhancement to help your business continue moving forward together.

You will enjoy unremitting the peace of mind by keeping your production databases under support with valid licensing, knowing that we'll always be there to support your business. When it's time to upgrade your database, you will have rights to the major product releases, so that you can benefit from the Oracle's technology leadership and keep pace with the world of business.

The following figure is a pictorial representation of the lifetime support policy of the Oracle database:

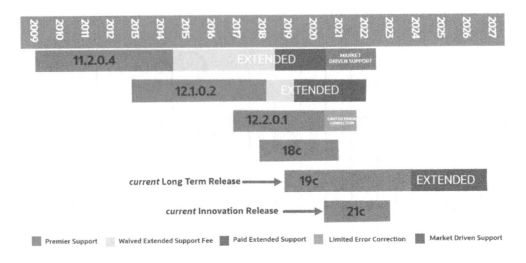

Figure 1.1: *Database Releases and Support Timelines*

Please refer to *'Release Schedule of Current Database Releases (Doc ID 742060.1)'* for more details and for the latest updates. This chapter provides an overview on upgrading an existing lower version of the Oracle databases starting from the 11.2.0.4 release to Oracle 19c using the AutoUpgrade utility.

Structure

In this chapter, we will cover the following topics:

- Introduction to the Oracle database upgrade
- Benefits of upgrading the database to 19C
- Oracle database 19c Direct upgrade – supported releases
- Oracle database 19c upgrade methods
- What is AutoUpgrade?
- Overview of the AutoUpgrade stages
- Overview of the AutoUpgrade stage operations and states
- AutoUpgrade processing modes
- Understanding the non-CDB to PDB upgrades with AutoUpgrade

Objective

After studying this chapter, you will be able to understand the database upgrade methods and have a quick overview of the AutoUpgrade utility and its uses.

Introduction to the Oracle database upgrade

As an Oracle Database Administrator, we are familiar with the terminology called Upgrading and Migrating the Databases. Before getting into the actual technical details, we would like to recall the differences between these two terminologies, which are as follows:

- **Database upgrade**: Upgrading an existing Oracle database into a higher release means that the data dictionary for the database is upgraded to the new release. During the database upgrade, we would not change or move the customer data which is inside the database.

- **Database migration**: This means that moving the data from one database to another in a new operating system or a new hardware or to a new character set. Migration does not include the database upgrade and it should be separately handled after the database migration is completed successfully.

Benefits of upgrading the database to 19c

Oracle has released a couple of new features in the Oracle database 19c; the following is a list of those that are majorly used in the daily DBA's activities:

- Automated installation, configuration, and patching

- AutoUpgrade and database utilities

- Database in-memory wait on populate

- Resource manager automatically enabled for database in-memory

- Memoptimized Rowstore Fast Ingest

- **Automatic Database Diagnostic Monitor (ADDM)** Support for **Pluggable Databases (PDBs)**

- Resource manager automatically enabled for database in-memory

- High-frequency SQL Plan Management Evolve Advisor Task

- Workload capture and replay in a PDB

- Automated PDB Relocation

- Zero-Downtime Oracle Grid Infrastructure Patching

- Automated transaction draining for Oracle Grid Infrastructure upgrades

- Oracle restart patching and upgrading

- Many other security features

Oracle database 19c direct upgrade – supported releases

We can perform a direct upgrade of the Oracle database to the new release from the following releases (refer *figure 1.2*):

- Oracle 11g (11.2.0.4)

- Oracle 12c (12.1.0.2)

- Oracle 12c (12.2.0.1)

- Oracle 18c

In case we want to upgrade the earlier database to the 11.2.0.4 release, then we cannot directly upgrade to the higher releases – 12c, 18c, or 19c. In such cases, we need to upgrade the database to the intermediate release before upgrading to 19c.

Take a look at the following example:

If you are planning to upgrade a database from release 9.2.0.8, then you must first upgrade to a sequence of intermediate Oracle database releases, i.e., upgrade from release 9.2.0.8 to release 11.2.0.4, and then upgrade from release 11.2.0.4 to Oracle 19c.

If you are planning to upgrade a database from release 10.1.0.5, 10.2.0.2, 10.2.0.3, 10.2.0.4, or 10.2.0.5, then you must upgrade the database to release 11.2.0.4 or 12.1.0.2. If you are planning to upgrade a database from release 11.2.0.2 or 11.1.0.7, then you must upgrade to the intermediate release – Oracle database 11g release 2 (11.2.0.4) – which is supported for direct upgrade to the Oracle database 19c.

Each and every case can be different from that of the examples provided here, as we have multiple available versions of the Oracle databases.

Figure 1.2 represents the pictorial representation of the supported releases for the Oracle 19c Database direct upgrade.

Figure 1.2: Oracle 19c Database direct upgrade – supported releases

Oracle database release with support dates

The following table illustrates the support date schedule for each Oracle database release:

Release	GA Date	Premier support ends	Extended support ends	Sustaining support ends
8.1.7	Sep 2000	Dec 2004	Dec 2006	Indefinite
9.2	Jul 2002	Jul 2007	Jul 2010	Indefinite
10.1	Jan 2004	Jan 2009	Jan 2012	Indefinite
10.2	Jul 200	5Jul 2010	Jul 2013	Indefinite
11.1	Aug 2007	Aug 2012	Aug 2015	Indefinite
11.2	Sep 2009	Jan 2015	Dec 2020	Indefinite
12.1(EE)	Jun 2013	Jul 2018	Jul 2022	Indefinite
12.1(SE)	Jun 2013	Aug 2016	Not Available	Indefinite
12.1(SE1)	Jun 2013	Aug 2016	Not Available	Indefinite
12.1 2(SE2)	Sep 2015	Jul 2018	Jul 2022	Indefinite
12.2.0.1	Mar 2017	Nov 30,2020	Not Available	Indefinite
18c	Jul 2018	Jun 2021	Not Available	Indefinite
19c	Apr 2019	Apr 2024	Apr 2027	Indefinite

Table 1.1: Oracle database release with support dates

Please refer to 'My Oracle Support (MOS)' (https://www.oracle.com/us/support/library/lsp-tech-chart-069290.pdf) for more details and for the latest updates.

Oracle database 19c upgrade methods

Oracle offers several methods to upgrade your database; the following are a few methods recommended by Oracle for upgrading the existing database:

- **Database Upgrade Assistant (DBUA)**: DBUA is the GUI utility which can be launched during the database installation and upgrade with the Oracle Universal Installer. This utility automates the upgrade processes by performing all the upgrade steps automatically, including the steps to upgrade the time zone. This method is fast and efficient and requires little manual intervention.

- **Manual upgrade**: Manual upgrade is a command-line utility to enable the Oracle database upgrades using the Shell scripts. Oracle provides multiple upgrade and downgrade scripts that we can use for upgrading and downgrading an Oracle database. If we go with this approach, we will have to perform all the steps manually, which includes the time zone upgrade with the Oracle provided scripts, update the oratab entries, and upgrade the Oracle clusterware information, if we are upgrading an Oracle RAC database.

- **Export/import**: We can create a new database and then use the Oracle `datapump` utility (`expdb/impdb`) to migrate the data from the lower version to the new higher version database. This process is very tedious as it will include many manual steps which includes the steps for pre-creating the tablespaces, roles, profiles, triggers, and a few other steps.

- **Oracle GoldenGate**: We can also use the Oracle Golden Gate to upgrade the database with minimum or zero downtime. For this method, we need to create a new database in the higher version, configure the Oracle Golden Gate setup between the source and the new database, perform the initial load in the new database, and then setup the data capture database sync from the source database to the new database and keep the new database in sync with the source database. During the cut-over day, we can make sure that the new database is in sync with the source database, stop the source database, and start using the new database. Please note that we will need a license to use the Oracle Golden Gate software.

AutoUpgrade

The *AutoUpgrade* utility is a new upgrade utility which allows you to upgrade the Oracle databases with minimal manual intervention. The AutoUpgrade tool is designed in such a way that when it is run, it not only identifies the issues before the database upgrade but also fixes them and then performs the database upgrade and runs any post upgrade steps. The AutoUpgrade tool can upgrade both the single instances and the cluster databases. It also supports both the **non-container database (non-cdb)** and the **container database (cdb)** upgrades (refer to *figure 1.3*). The AutoUpgrade tool supports upgrading a non-cdb database to a **pluggable database (pdb)** using one single command and supports all the operating systems. Take a look at the following diagram to understand this further:

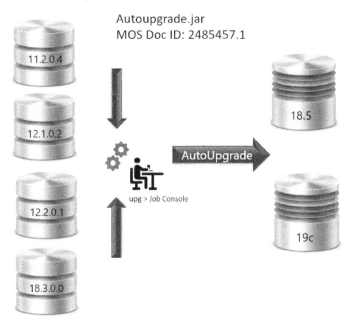

Figure 1.3: *Database Upgrade supports from Non-CDB to CDB*

For performing the database upgrade, *AutoUpgrade* processes through the various stages and processing modes and performs all the upgrade related activities.

Overview of AutoUpgrade stages

The following are the various stages and processing modes which the AutoUpgrade tool goes through:

- **Setup**: At this stage, the AutoUpgrade utility job manager creates a setup at the initial stages.

- **Pre-upgrade**: At this stage, AutoUpgrade performs a system check, and based on your current system configuration, determines its readiness for the upgrade.

- **Pre-checks**: At this stage, AutoUpgrade analyzes your source Oracle home to determine if the database meets the requirements for the upgrade.

- **Guaranteed Restore Point (GRP)**: At this stage, AutoUpgrade creates a GRP before starting the upgrade process. This option is only available for the Oracle Database Enterprise Edition releases. Even though AutoUpgrade creates a GRP by default, Oracle highly recommends that you perform a backup before starting your upgrade.

- **Pre-fixups**: At this stage, AutoUpgrade performs the pre-upgrade fixups before starting the database upgrade. For example, this is the stage at which AutoUpgrade gathers the dictionary statistics on the source database Oracle home.

- **Drain**: At this stage, AutoUpgrade shuts down the database.

- **DBupgrade**: At this stage, AutoUpgrade performs the upgrade, and compiles any invalid objects that are found after the upgrade completes.

- **Post-checks**: At this stage, AutoUpgrade performs the checks on the upgraded target database Oracle home before starting the post upgrade fixups.

- **Post-fixups**: At this stage, AutoUpgrade performs processing of the post upgrade fixups, such as upgrading the time zone.

- **Post-upgrade**: At this stage, AutoUpgrade copies or merges the source database Oracle home configuration files (`tnsnames.ora`, `sqlnet.ora`, and other files) to the target database Oracle home.

Overview of the AutoUpgrade stage operations and states

In AutoUpgrade, *operation* defines the actions performed during the stages, and *state* specifies the status of a stage operation.

Understanding the operation messages

There are the following two types of internal phase messages, also called as the operation messages, which describes what is happening during an AutoUpgrade state:

- **Preparing**: This is just an informative message, where no action is required to perform when you see it. For example, an AutoUpgrade instance is being created, initialized, or called, in preparation for completing an AutoUpgrade stage.

- **Executing**: AutoUpgrade is in the process of performing the main workflow of a stage. This is an informational message. There is no action for you to perform.

Understanding the state messages

There are four different state messages that indicate the status of the current workflow of the stage for which the message is displayed. They are listed as follows:

- **Aborted**: AutoUpgrade stopped performing the stage workflow, in response to a user request.

- **Error**: An error was encountered while the stage workflow was being performed. We can review the cause of the error.

- **Finished**: AutoUpgrade successfully completed the workflow for the stage.

- **Running**: AutoUpgrade is performing the stage workflow.

AutoUpgrade processing modes

AutoUpgrade can be run in multiple modes which include Analyze, Fixup, Deploy, and Upgrade, and each of these modes goes through some predefined stages that runs the predefined tasks and performs the database upgrade. Take a look at the following diagram for a pictorial representation of the AutoUpgrade processing modes:

Figure 1.4: AutoUpgrade processing modes

The following are the high-level details for each of these modes and the syntax for running the *AutoUpgrade* commands:

- **Analyze**: This AutoUpgrade processing mode (Analyze) checks your database to see if it is ready for upgrade:

```
$ORACLE_HOME/jdk8/bin/java -jar autoupgrade.jar -config <config_
file.txt> -mode analyze
```

- **Fixup**: This AutoUpgrade processing mode analyzes your database, and performs the fixups of the items that must be corrected before you can perform an upgrade:

```
$ORACLE_HOME/jdk8/bin/java -jar autoupgrade.jar -config <config_
file.txt> -mode fixups
```

- **Deploy**: This AutoUpgrade processing mode performs the actual upgrade of the database, and performs any pending fixups:

```
$ORACLE_HOME/jdk8/bin/java -jar autoupgrade.jar -config <config_
file.txt>  -mode deploy
```

- **Upgrade**: This AutoUpgrade processing mode enables you to upgrade the target database Oracle home, in cases where you do not have access to the source database Oracle home:

```
$ORACLE_HOME/jdk8/bin/java -jar autoupgrade.jar -config <config_
file.txt> -mode upgrade
```

The detailed steps in each process will be explained with all the phases in *Chapter 3, Upgrading Oracle Database from 11.2.0.4 to 19.9.0 (Using AutoUpgrade)*.

Understanding the non-CDB to PDB upgrades with AutoUpgrade

By using AutoUpgrade, in a single operation, you can convert and upgrade a non-CDB to a PDB in a new CDB, or upgrade and then convert a non-CDB database to a PDB in a pre-existing CDB, as shown in *figure 1.5*.

Oracle Database 19c is the terminal release in which the non-CDB Oracle Database architecture is supported. Oracle strongly recommends that you move to using **pluggable databases** (**PDBs**). When you migrate your database from the non-CDB architecture to the CDB architecture in Oracle Database 19c, Oracle offers you up to three user configurable PDBs in a **container database** (**CDB**), without requiring a multitenant license. If you need to configure four or more PDBs, then a multitenant license is required.

Figure 1.5: represents the pictorial representation of upgrading and converting a non-CDB to PDB using AutoUpgrade:

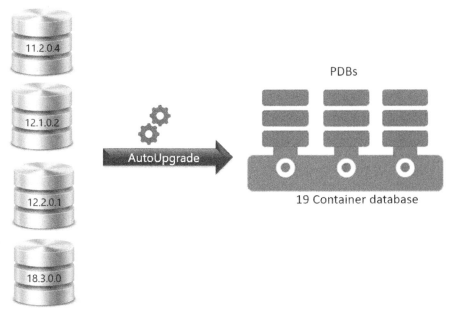

Figure 1.5: Upgrading and Converting a Non-CDB to PDB using AutoUpgrade

Conclusion

In this chapter, you got a good idea about the various methods of the Oracle Database upgrades, including a new feature called **AutoUpgrade** which has multiple stages, states, stage operations, and processing modes. We will have detailed instructions on the multiple AutoUpgrade scenarios, in the following chapters.

CHAPTER 2
Upgrading Oracle Database from 11.2.0.4 to 19.9.0 Using dbupgrade (Manual)

Introduction

In this chapter, we will upgrade the Oracle database from Oracle 11g (11.2.0.4) to Oracle 19c (19.9.0) using the Oracle parallel upgrade utility known as **dbupgrade**. This utility is a shell command which internally starts the catctl.pl script and upgrades the Oracle database components in parallel. This is a manual method and we will be running all the stages like pre-upgrade, upgrade, and post-upgrade steps manually. We will also upgrade the timezone version using the Oracle provided scripts. We have included the steps to downgrade the database from Oracle 19c (19.9.0) to Oracle 11g (11.2.0.4) using the *flashback to restore point* method later in this chapter.

Structure

In this chapter, we will cover the following topics:

- High level steps required for performing the Oracle database upgrade from version 11.2.0.4 to 19.9.0.0

- The source and target setup environments used to demonstrate the database upgrade

- The pre-requisite steps required for the database upgrade

- The Oracle parallel upgrade utility, **dbupgrade**.
- Performing the pre-upgrade steps and addressing any pre-upgrade issues
- Performing the database upgrade from version 11.2.0.4 to 19.9.0.0 using the Oracle parallel upgrade utility, **dbupgrade**
- Upgrade of the timezone version using the Oracle provided scripts
- Validation of the database upgrade
- Discuss the downgrade methods that can be used to downgrade the Oracle database from the upgraded version back to the source version
- Performing the database downgrade from 19.9.0.0 to 11.2.0.4
- Downgrade the timezone version back to the 11.2.0.4 version
- A few known issues that can occur during the database upgrade or the database downgrade

Objective

After reading this chapter, you will be able to upgrade your Oracle database from version 11.2.0.4 to 19c using the **dbupgrade** utility. You will also get familiar with the downgrade steps which will help you, in case you want to downgrade the database back from 19c to 11.2.0.4.

An overview of database upgrade

A picture is worth a thousand words; so *figure 2.1* is a high-level representation of our source database versions and the target database version after the database is upgraded using the Oracle provided script, **dbupgrade**:

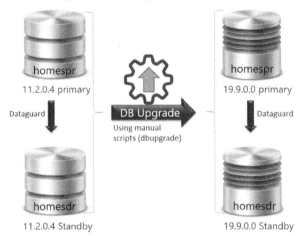

Figure 2.1: *Upgrade process from 11.2.0.4 Non-CDB to 19.9 Non-CDB (Manual approach)*

High-level steps performed as part of this upgrade activity

The following are the steps to be performed as part of the database upgrade activity:

1. Take a full backup of the primary database.

2. Enable the flashback feature in the primary source and the physical standby database.

3. Set the fast recovery area size to a higher value in both, the primary and the physical standby database.

4. Ensure that the physical standby database is in sync with the primary database.

5. Disable the **dataguard** broker in both the primary and the physical standby database.

6. Run the **preupgrade.jar** file in the primary database and fix any required and recommended issues as suggested by the pre-upgrade script.

7. Shutdown the physical standby database.

8. Upgrade the primary database.

9. Upgrade the timezone version.

10. Perform any post-upgrade steps, including upgrading the cluster configuration of the database using the **srvctl** command and updating the **/etc/oratab** entries to point to Oracle 19c.

11. Upgrade the physical standby database with the migrate redo data that it receives from the primary database.

12. Perform any post-upgrade steps for the physical standby database.

We have created the following two scripts which we can use to check the current database configuration and the standby database lag. We will be using these scripts throughout this chapter.

Script-1: This script will pull the current database details like, the mode and the role of the database:

```
[oracle@virtual-19crac1] cat /home/oracle/rac_database_info.sql

SQL> set lines 200
SQL> col DATABASE_HOST for a30;
SQL> col HOST_NAME for a15;
SQL> col DATABASE_ROLE for a10
```

```
SQL> col OPEN_MODE for a10
SQL> col STARTUP_TIME for a20
SQL> SELECT i.HOST_NAME "DATABASE_HOST" ,i.INSTANCE_NAME "DB_NAME",
d.DATABASE_ROLE " DATABASE_ROLE", d.OPEN_MODE " OPEN_MODE ", STARTUP_
TIME from GV$DATABASE d, gv$instance i where i.INST_ID=d.INST_ID;
```

Script-2: This script will check the current lag on the standby database and display the standby database role and mode info as well:

```
[oracle@virtual-19crac1] cat /home/oracle/standby_database_lag.sql
```

```
SQL> set lines 200
SQL> col DATABASE_HOST for a30;
SQL> col HOST_NAME for a15;
SQL> col DATABASE_ROLE for a10
SQL> col OPEN_MODE for a10
SQL> col STARTUP_TIME for a20
SQL> SELECT i.HOST_NAME "DATABASE_HOST" ,i.INSTANCE_NAME "DB_NAME",
d.DATABASE_ROLE " DATABASE_ROLE", d.OPEN_MODE " OPEN_MODE ", STARTUP_
TIME from GV$DATABASE d, gv$instance i  where i.INST_ID=d.INST_ID;
```

```
SQL> select inst_id,process, status, thread#, sequence#, block#, blocks
from gv$managed_standby where process='MRP0';
```

```
SQL> select a.thread#, (select max (sequence#)
```

from v$archived_log where archived='YES' and thread#=a.thread#) archived, max(a.sequence#) applied, (select max(sequence#) from v$archived_log where archived='YES' and thread#=a.thread#)-max(a.sequence#)gap from v$archived_log a where a.applied='YES' group by a.thread# order by thread#;

Environments used for the upgrade

The following are the source and the target database environments that are used to demonstrate the database upgrade.

Setting up the source environment

We have the primary database, which is a 2-node RAC database, and a physical standby database, which is also a 2-node RAC database. The primary database environment is Oracle 11g (11.2.0.4) database binaries being installed, and the Oracle home being patched with the April 2020 **Patch Set Update** (**PSU**). The **Grid Infrastructure** (**GI**) is Oracle 19c (19.9) in the primary database and the physical standby database. Please note that this book completely deals with the database upgrades with different versions.

The primary database version and the patch set is as shown as follows:

```
Cluster nodes        : virtual-19crac1
                       virtual-19crac2
OS version           : Oracle Enterprise Linux 7.1 64 bit
Oracle Home          : /u01/app/oracle/product/11.2.0.4/db_1
Database Version     : 11.2.0.4 with April 2020 Database Patch Set Update
Grid Version         : 19.9.0

[oracle@virtual-19crac1 ]$ export ORACLE_HOME=/u01/app/oracle/
product/11.2.0.4/db_1
[oracle@virtual-19crac1 ]$ export PATH=$ORACLE_HOME/bin:$PATH

[oracle@virtual-19crac1 ]$ $ORACLE_HOME/OPatch/opatch lspatches
30670774; Database Patch Set Update: 11.2.0.4.200414 (30670774)
29938455; OCW Patch Set Update: 11.2.0.4.191015 (29938455)
OPatch succeeded.
```

The primary database name is **homespr**, and the following are its RAC instances:

```
SQL> @/home/oracle/rac_database_info.sql
DATABASE_HOST      DB_NAME       DATABASE_ROLE      OPEN_MODE   STARTUP_TIME
----------------   ------------  ----------------   ---------   -----------
virtual-19crac1    homespr1      PRIMARY            READ WRITE  10-MAR-21
virtual-19crac2    homespr2      PRIMARY            READ WRITE  10-MAR-21
```

The Physical Standby database version and the patch set is shown as follows:

(The Physical standby database environment is the same version as the primary database, that is, Oracle 11g (11.2.0.4) database binaries patched with April 2020 **Patch Set Update (PSU)**)

```
Cluster nodes        : virtual-dr-19crac1
                       virtual-dr-19crac2
OS version           : Oracle Enterprise Linux 7.1 64 bit
Oracle Home          : /u01/app/oracle/product/11.2.0.4/db_1
Database Version     : 11.2.0.4 with April 2020 Database Patch Set Update
Grid Version         : 19.9.0
[oracle@virtual-dr-19crac1 ~]$ export ORACLE_HOME=/u01/app/oracle/
product/11.2.0.4/db_1

[oracle@virtual-dr-19crac1 ~]$ export PATH=$ORACLE_HOME/bin:$PATH
[oracle@virtual-dr-19crac1 ~]$ $ORACLE_HOME/OPatch/opatch lspatches
30670774; Database Patch Set Update : 11.2.0.4.200414 (30670774)
29938455; OCW Patch Set Update : 11.2.0.4.191015 (29938455) OPatch
succeeded.
```

The Physical standby database is **homesdr** and the following are its RAC instances:

```
SQL> @/home/oracle/rac_database_info.sql
DATABASE_HOST        DB_NAME     DATABASE_ROLE      OPEN_MODE   STARTUP_TIME
-----------------    --------    ---------------    --------    -----------
virtual-dr-19crac1   homesdr1    PHYSICAL STANDBY   MOUNTED     10-MAR-21
virtual-dr-19crac2   homesdr2    PHYSICAL STANDBY   MOUNTED     10-MAR-21
```

Setting up the target environment setup

We installed Oracle 19c (19.3.0) on both the primary and the physical standby database servers and applied the October 2020 PSU. If you want to use the latest patch set, check, and download the latest patch set from the **My Oracle Support (MOS)**.

The target primary database binary version and its patch set is given as follows:

```
Cluster nodes       : virtual-19crac1
                      virtual-19crac2
OS version          : Oracle Enterprise Linux 7.1 64 bit
Oracle Home         : /u01/app/oracle/product/19c/db_1
Database Version    : 19.3.0.0 with October 2020 Database Bundle Patch
Grid Version        : 19.9.0

[oracle@virtual-19crac1 ~]$ $ORACLE_HOME/OPatch/opatch lspatches
31771877;Database Release Update : 19.9.0.0.201020 (31771877)
29585399;OCW RELEASE UPDATE 19.3.0.0.0 (29585399)
OPatch succeeded.
```

The target physical standby database binary version and its patch set is given as follows:

```
Cluster nodes       : virtual-dr-19crac1
                      virtual-dr-19crac2
OS version          : Oracle Enterprise Linux 7.1 64 bit
Oracle Home         : /u01/app/oracle/product/19c/db_1
Database Version    : 19.3.0.0 with October 2020 Database Bundle Patch
Grid Version        : 19.9.0

[oracle@virtual-dr-19crac1 ~]   $ORACLE_HOME/OPatch/opatch lspatches
31771877;Database Release Update : 19.9.0.0.201020 (31771877)
29585399;OCW RELEASE UPDATE 19.3.0.0.0 (29585399)
OPatch succeeded.
```

Pre-requisites of the database upgrade

Check some of the pre-requisites and a few upfront tasks that we can perform before planning and starting the database upgrade.

Perform full backup of primary source database

Before staring any database upgrade activity, always take a **FULL** level 0 **RMAN** backup of the source database. The following is the sample **rman** script that we can use to take a full level 0 backup of the primary source database; you can use your scripts that work for your environment:

```
RMAN >
run
{
allocate channel ch1 device type disk format '/u01/19cupgrade/DATA_
L0_%d_%Y%M%D_%s-%p-%t';
allocate channel ch2 device type disk format '/u01/19cupgrade/DATA_
L0_%d_%Y%M%D_%s-%p-%t';
allocate channel ch3 device type disk format '/u01/19cupgrade/DATA_
L0_%d_%Y%M%D_%s-%p-%t';
allocate channel ch4 device type disk format '/u01/19cupgrade/DATA_
L0_%d_%Y%M%D_%s-%p-%t';
backup incremental level 0 database plus archivelog TAG='FULL_BACKUP_B4_
UPGRADE' format '/u01/19cupgrade/DATA_L0_%d_%Y%M%D_%s-%p-%t';
backup tag 'CONTROL_BACKUP_B4_UPGRADE' current controlfile format '/
u01/19cupgrade/DATA_CONTROL_%d_%Y%M%D_%s-%p-%t';
release channel ch1;
release channel ch2;
release channel ch3;
release channel ch4;
}
```

Enable the flashback feature in the primary source database

Ensure that the flashback feature is enabled in both the primary source and the physical standby database. We need the flashback to be enabled for creating a **guaranteed restore point** (**GRP**) before starting the upgrade process. We can use the guaranteed restore to flashback the database to the previous version in case we see any issues during or after the database upgrade.

Login to the primary source database and enable the flashback feature using the following SQL statement:

```
SQL> alter database flashback on;
Database altered.
```

Ensure that the flashback feature is enabled successfully using the following SQL statement:

```
SQL> select name, db_unique_name, database_role, log_mode, force_
logging, flashback_on from gv$database;
```

NAME	DB_UNIQUE_NAME	DATABASE_ROLE	LOG_MODE	FORCE_LOGGING	FLASHBACK_ON
HOMESPR	homespr	PRIMARY	ARCHIVELOG	YES	YES
HOMESPR	homespr	PRIMARY	ARCHIVELOG	YES	YES

Enable Flashback feature in physical standby database

In order to enable the flashback feature in the physical standby database, we have to cancel the **managed recovery process (MRP)** and then enable the flashback feature and re-start the MRP.

Login to the physical standby database and run the following SQL statements:

```
SQL> alter database recover managed standby database cancel;
Database altered.
```

```
SQL> alter database flashback on;
Database altered.
```

```
SQL> alter database recover managed standby database using current
logfile disconnect;
Database altered.
```

Ensure that the flashback feature is enabled successfully using the following SQL statement in the physical standby database:

```
SQL> select name, db_unique_name, database_role, log_mode, force_
logging, flashback_on from gv$database;
```

NAME	DB_UNIQUE_NAME	DATABASE_ROLE	LOG_MODE	FORCE_LOGGING	FLASHBACK_ON
HOMESPR	homesdr	PHYSICAL STANDBY	ARCHIVELOG	YES	YES
HOMESPR	homesdr	PHYSICAL STANDBY	ARCHIVELOG	YES	YES

Ensure enough space is available in Fast Recovery Area (FRA)

Ensure that we have enough free space in the **Fast Recovery Area** (**FRA**) and set the recovery destination size to enough as we need the recovery logs until we change the compatible parameter to 19.0.0 after upgrade. Also, the FRA will store all the flashback logs, which we would need, in case we have to downgrade the Oracle database back to Oracle 11g (11.2.0.4) after the upgrade using the **flashback** method. Check and set the **db_recovery_file_dest_size** parameter to a higher value. We need to set this parameter to a higher value in both the primary and the physical standby database (that is, 11g databases). In our case, as you can see in the following section, we are setting this parameter value to 20G:

```
SQL> show parameter recovery

NAME                                    TYPE        VALUE
--------------------------------------- ----------- ----------------
db_recovery_file_dest                   string      +DATA1
db_recovery_file_dest_size              big integer 5G
recovery_parallelism                    integer     0


SQL> alter system set db_recovery_file_dest_size=20G scope=both sid='*';
System altered.


SQL> show parameter recovery

NAME                                    TYPE        VALUE
--------------------------------------- ----------- ----------------
db_recovery_file_dest                   string      +DATA1
db_recovery_file_dest_size              big integer 20G
recovery_parallelism                    integer     0
```

Upgrade of Application Express (APEX)

If the source database has the Oracle **Application Express** (**APEX**) installed, we can upgrade it upfront as the APEX upgrade does not depend on the database upgrade. We can refer the following MOS note for the APEX upgrade. We can also do this step upfront to save time during the actual upgrade process.

For more details and the latest updates, refer to *Master Note for Oracle Application Express (APEX) Upgrades (Doc ID 1088970.1).*

Purge recyclebin

Check the **recyclebin** and purge it. In some cases, purging of the recycle bin might take more time if the recycle bin has too many objects in it. It's always a good idea to purge the recycle bin before starting the upgrade process, as this can significantly reduce the overall time taken for the database upgrade. It might be a good idea if we can check this well ahead of time and purge the **recyclebin** in the source primary database. If the **recyclebin** is having too many objects, sometimes it might even take at least a couple of hours to get them purged, which will significantly increase the downtime required for the database upgrade.

Check the object count in the **recyclebin**, using the following command:

```
SQL> select count(*)  from recyclebin;
```

Purge the recycle bin using the following SQL statement:

```
SQL> purge dba_recyclebin;
DBA Recyclebin purged.
```

Re-check the object count in the **recyclebin**, using the following command:

```
SQL> select count(*)  from recyclebin;
```

Gather dictionary statistics

It's always good to collect the dictionary statistics before the database upgrade process. Having good statistics on the dictionary tables and fixed objects can help the database upgrade to run faster, and thus, help in reducing the overall downtime required for the database upgrade.

Use the following SQL statement to check the dictionary statistics' last collected time:

```
SQL> col operation for a33
SQL> set lines 200
SQL> select operation, to_char(max(end_time),'dd-mon-yy hh24:mi') latest
    from dba_optstat_operations
    where operation in ('gather_fixed_objects_stats','gather_dictionary_
stats') group by operation;


OPERATION                           LATEST
---------------------------------   ---------------
gather_fixed_objects_stats          09-MAR-21 08:11
gather_dictionary_stats             09-MAR-21 09:23
```

We can gather the dictionary statistics using the following SQL statements:

```
SQL> EXECUTE DBMS_STATS.GATHER_DICTIONARY_STATS;
```

```
PL/SQL procedure successfully completed.

SQL> EXECUTE DBMS_STATS.GATHER_FIXED_OBJECTS_STATS;
PL/SQL procedure successfully completed.
```

Ensure that the physical standby database is in sync with the primary database

In the **Primary** database, execute a couple of log switches and check the current archive log list using the following SQL statements:

```
SQL> @/home/oracle/rac_database_info.sql
```

DATABASE_HOST	DB_NAME	DATABASE_ROLE	OPEN_MODE	STARTUP_TIME
virtual-19crac1	homespr1	PRIMARY	READ WRITE	10-MAR-21
virtual-19crac2	homespr2	PRIMARY	READ WRITE	10-MAR-21

```
SQL> alter system switch all logfile;
System altered.

SQL> archive log list;
Database log mode              Archive Mode
Automatic archival             Enabled
Archive destination            USE_DB_RECOVERY_FILE_DEST
Oldest online log sequence     27
Next log sequence to archive   28
Current log sequence           28
SQL>
```

In the Physical Standby database, check if it is receiving the redo logs from the primary database and if the MRP is applying the logs to keep it in sync with the primary database. Check the following SQL statements:

```
SQL> @/home/oracle/rac_database_info.sql
```

DATABASE_HOST	DB_NAME	DATABASE_ROLE	OPEN_MODE	STARTUP_TIME
virtual-dr-19crac1	homesdr1	PHYSICAL STANDBY	MOUNTED	10-MAR-21
virtual-dr-19crac2	homesdr2	PHYSICAL STANDBY	MOUNTED	10-MAR-21

INST_ID	PROCESS	STATUS	THREAD#	SEQUENCE#	BLOCK#	BLOCKS
1	MRP0	APPLYING_LOG	2	23	149	102400

THREAD#	ARCHIVED	APPLIED	GAP

```
1          30         30         0
2          22         21         1
```

As we can see, the physical standby database is in SYNC with the primary database. This completes our physical standby database setup. Let's move on to the next steps.

Upgrading the Oracle 11g (11.2.0.4) database to Oracle 19c (19.9.0)

In this section, we will upgrade both the primary and the physical standby database from the version Oracle 11g (11.2.0.4) to version Oracle 19c (19.9.0). Let's start the process by completing the pre-upgrade steps.

For this upgrade, we will use the database parallel upgrade utility (**dbupgrade**) to upgrade the database from 11g to 19c, and we will also use the Oracle provided scripts to upgrade the Timezone version.

About the parallel upgrade utility (catctl.pl and dbupgrade)

The parallel upgrade utility was introduced in 12.1.0.2. This utility upgrades the Oracle components in parallel, thus reducing the overall time taken to upgrade the Oracle database. This utility can be run as a **perl** command (**catctl.pl**) or it can be run as a shell command (**dbupgrade**). The **dbupgrade** utility, when run, starts the **catctl.pl** script, and it uses the other Oracle files to perform the upgrade in parallel. It is a fast and efficient tool. Both the **dbupgrade** and **catctl.pl** scripts are located in the **$ORACLE_HOME/bin** directory of the new Oracle home. We can also download the latest **dbupgrade** utility from MOS.

For more details and the latest updates, please refer to *'How to Download and Run Oracle's Database Pre-Upgrade Utility (Doc ID 884522.1)'*.

Once we download the latest dbupgrade utility, we can either copy it to $ORACLE_HOME/bin or stage it in other location and set the PATH to this location and run it from there.

Disable the dataguard broker

We have to disable the **dataguard** broker before the database upgrade and enable it back after the upgrade. Ensure that the standby database is in sync with the primary database and then disable the **dataguard** broker.

For the **Primary** database, ensure that the standby database is in sync. In the primary database, switch the logfiles and take a snapshot of the current archive log files info, as shown as follows:

```
SQL> @/home/oracle/rac_database_info.sql

DATABASE_HOST       DB_NAME    DATABASE_ROLE    OPEN_MODE     STARTUP_TIME
----------------    --------   --------------   ----------    --------------
virtual-19crac1     homespr1   PRIMARY          READ WRITE    10-MAR-21
virtual-19crac2     homespr2   PRIMARY          READ WRITE    10-MAR-21

SQL> archive log list;
Database log mode                 Archive Mode
Automatic archival                Enabled
Archive destination               USE_DB_RECOVERY_FILE_DEST
Oldest online log sequence        27
Next log sequence to archive      28
Current log sequence              28
SQL>
```

In the **Physical Standby** database, check to see whether the physical standby database is receiving the redo logs from the primary database, and whether the MRP process is applying the logs to keep it in sync with the primary database, as shown as follows:

```
@/home/oracle/standby_database_lag.sql

DATABASE_HOST        DB_NAME    DATABASE_ROLE      OPEN_MODE    STARTUP_TIME
----------------     --------   ----------------   ----------   ----------
virtual-dr-19crac1   homesdr1   PHYSICAL STANDBY   MOUNTED      10-MAR-21
virtual-dr-19crac2   homesdr2   PHYSICAL STANDBY   MOUNTED      10-MAR-21


INST_ID   PROCESS   STATUS         THREAD#   SEQUENCE#   BLOCK#   BLOCKS
--------- --------- ------------   --------  ----------  -------  ------
      1   MRP0      APPLYING_LOG          2          23      149   102400


THREAD#      ARCHIVED    APPLIED        GAP
----------  ----------  ----------  ----------
        1          30          30           0
        2          22          21           1
```

We can check the current configuration and disable the broker configuration, as follows:

```
[oracle@virtual-19crac1]$ dgmgrl
DGMGRL for Linux: Version 11.2.0.4.0 - 64bit Production
Copyright (c) 2000, 2009, Oracle. All rights reserved.
Welcome to DGMGRL, type "help" for information.
DGMGRL> connect sys
Password:
Connected.
```

```
DGMGRL>

DGMGRL> SHOW CONFIGURATION;
      Configuration - homesdg
        Protection Mode: MaxPerformance
        Databases:
          homespr - Primary database
          homesdr - Physical standby database
             Fast-Start Failover: DISABLED

      Configuration Status:
      SUCCESS
DGMGRL>
```

Disable the Fast Start Failover (FSFO) if it's enabled

Fast start failover (**FSFO**) is a feature which allows the dataguard broker to failover a failed primary database to one of the configured physical standby databases. If it is enabled, we can disable it, as follows:

```
DGMGRL>DISABLE FAST_START FAILOVER;
```

Disable the dataguard broker configuration

We can disable the configuration and re-verify the broker configuration. When we run the following command, it will disable the broker's active management of the databases in the Oracle dataguard configuration:

```
DGMGRL> DISABLE CONFIGURATION;
Disabled.

DGMGRL> SHOW CONFIGURATION;

 Configuration - homesdg
       Protection Mode: MaxPerformance
       Databases:
         homespr - Primary database
         homesdr - Physical standby database
            Fast-Start Failover: DISABLED
            Configuration Status:
      DISABLED
DGMGRL>
```

Stop the data guard broker (DMON) process in the primary database

We can disable the **dataguard** broker in the primary database by setting the **DG_BROKER_START** parameter to false. Check the following code:

```
SQL> @/home/oracle/rac_database_info.sql


DATABASE_HOST      DB_NAME      DATABASE_ROLE     OPEN_MODE     STARTUP_TIME
----------------   -----------  -------------     ----------    -------------
virtual-19crac1    homespr1     PRIMARY           READ WRITE    10-MAR-21
virtual-19crac2    homespr2     PRIMARY           READ WRITE    10-MAR-21


SQL> show parameter broker

NAME                          TYPE          VALUE
-------------------------     ----------    -------------------------------
dg_broker_config_file1        string        +DATAC1/homespr/dr1homespr.dat
dg_broker_config_file2        string        +DATAC1/homespr/dr2homespr.dat
dg_broker_start               boolean       TRUE

SQL> ALTER SYSTEM SET DG_BROKER_START=FALSE;
System altered.

SQL> show parameter DG_BROKER_START

NAME                          TYPE          VALUE
-------------------------     ----------    -------------------------------
dg_broker_config_file1        string        +DATAC1/homespr/dr1homespr.dat
dg_broker_config_file2        string        +DATAC1/homespr/dr2homespr.dat
dg_broker_start               boolean       FALSE
```

Backup DB broker configuration files

It's always a good idea to back up the broker configuration files. In our case, we have these files in the ASM instance. So, we will login to the ASM instance and make a copy of the broker configuration files, as shown as follows:

```
[oracle@virtual-19crac1]$ . oraenv

ORACLE_SID = [homespr] ? +ASM1
The Oracle base remains unchanged with value /u01/app/oracle
[oracle@virtual-19crac1]$ asmcmd
ASMCMD>

ASMCMD>cp +DATAC1/homespr/dr1homespr.dat +DATAC1/homespr/dr1homespr.dat.
bak
Copying +DATAC1/homespr/dr1homespr.dat +DATAC1/homespr/dr1homespr.
dat.bak

ASMCMD>cp +DATAC1/homespr/dr2homespr.dat +DATAC1/homespr/dr2homespr.dat.
bak
Copying +DATAC1/homespr/dr2homespr.dat +DATAC1/homespr/dr2homespr.dat.
bak
```

This completes the disabling broker steps on the primary database. Now, let's complete the same steps in the physical standby database.

Since we have already disabled the dataguard broker configuration from the primary database, we just need to stop the dataguard broker (**DMON**) process in the physical standby database, as shown as follows:

```
SQL> @/home/oracle/rac_database_info.sql

DATABASE_HOST        DB_NAME   DATABASE_ROLE    OPEN_MODE   STARTUP_TIME
------------------   --------  --------------   ---------   ------------
virtual-dr-19crac1   homesdr1  PHYSICAL STANDBY MOUNTED     10-MAR-21
virtual-dr-19crac2   homesdr2  PHYSICAL STANDBY MOUNTED     10-MAR-21


SQL> SHOW PARAMETER DG_BROKER

NAME                     TYPE         VALUE
--------------------     ----------   ------------------------------
dg_broker_config_file1   string       +DATAC1/homesdr/dr1homesdr.dat
dg_broker_config_file2   string       +DATAC1/homesdr/dr2homesdr.dat
dg_broker_start          boolean      TRUE


SQL> ALTER SYSTEM SET DG_BROKER_START=FALSE;
System altered.

SQL> SHOW PARAMETER DG_BROKER

NAME                     TYPE         VALUE
--------------------     ----------   ------------------------------
dg_broker_config_file1   string       +DATAC1/homesdr/dr1homesdr.dat
dg_broker_config_file2   string       +DATAC1/homesdr/dr2homesdr.dat
dg_broker_start          boolean      FALSE
```

Backup the dataguard broker configuration files on the physical standby database, as follows:

```
[oracle@virtual-dr-19crac1 ~]$ . oraenvORACLE_SID = [oracle] ? +ASM1
The Oracle base has been set to /u01/app/oracle

[oracle@virtual-dr-19crac1 ~]$ asmcmd

ASMCMD>cp +DATAC1/homesdr/dr1homesdr.dat +DATAC1/homesdr/dr1homesdr.dat.bak
Copying +DATAC1/homesdr/dr1homesdr.dat +DATAC1/homesdr/dr1homesdr.dat.bak

ASMCMD>cp +DATAC1/homesdr/dr2homesdr.dat +DATAC1/homesdr/dr2homesdr.dat.bak
Copying +DATAC1/homesdr/dr2homesdr.dat +DATAC1/homesdr/dr2homesdr.dat.bak
```

This completes the step for disabling the data guard broker on both the primary and the standby databases. Let's move on to the next section, where we will start the prep work for the upgrade and the actual upgrade task.

Working directories

Create a staging directory with the primary database name. We will use this directory as a working directory to save all the required log files, as follows:

```
[oracle@virtual-19crac1 ~]$ mkdir -p /u01/software/upgrade/homespr
```

Copy the network related files (**tnsnames.ora** and **sqlnet.ora**) and the password files and the **init.ora** parameter files from the 11.2.0.4 database home to the 19c database home.

Network files

Add the source database TNS entry in the **tnsnames.ora** file of the　Oracle 19c (19.9) database home; take a backup of the current **tnsnames.ora** file in　the Oracle 19c (19.9) database home, as follows:

```
[oracle@virtual-19crac1 ~]$ cd /u01/app/oracle/product/19c/db_1/network/
admin

[oracle@virtual-19crac1 ~]$ cp tnsnames.ora tnsnames.ora.March10
[oracle@virtual-19crac1 ~]$
```

Add the primary and the physical standby database entries to the Oracle 19c (19.9) database home **tnsnames.ora** file, as follows:

```
[oracle@virtual-19crac1 ~]$ vi tnsnames.ora
homespr =
 (DESCRIPTION =
   (ADDRESS = (PROTOCOL = TCP)(HOST = virtual-19crac-scan)(PORT = 1521))
   (CONNECT_DATA =
     (SERVER = DEDICATED)
     (SERVICE_NAME = homespr)
   )
 )

homesdr =
 (DESCRIPTION = (ADDRESS = (PROTOCOL = TCP)(HOST = virtual-dr-19crac-
scan)(PORT = 1521))
    (CONNECT_DATA =
    (SERVER = DEDICATED)
```

```
    (SERVICE_NAME = homesdr)
  )
)
```

Primary database initialization parameter (pfile/spfile) files

Copy the primary database initialization parameter files (**pfile** and **spfile**) from Oracle 11g (11.2.0.4) to Oracle 19c (19.9) database home, as follows:

```
[oracle@virtual-19crac1 ~]$  cp /u01/app/oracle/product/11.2.0.4/db_1/
dbs/*homes*ora  /u01/app/oracle/product/19c/db_1/dbs/
```

Password files

Copy the password file from the source database home to Oracle 19c (19.9), as follows:

```
[oracle@virtual-19crac1 ~]$ cp /u01/app/oracle/product/11.2.0.4/db_1/
dbs/*homes* /u01/app/oracle/product/19c/db_1/dbs/
```

Check the INVALID objects count in the primary database

It's always a good idea to take the snapshot of the invalid objects' count before starting the database upgrade process.

In the Primary database, complete the following steps:

1. Run the **utlrp** script to compile any INVALID objects and then take a count of the invalid objects, so that we can compare the count after the database upgrade, as follows:

    ```
    SQL> @$ORACLE_HOME/rdbms/admin/utlrp

    SQL> select count(*) from dba_objects where status='INVALID';
    ```

2. Take the count of the invalid objects in the **SYS** and **SYSTEM** schemas, as follows:

    ```
    SQL> spool /u01/software/upgrade/homespr/pre-upgrade_SYS_SYSTEM_
    invalid_Objects.log

    SQL> col owner for a25
    SQL> set lines 200
    SQL> col object_type for a30;
    SQL> col DATABASE_HOST for a40;
    SQL> col HOST_NAME for a15;
    SQL> col DATABASE_ROLE for a10
    ```

```
SQL> col OPEN_MODE for a10
SQL> col STARTUP_TIME for a20
SQL> col OBJECT_NAME for a30
SQL> SELECT i.HOST_NAME "DATABASE_HOST" ,
     i.INSTANCE_NAME "DB_NAME", d.DATABASE_ROLE "DATABASE_ROLE",
     d.OPEN_MODE " OPEN_MODE ", STARTUP_TIME
     from GV$DATABASE d, gv$instance i
     where i.INST_ID=d.INST_ID;

SQL> select owner,object_name,object_type,status
     from dba_objects
     where status='INVALID' and owner in ('SYS','SYSTEM')
order by owner;
spool off;
```

3. Next, take the invalid object count for the other schemas, as follows:

```
SQL> spool /u01/software/upgrade/homespr/pre-upgrade_non-SYS_
invalid_objects.log

SQL> col owner for a25
SQL> set lines 200
SQL> col object_type for a30;
SQL> col DATABASE_HOST for a40;
SQL> col HOST_NAME for a15;
SQL> col DATABASE_ROLE for a10
SQL> col OPEN_MODE for a10
SQL> col STARTUP_TIME for a20
SQL> col OBJECT_NAME for a30
SQL> SELECT i.HOST_NAME "DATABASE_HOST" ,
     i.INSTANCE_NAME "DB_NAME", d.DATABASE_ROLE "DATABASE_ROLE",
     d.OPEN_MODE " OPEN_MODE ", STARTUP_TIME
     from GV$DATABASE d, gv$instance i
     where i.INST_ID=d.INST_ID;

SQL> select count(*)
     from dba_objects
     where status='INVALID' and owner not in ('SYS','SYSTEM');

SQL> select owner,object_type,count(*)
     from dba_objects
     where status='INVALID' and owner not in ('SYS','SYSTEM')
group by owner,object_type order by owner ;

SQL> col object_name for a37
SQL> select owner,object_name,object_type,status
     from dba_objects
     where status='INVALID' and owner not in ('SYS','SYSTEM')
order by owner ;
spool off;
```

4. Check if both the spool files are created using following command:

```
[oracle@virtual-19crac1 homespr]$ ls -ltr

total 8

-rw-r--r-- 1 oracle oinstall 1650 Mar 10 21:02 pre-upgrade_SYS_
SYSTEM_invalid_Objects.log
-rw-r--r-- 1 oracle oinstall 2383 Mar 10 21:02 pre-upgrade_non-
SYS_invalid_objects.log
```

5. For testing purpose in the **Primary** database, let's create a table called **before_upgrade**, just to crosscheck after the upgrade to see if it comes to the physical standby database confirming that the upgrade is successful, as follows:

```
SQL> Create table BEFORE_UPGRADE (NAME Varchar(30));
Table created.

SQL> insert into BEFORE_UPGRADE values ('Table Before Upgrade');
1 row created.

SQL> commit;
Commit complete.
```

Running the pre-upgrade script pre-upgrade jar file

Before upgrading the database, we should always run the Oracle provided preupgrade.jar script which runs against the source database. This script will read the source database and gather all the required information from the database. It will also check all the parameters and settings and then report about any issues that needs to be addressed before starting the database upgrade.

Always download the latest preupgrade.jar file. _For more details and the latest updates, please refer to *'How to Download and Run Oracle's Database Pre-Upgrade Utility (Doc ID 884522.1)'*.

Once downloaded, we can stage it in the following location and you can copy it to the 19c database home, as follows:

```
[oracle@virtual-19crac1 homespr]$ /u01/app/oracle/product/19.3.0.0/
DbHome_1/rdbms/admin/preupgrade.jar
```

Run the pre-upgrade script in the source primary database, as follows:

```
[oracle@virtual-19crac1 homespr]$ /u01/app/oracle/product/11.2.0.4/
db_1/jdk/bin/java -jar /u01/app/oracle/product/19c/db_1/rdbms/admin/
preupgrade.jar TERMINAL DIR /u01/software/upgrade/homespr/homespr-
preupgrade
```

The output of the preceding **preupgrade** command is as follows:

```
[oracle@virtual-19crac1 homespr]$ /u01/app/oracle/product/11.2.0.4/
db_1/jdk/bin/java -jar /u01/app/oracle/product/19c/db_1/rdbms/admin/
preupgrade.jar TERMINAL DIR /u01/software/upgrade/homespr/homespr-
preupgrade
Report generated by Oracle Database Pre-Upgrade Information Tool Version
19.0.0.0.0 Build: 1 on 2021-03-10T21:21:51
Upgrade-To version: 19.0.0.0.0
========================================
Status of the database prior to upgrade
========================================
      Database Name:  HOMESPR
     Container Name:  Not Applicable in Pre-12.1 database
       Container ID:  Not Applicable in Pre-12.1 database
            Version:  11.2.0.4.0
     DB Patch Level:  PSU 11.2.0.4.200414
         Compatible:  11.2.0.4.0
          Blocksize:  8192
           Platform:  Linux x86 64-bit
      Timezone File:  14
  Database log mode:  ARCHIVELOG
           Readonly:  FALSE
            Edition:  EE

Oracle Component                      Upgrade Action     Current Status
----------------                      --------------     -------------
Oracle Server                         [to be upgraded]   VALID
JServer JAVA Virtual Machine          [to be upgraded]   VALID
Oracle XDK for Java                   [to be upgraded]   VALID
Real Application Clusters             [to be upgraded]   VALID
Oracle Workspace Manager              [to be upgraded]   VALID
OLAP Analytic Workspace               [to be upgraded]   VALID
Oracle Enterprise Manager Repository  [to be upgraded]   VALID
Oracle Text                           [to be upgraded]   VALID
Oracle XML Database                   [to be upgraded]   VALID
Oracle Java Packages                  [to be upgraded]   VALID
Oracle Multimedia                     [to be upgraded]   VALID
Oracle Spatial                        [to be upgraded]   VALID
Expression Filter                     [to be upgraded]   VALID
Rule Manager                          [to be upgraded]   VALID
Oracle OLAP API                       [to be upgraded]   VALID

==============
BEFORE UPGRADE
==============
```

REQUIRED ACTIONS
================
None

RECOMMENDED ACTIONS
===================

1. Update NUMERIC INITIALIZATION PARAMETERS to meet the estimated minimums.

   This action may be done now or when starting the database in the upgrade mode using the 19 ORACLE HOME.

Parameter	Currently	19 minimum
processes	150	300

   The database upgrade process requires certain initialization parameters to meet the minimum values. The Oracle upgrade process itself has the minimum values which may be higher and are marked with an asterisk. After upgrading, those asterisked parameter values may be reset if needed.

2. Remove the EM repository.

   - Copy the $ORACLE_HOME/rdbms/admin/emremove.sql script from the target 19 ORACLE_HOME into the source 11.2.0.4.0 ORACLE_HOME.

   Step 1: If the database control is configured, stop the EM Database Control, using the following command:
   ```
   $> emctl stop dbconsole
   ```
   Step 2: Connect to the database using the SYS account AS SYSDBA:
   ```
   SET ECHO ON;
   SET SERVEROUTPUT ON;
   @emremove.sql
   ```

   Without the set echo and serveroutput commands, we will not be able to follow the progress of the script.

   The database has an Enterprise Manager Database Control repository.

   Starting with Oracle Database 12c, the local Enterprise Manager Database Control does not exist anymore. The repository will be removed from your database during the upgrade. This step can manually be performed before the upgrade to reduce downtime.

3. Remove the OLAP Catalog by running the 11.2.0.4.0 SQL script $ORACLE_HOME/olap/admin/catnoamd.sql script.

The OLAP Catalog component, AMD, exists in the database.

Starting with Oracle Database 12c, the OLAP Catalog (OLAP AMD) is desupported and will automatically be marked as OPTION OFF during the database upgrade, if present. Oracle recommends removing the OLAP Catalog (OLAP AMD) before the database upgrade. This step can manually be performed before the upgrade to reduce downtime.

4. Upgrade Oracle Application Express (APEX) manually before the database upgrade.

    The database contains the APEX version 3.2.1.00.12. Upgrade APEX to at least version 18.2.0.00.12.

    Starting with Oracle Database Release 18, APEX is not upgraded automatically as part of the database upgrade. Refer to My Oracle Support

    Note 1088970.1 for more information about the APEX installation and upgrades.

5. (AUTOFIXUP) Gather stale data dictionary statistics prior to the database upgrade in the off-peak time using the following:

    EXECUTE DBMS_STATS.GATHER_DICTIONARY_STATS;

    Dictionary statistics do not exist or are stale (not up-to-date).

    Dictionary statistics help the Oracle optimizer find efficient SQL execution plans and are essential for proper upgrade timing. Oracle

    recommends gathering the dictionary statistics in the last 24 hours before the database upgrade.

    For information on managing tbe optimizer statistics, refer to the 11.2.0.4 Oracle Database Performance Tuning Guide.

6. (AUTOFIXUP) Directly grant ADMINISTER DATABASE TRIGGER privilege to the owner of the trigger or drop and re-create the trigger with a user that was granted directly with such. We can list those triggers using SELECT OWNER, TRIGGER_NAME FROM DBA_TRIGGERS, where TRIM(BASE_OBJECT_TYPE)='DATABASE' AND OWNER NOT IN (SELECT GRANTEE FROM DBA_SYS_PRIVS WHERE PRIVILEGE='ADMINISTER DATABASE TRIGGER').

    There are one or more database triggers whose owner does not have the right privilege on the database.

The creation of the database triggers must be done by the users with the ADMINISTER DATABASE TRIGGER privilege. Privilege must have been granted directly.

7. (AUTOFIXUP) Gather statistics on fixed objects prior to the upgrade.

   None of the fixed object tables have had the stats collected.

   Gathering the statistics on fixed objects, if none have been gathered yet, is recommended prior to upgrading.

   For information on managing the optimizer statistics, refer to the 11.2.0.4 Oracle Database Performance Tuning Guide.

INFORMATION ONLY

=================

8. To help you keep track of your tablespace allocations, the following AUTOEXTEND tablespaces are expected to successfully EXTEND during the upgrade process.

Tablespace	Size	Min Size For Upgrade
SYSAUX	560 MB	787 MB
SYSTEM	750 MB	1182 MB
TEMP	20 MB	150 MB
UNDOTBS1	65 MB	446 MB

   Minimum tablespace sizes for upgrade are estimates.

9. Run $ORACLE_HOME/rdbms/admin/catnoexf.sql located in the new Oracle Database Oracle home to remove both EXF and RUL.

   Expression Filter (EXF) or Rules Manager (RUL) exist in the database.

   Starting with Oracle Database release 12.1, the Expression Filter (EXF) and Database Rules Manager (RUL) features are desupported, and are removed during the upgrade process. This step can manually be performed before the upgrade to reduce downtime.

10. Check the Oracle Backup and Recovery User's Guide for information on how to manage an RMAN recovery catalog schema.

    If you are using a version of the recovery catalog schema that is older than that required by the RMAN client version, then you must upgrade the catalog schema.

    It is a good practice to have the catalog schema as the same or a higher version than the RMAN client version you are using.

```
ORACLE GENERATED FIXUP SCRIPT

==============================
```

All the issues in database HOMESPR, which were identified earlier as BEFORE UPGRADE "(AUTOFIXUP)" can be resolved by executing the following:

```
    SQL>@/u01/software/upgrade/homespr/homespr-preupgrade/
preupgrade_fixups.sql

=============
AFTER UPGRADE
=============

REQUIRED ACTIONS
================
None

RECOMMENDED ACTIONS
===================
```

11. Upgrade the database time zone file using the DBMS_DST package.

    The database is using the time zone file version 14 and the target 19 release ships with the time zone file version 32.

    Oracle recommends upgrading to the desired (latest) version of the time zone file. For more information, refer to "Upgrading the Time Zone File and Timestamp with Time Zone Data" in the 19 Oracle Database Globalization Support Guide.

12. (AUTOFIXUP) Gather the dictionary statistics after the upgrade using the following command:
    ```
    EXECUTE DBMS_STATS.GATHER_DICTIONARY_STATS;
    ```
    Oracle recommends gathering the dictionary statistics after upgrade.

    Dictionary statistics provide essential information to the Oracle optimizer to help it find efficient SQL execution plans. After a database upgrade, the statistics need to be re-gathered as there can now be bles that have significantly changed during the upgrade or new tables that do not have statistics gathered yet.

13. Gather statistics on fixed objects after the upgrade and when there is a representative workload on the system using the following command:
    ```
    EXECUTE DBMS_STATS.GATHER_FIXED_OBJECTS_STATS;
    ```

This recommendation is given for all the pre-upgrade runs.

Fixed object statistics provide the essential information to the Oracle optimizer to help it find efficient SQL execution plans. Those statistics are specific to the Oracle Database release that generates them, and can be stale upon the database upgrade.

For information on managing optimizer statistics, refer to the 11.2.0.4 Oracle Database Performance Tuning Guide.

INFORMATION ONLY

================

14. Check the Oracle documentation for the identified components for their specific upgrade procedure.

The database upgrade script will not upgrade the following Oracle components: OLAP Catalog,OWB

The Oracle database upgrade script upgrades most, but not all the Oracle Database components that may be installed. Some components that are not upgraded may have their own upgrade scripts, or they may be deprecated or obsolete.

ORACLE GENERATED FIXUP SCRIPT

============================== All the issues in the database HOMESPR, which were identified earlier as AFTER   UPGRADE "(AUTOFIXUP)" can be resolved by executing the following:

    SQL>@/u01/software/upgrade/homespr/homespr-preupgrade/
postupgrade_fixups.sql

==================
PREUPGRADE SUMMARY
==================

/u01/software/upgrade/homespr/homespr-preupgrade/preupgrade.log
/u01/software/upgrade/homespr/homespr-preupgrade/preupgrade_
ixups.sql
/u01/software/upgrade/homespr/homespr-preupgrade/postupgrade_
fixups.sql

Execute the fixup scripts indicated as follows:

Before the upgrade:
Log into the database and execute the pre-upgrade fixups:

@/u01/software/upgrade/homespr/homespr-preupgrade/preupgrade_
fixups.sql

```
After the upgrade:

Log into the database and execute the post-upgrade fixups:
@/u01/software/upgrade/homespr/homespr-preupgrade/postupgrade_
fixups.sql

Preupgrade complete: 2021-03-10T21:21:51
```

We should check the preceding output to identify any potential issues. If you find any critical issues, then we must address them first before proceeding to the next step. The preceding output also gives recommendations that can be done before moving to the next step which saves some time. A few recommendations include purging of the recycle bin, gathering statistics, and so on. It would be a very good idea if we can purge the recycle bin before, as this would reduce the downtime. We have seen in a few cases where the upgrade step has to spend more than one hour on the purging of the recycle bin step. So, we must check if the database has too many objects in the recycle bin and purge them before starting the upgrade.

The preceding script also generates the fixup scripts which includes the fixup scripts for both the pre-upgrade and the post-upgrade stages, as follows:

```
[oracle@virtual-19crac1 ~]$ /u01/software/upgrade/homespr/homespr-
preupgrade/preupgrade_fixups.sql
[oracle@virtual-19crac1 ~]$/u01/software/upgrade/homespr/homespr-
preupgrade/postupgrade_fixups.sql
```

We should run the **preupgrade_fixup.sql** script before starting the database upgrade and the **postupgrade_fixup.sql** script after the database upgrade.

Creating Guaranteed Restore Point (GRP) in physical standby database

We must create a guarantee restore point in both the primary and the standby databases, so that we can safely downgrade both the primary and the standby databases using the flashback method. It is very important that we create a guarantee restore point in the **Standby** database, before creating the restore point in the primary database. If create the restore point in the primary database before doing the same in the **Standby** database, we will have issues while downgrading the standby database and we might end up rebuilding the standby database after downgrading the primary database. So, please ensure that we create the guaranteed restore point in the standby database first.

Before creating the restore point, ensure that both the primary database and the standby databases are in sync with each other. Once that is confirmed, we will then stop the log shipping from the primary database to the standby database. We can defer the log shipping on the primary using the SQL command or the broker command as given in the following section. Here, we have used the **sqlplus** command to defer the log shipping on the primary and to cancel the MRP on the standby database.

If you are not using the data guard broker, then we can cancel the log shipping and the managed recover process on the physical standby database using the following SQL commands.

On the Primary database, defer the log shipping as follows:

```
SQL> alter system set log_archive_dest_state_2='DEFER' scope=both
sid='*';
System altered.
```

On the Physical **standby** database, cancel the MRP process as follows:

```
SQL> alter database recover managed standby database cancel;
Database altered.
```

If we have the data guard broker set up in the primary database, we can disable the log shipping and reapply, as follows:

1. Login to the primary database, as follows:

   ```
   SQL> ALTER SYSTEM SET DG_BROKER_START=TRUE;
   System altered.
   ```

2. Login to the dataguard broker of the primary database, as follows:

   ```
   [oracle@virtual-19crac1]$ dgmgrl
   DGMGRL for Linux: Version 11.2.0.4.0 - 64bit Production
   Copyright (c) 2000, 2009, Oracle. All rights reserved.
   Welcome to DGMGRL, type "help" for information.
   DGMGRL> connect sys
   Password:
   Connected.
   DGMGRL>
   ```

3. Enable the configuration as it has been disabled previously, as follows:

   ```
   DGMGRL> enable configuration
   Enabled.
   ```

4. Disable the log shipping on the primary database and log applying on the standby database, as follows:

   ```
   DGMGRL> edit database homespr set state = 'TRANSPORT-OFF';
   Succeeded.
   DGMGRL> edit database homesdr set state = 'APPLY-OFF';
   Succeeded.
   ```

5. Once the MRP is cancelled, we can create the GRP, as follows:

```
SQL> create restore point standby_before_19c_upgrade guarantee
flashback database;
Restore point created.
```

Enable the log shipping back in the **Primary** database and start the MRP in the **standby** database using the following steps.

If we have the **dataguard** broker configured in the **Primary** database, we can enable the log shipping on the primary database and start reapplying on the **standby** database as follows:

1. Login to the primary database, as follows:

```
SQL> ALTER SYSTEM SET DG_BROKER_START=TRUE;
System altered.
```

2. Login to the **dataguard** broker of the primary database, as follows:

```
[oracle@virtual-19crac1]$ dgmgrl

DGMGRL for Linux: Version 11.2.0.4.0 - 64bit Production
Copyright (c) 2000, 2009, Oracle. All rights reserved.
Welcome to DGMGRL, type "help" for information.
DGMGRL> connect sys
Password:
Connected.
DGMGRL>
DGMGRL> edit database homespr set state = 'TRANSPORT-ON';
Succeeded.
DGMGRL> edit database homesdr set state = 'APPLY-ON';
Succeeded.
```

If we are not using the data guard broker, we can cancel the log shipping and the recover process on the standby database as shown in the following section.

In the Primary database, enable the log shipping using the following command:

```
SQL> alter system set log_archive_dest_state_2='ENABLE' scope=both
sid='*';
System altered.
```

In the Physical Standby database, start the MRP process as follows:

```
SQL> alter database recover managed standby database disconnect from
session;
Database altered.
```

Shutdown the Physical standby database

Once confirmed that the standby database is in sync with the primary database, we can then stop the physical standby database. If this is an RAC database, we can use the server control utility to check the status and stop the physical standby database, as follows:

1. Check the current status of the physical standby database using the following **srvctl** command:

```
[oracle@virtual-dr-19crac1 admin]$ srvctl status database -d
homesdr

Instance homesdr1 is running on node virtual-dr-19crac1
Instance homesdr2 is running on node virtual-dr-19crac2
```

2. Stop the physical standby database using the following **srvctl** command:

```
[oracle@virtual-dr-19crac1 admin]$ srvctl stop database -d
homesdr
```

3. Check the current status using the following **srvctl** command again:

```
[oracle@virtual-dr-19crac1 admin]$ srvctl status database -d
homesdr
Instance homesdr1 is not running on node virtual-dr-19crac1
Instance homesdr2 is not running on node virtual-dr-19crac2
```

Run preupgrade fixup scripts in the source primary database

We can now run the **preupgrade_fixup.sql** script on the source database, and also fix any of the issues reported by the **preupgrade.jar** script and it can be fixed automatically by **dbupgrade**. Now, if we have any issues that need human intervention, those need to be addressed by the DBA.

@Primary database

Log into the primary database and execute the pre-upgrade fixups, as follows:

Script: @/u01/software/upgrade/homespr/homespr-preupgrade/preupgrade_
fixups.sql

The output of this command is shown as follows:

```
SQL> @/u01/software/upgrade/homespr/homespr-preupgrade/preupgrade_fixups.
sql

Executing Oracle PRE-Upgrade Fixup Script
```

```
Auto-Generated by:          Oracle Preupgrade Script
                            Version: 19.0.0.0.0 Build: 1
Generated on:               2021-03-10 21:21:49
For Source Database:        HOMESPR
Source Database Version:    11.2.0.4.0
For Upgrade to Version:     19.0.0.0.0


Preup                            Preupgrade
Action                           Issue Is
Number  Preupgrade Check Name    Remedied    Further DBA Action
------  ---------------------    ----------  ------------------------
    1.  parameter_min_val        NO          Manual fixup recommended.
    2.  em_present               NO          Manual fixup recommended.
    3.  amd_exists               NO          Manual fixup recommended.
    4.  apex_manual_upgrade      NO          Manual fixup recommended.
    5.  dictionary_stats         YES         None.
    6.  trgowner_no_admndbtrg    YES         None.
    7.  pre_fixed_objects        YES         None.
    8.  tablespaces_info         NO          Informational only.
                                             Further action is optional.
    9.  exf_rul_exists           NO          Informational only.
                                             Further action is optional.
   10.  rman_recovery_version    NO          Informational only.
                                             Further action is optional.
```

The fixup scripts have been run and they have resolved what they can. However, there are still issues originally identified by the preupgrade that have not been remedied and are still present in the database.

Depending on the severity of the specific issue, and the nature of the issue itself, that could mean that your database is not ready for upgrade. To resolve the outstanding issues, start by reviewing the preupgrade_fixups. sql and searching it for the name of the failed CHECK NAME or Preupgrade Action Number listed earlier.

There you will find the original corresponding diagnostic message from the preupgrade which explains in more detail what still needs to be done.

```
PL/SQL procedure successfully completed.
```

Create Flashback GRP in the primary database

As mentioned earlier, for any database upgrade, it's a must to have a solid backup plan. In this case, we will use the **flashback** method to downgrade the database. We already created the restore point in the **Standby** database; now, let's create a GRP in the primary database, as follows:

```
SQL> create restore point BEFORE_19C_UPGRADE guarantee flashback
database;
Restore point created.

SQL> @/home/oracle/rac_database_info.sql

DATABASE_HOST      DB_NAME    DATABASE_ROLE   OPEN_MODE    STARTUP_TIME
---------------    --------   -------------   ----------   -------------
virtual-19crac1    homespr1   PRIMARY         READ WRITE   10-MAR-21
virtual-19crac2    homespr2   PRIMARY         READ WRITE   10-MAR-21

SQL> set lines 200
SQL> col name for a20
SQL> col GUARANTEE_FLASHBACK_DATABASE for a10
SQL> SQL> col TIME for a60
SQL> select NAME, GUARANTEE_FLASHBACK_DATABASE, TIME
    from V$restore_point;

NAME                    GUARANTEE_FLASHBACK_DATABASE   TIME
------------------      ----------------------------   -------------------------
BEFORE_19C_UPGRADE      YES                            11-MAR-21
                                                       09.06.38.000000000 AM
```

Start the primary database in the upgrade mode from the 19c homes

We can now stop the primary database which is running from the 11.2.0.4 home and start it in the upgrade mode from the 19c home. As this an RAC database, we need to set the **cluster_database** parameter to false and stop the database using the **srvctl** command and start the first instance in the upgrade mode. Complete the following steps:

1. Set the **cluster_database** parameter to false and stop the primary database as follows:

    ```
    SQL>  alter  system  set  cluster_database=FALSE  SCOPE=spfile;
    System altered.

    [oracle@virtual-19crac1 dbs]$ srvctl status database -d homespr
    Instance homespr1 is running on node virtual-19crac1
    Instance homespr2 is running on node virtual-19crac2

    [oracle@virtual-19crac1 dbs]$ srvctl stop database -d homespr

    [oracle@virtual-19crac1 dbs]$ srvctl status database -d homespr
    Instance homespr1 is not running on node virtual-19crac1
    ```

```
Instance homespr2 is not running on node virtual-19crac2
```

2. Start the first instance of the **primary** database in the upgrade mode. For this, first let's update the database entry in **/etc/oratab** to point its home to **19c**, as follows:

```
[oracle@virtual-19crac1 dbs]$ vi /etc/oratab
```

```
[oracle@virtual-19crac1 dbs]$ cat /etc/oratab | grep homes
homespr:/u01/app/oracle/product/19c/db_1:N
homespr1:/u01/app/oracle/product/19c/db_1:N
[oracle@virtual-19crac1 dbs]$
```

3. Now, source the environment (as shown here), so that we can start the database from the **19c** home in the upgrade mode, as follows:

```
[oracle@virtual-19crac1 dbs]$ . oraenv
ORACLE_SID = [homespr1] ? homespr1
```

```
The Oracle base remains unchanged with value /u01/app/oracle
```

```
[oracle@virtual-19crac1 dbs]$ echo $ORACLE_HOME
/u01/app/oracle/product/19c/db_1
```

4. Since we already copied the **primary** database parameter file (**init.ora** file) from 11g to 19c home, we can use it to start the first instance. However, if we have not copied the **init** file yet, we can copy it as follows:

```
[oracle@virtual-19crac1 dbs]$ ls -ltr /u01/app/oracle/
product/11.2.0.4/db_1/dbs/inithomespr1.ora
-rw-r----- 1 oracle oinstall 43 Mar  9 08:44 /u01/app/oracle/
product/11.2.0.4/db_1/dbs/inithomespr1.ora
```

```
[oracle@virtual-19crac1 dbs]$ cp /u01/app/oracle/
product/11.2.0.4/db_1/dbs/inithomespr1.ora /u01/app/oracle/
product/19c/db_1/dbs/
```

```
[oracle@virtual-19crac1 dbs]$ ls -ltr /u01/app/oracle/
product/19c/db_1/dbs/inithomespr1.ora
```

```
-rw-r----- 1 oracle oinstall 43 Mar 11 09:31 /u01/app/oracle/
product/19c/db_1/dbs/inithomespr1.ora
```

5. Start the primary database in the upgrade mode, as follows:

```
[oracle@virtual-19crac1 dbs]$ . oraenv
ORACLE_SID = [homespr1] ? homespr1
The Oracle base remains unchanged with value /u01/app/oracle
[oracle@virtual-19crac1 dbs]$ echo $ORACLE_HOME
/u01/app/oracle/product/19c/db_1
```

6. Start the database in the upgrade mode, as follows:

```
[oracle@virtual-19crac1 dbs]$ sqlplus / as sysdba

SQL*Plus: Release 19.0.0.0.0 - Production on Thu Mar 11 09:34:47
2021
Version 19.9.0.0.0
Copyright (c) 1982, 2019, Oracle.  All rights reserved.
Connected to an idle instance.

SQL> startup upgrade;
ORACLE instance started.
Total System Global Area 3607099536 bytes
Fixed Size                  8902800 bytes
Variable Size             788529152 bytes
Database Buffers         2801795072 bytes
Redo Buffers                7872512 bytes
Database mounted.
Database opened.

SQL> select name,open_mode,cdb,version,status from
gv$database,gv$instance;
NAME       OPEN_MODE            CDB VERSION       STATUS
---------  -------------------- --- ------------  ------------
HOMESPR    READ WRITE           NO  19.0.0.0.0    OPEN MIGRATE
```

The physical standby database is still down and will be down until all the steps are completed for the primary database upgrade. We will start the standby database after the primary database upgrade completes.

It's now time to upgrade the database using the **dbupgrade** utility.

About dbupgrade utility

As mentioned earlier, **dbupgrade** is a database upgrade wrapper script which is basically a shell script that internally starts catctl.pl when we run the command. The main advantage of this utility is that it takes advantage of the CPU capacity by performing upgrades of the Oracle components in parallel. It also reduces the overall upgrade time as it operates and upgrades the components in parallel. The default parallel degree it uses is 4, but we can give a higher parallel degree during its run time. The **dbupgrade** command is located in the bin directory of the Oracle home. In our case, it's located in the following location:

```
[oracle@virtual-19crac1 dbs]$ ls -ltr /u01/app/oracle/product/19c/db_1/
bin/dbupgrade-rwxr-x---. 1 oracle oinstall 3136 Jan 19 2021 /u01/app/
oracle/product/19c/db_1/bin/dbupgrade
```

In our case, let's give the parallel of 16 and upgrade the database as follows:

```
[oracle@virtual-19crac1 dbs]$ $ORACLE_HOME/bin/dbupgrade -n 16
```

The following is the part output that is displayed on the screen after executing the preceding script:

```
[oracle@virtual-19crac1 dbs]$ $ORACLE_HOME/bin/dbupgrade -n 16

Argument list for [/u01/app/oracle/product/19c/db_1/rdbms/admin/catctl.
pl]
For Oracle internal use only A = 0
Run in                       c = 0
Do not run in                C = 0
Input Directory              d = 0
Echo OFF                     e = 1
Simulate                     E = 0
Forced cleanup               F = 0
Log Id                       i = 0
Child Process                I = 0
Log Dir                      l = 0
Priority List Name           L = 0
Upgrade Mode active          M = 0
SQL Process Count            n = 16
SQL PDB Process Count        N = 0
Open Mode Normal             o = 0
Start Phase                  p = 0
End Phase                    P = 0
Reverse Order                r = 0
AutoUpgrade Resume           R = 0
Script                       s = 0
Serial Run                   S = 0
RO User Tablespaces          T = 0
Display Phases               y = 0
Debug catcon.pm              z = 0
Debug catctl.pl              Z = 0
catctl.pl VERSION: [19.0.0.0.0]
           STATUS: [Production]
            BUILD: [RDBMS_19.9.0.0.0DBRU_LINUX.X64_200930]

Log file directory = [/u01/app/oracle/product/19c/db_1/cfgtoollogs/
homespr/upgrade20210311095624]

Parallel SQL Process Count              = 8
Components in [homespr]
    Installed [APEX APS CATALOG CATJAVA CATPROC CONTEXT EM JAVAVM ORDIM
WM RAC SDO XDB XML XOQ]
```

```
Not Installed [DV MGW ODM OLS WK]
DataBase Version      = 11.2.0.4.0
------------------------------------------------------
Phases [0-107]          Start Time:[2021_03_11 09:56:26]
------------------------------------------------------
***********   Executing Change Scripts   ***********
Serial    Phase #:0    [homespr] Files:1     Time: 58s
***************   Catalog Core SQL   ***************
Serial    Phase #:1    [homespr] Files:5     Time: 41s
Restart   Phase #:2    [homespr] Files:1     Time: 0s
***********   Catalog Tables and Views   ***********
Parallel Phase #:3     [homespr] Files:19    Time: 20s
Restart   Phase #:4    [homespr] Files:1     Time: 1s
*************   Catalog Final Scripts   ***********
Parallel Phase #:19    [homespr] Files:32    Time: 18s
Restart   Phase #:20   [homespr] Files:1     Time: 0s
Serial    Phase #:21   [homespr] Files:3     Time: 6s
Restart   Phase #:22   [homespr] Files:1     Time: 1s
Parallel Phase #:23    [homespr] Files:25    Time: 112s
Restart   Phase #:24   [homespr] Files:1     Time: 0s
Parallel Phase #:25    [homespr] Files:12    Time: 65s

Grand Total Time: 1668s

 LOG FILES: (/u01/app/oracle/product/19c/db_1/cfgtoollogs/homespr/
upgrade20210311095624/catupgrd*.log) Upgrade Summary Report Located in:

/u01/app/oracle/product/19c/db_1/cfgtoollogs/homespr/
upgrade20210311095624/upg_summary.log

Grand Total Upgrade Time:    [0d:0h:27m:48s]
```

The preceding **dbupgrade** script creates various logs which can be found in **cfgtoolslogs** of the 19c home. Please see as follows:

```
[oracle@virtual-19crac1 ~]$ cd /u01/app/oracle/product/19c/db_1/
cfgtoollogs/homespr/upgrade20210311095624/
[oracle@virtual-19crac1 upgrade20210311095624]$ ls -ltr
total 36840
-rw------- 1 oracle oinstall     540 Mar 11 09:56 catupgrd_catcon_7146.lst
-rw-r--r-- 1 oracle oinstall    5142 Mar 11 09:56
catupgrd_20210311095626_7146.ora
-rw-r--r-- 1 oracle oinstall    1312 Mar 11 10:01 catupgrd_catcon_kill_
sess_7146_ALL.sql
-rw-r--r-- 1 oracle oinstall      63 Mar 11 10:01 catupgrd_
catcon_12361.done
-rw------- 1 oracle oinstall 1727774 Mar 11 10:01 catupgrd7.log
-rw-r--r-- 1 oracle oinstall      63 Mar 11 10:01 catupgrd_
catcon_12355.done
-rw------- 1 oracle oinstall 1869054 Mar 11 10:01 catupgrd5.log
```

```
-rw-r--r-- 1 oracle oinstall       63 Mar 11 10:01 catupgrd_
catcon_12343.done
-rw------- 1 oracle oinstall 14894343 Mar 11 10:01 catupgrd0.log
-rw-r--r-- 1 oracle oinstall       63 Mar 11 10:01 catupgrd_
catcon_12346.done
-rw------- 1 oracle oinstall  2509583 Mar 11 10:01 catupgrd2.log
-rw-r--r-- 1 oracle oinstall       63 Mar 11 10:01 catupgrd_
catcon_12349.done
-rw------- 1 oracle oinstall  1717944 Mar 11 10:01 catupgrd3.log
-rw-r--r-- 1 oracle oinstall       63 Mar 11 10:01 catupgrd_catcon_12352.done

-rw------- 1 oracle oinstall  1592334 Mar 11 10:01 catupgrd4.log
-rw------- 1 oracle oinstall  2353175 Mar 11 10:01 catupgrd1.log
-rw------- 1 oracle oinstall  3302283 Mar 11 10:01 catupgrd6.log
```

In this, **catupgrd0.log** is the master log file and we can open a new session and do a tail on this **catupgrd0.log** file, as follows:

```
[oracle@virtual-19crac1 upgrade20210311095624]$ pwd
/u01/app/oracle/product/19c/db_1/cfgtoollogs/homespr/
upgrade20210311095624

[oracle@virtual-19crac1 upgrade20210311095624]$ tail -f catupgrd0.log
Oracle Database Release 19 Post-Upgrade Status Tool    03-11-2021
10:23:1
Database Name: HOMESPR
```

Component Name	Current Status	Full Version	Elapsed Time HH:MM:SS
Oracle Server	UPGRADED	19.9.0.0.0	00:10:03
JServer JAVA Virtual Machine	UPGRADED	19.9.0.0.0	00:02:22
Oracle XDK	UPGRADED	19.9.0.0.0	00:00:20
Oracle Database Java Packages	UPGRADED	19.9.0.0.0	00:00:07
OLAP Analytic Workspace	UPGRADED	19.9.0.0.0	00:00:08
OLAP Catalog	OPTION OFF	11.2.0.4.0	00:00:00
Oracle Text	UPGRADED	19.9.0.0.0	00:00:27
Oracle Workspace Manager	UPGRADED	19.9.0.0.0	00:00:32
Oracle Real Application Cluster	UPGRADED	19.9.0.0.0	00:00:00
Oracle XML Database	UPGRADED	19.9.0.0.0	00:01:22
Oracle Multimedia	UPGRADED	19.9.0.0.0	00:00:33
Spatial	LOADING	19.9.0.0.0	00:02:58
Oracle OLAP API	INVALID	19.9.0.0.0	00:00:11
Datapatch			00:05:06
Final Actions			00:05:37
Post Upgrade			00:00:18

```
Total Upgrade Time: 00:25:58
```

Database time zone version is 14. It is older than current release time zone version 32. Time zone upgrade is needed using the DBMS_DST package.

```
Grand Total Upgrade Time:      [0d:0h:27m:48s]
End of Summary Report
```

When we check our original session, where we started the **dbupgrade** script, we can see that it was completed in around 29 minutes. The following is the final part of the output of the **dbupgrade** command:

```
[oracle@virtual-19crac1 dbs]$ $ORACLE_HOME/bin/dbupgrade -n 16

Argument list for [/u01/app/oracle/product/19c/db_1/rdbms/admin/catctl.pl]

For Oracle internal use only A = 0

Run in                    c = 0
Do not run in             C = 0
Input Directory           d = 0
Oracle Database Release 19 Post-Upgrade Status Tool     03-11-2021
0:23:1
Database Name: HOMESPR
Component                       Current       Full       Elapsed Time
Name                            Status        Version    HH:MM:SS
Oracle Server                   UPGRADED      19.9.0.0.0 00:10:03
JServer JAVA Virtual Machine    UPGRADED      19.9.0.0.0 00:02:22
Oracle XDK                      UPGRADED      19.9.0.0.0 00:00:20
Oracle Database Java Packages   UPGRADED      19.9.0.0.0 00:00:07
OLAP Analytic Workspace         UPGRADED      19.9.0.0.0 00:00:08
OLAP Catalog                    OPTION OFF    11.2.0.4.0 00:00:00
Oracle Text                     UPGRADED      19.9.0.0.0 00:00:27
Oracle Workspace Manager        UPGRADED      19.9.0.0.0 00:00:32
Oracle Real Application Clusters UPGRADED     19.9.0.0.0 00:00:00
Oracle XML Database             UPGRADED      19.9.0.0.0 00:01:22
Oracle Multimedia               UPGRADED      19.9.0.0.0 00:00:33
Spatial                         LOADING       19.9.0.0.0 00:02:58
Oracle OLAP API                 INVALID       19.9.0.0.0 00:00:11
Datapatch                                                00:05:06
Final Actions                                            00:05:37
Post Upgrade                                             00:00:18
Total Upgrade Time: 00:25:58

Database time zone version is 14. It is older than current release time
zone version 32. Time zone upgrade is needed using the DBMS_DST package.
Grand Total Upgrade Time:      [0d:0h:27m:48s]
[oracle@virtual-19crac1 dbs]$
```

As you can see in the preceding section, the time zone upgrade is not done as part of the database upgrade. We will upgrade the timezone version using the Oracle provided scripts in the following section.

Running post upgrade fixup script

Now, since the **Primary** database upgrade is completed, let's start the database from the same 19c home in the normal mode using **sqlplus** and run the **postupgrade fixup** script, as follows:

```
[oracle@virtual-19crac1 dbs]$ sqlplus / as sysdba

SQL*Plus: Release 19.0.0.0.0 - Production on Thu Mar 11 10:47:18 2021
Version 19.9.0.0.0
Copyright (c) 1982, 2019, Oracle.  All rights reserved.

Connected to an idle instance.

SQL> startup;
ORACLE instance started.
Total System Global Area 3607099536 bytes
Fixed Size                  8902800 bytes
Variable Size             889192448 bytes
Database Buffers         2701131776 bytes
Redo Buffers                7872512 bytes
Database mounted.
Database opened.
SQL>
```

Check the status of the database instance, as follows:

```
SQL> @/home/oracle/rac_database_info.sql

DATABASE_HOST      DB_NAME      DATABASE_ROLE   OPEN_MODE    STARTUP_TIME
----------------   -----------  -------------   -----------  -----------
virtual-19crac1    homespr1     PRIMARY         READ WRITE   11-MAR-21

SQL> select name,open_mode,version,status
     from v$database,v$instance;
NAME       OPEN_MODE   VERSION            STATUS
---------  ----------  -----------------  -----------
HOMESPR    READ WRITE  19.0.0.0.0         OPEN
```

Connect to the **primary** database and run the **postupgrade fixup** script, as follows:

```
SQL> @/u01/software/upgrade/homespr/homespr-preupgrade/postupgrade_
fixups.sql

Session altered.
PL/SQL procedure successfully completed.
PL/SQL procedure successfully completed.
PL/SQL procedure successfully completed.
Package created.
```

```
No errors.
Package body created.

PL/SQL procedure successfully completed.
No errors.

Package created.
No errors.

Package body created.
No errors.

Executing Oracle POST-Upgrade Fixup Script

Auto-Generated by:         Oracle Preupgrade Script

                           Version: 19.0.0.0.0 Build: 1
Generated on:              2021-03-10 21:21:50

For Source Database:       HOMESPR
Source Database Version:   11.2.0.4.0
For Upgrade to Version:    19.0.0.0.0

Preup                            Preupgrade
Action                           Issue Is
Number   Preupgrade Check Name   Remedied    Further DBA Action
------   ---------------------   ---------   -------------------------
   11.   old_time_zones_exist    NO          Manual fixup recommended.
   12.   post_dictionary         YES         None.
   13.   post_fixed_objects      NO          Informational only.
                                             Further action is optional.
   14.   upg_by_std_upgrd        NO          Informational only.
                                             Further action is optional.
```

The fixup scripts have been run and they have resolved what they can. However, there are still issues originally identified by the preupgrade that have not been remedied and are still present in the database.

Depending on the severity of the specific issue, and the nature of the issue itself, that could mean that the database upgrade is not fully complete. To resolve the outstanding issues, start by reviewing the postupgrade_fixups.sql and searching it for the name of the failed CHECK NAME or Preupgrade Action Number listed earlier.

There we will find the original corresponding diagnostic message from the preupgrade which explains in more detail what still needs to be done.

```
PL/SQL procedure successfully completed.
Session altered.
```

As we can see in the preceding output, we still have a few things to take care of, like upgrading the Timezone version. Let's check the following steps.

Timezone upgrade

To upgrade the Timezone data in the primary database, we have a series of steps which we will run in the primary database, which are as follows:

1. First check the current Timezone version in the **primary** database, as follows:

    ```
    SQL> SELECT version FROM v$timezone_file;

    VERSION
    ----------
    14
    ```

2. Run the **utltz_countstar.sql** script to find the timezone data. This script will check and give the count for each table having the **TIMESTAMP WITH TIME ZONE (TSTZ)** data.

    ```
    SQL> @$ORACLE_HOME/rdbms/admin/utltz_countstar.sql
    ```

    The following output is displayed on the screen after executing the preceding script:

    ```
    SQL> @$ORACLE_HOME/rdbms/admin/utltz_countstar.sql
    Session altered.

    .

    Estimating amount of TSTZ data using COUNT(*).

    This might take some time ...

    .

    For SYS tables first ...

    Note: empty tables are not listed.

    Owner.TableName.ColumnName - COUNT(*) of that column

    SYS.AQ$_ALERT_QT_S.CREATION_TIME - 4
    SYS.AQ$_ALERT_QT_S.DELETION_TIME - 4
    SYS.AQ$_ALERT_QT_S.MODIFICATION_TIME - 4
    SYS.AQ$_AQ$_MEM_MC_S.CREATION_TIME - 3
    SYS.AQ$_AQ$_MEM_MC_S.DELETION_TIME - 3
    SYS.AQ$_AQ$_MEM_MC_S.MODIFICATION_TIME - 3
          Total count * of SYS TSTZ columns is : 196416
    There are in total 165 SYS TSTZ columns.
    .For non-SYS tables ...
    Note: empty tables are not listed.
    Owner.TableName.ColumnName - COUNT(*) of that column
    GSMADMIN_INTERNAL.AQ$_CHANGE_LOG_QUEUE_TABLE_S.CREATION_TIME - 1
    GSMADMIN_INTERNAL.AQ$_CHANGE_LOG_QUEUE_TABLE_S.DELETION_TIME - 1
    ```

```
GSMADMIN_INTERNAL.AQ$_CHANGE_LOG_QUEUE_TABLE_S.MODIFICATION_TIME
 1
WMSYS.AQ$_WM$EVENT_QUEUE_TABLE_S.CREATION_TIME - 1
WMSYS.AQ$_WM$EVENT_QUEUE_TABLE_S.DELETION_TIME - 1
WMSYS.AQ$_WM$EVENT_QUEUE_TABLE_S.MODIFICATION_TIME - 1
WMSYS.WM$WORKSPACES_TABLE$.CREATETIME - 1
WMSYS.WM$WORKSPACES_TABLE$.LAST_CHANGE - 1
Total count * of non-SYS TSTZ columns is :  8
There are in total 18 non-SYS TSTZ columns.
Total Minutes elapsed : 0
Session altered.
```

Time zone upgrade check script

Oracle provided the script to check if the timezone version was upgraded in the database and see if there is any new timezone version available to update. Run the following script in the **primary** database:

```
SQL> @$ORACLE_HOME/rdbms/admin/utltz_upg_check.sql
```

The following output is displayed on the screen after executing the preceding script:

```
SQL> @$ORACLE_HOME/rdbms/admin/utltz_upg_check.sql
Session altered.

INFO: Starting with RDBMS DST update preparation.
INFO: NO actual RDBMS DST update will be done by this script.
INFO: If an ERROR occurs the script will EXIT sqlplus.
INFO: Doing checks for known issues ...
INFO: Database version is 19.0.0.0 .
INFO: Database RDBMS DST version is DSTv14 .
INFO: No known issues detected.
INFO: Now detecting new RDBMS DST version.
A prepare window has been successfully started.
INFO: Newest RDBMS DST version detected is DSTv32 .
INFO: Next step is checking all TSTZ data.
|INFO: It might take a while before any further output is seen ...
|A prepare window has been successfully ended.
INFO: A newer RDBMS DST version than the one currently used is found.
INFO: Note that NO DST update was yet done.
INFO: Now run utltz_upg_apply.sql to do the actual RDBMS DST update.
INFO: Note that the utltz_upg_apply.sql script will
INFO: restart the database 2 times WITHOUT any confirmation or prompt.
Session altered.
```

Run the Timezone upgrade script

Oracle provided the script, **utltz_upg_apply** to upgrade the timezone version. This is the script that will actually upgrade the timezone version. Please note that this script will also restart the database a couple of times as part of updating the Timezone version.

```
SQL> @$ORACLE_HOME/rdbms/admin/utltz_upg_apply.sql
```

The following output is displayed on the screen after executing the preceding script:

```
SQL> @$ORACLE_HOME/rdbms/admin/utltz_upg_apply.sql
Session altered.

INFO: If an ERROR occurs, the script will EXIT SQL*Plus.

INFO: The database RDBMS DST version will be updated to DSTv32 .
WARNING: This script will restart the database 2 times
WARNING: WITHOUT asking ANY confirmation.
WARNING: Hit control-c NOW if this is not intended.
INFO: Restarting the database in UPGRADE mode to start the DST upgrade.
Database       closed.
Database dismounted.
|ORACLE instance shut down.
ORACLE instance started.
Total System Global Area 3607099536 bytes
Fixed Size                 8902800 bytes
Variable Size            889192448 bytes
Database  Buffers        2701131776 bytes
Redo Buffers               7872512 bytes
Database mounted.
Database opened.

INFO: Starting the RDBMS DST upgrade.
INFO: Upgrading all SYS owned TSTZ data.
INFO: It      might take time before any further output is seen ...
An upgrade window has been successfully started.
INFO: Restarting the database in NORMAL mode to upgrade non-SYS TSTZ
ata.
Database closed.
database dismounted.
ORACLE instance shut down.
ORACLE instance started.
Total System Global Area 3607099536 bytes
Fixed Size                 8902800 bytes
Variable Size            889192448 bytes
Database Buffers         2701131776 bytes
Redo Buffers               7872512 bytes
Database mounted.
Database opened.

INFO: Upgrading all non-SYS TSTZ data.
```

```
INFO: It might take time before any further output is seen ...
INFO: Do NOT start any application yet that uses TSTZ data!
INFO: Next is a list of all upgraded tables:
Table list: "MDSYS"."SDO_DIAG_MESSAGES_TABLE"
Number of failures: 0
Table list: "GSMADMIN_INTERNAL"."AQ$_CHANGE_LOG_QUEUE_TABLE_L"
Number of failures: 0
Table list: "GSMADMIN_INTERNAL"."AQ$_CHANGE_LOG_QUEUE_TABLE_S"
umber of failures: 0
INFO: Total failures during update of TSTZ data: 0 .
An upgrade window has been successfully ended.

INFO: Wer new Server RDBMS DST version is DSTv32 .
INFO: The RDBMS DST update is successfully finished.
INFO: Make sure to exit this SQL*Plus session.
INFO: Do not use it for timezone related selects.

Session altered.
```

Check the Timezone version now to see if it's changed to 32, which is the Timezone version in the 19c version, as follows:

```
SQL> @/home/oracle/rac_database_info.sql

DATABASE_HOST     DB_NAME       DATABASE_ROLE      OPEN_MODE    STARTUP_TIME
----------------  -----------   -----------------  ----------   ------------
virtual-19crac1   homespr1      PRIMARY            READ WRITE   11-MAR-21

1 row selected.
SQL>  SELECT version FROM v$timezone_file;

 VERSION
----------
     32
```

Run the **utlrp** script again in the primary database, as follows:

```
SQL> @$ORACLE_HOME/rdbms/admin/utlrp
```

Run the post upgrade status tool script to check if all the components look good and are in the valid state as follows:

```
SQL> @$ORACLE_HOME/rdbms/admin/utlusts.sql TEXT

Oracle Database Release 19 Post-Upgrade Status Tool    03-11-2021
11:40:1

Database Name: HOMESPR
```

```
Component                          Current      Full         Elapsed Time
Name                               Status       Version      HH:MM:SS
Oracle Server                      VALID        19.9.0.0.0   00:10:03
JServer JAVA Virtual Machine       VALID        19.9.0.0.0   00:02:22
Oracle XDK                         VALID        19.9.0.0.0   00:00:20
Oracle Database Java Packages      VALID        19.9.0.0.0   00:00:07
OLAP Analytic Workspace            VALID        19.9.0.0.0   00:00:08
OLAP Catalog                       OPTION OFF   11.2.0.4.0   00:00:00
Oracle Text                        VALID        19.9.0.0.0   00:00:27
Oracle Workspace Manager           VALID        19.9.0.0.0   00:00:32
Oracle Real Application Clusters   VALID        19.9.0.0.0   00:00:00
Oracle XML Database                VALID        19.9.0.0.0   00:01:22
Oracle Multimedia                  VALID        19.9.0.0.0   00:00:33
Spatial                            VALID        19.9.0.0.0   00:02:58
Oracle OLAP API                    VALID        19.9.0.0.0   00:00:11
Datapatch                                                    00:05:06
Final Actions                                                00:05:37
Post Upgrade                                                 00:00:18
Post Compile                                                 00:06:04
Total Upgrade Time: 00:32:03
Database time zone version is 32. It meets current release needs.
```

We can ignore the OLAP Catalog option as it is de-supported from 12. Run the **catuppst.sql** script, as follows:

```
SQL>  @$ORACLE_HOME/rdbms/admin/catuppst.sql
```

The following is the last part of the output from executing the preceding script:

```
SQL>  SELECT dbms_registry_sys.time_stamp('CATUPPST') as timestamp from
dual;

TIMESTAMP
-------------------------------------------------------------------
COMP_TIMESTAMP CATUPPST              2021-03-11 11:44:04
DBUA_TIMESTAMP CATUPPST     FINISHED 2021-03-11 11:44:04
DBUA_TIMESTAMP CATUPPST         NONE 2021-03-11 11:44:04
```

Re-run the post upgrade fixup script

Since we have upgraded the timezone version after the database upgrade, we can re-run the post upgrade script once more. This will fix any issues that's reported during its first run and it will also check and fix any issues related to the timezone version, as follows:

```
SQL> @/u01/software/upgrade/homespr/homespr-preupgrade/postupgrade_
fixups.sql
```

```
No errors.
No errors.
No errors.
No errors.

Executing Oracle POST-Upgrade Fixup Script
Auto-Generated by:         Oracle Preupgrade Script
                           Version: 19.0.0.0.0 Build: 1
Generated on:              2021-03-10 21:21:50
For Source Database:       HOMESPR
Source Database Version:   11.2.0.4.0
For Upgrade to Version:    19.0.0.0.0

Preup                           Preupgrade
Action                          Issue Is
Number   Preupgrade Check Name  Remedied     Further DBA Action
------   --------------------   ----------   -------------------------
   11.   old_time_zones_exist   YES          None.
   12.   post_dictionary        YES          None.
   13.   post_fixed_objects     NO           Informational only.
                                             Further action is optional.
   14.   upg_by_std_upgrd       NO           Informational only.
                                             Further action is optional.
```

The fixup scripts have been run and they have resolved what they can. However, there are still issues originally identified by the preupgrade that have not been remedied and are still present in the database.

Depending on the severity of the specific issue, and the nature of the issue itself, that could mean that the database upgrade is not fully complete. To resolve the outstanding issues, start by reviewing the postupgrade_fixups.sql and searching it for the name of the failed CHECK NAME or Preupgrade Action Number listed earlier.

There we will find the original corresponding diagnostic message from the preupgrade which explains in more detail what still needs to be done.

```
SQL>
```

Upgrade clusterware configuration of a database

We can skip this step if the database is not an RAC database and start the database in the normal mode using **sqlplus**. Since in our case, our primary and standby databases are RAC databases, we must upgrade the cluster configuration information using the server control utility (**srvctl**), as follows:

1. First, set the **cluster_database** parameter to 'true' and shutdown the database using the following **sqlplus** commands:

    ```
    [oracle@virtual-19crac1 dbs]$ sqlplus / as sysdba
    ```

```
SQL*Plus: Release 19.0.0.0.0 - Production on Thu Mar 11 12:01:01
2021

Version 19.9.0.0.0
Copyright (c) 1982, 2019, Oracle.  All rights reserved.

Connected to:
Oracle Database 19c Enterprise Edition Release 19.0.0.0.0 -
Production
Version 19.9.0.0.0

SQL> alter system set cluster_database=true scope=spfile;
System altered.

SQL> shutdown immediate;
Database closed.
Database dismounted.
ORACLE instance shut down.
SQL>
```

2. Now, using the following **srvctl upgrade** command, upgrade the configuration of the database and its services to the **19c**:

```
[oracle@virtual-19crac1 dbs]$ srvctl upgrade database -d homespr
-o /u01/app/oracle/product/19c/db_1
```

3. Using the following command, verify if the configuration has been upgraded. The Oracle home should point to **19c**:

```
[oracle@virtual-19crac1 dbs]$ srvctl config database -d homespr
Database unique name: homespr
Database name: homespr
Oracle home: /u01/app/oracle/product/19c/db_1
Oracle user: oracle
Spfile: +DATAC1/homespr/spfilehomespr.ora
Password file:
Domain:
Start options: open
Stop options: immediate
Database role: PRIMARY
Management policy: AUTOMATIC
Server pools:
Disk Groups: DATAC1
Mount point paths:
Services:
Type: RAC
Start concurrency:
Stop concurrency:
OSDBA group: oinstall
OSOPER group: oinstall
Database instances: homespr1,homespr2
```

```
Configured nodes: virtual-19crac1,virtual-19crac2
CSS critical: no

CPU count: 0
Memory target: 0
Maximum memory: 0
Default network number for database services:
Database is administrator managed
```

4. Start the **primary** database in the normal mode. This will start the database from the **19c** binaries, as follows:

```
[oracle@virtual-19crac1 dbs]$ srvctl start database -d homespr
[oracle@virtual-19crac1 dbs]$ srvctl status database -d homespr
Instance homespr1 is running on node virtual-19crac1
Instance homespr2 is running on node virtual-19crac2
```

5. Run the **utlrp** script in the **primary** database and check the registry to see if all the components are upgraded and in valid state, as follows:

```
SQL > @$ORACLE_HOME/rdbms/admin/utlrp
```

```
SQL> select count(*) from dba_objects where status='INVALID';
```

Check for the post upgrade invalid objects

It's always a good idea to take the snapshot of the invalid object count after the database upgrade. We can compare it with the pre-upgrade invalid count to make sure that they are both the same. On the **primary** database, first run the **utlrp** script to compile any **INVALID** objects and then take a count of the invalid objects, so that we can compare the count after the database upgrade; complete the following steps to check for the post-upgrade invalid objects:

1. First take the count of the invalid objects in the **SYS** and **SYSTEM** schemas, as follows:

```
SQL> spool /u01/software/upgrade/homespr/post-upgrade_SYS_SYSTEM_
invalid_Objects.log
```

```
SQL> SELECT i.HOST_NAME "DATABASE_HOST" ,
        i.INSTANCE_NAME "DB_NAME",
        d.DATABASE_ROLE " DATABASE_ROLE",
        d.OPEN_MODE " OPEN_MODE ", STARTUP_TIME
        from GV$DATABASE d, gv$instance i
        where i.INST_ID=d.INST_ID;
```

```
SQL> select owner,object_name,object_type,status
        from dba_objects
        where status='INVALID' and owner in ('SYS','SYSTEM')
        order by owner ;
```

```
spool off;
```

2. Next, take the invalid object count for the other schemas, as follows:

```
SQL> spool /u01/software/upgrade/homespr/post-upgrade_non-SYS_
invalid_objects.log
SQL> SELECT i.HOST_NAME "DATABASE_HOST" ,
        i.INSTANCE_NAME "DB_NAME",
        d.DATABASE_ROLE " DATABASE_ROLE",
        d.OPEN_MODE " OPEN_MODE ", STARTUP_TIME
        from GV$DATABASE d, gv$instance i
        where i.INST_ID=d.INST_ID;
SQL> select count(*)
        from dba_objects
        where status='INVALID' and owner not in ('SYS','SYSTEM');
SQL> select owner,object_type,count(*)
        from dba_objects
        where status='INVALID' and owner not in ('SYS','SYSTEM')
        group by owner,object_type order by owner ;
SQL> col object_name for a37
SQL> select owner,object_name,object_type,status
        from dba_objects
        where status='INVALID' and owner not in ('SYS','SYSTEM')
        order by owner ;
spool off;
```

3. Check if both the spool files are created, as follows:

```
[oracle@virtual-19crac1 homespr]$ pwd
/u01/software/upgrade/homespr

[oracle@virtual-19crac1 homespr]$ ls -ltr post_*

total 20
-rw-r--r-- 1 oracle oinstall 1650 Mar 11 12:13 post-upgrade_SYS_
SYSTEM_invalid_Objects.log
-rw-r--r-- 1 oracle oinstall 2389 Mar 11 12:13 post-upgrade_non-
SYS_invalid_objects.log
```

We can now check both the pre-upgrade and the post-upgrade invalid objects' counts to see if anything new came in the post upgrade. If the post-upgrade invalid log file contains more objects, then we must check on them and see if they can be fixed and be made valid.

With this step, the **primary** database upgrade is completed. Let's upgrade the **standby** database in the next step.

Upgrading the physical standby database to Oracle 19c (19.9.0)

Once the primary database is upgraded to Oracle 19c, let's upgrade the physical standby database. The physical standby database upgrade will happen by the migrating redo logs that it receives from the primary database. As of now, the physical standby database is down. Depending upon the environment, the primary database will generate, the archive logs. The following is the archive log list info from the primary database before and after the database upgrade:

The archive logs in the primary before the database upgrade are as follows:

```
SQL> archive log list;
Database log mode              Archive Mode
Automatic archival             Enabled
Archive destination            USE_DB_RECOVERY_FILE_DEST
Oldest online log sequence     27
Next log sequence to archive   28
Current log sequence           28
SQL>
```

The archive logs in the **primary** database after the database upgrade are as follows:

```
SQL> archive log list;
Database log mode              Archive Mode
Automatic archival             Enabled
Archive destination            USE_DB_RECOVERY_FILE_DEST
Oldest online log sequence     166
Next log sequence to archive   167
Current log sequence           167
SQL>
```

As you can see, the **primary** database has generated around 150 archive logs in the **primary** database.

Standby database upgrade precheck steps

Let's check the prechecks and ensure that they are completed:

1. Keep in mind to first copy the password files/parameter files and database **tnsnames.ora** entry from Oracle 11g to Oracle 19c home. We need to do this step in all the nodes of the cluster.

    In the **Physical Standby** database server, copy the password and parameter files as show below.

    ```
    [oracle@virtual-dr-19crac1 dbs]$ cp /u01/app/oracle/
    ```

```
product/11.2.0.4/db_1/dbs/*homes*
/u01/app/oracle/product/19c/db_1/dbs

[oracle@virtual-dr-19crac1 dbs]$ cp /u01/app/oracle/
product/11.2.0.4/network/admin/*homes* /u01/app/oracle/
product/19c/db_1/network/admin/
```

2. Modify the database entry in **/etc/oratab** to point to the Oracle 19c (19.3.0) home. We need to do this step in all the nodes of the cluster, as follows:

```
[oracle@virtual-dr-19crac1 dbs]$ cat /etc/oratab | grep homesdr
```

```
homesdr:/u01/app/oracle/product/19c/db_1:N
homesdr1:/u01/app/oracle/product/19c/db_1
```

3. Upgrade the clusterware configuration information of the physical standby database. We can upgrade the clusterware configuration information of the physical standby database using the **srvctl upgrade** command, shown as follows:

```
[oracle@virtual-dr-19crac1 dbs]$
export ORACLE_HOME=/u01/app/oracle/product/19c/db_1
```

```
[oracle@virtual-dr-19crac1 dbs]$
export PATH=$ORACLE_HOME/bin:$PATH
```

```
[oracle@virtual-dr-19crac1 dbs]$
srvctl upgrade database -d homesdr -o /u01/app/oracle/
product/19c/db_1
```

4. Start the physical standby database in the **MOUNT** mode. From the node-1 of the physical standby database server, start the physical standby database in the mount stage, as follows:

```
[oracle@virtual-dr-19crac1 dbs]$ srvctl start  database -d
homesdr
```

```
[oracle@virtual-dr-19crac1 dbs]$ srvctl status database -d
homesdr
Instance homesdr1 is running on node virtual-dr-19crac1
Instance homesdr2 is running on node virtual-dr-19crac2
```

```
SQL> @/home/oracle/rac_database_info.sql
```

```
DATABASE_HOST       DB_NAME   DATABASE_ROLE      OPEN_MODE   STARTUP_TIME
----------------    --------  -----------------  ---------   -----------
virtual-dr-19crac1  homesdr1  PHYSICAL STANDBY   MOUNTED     11-MAR-21
virtual-dr-19crac2  homesdr2  PHYSICAL STANDBY   MOUNTED     11-MAR-21
```

5. Enable the log shipping on the **primary** database, as follows:

```
SQL> ALTER SYSTEM SET log_archive_dest_state_2=enable SCOPE=BOTH
sid='*';
System altered.
```

The primary database will now start shipping all the redo logs to the standby database.

6. Start the recovery process in the **Standby** database, as follows:

```
SQL> ALTER DATABASE RECOVER managed standby database using
current logfile disconnect;

Database altered.
```

The MRP will now start applying all the logs that it has received from the primary database. This might take some time depending upon the number of archive log files that the primary database has generated during its upgrade. The physical standby database will be upgraded with all the migrated redo data that it received from the primary database.

7. Stop the database and start it by using the **srvctl** command.

Wait until the **standby** database catches up with the primary and then stop the database and start it by using the **srvctl** command in the *Read Only* mode, as follows:

```
[oracle@virtual-dr-19crac1 dbs]$ srvctl modify database -d
homesdr -startoption "READ ONLY"
[oracle@virtual-dr-19crac1 dbs]$ srvctl stop database -d homesdr

[oracle@virtual-dr-19crac1 dbs]$ srvctl start database -d homesdr

[oracle@virtual-dr-19crac1 dbs]$ srvctl status database -d
homesdr
Instance homesdr1 is running on node virtual-dr-19crac1
Instance homesdr2 is running on node virtual-dr-19crac2
```

If we are using the data guard broker, then we can also enable the log shipping and start the log apply process (mrp) on the standby database by completing following steps:

1. Start the broker in both the primary and the standby databases. Check and start the data guard broker if it is not started in both the primary database and the standby database, as follows:

@Primary database:

```
SQL> @/home/oracle/rac_database_info.sql
```

```
DATABASE_HOST      DB_NAME   DATABASE_ROLE  OPEN_MODE    STARTUP_TIME
----------------   --------  -------------  ----------   ----------
virtual-19crac1    homespr1  PRIMARY        READ WRITE   11-MAR-21
virtual-19crac2    homespr2  PRIMARY        READ WRITE   11-MAR-21

SQL> show parameter broker

NAME                     TYPE        VALUE
--------------------     ----------  --------------------------------
dg_broker_config_file1   string      +DATAC1/homespr/dr1homespr.dat
dg_broker_config_file2   string      +DATAC1/homespr/dr2homespr.dat
dg_broker_start          boolean     FALSE

SQL> ALTER SYSTEM SET DG_BROKER_START=TRUE;
System altered.

SQL> show parameter DG_BROKER_START

NAME                     TYPE        VALUE
--------------------     ----------  --------------------------------
dg_broker_config_file1   string      +DATAC1/homespr/dr1homespr.dat
dg_broker_config_file2   string      +DATAC1/homespr/dr2homespr.dat
dg_broker_start          boolean     TRUE
```

@Physcial Standby database:

```
SQL> @/home/oracle/rac_database_info.sql

DATABASE_HOST       DB_NAME   DATABASE_ROLE     OPEN_MODE             STARTUP_T
----------------    --------  -------------     --------------------  ---------
virtual-dr-19crac1  homesdr1  PHYSICAL STANDBY  READ ONLY WITH APPLY  11-MAR-21
virtual-dr-19crac2  homesdr2  PHYSICAL STANDBY  READ ONLY WITH APPLY  11-MAR-21

SQL> SHOW PARAMETER DG_BROKER

NAME                     TYPE        VALUE
--------------------     ----------  ----------------
dg_broker_config_file1   string      +DATAC1/homesdr/dr1homesdr.dat
dg_broker_config_file2   string      +DATAC1/homesdr/dr2homesdr.
datdg_broker_start       boolean     FALSE

SQL> ALTER SYSTEM SET DG_BROKER_START=TRUE;
System altered.

SQL> SHOW PARAMETER DG_BROKER
```

```
NAME                                    TYPE         VALUE
--------------------                    -----------  ----------------------------
dg_broker_config_file1                  string       +DATAC1/homesdr/dr1homesdr.dat
dg_broker_config_file2                  string       +DATAC1/homesdr/dr2homesdr.dat
dg_broker_start                         boolean      TRUE
```

2. Enable the broker configuration from the **primary** database. Check and enable the data guard broker configuration if it is disabled in the **primary** database, as follows:

```
[oracle@virtual-19crac1 admin]$ dgmgrl

DGMGRL for Linux: Release 19.0.0.0.0 - Production on Thu Mar 11
15:56:42 2021 Version 19.9.0.0.0
Copyright (c) 1982, 2019, Oracle and/or its affiliates.  All rights
reserved.

Welcome to DGMGRL, type "help" for information.

DGMGRL> connect sys
Password:
Connected to "homespr"
Connected as SYSDBA.
DGMGRL>
```

3. Check the current configuration, as follows:

```
DGMGRL> show configuration;

Configuration - homesdg

  Protection Mode: MaxPerformance
  Members:
  homespr - Primary database
    homesdr - Physical standby database

Fast-Start Failover:  Disabled
Configuration Status:
DISABLED
```

4. Enable the configuration, as follows:

```
DGMGRL> enable configuration;
Enabled.
```

5. Re-check the current configuration, as follows:

```
DGMGRL> show configuration;

Configuration - homesdg

  Protection Mode: MaxPerformance
```

```
       Members:
       homespr - Primary database
         homesdr - Physical standby database
            Fast-Start Failover:  Disabled
            Configuration Status:
       WARNING    (status updated 36 seconds ago)

       DGMGRL>
```

If we see any issues in the broker configuration, we can remove and recreate the configuration. We have seen this in a few cases, where the **dataguard** broker doesn't work after the database upgrades or after the database downgrades, and we end up removing and recreating the broker configuration.

In the Physical standby database, perform the following steps:

1. Start the managed recovery process using the following SQL statement and check the Lag to see if the MRP process in the standby database is applying the redo logs:

```
SQL> ALTER DATABASE RECOVER managed standby database using
current logfile disconnect;
Database altered.
```

2. Check if the **standby** database is opened in the **READ ONLY** mode and if it is in sync with the primary database, as follows:

```
@/home/oracle/standby_database_lag.sql

DATABASE_HOST      DB_NAME  DATABASE_ROLE   OPEN_MODE            STARTUP_T
------------------ -------- --------------- -------------------- ---------
virtual-dr-19crac1 homesdr1 PHYSICAL STANDBY READ ONLY WITH APPLY 11-MAR-21
virtual-dr-19crac2 homesdr2 PHYSICAL STANDBY READ ONLY WITH APPLY 11-MAR-21


INST_ID    PROCESS STATUS        THREAD#    SEQUENCE#  BLOCK# BLOCKS
---------- ------- ------------- ---------- ---------- ------ ------
1          MRP0    APPLYING_LOG  1          167        3774   102400

THREAD#    ARCHIVED   APPLIED    GAP
---------- ---------- ---------- ------
        1  166        166        0
        2  28         28         0
```

3. Check the components' status in the physical standby database, as follows:

```
SQL> select COMP_ID,COMP_NAME,VERSION,STATUS from dba_registry;

COMP_ID    COMP_NAME                             VERSION    STATUS
---------- ------------------------------------- ---------- ------
CATALOG    Oracle Database Catalog Views         19.0.0.0.0 VALID
CATPROC    Oracle Database Packages and Types    19.0.0.0.0 VALID
```

```
JAVAVM    JServer JAVA Virtual Machine      19.0.0.0.0   VALID
XML       Oracle XDK                        19.0.0.0.0   VALID
CATJAVA   Oracle Database Java Packages     19.0.0.0.0   VALID
APS         OLAP Analytic Workspace         19.0.0.0.0   VALID
RAC         Oracle Real Application Clusters 19.0.0.0.0  VALID
OWM         Oracle Workspace Manager        19.0.0.0.0   VALID
CONTEXT   Oracle Text                       19.0.0.0.0   VALID
XDB       Oracle XML Database               19.0.0.0.0   VALID
ORDIM     Oracle Multimedia                 19.0.0.0.0   VALID
SDO       Spatial                           19.0.0.0.0   VALID
XOQ       Oracle OLAP API                   19.0.0.0.0   VALID
AMD       OLAP Catalog                      11.2.0.4.0   OPTION
                                                         OFF

APEX        Oracle Application Express      3.2.1.00.12  VALID
15 rows selected.
```

Check for the **TEST** table in the standby database.

4. In the physical standby database, we can check for the table that we created in the primary database to see if it came through to the standby database.

```
@Physical Standby database:

SQL> select * from BEFORE_UPGRADE;
NAME
------------------------------
Table Before Upgrade
```

This completes the upgrade of the Oracle database from version Oracle 11g (11.2.0.4) to version Oracle 19c (19.9.0).

Post upgrade tasks

For the post upgrade tasks, we can complete the following steps both in the primary and the physical standby databases:

Please note that we did not implement these steps as we will test the downgrade using the flashback method. We cannot downgrade if we change the compatible parameter to 19c. If you want to downgrade, skip this step, and go to next section. However, if you don't want to downgrade the database, you can follow these steps to complete the post upgrade tasks.

1. **FRA space usage**: Until we drop the restore point, keep checking the FRA space usage and increase the space as necessary.

2. **Dropping GRP**: We can also drop the restore point in both the primary and the standby databases.

   ```
   SQL>DROP RESTORE POINT BEFORE_19C_UPGRADE;
   ```

3. **Database compatibility**: We can change the compatible parameter after waiting for one week as we cannot downgrade the database after changing this parameter to 19.

   Since this is a permanent change, once we change the compatible parameter to 19.9, we CANNOT revert, so please wait for 1 week and then change it, as follows:

   ```
   SQL > ALTER SYSTEM SET COMPATIBLE = '19.0.0' SCOPE=SPFILE
   sid='*';
   ```

With this step, we have successfully upgraded both the primary and the standby 11.2.0.4 database to 19.9.0.

In the following section, we will test the downgrade option using the **FLASHBACK** method.

Fallback using Flashback to GRP

The fastest way to downgrade a database from any upgraded version to its previous version is to flashback the database to a previously created guaranteed restore point that was created before starting the upgrade. This method will work as long as we don't change the database compatibility to the upgraded version.

In the **dataguard** environment, for this strategy to work, the flashback database should be enabled in both the **primary** and the **standby** databases and we should create a guaranteed restore point in the **standby** database first, before we start the database upgrade task. Also, we need to make sure that the **db_recovery_dest_size** parameter is set to a bigger value in both the primary and the standby databases. Let's test it out.

We will now downgrade both the primary database (**homespr**) and the physical standby database (**homesdr**) from 19.9.0 to 11.2.0.4, as shown in *Figure 2.2*:

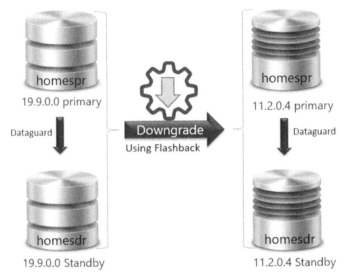

Figure 2.2: *Downgrade process from 19.9.0 database to 11.2.0.4 using flashback*

Downgrading the primary database

Let's look at the following steps to be completed for downgrading the primary database:

1. Stop the log shipping on the **Primary** and redo applying on the **Standby** databases.

2. If we don't have the dataguard broker configured, we can disable the log shipping on the primary and cancel the recovery on the standby database, as follows:

   @Primary database:
   ```
   SQL> alter system set log_archive_dest_state_2='defer' scope=both
   sid='*';
   System altered.
   ```

   @Physcial Standby database:
   ```
   SQL> alter database recover managed standby database cancel;
   Database altered.
   ```

3. If we have the **dataguard** broker configured, we can disable the log shipping and log applying as follows:

@Primary database

```
DGMGRL> edit database homespr set state = 'TRANSPORT-OFF';
DGMGRL> edit database homesdr set state = 'APPLY-OFF';
```

4. Shutdown the **primary** database running from the **19c** home and start only one instance in the mount state. If this is an **RAC** database, you can use the **srvctl** command for this, and if this is not an **RAC** database, you can use the **sqlplus** command to start the database.

5. Stop the database and check its status as follows:

```
[oracle@virtual-19crac1 admin]$srvctl stop database -d homespr

[oracle@virtual-19crac1 admin]$ srvctl status database -d homespr
Instance homespr1 is not running on node virtual-19crac1
Instance homespr2 is not running on node virtual-19crac2
```

6. Start the first instance of the database on **node1** and check the status of the database as follows:

```
[oracle@virtual-19crac1 admin]$srvctl start instance -d homespr
-n virtual-19crac1 -o mount

[oracle@virtual-19crac1 admin]$ srvctl status database -d homespr
Instance homespr1 is running on node virtual-19crac1
Instance homespr2 is not running on node virtual-19crac2
[oracle@virtual-19crac1 admin]$
```

7. Downgrade the **primary** database. Check the restore point that we created in the **primary** database before we started the database and let's flashback the **primary** database to that restore point.

@Primary database

```
SQL> @/home/oracle/rac_database_info.sql

DATABASE_HOST     DB_NAME    DATABASE_ROLE    OPEN_MODE   STARTUP_TIME
----------------  --------   -------------    ---------   ------------
virtual-19crac1   homespr1   PRIMARY          MOUNTED     11-MAR-21

SQL> set lines
SQL> col name for a20
SQL> col GUARANTEE_FLASHBACK_DATABASE for a10
SQL> SQL> col TIME for a60
SQL> set lines 190
SQL> select NAME,GUARANTEE_FLASHBACK_DATABASE,TIME
     from $restore_point;
```

```
NAME                GUARANTEE_F  TIME
------------------  -----------  ------------------------------
BEFORE_19C_UPGRADE  YES          11-MAR-21 09.06.38.000000000 AM
```

8. Flashback the **primary** database to the preceding GRP, as follows:

```
SQL> flashback database to RESTORE POINT BEFORE_19C_UPGRADE;
Flashback complete.
```

9. Create a new **pfile** from the current **spfile** in the primary database and remove all the hidden parameters as they are from 19c and then recreate the **spfile** from the modified **pfile**:

```
SQL>create pfile='/u01/app/oracle/product/11.2.0.4/db_1/dbs/after_
downgrade.ora' from spfile='+DATAC1/homespr/spfilehomespr.ora';
File created.
```

10. Modify the database init parameter file (**pfile**) (**/u01/app/oracle/ product/11.2.0.4/db_1/dbs/after_downgrade.ora**) and remove all the underscore parameters from it. Once we modify the **pfile**, we can shut down the primary database and create the server parameter file (**spfile**) from the modified **pfile**, as follows:

```
[oracle@virtual-19crac1 admin]$srvctl stop database -d homespr
```

```
SQL>create spfile='+DATAC1/homespr/spfilehomespr.ora' from pfile='/
u01/app/oracle/product/11.2.0.4/db_1/dbs/after_downgrade.ora';
File created.
```

11. Downgrade the Oracle Clusterware database configuration.

12. We now need to downgrade the cluster configuration of the **Primary** database and start the database in the mount mode from the 11.2.0.4 home using the **srvctl** command, as follows:

```
[oracle@virtual-19crac1 dbs]$
export ORACLE_HOME=/u01/app/oracle/product/19c/db_1
[oracle@virtual-19crac1 dbs]$
export PATH=$ORACLE_HOME/bin:$PATH
```

```
[oracle@virtual-19crac1 dbs]$ srvctl downgrade database -d
homespr  -o /u01/app/oracle/product/11.2.0.4/db_1 -t 11.2.0.4
```

13. Also, update the entries in **/etc/oratab** to change the database home from 19c to 11.2.0.4, as follows:

```
[oracle@virtual-19crac1 dbs]$ vi /etc/oratab
```

```
[oracle@virtual-19crac1 dbs]$ cat /etc/oratab | grep homes
```

```
homespr1:/u01/app/oracle/product/11.2.0.4/db_1:N
[oracle@virtual-19crac1 dbs]$
```

14. Start the database instance from the 11.2.0.4 home in the **MOUNT** mode on node-1 from the 11.2.0.4 home. If this is the **RAC** database, we can use the **srvctl** command, and if this is not an **RAC** database, we can use the **sqlplus** commands to start the instance in the mount mode, as follows:

```
[oracle@virtual-19crac1 dbs]$ export ORACLE_HOME=/u01/app/oracle/
product/11.2.0.4/db_1

[oracle@virtual-19crac1 dbs]$ export PATH=$ORACLE_HOME/bin:$PATH

[oracle@virtual-19crac1 admin]$srvctl start instance -d homespr
-n virtual-19crac1 -o mount
[oracle@virtual-19crac1 dbs]$ srvctl status database -d homespr
Instance homespr1 is running on node virtual-19crac1
Instance homespr2 is not running on node virtual-19crac2
```

15. Open the database in the reset logs mode. Once the database is open in the **mount** mode, we can open the database with **resetlogs** as we have downgraded the database, as follows:

```
[oracle@virtual-19crac1 dbs]$ sqlplus / as sysdba

SQL*Plus: Release 11.2.0.4.0 Production on Thu Mar 11 19:48:46
2021
Copyright (c) 1982, 2013, Oracle.  All rights reserved.
Connected to:
Oracle Database 11g Enterprise Edition Release 11.2.0.4.0 - 64bit
Production
With the Partitioning, Real Application Clusters, Automatic
Storage Management, OLAP, Data Mining and Real Application
Testing options

SQL> alter database open resetlogs;
Database altered.
SQL> exit
```

16. Stop the **primary** database and start it in the normal mode, as follows:

```
[oracle@virtual-19crac1 dbs]$ srvctl stop database -d homespr
[oracle@virtual-19crac1 dbs]$ srvctl start database -d homespr

[oracle@virtual-19crac1 dbs]$ srvctl status database -d homespr
Instance homespr1 is running on node virtual-19crac1
Instance homespr2 is running on node virtual-19crac2
```

17. Check the registry components to see if they have been successfully downgraded to 11.2.0.4, as follows:

```
SQL> @/home/oracle/rac_database_info.sql
DATABASE_HOST    DB_NAME   DATABASE_ROLE   OPEN_MODE   STARTUP_TIME
---------------  --------  -------------   ----------  -----------
virtual-19crac1  homespr1  PRIMARY         READ WRITE  11-MAR-21
virtual-19crac2  homespr2  PRIMARY         READ WRITE  11-MAR-21


SQL> select COMP_ID,COMP_NAME,VERSION,STATUS from dba_registry;
COMP_ID     COMP_NAME                              VERSION       STATUS
----------  -------------------------------------  ----------    ------
OWB         OWB                                    11.2.0.4.0    VALID
APEX        Oracle Application Express             3.2.1.00.12   VALID
EM          Oracle Enterprise Manager              11.2.0.4.0    VALID
AMD         OLAP Catalog                           11.2.0.4.0    VALID
SDO         Spatial                                11.2.0.4.0    VALID
ORDIM       Oracle Multimedia                      11.2.0.4.0    VALID
XDB         Oracle XML Database                    11.2.0.4.0    VALID
CONTEXT     Oracle Text                            11.2.0.4.0    VALID
EXF         Oracle Expression Filter               11.2.0.4.0    VALID
RUL         Oracle Rules Manager                   11.2.0.4.0    VALID
OWM         Oracle Workspace Manager               11.2.0.4.0    VALID
CATALOG     Oracle Database Catalog Views          11.2.0.4.0    VALID
CATPROC     Oracle Database Packages and Types     11.2.0.4.0    VALID
JAVAVM      JServer JAVA Virtual Machine           11.2.0.4.0    VALID
XML         Oracle XDK                             11.2.0.4.0    VALID
CATJAVA     Oracle Database Java Packages          11.2.0.4.0    VALID
APS         OLAP Analytic Workspace                11.2.0.4.0    VALID
XOQ         Oracle OLAP API                        11.2.0.4.0    VALID
RAC         Oracle Real Application Clusters       11.2.0.4.0    VALID

19 rows selected.
```

18. Now check the Timezone version, as follows:

```
SQL> SELECT version FROM v$timezone_file;

    VERSION
    ----------
    14
```

This completes the steps to the downgrade of the **Primary** database using the flashback to restore the point method. Now, let's downgrade the **standby** database using the same method.

Downgrading the physical standby database

For downgrading the standby database using flashback to restore the point method, we will be using the restore point that we created before starting the database upgrade to 19.9.0 by completing the following steps:

1. Shutdown the **standby** database from the current home (**19c**) and start only one instance in the mount mode, as follows:

   ```
   [oracle@virtual-dr-19crac1 dbs]$ srvctl stop  database -d homesdr

   [oracle@virtual-dr-19crac1 dbs]$ srvctl start instance -d homesdr
   -n virtual-dr-19crac1 -o mount

   [oracle@virtual-dr-19crac1 dbs]$ srvctl status database -d
   homesdr
   Instance homesdr1 is running on node virtual-dr-19crac1
   Instance homesdr2 is not running on node virtual-dr-19crac2
   ```

2. Check the restore point that we created in the **standby** database before starting the upgrade activity, as follows:

   ```
   SQL> @/home/oracle/rac_database_info.sql

   DATABASE_HOST        DB_NAME    DATABASE_ROLE      OPEN_MODE   STARTUP_TIME
   ------------------   --------   ----------------   --------   ------------
   virtual-dr-19crac1   homesdr1   PHYSICAL STANDBY   MOUNTED    11-MAR-21


   SQL> select NAME,GUARANTEE_FLASHBACK_DATABASE,TIME
        from V$restore_point;
   NAME                          GUARANTEE_F       TIME
   ---------------------------   ---------------   -----------------------
   STANDBY_BEFORE_19C_UPGRADE    YES               11-MAR 2107.08.42.000000000 AM
   ```

   Please keep in mind the restore point creation of the standby database. You will observe that the Standby database restore point's timestamp is before the primary database restore point creation time.

   The restore point time in the standby database must always be before that of its primary database.

3. On the **standby** database, first cancel the MRP using the following SQL statement:

   ```
   SQL> alter database recover managed standby database cancel;
   Database altered.
   ```

4. On the **standby** database, **flashback** the standby database to the preceding restore point, as follows:

```
SQL> flashback database to RESTORE POINT  STANDBY_BEFORE_19C_
UPGRADE;
Flashback complete.
```

5. Create a temporary **pfile** from the current **spfile**. On the **Standby** database, create **pfile** and remove all the hidden parameters as they are from **19c** and recreate the **spfile**, as follows:

```
SQL> create pfile='/u01/app/oracle/product/11.2.0.4/db_1/dbs/
after_downgrade.ora' from spfile='+DATAC1/homesdr/PARAMETERFILE/
spfilehomesdr1.ora';

File created.
```

6. Shutdown the **standby** database and modify the **pfile** created in the preceding step and remove all the underscore parameters which belongs to the **19c** database from it:

```
[oracle@virtual-dr-19crac1 dbs]$ srvctl stop  database -d homesdr
```

7. Now, create the **spfile** from the modified **pfile**:

```
[oracle@virtual-dr-19crac1 dbs]$ vi /u01/app/oracle/
product/11.2.0.4/db_1/dbs/after_downgrade.ora


[oracle@virtual-dr-19crac1 dbs]$ sqlplus / as sysdba
SQL*Plus: Release 19.0.0.0.0 - Production on Thu Mar 11 20:18:56
2021
Version 19.9.0.0.0
Copyright (c) 1982, 2019, Oracle.  All rights reserved.
Connected to an idle instance.
```

```
SQL> create spfile='+DATAC1/homesdr/PARAMETERFILE/spfilehomesdr1.
ora' from pfile='/u01/app/oracle/product/11.2.0.4/db_1/dbs/after_
downgrade.ora';
File created.
```

Downgrade the standby database's clusterware configuration of the database

Downgrade the cluster configuration of the physical **standby** database and start the database in the **mount** mode from the 11.2.0.4 home using the **srvctl** command, by completing the following steps:

1. Downgrade the clusterware configuration as follows:

```
[oracle@virtual-dr-19crac1 dbs]$ export ORACLE_HOME=/u01/app/
oracle/product/19c/db_1
[oracle@virtual-dr-19crac1 dbs]$ export PATH=$ORACLE_HOME/
bin:$PATH

[oracle@virtual-dr-19crac1 dbs]$ srvctl downgrade database -d
homesdr  -o /u01/app/oracle/product/11.2.0.4/db_1 -t 11.2.0.4
```

2. Also change the **oratab** entry for the standby database to point to the 11.2.0.4 home, as follows:

```
[oracle@virtual-dr-19crac1 dbs]$ vi /etc/oratab
```

3. Start the first database instance in the mount mode from the 11.2.0.4 home, as follows:

```
[oracle@virtual-dr-19crac1 dbs]$ srvctl export ORACLE_HOME=/u01/
app/oracle/product/11.2.0.4/db_1
```

```
[oracle@virtual-dr-19crac1 dbs]$ srvctl  export PATH=$ORACLE_
HOME/bin:$PATH
```

```
[oracle@virtual-dr-19crac1 dbs]$ srvctl start instance -d homesdr
-n virtual-dr-19crac1 -o mount
```

```
[oracle@virtual-dr-19crac1 dbs]$ srvctl status database -d
homesdr
Instance homesdr1 is running on node virtual-dr-19crac1
Instance homesdr2 is not running on node virtual-dr-19crac2
```

This completes the step of downgrading the standby database.

Recreate the data guard broker configuration

Since we have downgraded the database, we will need to recreate the dataguard broker configuration, by completing the following steps:

1. Make sure that the broker is started in both the primary and the standby databases. If it's not started, we can start it by using the following command:

For Primary database:

```
SQL> ALTER SYSTEM SET DG_BROKER_START=TRUE;
System altered.
```

```
For Physical Standby database:
```

```
SQL> ALTER SYSTEM SET DG_BROKER_START=TRUE;
System altered.
```

2. Remove the existing configuration and re-create the new configuration as follows:

```
[oracle@virtual-19crac1 dbs]$ dgmgrl

DGMGRL for Linux: Version 11.2.0.4.0 - 64bit Production
Copyright (c) 2000, 2009, Oracle. All rights reserved.
Welcome to DGMGRL, type "help" for information.
DGMGRL> connect sys
Password:
Connected.

DGMGRL> show configuration;
Configuration details cannot be determined by DGMGRL
```

3. As we can see, it's not able to determine the old configuration. Let's remove the old configuration and create a new configuration and enable it, as follows:

```
DGMGRL> remove configuration;
Removed configuration

DGMGRL > create configuration homespr as primary database is
'homespr' connect identifier is 'homespr';

DGMGRL > add database 'homesdr' as connect identifier is
'homesdr';

DGMGRL> enable configuration;
Enabled.

DGMGRL> show configuration;
Configuration – homespr
  Protection Mode: MaxPerformance
  Databases:
    homespr - Primary database
    homesdr - Physical standby database
Fast-Start Failover: DISABLED
Configuration Status:
SUCCESS
```

Once we enable the broker configuration, we can see that the primary database starts shipping all the redo data including the migrate data to the standby database, and the MRP process, which is started by the broker, will start applying the all the migrated redo data to the standby database. At this time, we can keep checking the standby database alert log, and we will see that the MRP process will start applying all the log files, including the logs containing the downgraded redo data.

In case we don't have the dataguard broker configured, we can enable the log shipping on the primary and start the recovery on the standby database, as follows:

@Primary database:

```
SQL> alter system set log_archive_dest_state_2='ENABLE' scope=sid='*';
Database altered.
```
@Physical Standby database:
```
SQL> ALTER DATABASE RECOVER managed standby database using current
logfile disconnect;
Database altered.
```

Once the MRP applies all the redo data to the standby database, we can stop and start the **standby** database in the read only mode and check the registry components status and the timezone version to see if they have downgraded successfully, by completing the following steps:

1. First set the **cluster_database** parameter to '**true**' and bounce the database, as follows:

   ```
   [oracle@virtual-dr-19crac1 dbs]$ sqlplus / as sysdba
   SQL> alter system set cluster_database=TRUE scope=spfile  sid='*';
   System altered.
   ```

   Stop the database
   ```
   [oracle@virtual-dr-19crac1 dbs]$srvctl stop database -d homesdr
   ```

   Start the database in read only mode

   ```
   [oracle@virtual-dr-19crac1 dbs]$ srvctl start  database -d
   homesdr  -o 'READ ONLY'
   ```

   ```
   [oracle@virtual-dr-19crac1 dbs]$ srvctl status database -d
   homesdr
   Instance homesdr1 is running on node virtual-dr-19crac1
   Instance homesdr2 is running on node virtual-dr-19crac2
   ```

2. Next, check the registry component status in the standby database, as follows:

   ```
   SQL> @/home/oracle/rac_database_info.sql
   ```

```
DATABASE_HOST       DB_NAME   DATABASE_ROLE     OPEN_MODE             STARTUP_TIME
-----------------   --------  ---------------   --------------------  -------------
virtual-dr-19crac1  homesdr1  PHYSICAL STANDBY  READ ONLY WITH APPLY  11-MAR-21
virtual-dr-19crac2  homesdr2  PHYSICAL STANDBY  READ ONLY WITH APPLY  11-MAR-21
```

```
SQL> select COMP_ID,COMP_NAME,VERSION,STATUS from dba_registry;
COMP_ID     COMP_NAME                              VERSION      STATUS
----------- -------------------------------------- ------------ ------
OWB         OWB                                    11.2.0.4.0   VALID
APEX        Oracle Application Express             3.2.1.00.12  VALID
EM          Oracle Enterprise Manager             11.2.0.4.0   VALID
AMD         OLAP Catalog                          11.2.0.4.0   VALID
SDO         Spatial                               11.2.0.4.0   VALID
ORDIM       Oracle Multimedia                     11.2.0.4.0   VALID
XDB         Oracle XML Database                   11.2.0.4.0   VALID
CONTEXT     Oracle Text                           11.2.0.4.0   VALID
EXF         Oracle Expression Filter              11.2.0.4.0   VALID
RUL         Oracle Rules Manager                  11.2.0.4.0   VALID
OWM         Oracle Workspace Manager              11.2.0.4.0   VALID
CATALOG     Oracle Database Catalog Views         11.2.0.4.0   VALID
CATPROC     Oracle Database Packages and Types    11.2.0.4.0   VALID
JAVAVM      JServer JAVA Virtual Machine          11.2.0.4.0   VALID
XML         Oracle XDK                            11.2.0.4.0   VALID
CATJAVA     Oracle Database Java Packages         11.2.0.4.0   VALID
APS         OLAP Analytic Workspace               11.2.0.4.0   VALID
XOQ         Oracle OLAP API                       11.2.0.4.0   VALID
RAC         Oracle Real Application Clusters      11.2.0.4.0   VALID
19 rows selected.
```

3. Now, check the Timezone version in the physical standby database, as follows:

```
SQL> SELECT version FROM v$timezone_file;

        VERSION
        ----------
            14
```

The Timezone has now been successfully downgraded from 32(19c) to 14(11g).

Let's do the final check to ensure that both the primary and the standby databases are in sync with each other. On the **Primary** database, we switch a couple of **logfiles** and check if the **standby** database is receiving and applying them, as follows:

@Primary database

```
SQL> @/home/oracle/rac_database_info.sql

DATABASE_HOST     DB_NAME    DATABASE_ROLE   OPEN_MODE    STARTUP_TIME
---------------   --------   -------------   ----------   ------------
virtual-19crac1   homespr1   PRIMARY         READ WRITE   11-MAR-21
virtual-19crac2   homespr2   PRIMARY         READ WRITE   11-MAR-21

SQL> alter system switch all logfile;
System altered.
```

```
SQL> archive log list;
Database log mode               Archive Mode
Automatic archival              Enabled
Archive destination             USE_DB_RECOVERY_FILE_DEST
Oldest online log sequence      15
Next log sequence to archive    15
Current log sequence            16
SQL>
```

@Physcial Standby Database:

@/home/oracle/standby_database_lag.sql

```
DATABASE_HOST       DB_NAME   DATABASE_ROLE     OPEN_MODE               STARTUP_TIME
----------------    --------  ---------------   --------------------    --------------
virtual-dr-19crac1  homesdr1  PHYSICAL STANDBY  READ ONLY WITH APPLY    11-MAR-21
virtual-dr-19crac2  homesdr2  PHYSICAL STANDBY  READ ONLY WITH APPLY    11-MAR-21

INST_ID     PROCESS     STATUS          THREAD#     SEQUENCE#   BLOCK#    BLOCKS
----------  ----------  ------------    ----------  ----------  -------   ------
        1 MRP0          APPLYING_LOG  1             16          6         102400

THREAD#     ARCHIVED    APPLIED     GAP
----------  ----------  ----------  ----------
      1         16          16          0
      2         14          13          0
```

With this step, we have successfully downgraded the database from 19c to 11.2.0.4 using the **flashback** method.

Conclusion

In this chapter, we upgraded the database using the database parallel upgrade utility, the Timezone data using Oracle provided scripts, and the cluster configuration manually. We also downgraded both the primary and the physical standby database using the **flashback** method. The database parallel upgrade utility is a good utility which helps in upgrading the Oracle database in the best possible way, but we still need to perform most of the steps manually which includes, updating the **/etc/oratab** entries with the new home, upgrading the cluster configuration of the database using the **srvctl** command, and creating the guaranteed restore point in the primary database. We can avoid doing most of these manual steps, if we use Oracle's AutoUpgrade utility. The AutoUpgrade tool is an extraordinary tool which automates most of these steps for us. Along with upgrading the database, it also takes care of upgrading the cluster configuration of the Oracle database, upgrades the timezone version, updates the entries **/etc/oratab**, and a few other things. We will use the AutoUpgrade utility in all the following chapters and test upgrading the Oracle 11g/12c and 18c databases to 19c. In the next chapter, we will learn what the AutoUpgrade utility is, and see how we can use this tool to upgrade the Oracle database from version 11.2.0.4 to 19.9.0.0.

Multiple choice questions

1. **What is the default parallel degree for the database parallel upgrade utility, dbupgrade?**

    a) 2

    b) 4

    c) 6

    d) 8

2. **Does the database upgrade utility create a guaranteed restore point by itself?**

    a) Yes

    b) No

3. **How many fixup scripts does the dbupgrade command produce after running the preupgrade.jar?**

    a) 1

    b) 6

    c) 3

    d) 2

4. **Does the database parallel upgrade utility upgrade the Timezone version?**

    a) Yes

    b) No

Answers

1. b

2. b

3. d

4. b

CHAPTER 3
Upgrading Oracle Database from 11.2.0.4 to 19.9.0 (Using AutoUpgrade)

Introduction

In the previous chapter, we saw how to upgrade an Oracle database version from 11.2.0.4 to 19.9.0 using the parallel upgrade utility called **dbupgrade**, which is a manual method and involves many steps that need to be performed.

In this chapter, we will upgrade the Oracle database version from 11.2.0.4 to 19.9.0 using a utility called **AutoUpgrade**, understand how the AutoUpgrade utility works, and how we can upgrade an Oracle database with minimal human intervention.

Structure

In this chapter, we will cover the following topics:

- Introduction to the AutoUpgrade utility
- Installation of the AutoUpgrade utility
- The configuration file used in AutoUpgrade and its different parameters
- AutoUpgrade error codes
- The stages and the processing modes in the AutoUpgrade

- Logs generated from the upgrade activity

- 11.2.0.4 primary database upgrade to 19c using AutoUpgrade utility

- Running AutoUpgrade in 'analyze' mode and fixing issues

- AutoUpgrade log locations

- Post-upgrade checks

- Upgrading the physical standby database from 11.2.0.4 to 19c

- Validation of the primary and the physical standby database upgrade

- Oracle downgrade methods

- Downgrading the primary and the standby databases using Oracle provided scripts

- Issues occurring when downgrading a 19c database to 11.2.0.4 and its solutions

- Downgrading the timezone version using the Oracle provided scripts

- A few known issues and solutions

Objectives

After studying this chapter, you will gain knowledge on what an AutoUpgrade utility is, what its different components are, and how we can use it to upgrade the Oracle database from the lower versions to 19c. You will get familiar with the different processing modes that AutoUpgrade can be run with and the various stages that the utility goes through when it is used to upgrade the database. You will know about the configuration file that is used by the AutoUpgrade tool. You will also see how to downgrade the database from 19c to its source version by using the Oracle provided scripts.

The AutoUpgrade utility

The **AutoUpgrade** tool is a new upgrade utility which allows you to upgrade your Oracle databases with minimal manual intervention. The AutoUpgrade tool is designed in such a way that when it's run, it not only identifies the issues before the database upgrade but also fixes them, and then performs the database upgrade and runs any post upgrade steps. Please note that the AutoUpgrade tool cannot be used to upgrade the grid infrastructure; it is used only to upgrade the Oracle database.

Figure 3.1 shows the flow of the high-level steps that the AutoUpgrade utility performs when upgrading the Oracle database:

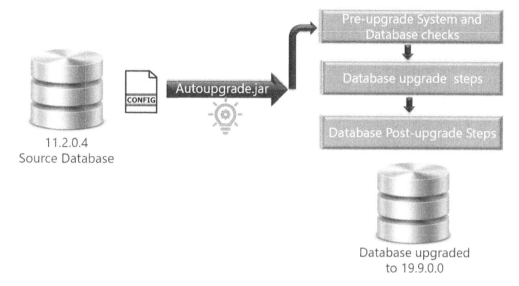

Figure 3.1*: AutoUpgrade utility*

The AutoUpgrade tool can upgrade both the single instances and the cluster databases. It also supports both the **non-container database (non-cdb)** and the **container database (cdb)** upgrades. The AutoUpgrade tool supports upgrading a non-cdb database to a **pluggable database (pdb)** using one single command, and also supports all the operating systems where we can have the Oracle databases configured, and it upgrades multiple databases in one single operation.

Support of the AutoUpgrade utility

The AutoUpgrade tool can be used to upgrade the Oracle databases to the following target database versions:

- Oracle Database version 12c (12.2.0 with Jan 2019 release update and later)

- Oracle Database version 18c (18.5.0 and later)

- Oracle Database version 19c (19.3.0 and later)

The minimum Oracle database version that the AutoUpgrade utility can upgrade from is Oracle Database 11.2.0.4. As of today, the AutoUpgrade tool can be used to upgrade the Oracle databases from the following versions to Oracle 19c:

- Oracle Database version 18c

- Oracle Database version 12.2.0.1

- Oracle Database version 12.1.0.2

- Oracle Database version 11.2.0.4

Installing the AutoUpgrade utility

The AutoUpgrade utility uses an autoupgrade.jar file to upgrade the Oracle database and this jar file comes, by default, with the Oracle 19c (19.3.0) installation and later, but Oracle strongly recommends downloading and using the latest version of the AutoUpgrade tool which can be downloaded from the **My Oracle support** (**MOS**) (Doc ID 2485457.1).

Configuration File of AutoUpgrade Utility

The AutoUpgrade configuration file contains all the information required by the AutoUpgrade tool to upgrade the Oracle database. It is the only file that we need to provide the information to the AutoUpgrade utility. This tool basically reads a configuration file and then starts upgrading the Oracle database based on the information defined in the configuration file. We can create a sample configuration file by running the **AutoUpgrade** jar file, and later we can rename it with any user defined name and pass an argument when we run the AutoUpgrade tool, as follows:

```
[oracle@chapvm-19crac1 vicedbpr]$ $ORACLE_HOME/jdk/bin/java -jar
$ORACLE_HOME/rdbms/admin/autoupgrade.jar -create_sample_file config

Sample Configuration file.
-------------------------

[oracle@chapvm-19crac1 vicedbpr]$ cat Sample_upgrade.cfg

### Global parameters ###############################
global.autoupg_log_dir=/u01/software/upgrade/texapr

## First database ###################################
upg1.log_dir=/u01/software/upgrade
upg1.sid=texapr1
upg1.source_home=/u01/app/Oracle/product/12c/db_1
upg1.target_home=/u01/app/Oracle/product/19c/db_1
upg1.upgrade_node=virtual-19crac1
upg1.run_utlrp=yes
upg1.timezone_upg=yes
upg1.target_version=19

### Second database #################################
upg2.sid=database1
upg2.source_home=/u01/app/Oracle/product/111.2.0.4/db_1
upg2.target_home=/u01/app/Oracle/product/19c/db_1
```

```
[oracle@chapvm-19crac1 vicedbpr]$
```

Note: upg1 and upg2 mentioned earlier are user defined; you can use any names for these parameters.

Configuration file parameters of AutoUpgrade

The configuration file used by AutoUpgrade can contain parameters for one database or multiple databases. We can define the local parameters for each database and also, we can define the global parameters to work globally for all the databases defined in the configuration file. When the parameters are specified for multiple databases running from the different database homes, the AutoUpgrade tool has the capability to upgrade all the databases from the different versions mentioned in the configuration file to Oracle 19c in one single operation.

Global parameters

The global parameters are the parameters which specifies the behavior for all the databases defined in the configuration file. The global parameters are optional. Some of the few global parameters are listed as follows:

```
global.autoupg_log_dir  : Log location for all the log files.
drop_grp_after_upgrade  : Specify to drop restore point after the
                          database upgrade.
before_action           : Specify custom scripts to run before starting
                          upgrade.
after_action            : Specify custom scripts to run after
                          completing upgrade.
```

Local parameters

The local parameters are specific to a specific database defined in the configuration file. You can refer to the following Oracle official document for a complete set of parameters:

https://docs.Oracle.com/en/database/Oracle/Oracle-database/19/upgrd/autoupgrade-utility-configuration-files.html#GUID-5C5542C0-F21E-4DBF-A878-27F5F4AF6519

AutoUpgrade version

Oracle keeps updating the **AutoUpgrade** jar file with new features on a regular basis and that is the reason why Oracle strongly recommends using the latest version for performing any Oracle database upgrade. We can check the current version of AutoUpgrade by using the following command:

```
[oracle@chapvm-19crac1]$ $ORACLE_HOME/jdk/bin/java -jar $ORACLE_HOME/
rdbms/admin/autoupgrade.jar -version
build.hash 8ee6880
build.version 21.1.1    <-Version
build.date 2020/12/14 14:41:34
build.max_target_version 21
build.supported_target_versions 12.2,18,19,21
build.type production
```

We will use AutoUpgrade version 21.1.1 for all the database upgrades demonstrated in all the chapters in this book.

AutoUpgrade jar file options

AutoUpgrade can be run with various options. We can run AutoUpgrade with '-help' option to see all the available options, as follows:

```
[oracle@chapvm-19crac1]$ $ORACLE_HOME/jdk/bin/java -jar $ORACLE_HOME/
rdbms/admin/autoupgrade.jar -help
```

AutoUpgrade error codes

Whenever AutoUpgrade hits with an error, it displays an error code. A few of the error codes might be obvious and easy to understand the error, whereas a few might be a little ambiguous, and we may need to check the log files to find more details about the error. We can check all the error codes using the latest version of AutoUpgrade (version, 21.1.3) using the following command (Please note this option (**-error_code**) is not available with the older version of AutoUpgrade tool.):

```
[oracle@chapvm-19crac1]$ $ORACLE_HOME/jdk/bin/java -jar $ORACLE_HOME/
rdbms/admin/autoupgrade.jar -version
build.hash 57ab246
build.version 21.1.3    <-Version
build.date 2021/04/21 13:32:13
build.supported_target_versions 12.2,18,19,21
build.type production
[oracle@chapvm-19crac1]$ 19crac1 software]$ $ORACLE_HOME/jdk/bin/java
-jar $ORACLE_HOME/rdbms/admin/autoupgrade.jar -error_code
```

The preceding command displays almost over 120 error codes. we cannot display all the codes here but below are few of them.

```
ERROR3106.ERROR  = UPG-3106
ERROR3106.CAUSE  = Unable to upgrade RAC database on CRS
ERROR3107.ERROR  = UPG-3107
ERROR3107.CAUSE  = Unable to update spfile information on CRS
ERROR3108.ERROR  = UPG-3108
```

```
ERROR3108.CAUSE  = Failed to enable RAC database on CRS
ERROR3109.ERROR  = UPG-3109
ERROR3109.CAUSE  = Unable to stop current instance
ERROR3110.ERROR  = UPG-3110
ERROR3110.CAUSE  = Unable to downgrade RAC database
                   source binaries on CRS
ERROR3111.ERROR  = UPG-3111
ERROR3111.CAUSE  = Failed to enable RAC database source binaries on CRS
ERROR3112.ERROR  = UPG-3112
ERROR3112.CAUSE  = Unable to start RAC database
                   after downgrade source binaries on CRS
```

Oracle database upgrade process using AutoUpgrade

The AutoUpgrade utility goes through the various pre-defined modes and stages while it is upgrading the database.

Processing modes of AutoUpgrade

AutoUpgrade can be run in multiple modes which include Analyze, Fixup, Deploy, and Upgrade, and each of these modes goes through some predefined stages which runs predefined tasks and performs the database upgrade.

Figure 3.2 shows the various stages of the AutoUpgrade utility:

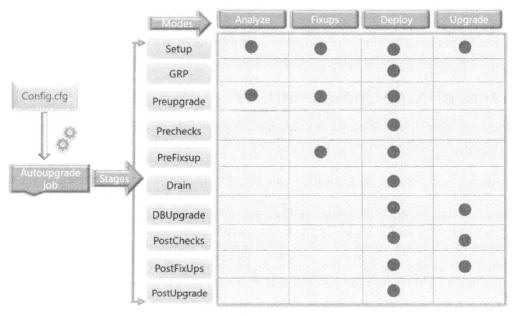

Figure 3.2: *AutoUpgrade tool different stages and modes*

When we run the AutoUpgrade, the following is the sequence of steps that it performs, depending upon the mode that we selected:

- **Analyze mode**: The Analyze mode is the first mode that the AutoUpgrade utility runs as part of the database upgrade. In this mode, it reads the source database and preforms all the prechecks and prepares the database for the upgrade. The AutoUpgrade process only reads the database, and this mode will not make any changes to the source database, and the source database can continue to be available during in Analyze mode. This mode will generate the log files which needs to be reviewed to identify any potential issues and fix them before going to the upgrade process.

- **Fixup mode**: The Fixup mode also reads the source database and identifies any potential issues that needs to be fixed before the database upgrade. The identified fixes can either be fixed automatically by the AutoUpgrade utility when we run the upgrade in the deploy mode, or fixed manually before initiating the database upgrade execution in the deploy mode.

- **Deploy mode**: The Deploy mode is the mode which actually executes the database upgrade, based on the information defined in the configuration file. This mode will start by performing a pre-check in the source database and fix any issues that can be fixed automatically and ensure that the database is ready for the database upgrade. It will then perform the database upgrade and once the upgrade completes, it will also perform the post upgrade tasks including the Timezone version upgrade and any custom scripts that we defined in the configuration file (like running **utlrp** script).

- **Upgrade mode**: The Upgrade mode also performs the same steps as the Deploy mode, the only difference is that this mode is used when you don't have access to the source database home.

Stages of AutoUpgrade utility

When the AutoUpgrade utility is started with any of the modes mentioned earlier, the Oracle AutoUpgrade job manager process will be started, and this process will parse the configuration file and create the required jobs depending on the processing mode. Each of these jobs goes through the various stages and performs a set of specific actions to perform the actual upgrade work. Each of these AutoUpgrade jobs generates a unique ID, called **jobid**, specific for each of the database mentioned in the configuration file. AutoUpgrade uses **jobid** as an option to detect its current stage and if it has to resume the operation, it will resume from the previously stopped point without starting from the beginning of the operation. The various series of stages that the AutoUpgrade process goes through are given as follows:

- **Setup stage**: This is the first stage where the AutoUpgrade job manager process creates the upgrade job and starts the job.

- **GRP stage**: In this stage, the AutoUpgrade tool creates the GRP before starting any upgrade process in the source database. We can use this restore point to downgrade the database using the flashback method.

- **Pre-upgrade stage**: In this stage, AutoUpgrade performs various pre-upgrade checks in the source database which includes the checks like free space, available memory, and so on.

- **Pre-checks stage**: In this stage, AutoUpgrade will read the source database and perform readiness checks to see if the source database meets all the requirements to get upgraded.

- **Pre-fixups stage**: In this stage, AutoUpgrade performs the pre-upgrade fixups which it has identified in the precheck stage like gathering the statistics, purging the recycle bin, and so on.

- **Drain stage**: In this stage, the AutoUpgrade process will start shutting down the source listener and the source database.

- **Dbupgrade stage**: This is the stage where the AutoUpgrade process will perform the actual upgrade process. After the upgrade task, it also runs the **utlrp** script to compile the invalid objects in the upgraded database.

- **Postchecks stage**: In this stage, the AutoUpgrade process will run the post upgrade checks to ensure that the database is upgraded successfully. If it finds everything alright, it will then move to running the post upgrade fixup scripts in the next stage.

- **Postfixups stage**: In this stage, the AutoUpgrade process will perform the post upgrade tasks including the timezone upgrade.

- **PostUpgrade stage**: This is the final stage of the upgrade process where the AutoUpgrade will upgrade the database configuration to the target database version and start the database from the target database home. It will also copy all the database configuration files (like **tnsnames.ora**, **sqlnet.ora**, etc.) from the source database home and add them to the target database home. It will then update the configuration file called **/etc/oratab** to point to the new database home.

Console commands of AutoUpgrade

Some of the AutoUpgrade commands which you can use while the AutoUpgrade process is running are given in the following section. We have to run these following commands from the AutoUpgrade Command Prompt:

```
Command                           Action

------------------------          -------------------------------------
lsj                               List the running jobs
status   -job (job number)        Status of specific job
abort    -job (job number)        Aborts a specific job
resume   -job (job number)        Resume a specific job
Restore  -job (job number)        restores a database from GRP
```

Restarting an AutoUpgrade job

As mentioned earlier, we can use the **resume** option from the AutoUpgrade command prompt and, by default, the AutoUpgrade will resume the job from the point where it was halted. This is a good point, as let's say, if you cancelled the upgrade job by mistake, you can then simply resume the job using the resume option and it will pick it up from where it was stopped. However, if you want to start the AutoUpgrade process from the beginning, first you must remove the recovery checkpoint that it had created for the current run by using the following command and then if you start the **autoupgrade**, it will start from the beginning with a new job number:

```
[oracle@chapvm-19crac1]$ORACLE_HOME/jdk/bin/java -jar $ORACLE_HOME/
rdbms/admin/autoupgrade.jar -create_sample_file -clear_recovery_
checkpoint
```

Logs of AutoUpgrade

AutoUpgrade generates a few logs in the html format and most of them in the text format. It generates the logs in the location defined with the parameter **autoupg_log_dir** in the configuration file. So far, we saw what is AutoUpgrade tool and how it works; now, let's see how we can upgrade the database using the AutoUpgrade utility in the following section.

Upgrading RAC database from Oracle 11g (11.2.0.4) to Oracle 19c (19.9.0)

In the first part of this section, we will upgrade a two-node RAC database from the version Oracle 11g (11.2.0.4) to Oracle 19c (19.9.0) using the AutoUpgrade utility. We will also upgrade its physical standby database using the redo logs. In the latter part of this section, we will downgrade both the primary and the physical standby database from the version Oracle 19c (19.9.0) to Oracle 11g (11.2.0.4) using the Oracle provided downgrade scripts. *Figure 3.3* provides a pictorial representation of this database upgrade:

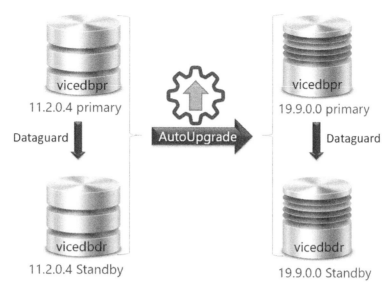

Figure 3.3: *Database Upgrade using AutoUpgrade from Oracle 11g (11.2.0.4) to Oracle 19c (19.9.0)*

High-level steps of the AutoUpgrade process

The following are a few high-level steps that are performed as part of upgrading the 11.2.0.4 database to 19c using the AutoUpgrade utility. This provides the covers points including the pre-upgrade, upgrade, and post upgrade steps, as follows:

1. Take a full backup of the primary database.

2. Enable the flashback feature in the primary and the physical standby database.

3. Set the fast recovery area size to a higher value in both the primary and the physical standby database.

4. Gather the dictionary statistics to the latest as this will help the database upgrade process to run faster.

5. Purge the **recyclebin** as this will help us to save time during the database upgrade and in reducing the downtime needed for the database upgrade.

6. Ensure that the physical standby database is in sync with the primary database before starting the database upgrade process.

7. Create a GRP in the physical standby database.

8. Disable the **dataguard** broker in both the primary and the physical standby database.

9. Shutdown the physical standby database.

10. Run the AutoUpgrade script in the ANALYZE mode in the primary database and fix any issues that are identified by the AutoUpgrade tool.

11. Upgrade the primary database by running the AutoUpgrade script in the **DEPLOY** mode.

12. Perform any post upgrade checks on the primary database.

13. Upgrade the physical standby database with the migrate redo data that it receives from the primary database.

14. Enable the **dataguard** broker and perform a final check on both the primary database and the physical standby database.

15. Perform any post upgrade steps for the physical standby database.

We created the following two scripts which we can use to check the primary database configuration and the physical standby database lag. We will be using these scripts throughout this chapter.

Script-1: This script will pull the primary database details like, the mode and the role of the database.

```
[oracle@chapvm-19crac1] cat /home/Oracle/rac_database_info.sql


set lines 200
col DATABASE_HOST for a30;
col HOST_NAME for a15;
col DATABASE_ROLE for a10
col OPEN_MODE for a10
col STARTUP_TIME for a20
SELECT i.HOST_NAME "DATABASE_HOST" ,i.INSTANCE_NAME "DB_NAME",
d.DATABASE_ROLE " DATABASE_ROLE", d.OPEN_MODE "OPEN_MODE", STARTUP_TIME
from GV$DATABASE d, gv$instance i
where i.INST_ID=d.INST_ID;
```

Script-2: This script will check the current lag on the physical **standby** database and display the physical **standby** database role and mode info as well.

```
[oracle@chapvm-19crac1] cat /home/Oracle/standby_database_lag.sql


set lines 200
```

```
col DATABASE_HOST for a30;
col HOST_NAME for a15;
col DATABASE_ROLE for a10
col OPEN_MODE for a10
col STARTUP_TIME for a20
SELECT i.HOST_NAME "DATABASE_HOST" ,i.INSTANCE_NAME "DB_NAME",
d.DATABASE_ROLE " DATABASE_ROLE", d.OPEN_MODE " OPEN_MODE ", STARTUP_
TIME from GV$DATABASE d, gv$instance i  where i.INST_ID=d.INST_ID;

select inst_id,process, status, thread#, sequence#, block#, blocks
from gv$managed_standby
where process='MRP0';

select a.thread#, (select max (sequence#)
from v$archived_log  where archived='YES' and thread#=a.thread#)
archived, max(a.sequence#) applied,  (select max(sequence#)
from v$archived_log
where archived='YES' and thread#=a.thread#)-max(a.sequence#)gap from
v$archived_log a where a.applied='YES' group by a.thread# order by
thread#;
```

Check the configuration of primary database and physical standby database

In this demonstration, we have the primary database, which is a two-node RAC database and a physical standby database which is also a two-node RAC database. The primary database environment is the Oracle 11g (11.2.0.4) database binaries being installed, and the Oracle home being patched with the April 2020 **Patch Set Update** (**PSU**).

Setting up the source environment

The primary database version and the patch set is shown as follows:

```
Cluster Nodes       : chapvm-19crac1
                      chapvm-19crac2
OS version          : Oracle Enterprise Linux 7.1 64 bit
Oracle Home         : /u01/app/oracle/product/11.2.0.4/db_1
Database Version    : 11.2.0.4 with April 2020 Database Patch Set Update
Grid Version        : 19.9.0

[oracle@chapvm-19crac1 ]$ export ORACLE_HOME=/u01/app/oracle/
product/11.2.0.4/db_1
[oracle@chapvm-19crac1 ]$ export PATH=$ORACLE_HOME/bin:$PATH
[oracle@chapvm-19crac1 ]$ $ORACLE_HOME/OPatch/opatch lspatches
30670774;Database Patch Set Update : 11.2.0.4.200414 (30670774)
```

```
29938455;OCW Patch Set Update : 11.2.0.4.191015 (29938455)
OPatch succeeded.
```

The **primary** database name is **vicedbpr** and the following are its RAC instances:

```
SQL> @/home/Oracle/rac_database_info.sql


DATABASE_HOST    DB_NAME      DATABASE_ROLE    OPEN_MODE    STARTUP_TIME
--------------   ----------   --------------   -----------  ------------
chapvm-19crac1   vicedbpr1    PRIMARY          READ WRITE   15-FEB-21
chapvm-19crac2   vicedbpr2    PRIMARY          READ WRITE   15-FEB-21
```

The physical standby database environment is the same as the version of the primary database, that is, the Oracle 11g (11.2.0.4) database binaries installed and patched with April 2020 PSU, as follows:

```
Cluster Nodes              : chapstdby-19crac1
                             chapstdby-19crac2
OS version                 : Oracle Enterprise Linux 7.1 64 bit
Oracle Home                : /u01/app/oracle/product/11.2.0.4/db_1
Database Version           : 11.2.0.4 with April 2020 Database Patch Set
Update
Grid Version               : 19.9.0
```

```
[oracle@chapstdby-19crac1 ~]$ export ORACLE_HOME=/u01/app/oracle/
product/11.2.0.4/db_1
[oracle@chapstdby-19crac1 ~]$ export PATH=$ORACLE_HOME/bin:$PATH

[oracle@chapstdby-19crac1 ~]$  $ORACLE_HOME/OPatch/opatch lspatches
30670774;Database Patch Set Update : 11.2.0.4.200414 (30670774)
29938455;OCW Patch Set Update : 11.2.0.4.191015 (29938455)
OPatch succeeded.
```

The physical standby database name is **vicedbdr** and the following are its RAC instances:

```
SQL> @/home/Oracle/rac_database_info.sql


DATABASE_HOST      DB_NAME      DATABASE_ROLE      OPEN_MODE    STARTUP_TIME
----------------   ----------   ----------------   ---------    ------------
chapstdby-19crac1  vicedbdr1    PHYSICAL STANDBY   MOUNTED      15-FEB-21
chapstdby-19crac2  vicedbdr2    PHYSICAL STANDBY   MOUNTED      15-FEB-21
```

Setting up the target environment

We installed Oracle 19c (19.3.0) on both the primary and the physical standby database servers and applied the October 2020 PSU. If you want to use the latest patch set, then check and download the latest patch set from the **My Oracle Support** (**MOS**).

The target primary database binary version and its patch set is as follows:

```
Cluster Nodes        : chapvm-19crac1
                       chapvm-19crac2
OS version           : Oracle Enterprise Linux 7.1 64 bit
Oracle Home          : /u01/app/oracle/product/19c/db_1
Database Version     : 19.3.0.0 with October 2020 Database Bundle Patch
Grid Version         : 19.9.0


[oracle@chapvm-19crac1 ]$ export ORACLE_HOME=/u01/app/oracle/
product/19c/db_1
[oracle@chapvm-19crac1 ]$ export PATH=$ORACLE_HOME/bin:$PATH

[oracle@chapvm-19crac1 ]$ $ORACLE_HOME/OPatch/opatch lspatches
31668882;OJVM RELEASE UPDATE: 19.9.0.0.201020 (31668882)
31772784;OCW RELEASE UPDATE 19.9.0.0.0 (31772784)
31771877;Database Release Update : 19.9.0.0.201020 (31771877)
OPatch succeeded.
```

The target physical standby database binary version and its patch set is as follows:

```
Cluster Nodes        : chapstdby-19crac1
                       chapstdby-19crac2
OS version           : Oracle Enterprise Linux 7.1 64 bit
Oracle Home          : /u01/app/oracle/product/19c/db_1
Database Version     : 19.3.0.0 with October 2020 Database Bundle Patch
Grid Version         : 19.9.0

[oracle@chapstdby-19crac1 ~]$ export ORACLE_HOME=/u01/app/oracle/
product/19c/db_1
[oracle@chapstdby-19crac1 ~]$ export PATH=$ORACLE_HOME/bin:$PATH

[oracle@chapstdby-19crac1 ~]$  $ORACLE_HOME/OPatch/opatch lspatches
31668882;OJVM RELEASE UPDATE: 19.9.0.0.201020 (31668882)
31772784;OCW RELEASE UPDATE 19.9.0.0.0 (31772784)
31771877;Database Release Update : 19.9.0.0.201020 (31771877)
OPatch succeeded.
```

Pre-requisites

Check some of the pre-requisites, and also a few upfront tasks that we can perform for the database upgrade.

Perform full backup of primary source database

Before staring any database upgrade activity, always take a **FULL** level 0 **RMAN** backup of the source database. The following is a sample **rman** script that we can use to take Full level 0 backup of the primary source database (You can use your scripts that works for your environment.):

```
run
{
allocate channel ch1 device type disk format '/u01/19cupgrade/DATA_
L0_%d_%Y%M%D_%s-%p-%t';
allocate channel ch2 device type disk format '/u01/19cupgrade/DATA_
0_%d_%Y%M%D_%s-%p-%t';
allocate channel ch3 device type disk format '/u01/19cupgrade/DATA_
0_%d_%Y%M%D_%s-%p-%t';
allocate channel ch4 device type disk format '/u01/19cupgrade/DATA_
0_%d_%Y%M%D_%s-%p-%t';
backup incremental level 0 database plus archivelog TAG='FULL_BACKUP_B4_
UPGRADE'
format '/u01/19cupgrade/DATA_L0_%d_%Y%M%D_%s-%p-%t';
backup tag 'CONTROL_BACKUP_B4_UPGRADE' current controlfile
format '/u01/19cupgrade/DATA_CONTROL_%d_%Y%M%D_%s-%p-%t';
release channel ch1;
release channel ch2;
release channel ch3;
release channel ch4;
}
```

Enable flashback feature in primary source database

Ensure that the flashback is enabled in both the primary and the physical standby database. When we use the **AutoUpgrade** utility to upgrade the Oracle database, we need to have the flashback enabled in the database as the AutoUpgrade utility creates a guaranteed restore point during the upgrade process, and the upgrade process will fail in the early stages if the flashback is not enabled.

Login to the primary source database and enable the flashback feature using the following SQL statement:

```
SQL> alter database flashback on;
```

```
Database altered.
```

Make sure that the flashback is enabled successfully using the following SQL statement:

```
SQL> select name, db_unique_name, database_role, log_mode, force_
logging, flashback_on from gv$database;

NAME      DB_UNIQUE_NAME  DATABASE_ROLE  LOG_MODE    FORCE_LOGGING  FLASHBACK_ON
--------  --------------  -------------  ----------  -------------  -----------
VICEDBPR  vicedbpr        PRIMARY        ARCHIVELOG  YES            YES
VICEDBPR  vicedbpr        PRIMARY        ARCHIVELOG  YES            YES
```

Enable flashback in physical standby database

To enable the flashback in the physical standby database, we must cancel the **managed recovery process** (**MRP**) and then enable the flashback and re-start the MRP.

Login to the physical standby database and run the following SQL statements:

```
SQL> alter database recover managed standby database cancel;
Database altered.
```

```
SQL> alter database flashback on;
Database altered.
```

```
SQL> alter database recover managed standby database using current
logfile disconnect;
Database altered.
```

Make sure that the flashback is enabled successfully using the following SQL statement in the physical standby database:

```
SQL> select name, db_unique_name, database_role, log_mode, force_
logging, flashback_on from gv$database;

NAME      DB_UNIQUE_NAME  DATABASE_ROLE     LOG_MODE    FORCE_LOGGING  FLASHBACK
--------  --------------  ----------------  ----------  -------------  ---------
VICEPRPR  viceprdr        PHYSICAL STANDBY  ARCHIVELOG  YES            YES
VICEPRPR  viceprdr        PHYSICAL STANDBY  ARCHIVELOG  YES            YES
```

Ensure enough space in Fast Recovery Area (FRA)

Ensure we have enough free space in the Fast recovery area, and that we must set the recovery destination size to a sufficient number as we need the recovery logs until we change the compatible parameter to 19.0.0 after the upgrade. Also, the FRA will store all the flashback logs which we will need, in case we have to downgrade the

Oracle database back to Oracle 11g (11.2.0.4) after the upgrade using the flashback method. Check and set the **db_recovery_file_dest_size** parameter to a higher value. We need to set this parameter with a higher value in both the primary and the physical standby database (that is, 11g databases). In our case, we are setting it this parameter value to 20G, as follows:

```
SQL> show parameter recovery

NAME                          TYPE           VALUE
--------------------------    ------------   ----------------
db_recovery_file_dest         string         +DATA1
db_recovery_file_dest_size    big integer    10000M
recovery_parallelism          integer        0

SQL> alter system set db_recovery_file_dest_size=20G scope=both sid='*';
System altered.
SQL> show parameter recovery

NAME                          TYPE           VALUE
--------------------------    ------------   ----------------
db_recovery_file_dest         string         +DATA1
db_recovery_file_dest_size    big integer    20G
recovery_parallelism          integer        0
```

This completes the precheck steps. Ensure that both the primary and the physical standby database of Oracle 11g (11.2.0.4) are in sync with each other, and that we have enabled the flashback feature in both primary database and the physical standby database.

Gather dictionary statistics

It's always good to collect the dictionary statistics before the database upgrade process. Having good statistics on the dictionary tables and fixed objects can help the database upgrade to run faster and thus help in reducing the overall downtime required for the database upgrade.

Use the following SQL statement to check the dictionary statistics' last collected time:

```
SQL> col operation for a33
SQL> set lines 200
SQL> select operation, to_char(max(end_time),'dd-mon-yy hh24:mi') latest
     from dba_optstat_operations
     where operation in
     ('gather_fixed_objects_stats','gather_dictionary_stats')
     group by operation;
```

```
OPERATION                               LATEST
----------------------------------      ---------------
gather_fixed_objects_stats              14-FEB-21 16:38
gather_dictionary_stats                 14-FEB-21 19:50
```

We can gather the dictionary statistics using the following SQL statements:

```
SQL> EXECUTE DBMS_STATS.GATHER_DICTIONARY_STATS;
PL/SQL procedure successfully completed.


SQL> EXECUTE DBMS_STATS.GATHER_FIXED_OBJECTS_STATS;
PL/SQL procedure successfully completed.
```

Purge recyclebin

Check the **recyclebin** and purge it; in some cases, it might take more time if we have too many objects in the **recyclebin**. So, it's always a good idea to purge the recycle bin before starting the upgrade process, as this can significantly reduce the overall time taken for the database upgrade. It might be a good idea if we can check this well ahead of time and purge the **recyclebin** in the source primary database. If the **recyclebin** has too many objects, then sometimes it might even take at least a couple of hours to get them purged, which will significantly increase the downtime required for the database upgrade.

Now, let's look at the following steps:

1. Check the object count in the **recyclebin**, as follows:

    ```
    SQL> select count(*)  from recyclebin;
    ```

2. Purge the recycle bin using the following SQL statement:
    ```
    SQL> purge dba_recyclebin;
    DBA Recyclebin purged.
    ```

3. Re-check the object count in the **recyclebin**, as follows:
    ```
    SQL> select count(*)  from recyclebin;
    ```

Hidden parameters

If the source database has any hidden (underscore) parameters set, Oracle recommends to reset them before the database upgrade and set them back after the database upgrade. We can use the following scripts which generate the **SET/RESET** commands for all the hidden parameters in the database:

Script-1: The command to display the current hidden parameters is as follows:

```
SQL> col value for a44
SQL> col name for a55
SQL> set lines 200
SQL> set pages 0
SQL> select name,value
from SYS.V$PARAMETER
WHERE name LIKE '\_%' ESCAPE '\' order by name;

NAME                                    VALUE
-------------------------------------   ---------------------------
_ash_enable                             TRUE
_disable_file_resize_logging            TRUE
_file_size_increase_increment           2143289344
_parallel_cluster_cache_policy          ADAPTIVE
_report_capture_cycle_time              0
_smm_auto_max_io_size                   1024
_sqlmon_max_planlines                   2500
_swrf_mmon_metrics                      TRUE
8 rows selected.
```

Script-2: The SQL to generate a dynamic SQL for the **RESET** commands. We have to run the generated reset commands before starting the database upgrade, as follows:

```
SQL> col value for a44
SQL> col name for a55
SQL> set lines 200
SQL> set pages 0
SQL> select ' ALTER SYSTEM RESET "' || name || '" scope=spfile sid=' ||
'''*'';'
from SYS.V$PARAMETER
WHERE name LIKE '\_%' ESCAPE '\' order by name;

ALTER SYSTEM RESET "_ash_enable" scope=spfile sid='*';
ALTER SYSTEM RESET "_disable_file_resize_logging" scope=spfile sid='*';
ALTER SYSTEM RESET "_file_size_increase_increment" scope=spfile sid='*';
ALTER SYSTEM RESET "_parallel_cluster_cache_policy" scope=spfile sid='*';
ALTER SYSTEM RESET "_report_capture_cycle_time" scope=spfile sid='*';
ALTER SYSTEM RESET "_smm_auto_max_io_size" scope=spfile sid='*';
ALTER SYSTEM RESET "_sqlmon_max_planlines" scope=spfile sid='*';
ALTER SYSTEM RESET "_swrf_mmon_metrics" scope=spfile sid='*';
8 rows selected.
```

Script 3: The SQL to generate the dynamic SQL for the **SET** commands. We can run the generated commands after the database upgrade, as follows:

```
SQL> col value for a44
```

```
SQL> col name for a55
SQL> set lines 200
SQL> set pages 0
SQL> select ' ALTER SYSTEM SET "' || name || '"=' || value|| '
scope=spfile sid=' || '''*'';' from SYS.V$PARAMETER
WHERE name LIKE '\_%' ESCAPE '\'
order by name;

ALTER SYSTEM SET "_ash_enable"=TRUE scope=spfile sid='*';
ALTER SYSTEM SET "_disable_file_resize_logging"=TRUE scope=spfile sid='*';
ALTER SYSTEM SET "_file_size_increase_increment"=2143289344 scope=spfile
sid='*';
ALTER SYSTEM SET "_parallel_cluster_cache_policy"=ADAPTIVE scope=spfile
sid='*';
ALTER SYSTEM SET "_report_capture_cycle_time"=0 scope=spfile sid='*';
ALTER SYSTEM SET "_smm_auto_max_io_size"=1024 scope=spfile sid='*';
ALTER SYSTEM SET "_sqlmon_max_planlines"=2500 scope=spfile sid='*';
ALTER SYSTEM SET "_swrf_mmon_metrics"=TRUE scope=spfile sid='*';
8 rows selected.
```

Upgrade of Application Express (APEX)

If the source database has the Oracle **Application Express** (**APEX**) installed, we can upgrade it upfront as the APEX upgrade does not depend on the database upgrade. We can refer to the following MOS note for the APEX upgrade. We can also do this step upfront to save time during the actual upgrade process.

For more details, refer to *Master Note for Oracle Application Express (APEX) Upgrades (Doc ID 1088970.1).*

Ensure that the physical standby database is in sync with the primary database

Execute a couple of log switches and check the current archive log list using the following SQL statements:

SQL> @/home/Oracle/rac_database_info.sql

```
DATABASE_HOST    DB_NAME     DATABASE_ROLE    OPEN_MODE    STARTUP_TIME
--------------   ----------  --------------   -----------  ------------
chapvm-19crac1   vicedbpr1   PRIMARY          READ WRITE   15-FEB-21
chapvm-19crac2   vicedbpr2   PRIMARY          READ WRITE   15-FEB-21

SQL> alter system switch all logfile;
System altered.

SQL> archive log list;
```

```
Database log mode                  Archive Mode
Automatic archival                 Enabled
Archive destination                USE_DB_RECOVERY_FILE_DEST
Oldest online log sequence         21
Next log sequence to archive       22
Current log sequence               22
SQL>
```

In the Physical standby database, check to see if it is receiving the redo logs from the primary database and if the MRP is applying the logs to keep it in sync with the primary database. Check the following SQL statements:

```
SQL>@/home/Oracle/standby_database_lag.sql
```

DATABASE_HOST	DB_NAME	DATABASE_ROLE	OPEN_MODE	STARTUP_TIME
chapstdby-19crac1	vicedbdr1	PHYSICAL STANDBY	MOUNTED	15-FEB-21
chapstdby-19crac2	vicedbdr2	PHYSICAL STANDBY	MOUNTED	15-FEB-21

INST_ID	PROCESS	STATUS	THREAD#	SEQUENCE#	BLOCK#	BLOCKS
1	MRP0	APPLYING_LOG	1	22	398	102400

THREAD#	ARCHIVED	APPLIED	GAP
1	21	20	1
2	18	18	0

As we can see, the physical standby database is in SYNC with the primary database. This completes our physical standby database setup. Let's move to the next steps.

Creating Guaranteed Restore Point (GRP) in the physical standby database

Since we will downgrade the database using the flashback method, we have to create the guaranteed restore points for this purpose. In the primary database, the AutoUpgrade process will create the guaranteed restore point before it starts the database upgrade, but in the physical standby database, we need to create the guaranteed restore point manually. As mentioned in the first chapter, it is very important that we create a guaranteed restore point in the physical standby database. However, before starting the upgrade process in the primary database, if we do not create the restore point in the physical standby database first, we might encounter issues while downgrading the physical standby database and we might end up rebuilding the physical standby database after downgrading the primary database; so, ensure that you create the guaranteed restore point in the physical standby database first.

Before creating the guaranteed restore point, ensure that both the primary database and the physical standby databases are in sync. Once they are in the sync state, we can stop the log shipping from the primary database to the physical standby database. We can defer the log shipping on the primary database by using either the SQL command or the data guard broker environment.

If you are not using the data guard broker, then you can cancel the log shipping and the managed recover process on physical standby database using the following SQL commands.

On the primary database, defer the log shipping as follows:

```
SQL> alter system set log_archive_dest_state_2='DEFER' scope=both
sid='*';
System altered.
```

On the physical standby database, cancel the MRP process as follows:

```
SQL> Alter database recover managed standby database cancel;
Database altered.
```

If we have the data guard broker set up in the primary database, we can disable the log shipping and redo applying as follows:

1. Login to the primary database, as follows:

```
SQL> ALTER SYSTEM SET DG_BROKER_START=TRUE;
System altered.
```

2. Login to the **dataguard** broker of the primary database, as follows:

```
[oracle@chapvm-19crac1 vicedbpr]$ dgmgrl

DGMGRL for Linux: Version 11.2.0.4.0 - 64bit Production
Copyright (c) 2000, 2009, Oracle. All rights reserved.
Welcome to DGMGRL, type "help" for information.
DGMGRL> connect sys
Password:
Connected.
DGMGRL>

DGMGRL> enable configuration (Enable the configuration as it has
been disabled previously)
Enabled.
```

Disable the log shipping on the primary database and log applying on the standby database as follows:

```
DGMGRL> edit  database  vicedbpr  set  state  =  'TRANSPORT-OFF';
Succeeded.
```

```
DGMGRL> edit database vicedbdr set state = 'APPLY-OFF';
Succeeded.
```

Once the MRP is cancelled, we can create the guaranteed restore point as follows:

```
SQL> create restore point standby_before_19c_upgrade guarantee flashback
database;
Restore point created.
```

Next, we will enable the log shipping back in the primary and start the MRP in the physical standby database, as follows:

1. On the primary database, enable the log shipping as follows:

    ```
    SQL> alter system set log_archive_dest_state_2='ENABLE'
    scope=both sid='*';
    ```

2. On the physical standby database, start the MRP process as follows:

    ```
    SQL> alter database recover managed standby database disconnect
    from session;
    Database altered.
    ```

If we have the **dataguard** broker configured in the primary database, we can enable the log shipping on the primary database and start redo applying on the standby database as follows:

1. Login to the primary database, as follows:

    ```
    SQL> ALTER SYSTEM SET DG_BROKER_START=TRUE;
    System altered.
    ```

2. Login to the **dataguard** broker of the primary database, as follows:

    ```
    [oracle@chapvm-19crac1 vicedbpr]$ dgmgrl
    DGMGRL for Linux: Version 11.2.0.4.0 - 64bit Production
    Copyright (c) 2000, 2009, Oracle. All rights reserved.
    Welcome to DGMGRL, type "help" for information.
    DGMGRL> connect sys
    Password:
    Connected.
    DGMGRL>
    DGMGRL> edit database vicedbpr set state = 'TRANSPORT-ON';
    DGMGRL> edit database vicedbdr set state = 'APPLY-ON';
    ```

Upgrading Oracle 11g (11.2.0.4) database to 19c (19.9.0)

In this section, we will upgrade both the primary and the standby database from version Oracle 11g (11.2.0.4) to version Oracle 19c (19.9.0). Let's start the process by completing the pre-upgrade steps.

Disable Dataguard broker

We must disable the dataguard broker before the database upgrade and enable it back after the upgrade. Ensure that the standby database is in sync with the primary database and then disable the dataguard broker.

Standby sync check before disabling dataguard broker

In the primary database, switch the logfiles and take a snapshot of the current archive log files info, as follows:

```
SQL> @/home/Oracle/rac_database_info.sql

DATABASE_HOST    DB_NAME     DATABASE_ROLE    OPEN_MODE    STARTUP_TIME
--------------   ---------   --------------   ----------   ------------
chapvm-19crac1   vicedbpr1   PRIMARY          READ WRITE   15-FEB-21
chapvm-19crac2   vicedbpr2   PRIMARY          READ WRITE   15-FEB-21

SQL> alter system switch all logfile;
System altered.


SQL> archive log list;

Database log mode              Archive Mode
Automatic archival             Enabled
Archive destination            USE_DB_RECOVERY_FILE_DEST
Oldest online log sequence     50
Next log sequence to archive   51
Current log sequence           51
SQL>
```

Check to see whether the physical standby database is receiving the redo logs from the primary database and whether the MRP process is applying the logs to keep it in sync with the primary database. We can check these by using the following SQL statements:

```
SQL> @/home/Oracle/standby_database_lag.sql
```

```
DATABASE_HOST        DB_NAME    DATABASE_ROLE     OPEN_MODE    STARTUP_TIME
------------------   --------   ----------------  ----------   ------------
chapstdby-19crac1   vicedbdr1  PHYSICAL STANDBY  MOUNTED      15-FEB-21
chapstdby-19crac2   vicedbdr2  PHYSICAL STANDBY  MOUNTED      15-FEB-21


INST_ID   PROCESS     STATUS         THREAD#   SEQUENCE#  BLOCK#   BLOCKS
--------- ---------   ------------   --------  ---------  -------  -------
   1      MRP0        APPLYING_LOG      1       51          54      102400

THREAD#   ARCHIVED    APPLIED     GAP
--------- ---------   ----------  ----------
1         50          49          1
2         42          42          0
```

We can check the current configuration and disable the broker configuration as follows:

```
[oracle@chapvm-19crac1~]$ dgmgrl
DGMGRL for Linux: Version 11.2.0.4.0 - 64bit Production
Copyright (c) 2000, 2009, Oracle. All rights reserved.Welcome to DGMGRL,
type "help" for information.
DGMGRL> connect sys
Password:
Connected.
DGMGRL> show configuration
      Configuration - vicedbpr

        Protection Mode: MaxPerformance
        Databases:
          vicedbpr - Primary database
          vicedbdr - Physical standby database
      Fast-Start Failover: DISABLED
      Configuration Status:
      SUCCESS
DGMGRL>
```

Disable Fast start failover (FSFO) if it's enabled

Fast start failover (**FSFO**) is a feature which allows the dataguard broker to failover a failed primary database to one of the configured standby databases. If it is enabled, we can disable it as follows:

```
DGMGRL>DISABLE FAST_START FAILOVER;
```

Disable the dataguard broker configuration

We can disable the configuration and re-verify the broker configuration. When we run the following command, it will disable the broker's active management of the databases in the Oracle dataguard configuration:

```
DGMGRL> DISABLE CONFIGURATION;
Disabled.

DGMGRL>  SHOW CONFIGURATION;
 Configuration - vicedbpr

        Protection Mode: MaxPerformance
        Databases:
          vicedbpr - Primary database
          vicedbdr - Physical standby database
      Fast-Start Failover: DISABLED
      Configuration Status:
     DISABLED
```

Stop the data guard broker (DMON) process in the primary database

We can disable the **dataguard** broker in the primary database by setting the **DG_BROKER_START** parameter to false. Check the following:

```
SQL> @/home/Oracle/rac_database_info.sql


DATABASE_HOST      DB_NAME      DATABASE_ROLE   OPEN_MODE    STARTUP_TIME
- - - - - - - - -  - - - - - -  - - - - - - -   - - - - - -  - - - - - - -
chapvm-19crac1     vicedbpr1    PRIMARY         READ WRITE   15-FEB-21
chapvm-19crac2     vicedbpr2    PRIMARY         READ WRITE   15-FEB-21

SQL> show parameter broker

NAME                          TYPE         VALUE
- - - - - - - - - - - - - -   - - - - - -  - - - - - - - - - - - - -
dg_broker_config_file1        string       +DATA/vicedbpr/dr1vicedbpr.dat
dg_broker_config_file2        string       +DATA/vicedbpr/dr2vicedbpr.dat
dg_broker_start               boolean      TRUE
```

Stop the data guard broker process as follows:

```
SQL> ALTER SYSTEM SET DG_BROKER_START=FALSE;
System altered.

SQL> show parameter DG_BROKER_START
NAME                          TYPE         VALUE
- - - - - - - - - - - - - -   - - - - - -  - - - - - - - - - - - - - - - - -
dg_broker_config_file1        string       +DATA/vicedbpr/dr1vicedbpr.dat
dg_broker_config_file2        string       +DATA/vicedbpr/dr2vicedbpr.dat
dg_broker_start               boolean      FALSE
```

Backup the data guard broker configuration files for the primary database

It's always a good idea to back up the broker configuration files. In our case, we have these files in ASM, and we will login to the ASM instance and make a copy of the broker configuration files, as follows:

```
[oracle@chapvm-19crac1~]$ . oraenv
ORACLE_SID = [Oracle] ? +ASM1
The Oracle base has been set to /u01/app/Oracle
[oracle@chapvm-19crac1~]$ asmcmd
ASMCMD>

ASMCMD> cp +DATA/vicedbpr/dr1vicedbpr.dat +DATA/vicedbpr/dr1vicedbpr.
dat.bak
copying ++DATA/vicedbpr/dr1vicedbpr.dat +DATA/vicedbpr/dr1vicedbpr.dat.
bak

ASMCMD> cp +DATA/vicedbpr/dr2vicedbpr.dat +DATA/vicedbpr/dr2vicedbpr.
dat.bak
copying +DATA/vicedbpr/dr2vicedbpr.dat +DATA/vicedbpr/dr2vicedbpr.dat.
bak
```

This completes the steps for disabling dataguard broker in the primary database. Let's do the same in the physical standby database. Since we have already disabled the dataguard broker configuration from the primary database, we just need to stop the data guard broker (**DMON**) process in the physical standby database, as follows:

```
SQL> @/home/Oracle/rac_database_info.sql

DATABASE_HOST      DB_NAME     DATABASE_ROLE      OPEN_MODE   STARTUP_TIME
--------------     ---------   ----------------   ---------   -----------
chapstdby-19crac1  vicedbdr1   PHYSICAL STANDBY   MOUNTED     15-FEB-21
chapstdby-19crac2  vicedbdr2   PHYSICAL STANDBY   MOUNTED     15-FEB-21


SQL> SHOW PARAMETER DG_BROKER

NAME                    TYPE       VALUE
--------------------    --------   --------------------------------
dg_broker_config_file1  string     +DATA/vicedbdr/dr1vicedbdr.dat
dg_broker_config_file2  string     +DATA/vicedbdr/dr2vicedbdr.dat
dg_broker_start         boolean    TRUE
```

Stop the data guard broker process as follows:

```
SQL> ALTER SYSTEM SET DG_BROKER_START=FALSE;
System altered.

SQL> SHOW PARAMETER DG_BROKER
```

```
NAME                       TYPE        VALUE
------------------------   --------    --------------------------------
dg_broker_config_file1     string      +DATA/vicedbdr/dr1vicedbdr.dat
dg_broker_config_file2     string      +DATA/vicedbdr/dr2vicedbdr.dat
dg_broker_start            boolean     FALSE
```

Backup the DB broker configuration files of the physical standby database

Backup the data guard broker configuration files of the physical standby database. Since our broker configuration files are in the ASM instance, login to the ASM instance and copy the files as follows:

```
SQL> SHOW PARAMETER DG_BROKER

NAME                       TYPE          VALUE
------------------------   -----------   --------------------------------
dg_broker_config_file1     string        +DATA/vicedbdr/dr1vicedbdr.dat
dg_broker_config_file2     string        +DATA/vicedbdr/dr2vicedbdr.dat
dg_broker_start            boolean       FALSE
```

Login to the ASM and take a backup of the config files:

```
[oracle@chapstdby-19crac1 ~]$ . oraenv
ORACLE_SID = [Oracle] ? +ASM1
The Oracle base has been set to /u01/app/Oracle
[oracle@chapstdby-19crac1 ~]$ asmcmd
ASMCMD> cp +DATA/vicedbdr/dr1vicedbdr.dat +DATA/vicedbdr/dr1vicedbdr.
dat.bak
Copying +DATA/vicedbdr/dr1vicedbdr.dat +DATA/vicedbdr/dr1vicedbdr.dat.
bak

ASMCMD> cp +DATA/vicedbdr/dr2vicedbdr.dat +DATA/vicedbdr/dr2vicedbdr.
dat.bak
Copying +DATA/vicedbdr/dr2vicedbdr.dat +DATA/vicedbdr/dr2vicedbdr.dat.
bak
```

This completes the steps for disabling and stopping the data guard broker on both the primary database and the physical standby database.

Working directories

Create a staging directory with the primary database name. We will use this directory as a working directory to save all the required log files, as follows:

```
[oracle@chapvm-19crac1~]$ mkdir -p /u01/software/upgrade/vicedbpr
```

Copy the required Oracle files from the source database Oracle 11g (11.2.0.4) to Oracle 19c (19.9.0) database home.

Network files

For the network related files, complete the following steps:

1. Add the source database TNS entry in the **tnsnames.ora** file of Oracle 19c (19.9.0) database home.

2. Take a backup of the current **tnsnames.ora** file in Oracle 19c (19.9.0) database home, as follows:

```
[oracle@chapvm-19crac1 admin]$ cd /u01/app/oracle/product/19c/
db_1/network/admin
[oracle@chapvm-19crac1 admin]$ cp tnsnames.ora tnsnames.ora.Feb15
```

3. Add the primary and physical standby database entries to Oracle 19c (19.9.0) **tnsnames.ora** file, as follows:

```
[oracle@chapvm-19crac1 admin]$ cd /u01/app/oracle/product/19c/
db_1/network/admin

[oracle@chapvm-19crac1 admin]$ vi tnsnames.ora

vicedbpr =
 (DESCRIPTION =
   (ADDRESS = (PROTOCOL = TCP)(HOST = chapvm-19crac-scan)(PORT =
1521))
   (CONNECT_DATA =
     (SERVER = DEDICATED)
     (SERVICE_NAME = vicedbpr)
    )
 )
vicedbdr =

 (DESCRIPTION =
 (ADDRESS = (PROTOCOL = TCP)(HOST = chapstdby-19crac-scan)(PORT =
1521))
   (CONNECT_DATA =
    (SERVER = DEDICATED)
    (SERVICE_NAME = vicedbdr)
    )
 )
```

Primary database initialization parameter (pfile/spfile) files

Copy the primary database initialization parameter files (**pfile** and **spfile**) from Oracle 11g (11.2.0.4) to Oracle 19c (19.9.0) database home, as follows:

```
[oracle@chapvm-19crac1]$ cp /u01/app/oracle/product/11.2.0.4/db_1/
```

```
dbs/*vice*ora  /u01/app/oracle/product/19c/db_1/dbs/
```

Password files

The password file is in the **dbs** folder; we can copy it to the Oracle 19c (19.9.0) **dbs** folder, as follows:

```
[oracle@chapvm-19crac1]$ cp /u01/app/oracle/product/11.2.0.4/db_1/
dbs/*orapwvice* /u01/app/oracle/product/19c/db_1/dbs/
```

Check the INVALID objects' counts in the primary database

It's always a good idea to take the snapshot of the invalid objects' count before starting the database upgrade process.

In the primary database, complete the following steps:

1. First run the **utlrp** script to compile any **INVALID** objects and then take a count of the invalid objects, so that we can compare the count after the database upgrade, as follows:

   ```
   SQL > @$ORACLE_HOME/rdbms/admin/utlrp
   ```

   ```
   SQL> select count(*) from dba_objects where status='INVALID';
   ```

2. Let's take the count of the invalid objects in the **SYS** and **SYSTEM** schemas, as follows:

   ```
   SQL> spool /u01/software/upgrade/vicedbpr/pre-upgrade_SYS_SYSTEM_
   invalid_Objects.log

   SQL> col owner for a25
   SQL> set lines 200
   SQL> set pages 200
   SQL> col object_type for a30;
   SQL> set lines 200
   SQL> SELECT i.HOST_NAME "DATABASE_HOST" ,
       i.INSTANCE_NAME "DB_NAME", d.DATABASE_ROLE " DATABASE_ROLE",
       d.OPEN_MODE " OPEN_MODE ", STARTUP_TIME
       from GV$DATABASE d, gv$instance i
       where i.INST_ID=d.INST_ID;
   SQL> select owner,object_name,object_type,status
       from dba_objects
       where status='INVALID' and owner in ('SYS','SYSTEM')
       order by owner ;
   spool off;
   ```

3. Next, we can take the invalid object count for the non-sys and non-system schemas, as follows:

```
SQL> spool /u01/software/upgrade/vicedbpr/pre-upgrade_non-SYS_
invalid_objects.log
```

```
SQL> col owner for a25
SQL> set lines 200
SQL> set pages 200
SQL> col object_type for a30;
SQL> set lines 200
SQL> SELECT i.HOST_NAME "DATABASE_HOST" ,
 i.INSTANCE_NAME "DB_NAME", d.DATABASE_ROLE " DATABASE_ROLE",
        d.OPEN_MODE " OPEN_MODE ", STARTUP_TIME
    from GV$DATABASE d, gv$instance i
    where i.INST_ID=d.INST_ID;
```

```
SQL> select count(*)
    from dba_objects
    where status='INVALID' and owner not in ('SYS','SYSTEM');
```

```
SQL> select owner,object_type,count(*)
    from dba_objects
    where status='INVALID' and owner not in ('SYS','SYSTEM')
    group by owner,object_type order by owner ;
```

```
SQL> col object_name for a37
SQL> select owner,object_name,object_type,status
    from dba_objects
    where status='INVALID' and owner not in ('SYS','SYSTEM')
    order by owner ;
spool off;
```

4. Check if the spool files got created. We can use this information to compare with the post-upgrade invalid object count that we will be taking after the database upgrade, as follows:

```
[oracle@chapvm-19crac1 admin]$ cd /u01/software/upgrade/vicedbpr

[oracle@chapvm-19crac1 vicedbpr]$ ls -ltr
total 8
-rw-r--r-- 1 Oracle oinstall 1650 Feb 16 07:58 pre-upgrade_SYS_
SYSTEM_invalid_Objects.log
-rw-r--r-- 1 Oracle oinstall 2383 Feb 16 07:58 pre-upgrade_non-
SYS_invalid_objects.log
[oracle@chapvm-19crac1 vicedbpr]$
```

For testing purposes, in the primary database, let's create a table called **before_ upgrade**, just to crosscheck after the upgrade to see if it comes to the physical standby database confirming that the upgrade is successful.

Login to the primary database and create the test table as follows:

```
SQL> Create table BEFORE_UPGRADE (NAME Varchar(30));
Table created.
```

```
SQL> insert into BEFORE_UPGRADE values ('Table Before Upgrade');
1 row created.
```

```
SQL> commit;
Commit complete.
```

Download the latest AutoUpgrade tool

As mentioned earlier, Oracle strongly recommends downloading the latest version and using it instead of the default one that comes with Oracle 19c. We can download the latest AutoUpgrade tool from the following MOS Doc ID 2485457.1

Once downloaded, we can stage it in the following location and you can copy it to the **19c** database home, as follows:

```
[oracle@chovm-19crac1 ~]$ cd /u01/software/

[oracle@chovm-19crac1 software]$ ls -ltr autoupgrade.jar
-rwxrwxr-x. 1 Oracle oinstall 2868558 Jan 18 10:53 autoupgrade.jar

[oracle@chovm-19crac1 ~]$ ls -ltr  /u01/app/Oracle/product/19c/db_1/
rdbms/admin/autoupgrade.jar

[oracle@chovm-19crac1 ~]$ mv /u01/app/Oracle/product/19c/db_1/rdbms/
admin/autoupgrade.jar /u01/app/Oracle/product/19c/db_1/rdbms/admin/
autoupgrade.jar.default

[oracle@chovm-19crac1 ~]$  cp /u01/software/autoupgrade.jar /u01/app/
Oracle/product/19c/db_1/rdbms/admin/
```

Configuration file creation for AutoUpgrade

The AutoUpgrade utility requires a config file which it uses for performing the pre-upgrade and the actual upgrade of the database. The config file is a simple file that will contain the information like the source database version, target database version, log directory location, and so on. We can manually create the file, or we can create a sample config file using autoupgrade.jar and modify it to include the source and target database details, as shown in the following section.

We must create the sample file from the Oracle 19c home, and later we can modify as per the requirement, as follows:

```
[oracle@chapvm-19crac1 vicedbpr]$ cd /u01/software/upgrade/vicedbpr
[oracle@chapvm-19crac1 vicedbpr]$ export ORACLE_HOME=/u01/app/oracle/
product/19c/db_1
[oracle@chapvm-19crac1 vicedbpr]$ export PATH=$ORACLE_HOME/bin:PATH
[oracle@chapvm-19crac1 vicedbpr]$ echo $ORACLE_HOME
```

/u01/app/Oracle/product/19c/db_1

```
[oracle@chapvm-19crac1 vicedbpr]$ $ORACLE_HOME/jdk/bin/java -jar
$ORACLE_HOME/rdbms/admin/autoupgrade.jar -create_sample_file config
```

The preceding command will create a sample configuration file in the current directory:

```
[oracle@chapvm-19crac1 vicedbpr]$ ls -ltr
-rw-r--r-- 1 Oracle oinstall 1650 Feb 16 07:58 pre-upgrade_SYS_SYSTEM_
invalid_Objects.log
-rw-r--r-- 1 Oracle oinstall 2383 Feb 16 07:58 pre-upgrade_non-SYS_
invalid_objects.log
-rw-r--r-- 1 Oracle oinstall 5885 Feb 16 08:02 sample_config.cfg
```

We can check the sample config file; it will have the sample parameters that we can modify to match our requirement. For our requirement, we will include the following details:

- Source database home
- Target database home
- Source database version
- Target database version.
- Log directories
- Differ Log shipping to physical standby
- Timezone version upgrade
- Run **utlrp** script as part of the upgrade

We made a copy of the sample config file and modified the copied file as follows:

```
[oracle@chapvm-19crac1 vicedbpr]$ cd /u01/software/upgrade/vicedbpr
[oracle@chapvm-19crac1 vicedbpr]$ cp sample_config.cfg vicedbpr_19c.cfg
[oracle@chapvm-19crac1 vicedbpr]$ vi vicedbpr_19c.cfg
```

The following are the Contents of this config file:

```
[oracle@chapvm-19crac1 vicedbpr]$ cat vicedbpr_19c.cfg
# Global configurations
```

global.autoupg_log_dir=/u01/software/upgrade/vicedbpr

```
upg1.log_dir=/u01/software/upgrade/vicedbpr
upg1.sid=vicedbpr1
upg1.source_home=/u01/app/Oracle/product/11.2.0.4/db_1
upg1.target_home=/u01/app/Oracle/product/19c/db_1
upg1.start_time=NOW                          # Start time
upg1.upgrade_node=chapvm-19crac1.localdomain # Local node upg1.run_
utlrp=yes                                    # For Utlrp
upg1.timezone_upg=yes                        # Timezone upgrade
upg1.target_version=19                       # Target database version
upg1.defer_standby_log_shipping=yes          # AutoUpgrade can defer
the log-shipping to configured standby databases
```

upg1 is a just unique identifier that identifies one set of database configuration details. We can include multiple databases in the same configuration file and upgrade all the databases at once. For each of the second database that you add in the same configuration file, just specify a new identifier like upg2, upg3, and so on.

In the preceding configuration file, we specified the log directory, source, and the target database binaries' location, and we can see the parameter `timezone_upg` set to yes, which will upgrade the Timezone (`tstz`) data. The configuration file also has the parameter `defer_standby_log_shipping` set to yes, which should defer the log shipping to the physical standby databases of the primary database.

Running AutoUpgrade in the Analyze mode

We know all the modes; let's run the AutoUpgrade in the Analyze mode for our upgrade. As mentioned earlier, this mode will only read the source database and check if the database is ready for the upgrade.

This mode will not make any changes to the source database.

Export the Oracle home to 19c database home, as follows:

```
[oracle@chapvm-19crac1 vicedbpr]$ export ORACLE_HOME=/u01/app/oracle/
product/19c/db_1
[oracle@chapvm-19crac1 vicedbpr]$ export PATH=$ORACLE_HOME/bin:$PATH
```

Now run the AutoUpgrade in the ANALYZE mode as follows:

```
[oracle@chapvm-19crac1 vicedbpr]$ $ORACLE_HOME/jdk/bin/java -jar
$ORACLE_HOME/rdbms/admin/autoupgrade.jar -config vicedbpr_19c.cfg -mode
ANALYZE
```

If the preceding command is run successfully, it will start reading the source database for the upgrade and generate not only the log files, but also create the pre-upgrade and post-upgrade fixup scripts. The following is part of the output for the preceding command:

```
[oracle@chapvm-19crac1 vicedbpr]$ $ORACLE_HOME/jdk/bin/java -jar
$ORACLE_HOME/rdbms/admin/autoupgrade.jar -config vicedbpr_19c.cfg -mode
ANALYZE

AutoUpgrade tool launched with default options
Processing config file ...
+------------------------------+
| Starting AutoUpgrade execution |
+------------------------------+
1 databases will be analyzed
Type 'help' to list console commands
upg>
upj> Job 100 completed
------------------ Final Summary --------------------
Number of databases         [1]
Jobs finished               [1]
Jobs failed                 [0]
Jobs pending                [0]
Please check the summary report at:
/u01/software/upgrade/vicedbpr/cfgtoollogs/upgrade/auto/status/status.
html
/u01/software/upgrade/vicedbpr/cfgtoollogs/upgrade/auto/status/status.
log [oracle@chapvm-19crac1 vicedbpr]$
```

While it's still running, we can use the following commands to check the status of the job and we can monitor/manage/control the jobs from the autoupgrade:

- **lsj**: To list the jobs.

- **status**: To show the job status.

- **tasks**: To show the tasks are executed.

- **abort**: To abort a specific job.

- **resume**: To resume a specific job which might have been stopped. We can use **job_id** for resuming a job.

We also need to check the logs at a location that is mentioned in the following section, to identify any pre-checks that we might need to do any changes before upgrading the database. The AutoUpgrade utility creates multiple sub directories in the log location defined in the configuration file. Each time we run the AutoUpgrade utility in either the Analyze mode or the Deploy mode, it creates a sub directory with the naming conventions like 100,101…etc.

In this case, it created various **directories/logs** in the **/u01/software/upgrade/ vicedbpr** location. Let us list the locations and files of the log directories, as follows:

```
[oracle@chapvm-19crac1 vicedbpr]$ ls -ltr
```

```
-rwx------ 1 Oracle oinstall 1650 Feb 16 07:58 pre-upgrade_SYS_SYSTEM_
invalid_Objects.log
-rwx------ 1 Oracle oinstall 2383 Feb 16 07:58 pre-upgrade_non-SYS_
invalid_objects.log
-rwx------ 1 Oracle oinstall 5885 Feb 16 08:02 sample_config.cfg
-rwx------ 1 Oracle oinstall 1532 Feb 16 08:05 vicedbpr_19c.cfg
drwx------ 3 Oracle oinstall   21 Feb 16 08:09 cfgtoollogs
drwx------ 4 Oracle oinstall   29 Feb 16 08:09 vicedbpr1


[oracle@chapvm-19crac1 vicedbpr]$ ls -ltr vicedbpr1
drwx------ 2 Oracle oinstall 131 Feb 16 08:09 temp
drwx------ 3 Oracle oinstall 119 Feb 16 08:10 100

[oracle@chapvm-19crac1 vicedbpr]$ ls -ltr vicedbpr1/100
-rwx------ 1 Oracle oinstall      0 Feb 16 08:09 autoupgrade_err.log
-rwx------ 1 Oracle oinstall    302 Feb 16 08:09 autoupgrade_20210216_
user.log
drwx------ 2 Oracle oinstall   4096 Feb 16 08:10 prechecks
-rwx------ 1 Oracle oinstall 167807 Feb 16 08:10 autoupgrade_20210216.
log

[oracle@chapvm-19crac1 vicedbpr]$ ls -ltr vicedbpr1/100/prechecks

-rwx------ 1 Oracle oinstall 177470 Feb 16 08:10 prechecks_vicedbpr1.log
-rwx------ 1 Oracle oinstall  12282 Feb 16 08:10 vicedbpr_checklist.xml
-rwx------ 1 Oracle oinstall    154 Feb 16 08:10 vicedbpr_checklist.json
-rwx------ 1 Oracle oinstall   3388 Feb 16 08:10 vicedbpr_checklist.cfg
-rwx------ 1 Oracle oinstall  31451 Feb 16 08:10 vicedbpr_preupgrade.
html
-rwx------ 1 Oracle oinstall  16302 Feb 16 08:10 upgrade.xml
-rwx------ 1 Oracle oinstall  11876 Feb 16 08:10 vicedbpr_preupgrade.log
```

Among these log files, the log file with **dbname_preupgrade.log** (example, in this case, **vicedbpr_preupgrade.log**) is one of the important logfile to check. This logfile will have all the information on the pre-upgrade checks/post upgrade recommendations and the fixup scripts. It will also list all the issues that need to be addressed. The following is the sample output of **vicedbpr_preupgrade.log**:

```
[oracle@chapvm-19crac1 status]$ cd /u01/software/upgrade/vicedbpr/
vicedbpr1/100/prechecks/
[oracle@chapvm-19crac1 prechecks]$ cat vicedbpr_preupgrade.log

Report generated by AutoUpgrade 21.1.1 (#8ee6880) on 2021-02-16 08:10:03

Upgrade-To version: 19.0.0.0.0
=======================================
Status of the database prior to upgrade
=======================================
      Database Name:  vicedbpr1
```

```
          Container Name:  Not Applicable in Pre-12.1 database
            Container ID:  Not Applicable in Pre-12.1 database
                 Version:  11.2.0.4.0
          DB Patch Level:  PSU 11.2.0.4.200414
              Compatible:  11.2.0.4.0
               Blocksize:  8192
                Platform:  Linux x86 64-bit
           Timezone File:  14
      Database log mode:  ARCHIVELOG
                Readonly:  false
                 Edition:  EE

Oracle Component                        Upgrade Action      Current Status
----------------                        --------------      ------------
OLAP Analytic Workspace                 [to be upgraded]    VALID
Oracle Workspace Manager                [to be upgraded]    VALID
Rule Manager                            [to be upgraded]    VALID
Oracle Enterprise Manager Repository    [to be upgraded]    VALID
Oracle Text                             [to be upgraded]    VALID
Expression Filter                       [to be upgraded]    VALID
Oracle Server                           [to be upgraded]    VALID
Real Application Clusters               [to be upgraded]    VALID
Oracle XDK for Java                     [to be upgraded]    VALID
Oracle Java Packages                    [to be upgraded]    VALID
Oracle XML Database                     [to be upgraded]    VALID
Oracle Multimedia                       [to be upgraded]    VALID
JServer JAVA Virtual Machine            [to be upgraded]    VALID
Oracle OLAP API                         [to be upgraded]    VALID
Oracle Spatial                          [to be upgraded]    VALID

==============
BEFORE UPGRADE
==============

  REQUIRED ACTIONS
  ================

  1. (AUTOFIXUP) Set DB_RECOVERY_FILE_DEST_SIZE initialization parameter
     to at least 5662 MB (6 GB).  Check the alert log during the upgrade
     to ensure there is remaining free space available in the recovery
     area.

     DB_RECOVERY_FILE_DEST_SIZE is set at 4407 MB (4 GB).   There is
     currently  3695 MB (4 GB) of free space remaining, which may not
     be adequate for the upgrade.

     Currently:
      Fast recovery area :  +DATA
      Limit              :  4407 MB (4 GB)
      Used               :  729088 KB (712 MB)
```

```
Available            :   3695 MB (4 GB)
```

The database has archivelog and flashback enabled, and the upgrade process will need free space to generate the archived and flashback logs to the recovery area specified by the initialization parameter DB_RECOVERY_FILE_DEST.

The logs generated must not overflow the limit set by DB_RECOVERY_FILE_DEST_SIZE, as that can cause the upgrade to not proceed.

RECOMMENDED ACTIONS

====================

2. (AUTOFIXUP) Remove OLAP Catalog by running the 11.2.0.4.0 SQL script $ORACLE_HOME/olap/admin/catnoamd.sql script.

The OLAP Catalog component, AMD, exists in the database.

Starting with Oracle Database 12c, the OLAP Catalog (OLAP AMD) is esupported and will automatically be marked as OPTION OFF during the database upgrade if present. Oracle recommends removing OLAP Catalog (OLAP AMD) before the database upgrade. This step can manually be performed before the upgrade to reduce downtime.

3.   (AUTOFIXUP) Remove the EM repository.

- Copy the $ORACLE_HOME/rdbms/admin/emremove.sql script from the target 19 ORACLE_HOME into the source 11.2.0.4.0 ORACLE_HOME.

Step 1: If the database control is configured, stop EM Database Control, using the following command:

```
$> emctl stop dbconsole
```

Step 2: Connect to the database using the following SYS account AS SYSDBA:

```
SET ECHO ON;

SET SERVEROUTPUT ON;

@emremove.sql
```

Without the set echo and serveroutput commands, you will not be able to follow the progress of the script.

The database has an Enterprise Manager Database Control repository.

Starting with Oracle Database 12c, the local Enterprise Manager Database Control does not exist anymore. The repository will be removed from your database during the upgrade. This step can manually be performed before the upgrade to reduce downtime.

4. (AUTOFIXUP) Update NUMERIC INITIALIZATION PARAMETERS to meet the
   estimated minimums. This action may be done now or when starting
   the database in the upgrade mode using the 19 ORACLE HOME.

```
Parameter                        Currently 19    minimum
---------                        -------------   --------------
processes                        150             300
```

   The database upgrade process requires certain initialization
   parameters to meet the minimum values. The Oracle upgrade
   process itself has minimum values which may be higher and are
   marked with an asterisk. After upgrading, those asterisked
   parameter values may be reset if needed.

5. Upgrade Oracle Application Express (APEX) manually before or
   after the database upgrade.

   The database contains the APEX version 3.2.1.00.12, which is not
   supported on the target version 19.0.0.0.0. APEX must be upgraded
   to at least version 18.2.0.00.12 either before or after the
   database is upgraded.

   Starting with Oracle Database Release 18, APEX is not upgraded
   automatically as part of the database upgrade. Refer to My
   Oracle Support Note 1088970.1 for information about the APEX
   installation and upgrades. Refer to MOS Note 1344948.1 for the
   minimum APEX version supported for your target database release.
   The unsupported versions of APEX will be in an INVALID state
   when its database dependencies are not in sync with theupgraded
   database.

6. (AUTOFIXUP) Directly grant the ADMINISTER DATABASE TRIGGER
   privilege to the owner of the trigger or drop and re-create the
   trigger with a user that was granted directly with such. We can
   list those triggers using: SELECT OWNER, TRIGGER_NAME FROM DBA_
   TRIGGERS, WHERE: TRIM(BASE_OBJECT_TYPE)='DATABASE' AND OWNER NOT
   IN (SELECT GRANTEE FROM DBA_SYS_PRIVS WHERE PRIVILEGE='ADMINISTER
   DATABASE TRIGGER').

   There are one or more database triggers whose owner does not have
   the right privilege on the database.

   The creation of the database triggers must be done by users
   granted with the ADMINISTER DATABASE TRIGGER privilege. The
   privilege must have been granted directly.

7. (AUTOFIXUP) Gather statistics on fixed objects prior the upgrade.

   None of the fixed object tables have had stats collected.

   Gathering the statistics on fixed objects, if none have been gathered yet, is recommended prior to upgrading.

For information on managing the optimizer statistics, refer to the 11.2.0.4 Oracle Database Performance Tuning Guide.

    INFORMATION ONLY

    =================

8. (AUTOFIXUP) Run $ORACLE_HOME/rdbms/admin/catnoexf.sql located in the new Oracle Database Oracle home to remove both EXF and RUL.

Expression Filter (EXF) or Rules Manager (RUL) exist in the database.

Starting with Oracle Database release 12.1, the Expression Filter (EXF) and Database Rules Manager (RUL) features are desupported, and are moved during the upgrade process. This step can manually be performed before the upgrade to reduce downtime.

9. (AUTOFIXUP) Mandatory changes are applied automatically in the during_upgrade_pfile_dbname.ora file. Some of these changes maybe present in the after_upgrade_pfile_dbname.ora file. The during_upgrade_pfile_dbname.ora is used to start the database in the upgrade mode. The after_upgrade_pfile_dbname.ora is used to start the database once the upgrade has been completed successfully.

Parameter

----

cluster_database='FALSE'

Mandatory changes are required to perform the upgrade. These changes are implemented in the during_ and after_upgrade_pfile_dbname.ora files.

10. Check the Oracle Backup and Recovery User's Guide for information on how to manage an RMAN recovery catalog schema.

If you are using a version of the recovery catalog schema that is older than that required by the RMAN client version, then you must upgrade the catalog schema.

It is a good practice to have the catalog schema as the same or a higher version than the RMAN client version that you are using.

11. To help you keep track of your tablespace allocations, the following AUTOEXTEND tablespaces are expected to successfully EXTEND during the upgrade process:

Tablespace	Min Size	For Upgrade
SYSTEM	750 MB	984 MB

```
    TEMP                                 20 MB        240 MB
    UNDOTBS1                             60 MB        401 MB
    SYSAUX                              510 MB        723 MB
```

The minimum tablespace sizes for upgrade are estimates.

12. Follow the instructions in the Oracle Multimedia README.txt
    file in <19 ORACLE_HOME>/ord/im/admin/README.txt, or MOS note
    2555923.1 to determine if Oracle Multimedia is being used. If
    Oracle Multimedia is being used, refer to MOS note 2347372.1 for
    suggestions on replacing Oracle Multimedia.

    Oracle Multimedia component (ORDIM) is installed.

    Starting with release 19c, Oracle Multimedia is desupported. The
    object types still exist, but the methods and procedures will
    raise an exception. Refer to the 19 Oracle Database Upgrade
    Guide, the Oracle Multimedia README.txt file in <19 ORACLE_
    HOME>/ord/im/admin/README.txt, or MOS note 2555923.1 for more
    information.

    =============
    AFTER UPGRADE
    =============

        REQUIRED ACTIONS
        ================
        None

        RECOMMENDED ACTIONS
        ===================

13. (AUTOFIXUP) Upgrade the database time zone file using the DBMS_DST

    package.

    The database is using the time zone file version 14 and the target
    19 release ships with time zone file version 32.

    Oracle recommends upgrading to the desired (latest) version of
    the time zone file. For more information, refer to "Upgrading
    the Time Zone File and Timestamp with Time Zone Data" in the 19
    Oracle Database Globalization Support Guide.

14. (AUTOFIXUP) Recompile the objects with the timestamp mismatch.
     Please refer to MOS note 781959.1 for more details.

    There are objects whose timestamp are mismatched with its parent
    objects.

    Timestamp of the dependent objects must coincide with the
    timestamp of the parent objects.
```
```

15. (AUTOFIXUP) Gather the dictionary statistics after the upgrade using the following command:

    EXECUTE DBMS_STATS.GATHER_DICTIONARY_STATS;

    Oracle recommends gathering the dictionary statistics after the upgrade.

    Dictionary statistics provide essential information to the Oracle optimizer to help it find efficient SQL execution plans. After a database upgrade, the statistics need to be re-gathered as there can now be tables that have significantly changed during the upgrade or new tables that do not have the statistics gathered yet.

16. Gather the statistics on fixed objects after the upgrade and when there is a representative workload on the system using the following command:

    EXECUTE DBMS_STATS.GATHER_FIXED_OBJECTS_STATS;

    Oracle recommends gathering the fixed object statistics after upgrade. This recommendation is given for all the preupgrade runs.

    The fixed object statistics provide essential information to the Oracle optimizer to help it find efficient SQL execution plans. Those statistics are specific to the Oracle Database release that generates them, and can be stale upon database upgrade.

    For information on managing the optimizer statistics, refer to the 11.2.0.4 Oracle Database Performance Tuning Guide.

17. (AUTOFIXUP) Run @?/rdbms/admin/utlrp.sql in order to recompile any invalid objects.

    There are invalid objects in the database after the upgrade.

    The invalid database objects need to be recompiled after the upgrade.

It is mandatory that we fix any issues reported in the issues section and then proceed with the next steps. In the preceding case, everything looks good, so let's move to the next step.

Shutdown the physical standby database

We can now stop the physical standby database. If this is an RAC database, we can use the server control utility to check the status and stop the physical standby database as follows:

1. Check the current status of the physical standby database using the **srvctl** command, as follows:

```
[oracle@chapstdby-19crac1 dbs]$ srvctl status  database -d
vicedbdr
Instance vicedbdr1 is running on node chapstdby-19crac1
Instance vicedbdr2 is running on node chapstdby-19crac2
```

2. Stop the physical standby database using the **srvctl** command, as follows:

```
[oracle@chapstdby-19crac1 dbs]$ srvctl stop database -d vicedbdr
```

3. Check the current status using the **srvctl** command, as follows:

```
[oracle@chapstdby-19crac1 dbs]$ srvctl status  database -d
vicedbdr
Instance vicedbdr1 is not running on node chapstdby-19crac1
Instance vicedbdr2 is not running on node chapstdby-19crac2
```

Upgrade the primary database using AutoUpgrade

Run the **AutoUpgrade** command in the **DEPLOY** mode to upgrade the database. We need to run this from the Oracle **19c** home. So, lets export the Oracle home to point to Oracle **19c** first, and then run the **AutoUpgrade** command as follows:

```
[oracle@chapvm-19crac1]$ export ORACLE_HOME=/u01/app/oracle/product/19c/
db_1
[oracle@chapvm-19crac1]$ export PATH=$PATH:$ORACLE_HOME/bin:$PATH

[oracle@chapvm-19crac1 vicedbpr]$ echo $ORACLE_HOME

/u01/app/Oracle/product/19c/db_1

[oracle@chapvm-19crac1 vicedbpr]$ cd /u01/software/upgrade/vicedbpr

[oracle@chapvm-19crac1 vicedbpr]$ $ORACLE_HOME/jdk/bin/java -jar
$ORACLE_HOME/rdbms/admin/autoupgrade.jar -config vicedbpr_19c.cfg -mode
DEPLOY
```

The following is part of the output when the preceding command is run successfully:

```
[oracle@chapvm-19crac1 vicedbpr]$ $ORACLE_HOME/jdk/bin/java -jar
$ORACLE_HOME/rdbms/admin/autoupgrade.jar -config vicedbpr_19c.cfg -mode
DEPLOY

AutoUpgrade tool launched with default options
Processing config file ...
+-------------------------------+
| Starting AutoUpgrade execution |
```

```
+-------------------------------+
1 databases will be processed
Type 'help' to list console commands
upg> lsj
+----+---------+-----+---------+-------+--------------+--------+-------+
|Job#|  DB_NAME|STAGE|OPERATION| STATUS|    START_TIME| UPDATED|MESSAGE|
+----+---------+-----+---------+-------+--------------+--------+-------+
| 101|vicedbpr1|  GRP|EXECUTING|RUNNING|21/02/16 08:32|08:32:13|       |
+----+---------+-----+---------+-------+--------------+--------+-------+
Total jobs 1
upg> lsj
--+---------+-----+---------+-------+--------------+--------+----
|Job#|DB_NAME|STAGE|OPERATION| STATUS|START_TIME| UPDATED|MESSAGE|
+---------+-----+---------+-------+--------------+--------+------------

| 101|vicedbpr1|DRAIN|EXECUTING|RUNNING|21/02/16 08:32|08:35:58|Shutting
down database|
+---------+-----+---------+-------+--------------+--------+----------+
Total jobs 1 upg> lsj
----+---------+---------+---------+-------+-------------------+-------
|Job#|  DB_NAME|STAGE|OPERATION| STATUS|START_TIME|UPDATED|MESSAGE|
+----+---------+---------+---------+-------+--------------+--------+--
101|vicedbpr1|DBUPGRADE|EXECUTING|RUNNING|21/02/16
08:32|08:58:18|91%Upgraded |
+----+---------+---------+---------+-------+--------------+--------+---
Total jobs 1
upg> Job 101 completed
------------------ Final Summary -------------------
Number of databases        [1]
Jobs finished              [1]
Jobs failed                [0]
Jobs pending               [0]


---- Drop GRP at your convenience once you consider it is no longer
needed ----
Drop GRP from vicedbpr1: drop restore point AUTOUPGRADE_9212_
VICEDBPR1112040

Please check the summary report at:
/u01/software/upgrade/vicedbpr/cfgtoollogs/upgrade/auto/status/status.
html
/u01/software/upgrade/vicedbpr/cfgtoollogs/upgrade/auto/status/status.
log
[oracle@chapvm-19crac1 vicedbpr]$
```

While the AutoUpgrade process is running, we can open a new terminal and check the different directories that the AutoUpgrade tool creates for the various logs.

In this case, directory **/u01/software/upgrade/vicedbpr/vicedbpr1/100** was created when we ran AutoUpgrade with the **ANALYZE** mode, whereas, the directory **/u01/software/upgrade/vicedbpr/vicedbpr1/101** was created when we ran AutoUpgrade with the **DEPLOY** mode.

We can monitor the following logfile in **/u01/software/upgrade/vicedbpr/ vicedbpr1/101**, as follows:

```
[oracle@chapvm-19crac1 101]$ tail -f autoupgrade_20210216_user.log

[checkname]           POST_UTLRP
[stage]               POSTCHECKS
[fixup_available]     YES
[runfix]              YES
[severity]            RECOMMEND
----------------------------------------------------

2021-02-16 08:32:25.464 INFO Adding fixup PURGE_RECYCLEBIN PRECHECKS YES
true ERROR to execution queue of vicedbpr1

2021-02-16 08:35:15.135 INFO Updating parameter *.processes=150 to
*.processes=330 in /u01/software/upgrade/vicedbpr/vicedbpr1/temp/during_
upgrade_pfile_vicedbpr1.ora
2021-02-16 08:35:15.141 INFO Updating parameter *.processes=150 to
*.processes=330 in /u01/software/upgrade/vicedbpr/vicedbpr1/temp/after_
upgrade_pfile_vicedbpr1.ora
2021-02-16 08:35:15.181 INFO Updating parameter *.cluster_
database='true' to *.cluster_database='FALSE' in /u01/software/upgrade/
vicedbpr/vicedbpr1/temp/during_upgrade_pfile_vicedbpr1.ora

2021-02-16 08:35:23.053 INFO Analyzing vicedbpr1, 88 checks will run
using 2 threads
2021-02-16 08:35:58.255 INFO Defer redo log shipping to standby database
2021-02-16 08:36:43.275 INFO File [/u01/app/Oracle/product/19c/db_1/dbs/
orapwvicedbpr1] already exists
2021-02-16 08:36:43.308 INFO [chapvm-19crac2.localdomain] Password file /
u01/app/Oracle/product/11.2.0.4/db_1/dbs/orapwvicedbpr2 is not found on
remote host
2021-02-16 08:37:10.673 INFO Total Number of upgrade phases is 108
2021-02-16 08:37:10.681 INFO Begin Upgrade on Database [vicedbpr]
2021-02-16 08:37:16.005 INFO 0%Upgraded
2021-02-16 08:40:16.341 INFO 8%Upgraded
2021-02-16 08:43:16.548 INFO 21%Upgraded
2021-02-16 08:46:16.986 INFO 39%Upgraded
2021-02-16 08:49:17.240 INFO 49%Upgraded
2021-02-16 08:52:17.597 INFO 49%Upgraded
2021-02-16 08:55:18.010 INFO 75%Upgraded
2021-02-16 08:58:18.249 INFO 91%Upgraded
2021-02-16 09:01:18.849 INFO 91%Upgraded
```

```
2021-02-16 09:04:19.032 INFO 92%Upgraded
2021-02-16 09:06:31.241 INFO SUCCESSFULLY UPGRADED [vicedbpr]
2021-02-16 09:06:31.241 INFO End Upgrade on Database [vicedbpr]
2021-02-16 09:06:35.131 INFO SUCCESSFULLY UPGRADED [vicedbpr]
2021-02-16 09:06:35.149 INFO vicedbpr Return status is SUCCESS
```

We can also check the other log file, **upg_summary_report.log** that it has created in the **dbupgrade** directory of **101**. This log file will have the summary of the upgraded components status, as follows:

```
[oracle@chapvm-19crac1 dbupgrade]$ cd /u01/software/upgrade/vicedbpr/
vicedbpr1/101/dbupgrade
[oracle@chapvm-19crac1 dbupgrade]$ cat upg_summary_report.log

Grand Total Upgrade Time:    [0d:0h:29m:51s]
[oracle@chapvm-19crac1 dbupgrade]$ cat upg_summary.log

Oracle Database Release 19 Post-Upgrade Status Tool    02-16-2021
09:05:2
Database Name: VICEDBPR
```

Component Name	Current Status	Full Version	Elapsed Time HH:MM:SS
Oracle Server	UPGRADED	19.9.0.0.0	00:10:46
JServer JAVA Virtual Machine	VALID	19.9.0.0.0	00:02:48
Oracle XDK	UPGRADED	19.9.0.0.0	00:00:21
Oracle Database Java Packages	UPGRADED	19.9.0.0.0	00:00:07
OLAP Analytic Workspace	UPGRADED	19.9.0.0.0	00:00:12
Oracle Text	UPGRADED	19.9.0.0.0	00:00:34
Oracle Workspace Manager	UPGRADED	19.9.0.0.0	00:00:31
Oracle Real Application Clusters	UPGRADED	19.9.0.0.0	00:00:00
Oracle XML Database	UPGRADED	19.9.0.0.0	00:01:23
Oracle Multimedia	UPGRADED	19.9.0.0.0	00:00:28
Spatial	LOADING	19.9.0.0.0	00:02:46
Oracle OLAP API	INVALID	19.9.0.0.0	00:00:07
Datapatch			00:06:23
Final Actions			00:06:55
Post Upgrade			00:00:18

```
Total Upgrade Time: 00:27:26
Grand Total Upgrade Time:    [0d:0h:29m:51s]
[oracle@chapvm-19crac1 dbupgrade]$
```

Once the primary database upgrade is completed, let's verify a few things, as follows:

1. First, check the **/etc/oratab** in all the nodes to see if **AutoUpgrade** updated the **db** entry to point to the new Oracle **19c** home, as follows:

Node 1:

```
[oracle@chovm-19crac1 ~]$ cat /etc/oratab | grep vicedbpr1
vicedbpr1:/u01/app/Oracle/product/19c/db_1:N
```

Node 2:

```
[oracle@chovm-19crac2 ~]$ cat /etc/oratab | grep vicedbpr
vicedbpr2:/u01/app/Oracle/product/19c/db_1:N
```

Let's check if the AutoUpgrade has upgraded the cluster configuration, as follows:

```
[oracle@chapvm-19crac1 ~]$ . oraenv
ORACLE_SID = [Oracle] ? vicedbpr1
The Oracle base has been set to /u01/app/oracle

[oracle@chapvm-19crac1 ~]$ srvctl config database -d vicedbpr
Database unique name: vicedbpr
Database name: vicedbpr
Oracle home: /u01/app/Oracle/product/19c/db_1
Oracle user: Oracle
Spfile: +DATA/vicedbpr/spfilevicedbpr.ora
Password file:
Domain:
Start options: open
Stop options: immediate
Database role: PRIMARY
Management policy: AUTOMATIC
Server pools:
Disk Groups: DATA
Mount point paths:
Services:
Type: RAC
Start concurrency:
Stop concurrency:
OSDBA group: oinstall
OSOPER group: oinstall
Database instances: vicedbpr1,vicedbpr2
Configured nodes: chapvm-19crac1,chapvm-19crac2
CSS critical: no
CPU count: 0
Memory target: 0
Maximum memory: 0
Default network number for database services:
Database is administrator managed
```

2. Check if the AutoUpgrade utility has created the guaranteed restore point in the primary database, as follows:

```
SQL>select NAME, GUARANTEE_FLASHBACK_DATABASE, TIME from
V$restore_point;
NAME                             GUARANTEE_F  TIME
-------------------------------- -----------  -------------------------
AUTOUPGRADE_9212_VICEDBPR1112040  YES         16-FEB-21 08.32.13.0000 AM
```

3. Run the **utlrp** script in the primary database and check the registry to see if all the components are upgraded and all are in a valid state, as follows:

```
SQL> @/home/Oracle/rac_database_info.sql

DATABASE_HOST   DB_NAME    DATABASE_ROLE   OPEN_MODE   STARTUP_TIME
-------------   ---------  -------------   ---------   -----------
chapvm-19crac1  vicedbpr1  PRIMARY         READ WRITE  16-FEB-21
chapvm-19crac2  vicedbpr2  PRIMARY         READ WRITE  16-FEB-21
```

Run the utlrp script.

```
SQL> @$ORACLE_HOME/rdbms/admin/utlrp
```

Now check the Components status in the dba registry

```
SQL> select COMP_ID,COMP_NAME,VERSION,STATUS from dba_registry;
COMP_ID     COMP_NAME                               VERSION     STATUS
----------  --------------------------------------  ----------  -------
CATALOG     Oracle Database Catalog Views           19.0.0.0.0  VALID
CATPROC     Oracle Database Packages and Types      19.0.0.0.0  VALID
JAVAVM      JServer JAVA Virtual Machine            19.0.0.0.0  VALID
XML         Oracle XDK                              19.0.0.0.0  VALID
CATJAVA     Oracle Database Java Packages           19.0.0.0.0  VALID
APS         OLAP Analytic Workspace                 19.0.0.0.0  VALID
RAC         Oracle Real Application Clusters        19.0.0.0.0  VALID
OWM         Oracle Workspace Manager                19.0.0.0.0  VALID
CONTEXT     Oracle Text                             19.0.0.0.0  VALID
XDB         Oracle XML Database                     19.0.0.0.0  VALID
ORDIM       Oracle Multimedia                       19.0.0.0.0  VALID
SDO         Spatial                                 19.0.0.0.0  VALID
XOQ         Oracle OLAP API                         19.0.0.0.0  VALID
APEX        Oracle Application Express              3.2.1.00.12 VALID
14 rows selected.
```

Check the timezone version to ensure that the AutoUpgrade has upgraded its version to 32 (Oracle 19c Timezone version):

```
SQL > SELECT version FROM v$timezone_file;
VERSION
---------
```

```
32
1 row selected.
```

If this is the RAC database, we can check if the database is up in all the nodes. If it's not up in the other nodes of the cluster, we can start the database in all the nodes.

4. Set the **cluster_database** parameter to true and start the database using the **srvctl** command, as follows:

```
SQL> alter system set cluster_database=true scope=spfile sid='*';
System altered.

Oracle@chapvm-19crac1 ~]$ srvctl stop  database -d vicedbpr
Oracle@chapvm-19crac1 ~]$ srvctl start database -d vicedbpr

Oracle@chapvm-19crac1 ~]$ srvctl status database -d vicedbpr
Instance vicedbpr1 is running on node chapvm-19crac1
Instance vicedbpr2 is running on node chapvm-19crac2
```

Check for the post upgrade invalid objects

It's always a good idea to take the snapshot of the invalid objects count after the database upgrade, as we can compare it with the pre-upgrade invalid count to make sure that they are both the same. On the primary database, first run the **utlrp** script to compile any **INVALID** objects and then take a count of the invalid objects, so that we can compare the count after the database upgrade, as follows:

1. First take the count of the invalid objects in the **SYS** and **SYSTEM** schemas, as follows:

```
SQL> spool /u01/software/upgrade/vicedbpr/vicedbpr_postupgrade/
vicedbpr_post-upgrade_SYS_SYSTEM_invalid_Objects.log

SQL> col owner for a25
 SQL> set lines 200
 SQL> SELECT i.HOST_NAME "DATABASE_HOST" ,
        i.INSTANCE_NAME "DB_NAME", d.DATABASE_ROLE " DATABASE_ROLE",
        d.OPEN_MODE " OPEN_MODE ", STARTUP_TIME
        from GV$DATABASE d, gv$instance i
        where i.INST_ID=d.INST_ID;

SQL> select owner,object_name,object_type,status
        from dba_objects
        where status='INVALID' and owner in ('SYS','SYSTEM')
        order by owner ;
spool off;
```

2. Next, take the invalid object count for the other schemas, as follows:

```
SQL> spool /u01/software/upgrade/vicedbpr/vicedbpr_postupgrade/
vicedbpr_post-upgrade_non-SYS_invalid_objects.log

SQL> col owner for a25
SQL> set lines 200
SQL> set pages 200
SQL> col object_type for a30;
SQL> set lines 200
SQL> col DATABASE_HOST for a40;
SQL> SELECT i.HOST_NAME "DATABASE_HOST" ,
    i.INSTANCE_NAME "DB_NAME", d.DATABASE_ROLE " DATABASE_ROLE",
    d.OPEN_MODE " OPEN_MODE ", STARTUP_TIME
    from GV$DATABASE d, gv$instance i
    where i.INST_ID=d.INST_ID;

SQL> select count(*)
    from dba_objects
    where status='INVALID' and owner not in ('SYS','SYSTEM');
SQL> select owner,object_type,count(*)
    from dba_objects
    where status='INVALID' and owner not in ('SYS','SYSTEM')
    group by owner,object_type order by owner ;
SQL> col object_name for a37
SQL> select owner,object_name,object_type,status

    from dba_objects
    where status='INVALID' and owner not in ('SYS','SYSTEM')
    order by owner ;
spool off;
```

Next, we will create a second **TEST** table in the primary database.

3. Create a second test table just to crosscheck to see if it is coming to the physical standby database through the logs without any issues, as follows:

```
SQL> Create table AFTER_UPGRADE (NAME Varchar(30));
Table created.
```

```
SQL> insert into AFTER_UPGRADE values ('Table AFTER Upgrade');
1 row created.
SQL> commit;
Commit complete.
```

```
SQL> alter system switch all logfile;
System altered.
```

With this step, the primary database upgrade is completed. Let's upgrade the physical standby database.

Upgrading the physical standby database to Oracle 19c (19.9.0)

By this time, the primary database is upgraded to Oracle 19c. Now, let's upgrade the physical standby database. The physical standby database upgrade will happen with the migrating redo logs that it receives from the primary database. As of now, the physical standby database is down. Let's upgrade its configuration file first and then start the database using the server control utility. But first, let's take a look at a few pre-checks and ensure that they are completed, as follows:

1. First copy the password files/parameter files and the database **tnsnames. ora** entry from Oracle 11g to Oracle 19c home. We need to do this step in all the nodes of the cluster, as follows:

```
[oracle@chapstdby-19crac1 ~]$ cp /u01/app/oracle/
product/11.2.0.4/db_1/dbs/*vice*

/u01/app/oracle/product/19c/db_1/dbs

[oracle@chapstdby-19crac1 ~]$ cp /u01/app/oracle/
product/11.2.0.4/network/admin/*vicepr* /u01/app/oracle/
product/19c/db_1/network/admin/
```

2. Modify the database entry in **/etc/oratab** to point to the Oracle 19c (19.3.0) home. We need to do this step in all the nodes of the cluster, as follows:

```
[oracle@chapstdby-19crac1 ~]$  cat /etc/oratab | grep viceprdr

viceprdr:/u01/app/Oracle/product/19c/db_1:N
viceprdr1:/u01/app/Oracle/product/19c/db_1
```

3. Upgrade the cluster configuration information of the physical standby database using the **srvctl upgrade** command, as follows:

```
[oracle@chapstdby-19crac1 ~]$ export ORACLE_HOME=/u01/app/oracle/
product/19c/db_1
[oracle@chapstdby-19crac1 ~]$ export PATH=$ORACLE_HOME/bin:$PATH

[oracle@chapstdby-19crac1 ~]$ srvctl upgrade database -d vicedbdr
-o /u01/app/oracle/product/19c/db_1
[oracle@chapstdby-19crac1 ~]$ srvctl config database -d vicedbdr
[oracle@chapstdby-19crac1 ~]$ srvctl config database -db vicedbdr
Database unique name: vicedbdr
Database name:
Oracle home: /u01/app/Oracle/product/19c/db_1
Oracle user: Oracle
Spfile: +data/vicedbdr/PARAMETERFILE/spfilevicedbdr1.ora
```

```
Password file:
Domain:
Start options: open
Stop options: immediate
Database role: PHYSICAL_STANDBY
Management policy: AUTOMATIC
Server pools:
Disk Groups: DATA
Mount point paths:
Services:
Type: RAC
Start concurrency:
Stop concurrency:
OSDBA group: oinstall
OSOPER group: oinstall
Database instances: vicedbdr1,vicedbdr2
Configured nodes: chapstdby-19crac1,chapstdby-19crac2
CSS critical: no
CPU count: 0
Memory target: 0
Maximum memory: 0
Default network number for database services:
Database is administrator managed
[oracle@chapstdby-19crac1 ~]$
```

4. Start the physical standby database in the **MOUNT** mode. From the node-1 of the physical standby database server, start the physical standby database in mount stage, as follows:

```
[oracle@chapstdby-19crac1 ~]$ srvctl start database -d vicedbdr
-o mount
```

5. Enable the log shipping on the primary database, as follows:

```
SQL> ALTER SYSTEM SET log_archive_dest_state_2=enable SCOPE=BOTH
sid='*';
System altered.
```

The primary database will now start shipping all the redo logs to the physical standby database. Please note that at this point, if needed, we can also start the **dataguard** broker (**DMON**) process in both the primary and the standby databases and enable the **dataguard** broker using **DGMGRL**.

6. Start the MRP in the physical standby database, as follows:

```
[oracle@chapstdby-19crac1 ~]$ sqlplus / as sysdba

SQL*Plus: Release 19.0.0.0.0 - Production on Tue Feb 16 09:45:35
2021
```

```
Version 19.9.0.0.0
Copyright (c) 1982, 2020, Oracle.  All rights reserved.
Connected to:
Oracle Database 19c Enterprise Edition Release 19.0.0.0.0 -
Production
Version 19.9.0.0.0

SQL> ALTER DATABASE RECOVER managed standby database using
current logfile disconnect;
Database altered.
```

For the physical standby database, the MRP will now start applying all the logs that it has received from the primary database. This might take some time, depending upon the number of archive log files that the primary database has generated during its upgrade. The physical standby database will be upgraded with all the migrate redo data that it receives from the primary database.

We can tail the alert log and wait for some time for the standby database to catchup with the primary, as follows:

```
Alert Log of standby database:

--------------------------------

2021-02-16T09:51:22.018941-06:00

MRP0 (PID:22352): Media Recovery Log +DATA/VICEDBDR/
ARCHIVELOG/2021_02_16/thread_1_seq_185.2953.1064656003
2021-02-16T09:51:22.082779-06:00
MRP0 (PID:22352): Media Recovery Log +DATA/VICEDBDR/
ARCHIVELOG/2021_02_16/thread_2_seq_62.2823.1064655919

2021-02-16T09:51:22.245507-06:00
MRP0 (PID:22352): Media Recovery Log +DATA/VICEDBDR/
ARCHIVELOG/2021_02_16/thread_1_seq_186.2954.1064656003
MRP0 (PID:22352): Media Recovery Waiting for T-1.S-187 (in
transit)
2021-02-16T09:51:22.570497-06:00
Recovery of Online Redo Log:Thread 1 Group 5 Seq 187 Reading mem
0
  Mem# 0: +DATA/vicedbdr/onlinelog/group_5.2703.1064586089
  Mem# 1: +DATA/vicedbdr/onlinelog/group_5.2699.1064586089
MRP0 (PID:22352): Media Recovery Waiting for T-2.S-63 (in
transit)
2021-02-16T09:51:22.591523-06:00
Recovery of Online Redo Log: Thread 2 Group 9 Seq 63 Reading mem
  Mem# 0: +DATA/vicedbdr/onlinelog/group_9.2674.1064586095
  Mem# 1: +DATA/vicedbdr/onlinelog/group_9.2671.1064586095
```

```
Resize operation completed for file# 2, old size 675840K, new size
86080K
```

7. Stop the database and start it by using the **srvctl** command.

8. Wait until the standby database catches up with the primary and then stop the database and start it by using the **srvctl** command, as follows:

```
[oracle@chostdby-19crac1]$ sqlplus / as sysdba
SQL> shutdown immediate;

[oracle@chapstdby-19crac1]$ srvctl modify database -d vicedbdr
-startoption "READ ONLY"

[oracle@chapstdby-19crac1]$ srvctl start database -d vicedbdr
[oracle@chapstdby-19crac1]$ srvctl status database -d vicedbdr
Instance vicedbdr1 is running on node chapstdby-19crac1
Instance vicedbdr2 is running on node chapstdby-19crac2
```

9. Start the MRP and check the lag in the standby database, as follows:

```
SQL> ALTER DATABASE RECOVER managed standby database using
current logfile disconnect;

@/home/Oracle/standby_database_lag.sql
```

DATABASE_HOST	DB_NAME	DATABASE_ROLE	OPEN_MODE	STARTUP_TIME
chapstdby-19crac1	vicedbdr1	PHYSICAL STANDBY	MOUNTED	16-FEB-21
chapstdby-19crac2	vicedbdr2	PHYSICAL STANDBY	MOUNTED	16-FEB-21

INST_ID	PROCESS	STATUS	THREAD#	SEQUENCE#	BLOCK#	BLOCKS
1	MRP0	APPLYING_LOG	1	195	64	102400

THREAD#	ARCHIVED	APPLIED	GAP
1	196	195	1
2	68	68	0

10. Check the components' status in the physical standby database, as follows:

```
SQL> @/home/Oracle/rac_database_info.sql
```

DATABASE_HOST	DB_NAME	DATABASE_ROLE	OPEN_MODE	STARTUP
chapstdby-19crac1	vicedbdr1	PHYSICAL STANDBY	READ ONLY WITH APPLY	16-FEB-21
chapstdby-19crac2	vicedbdr2	PHYSICAL STANDBY	READ ONLY WITH APPLY	16-FEB-21

```
SQL> select COMP_ID,COMP_NAME,VERSION,STATUS from dba_registry;
```

```
COMP_ID     COMP_NAME                               VERSION      STATUS
----------  --------------------------------------  -----------  --------
CATALOG     Oracle Database Catalog Views           19.0.0.0.0   VALID
CATPROC     Oracle DatabasePackages and Types19.0.0.0.0          VALID
JAVAVM      JServer JAVA Virtual Machine            19.0.0.0.0   VALID
XML         Oracle XDK                              19.0.0.0.0   VALID
CATJAVA     Oracle Database Java Packages           19.0.0.0.0   VALID
APS         OLAP Analytic Workspace                 19.0.0.0.0   VALID
RAC         Oracle Real Application Clusters 19.0.0.0.0           VALID
OWM         Oracle Workspace Manager                19.0.0.0.0   VALID
CONTEXT     Oracle Text                             19.0.0.0.0   VALID
XDB         Oracle XML Database                     19.0.0.0.0   VALID
ORDIM       Oracle Multimedia                       19.0.0.0.0   VALID
SDO         Spatial                                 19.0.0.0.0   VALID
XOQ         Oracle OLAP API                         19.0.0.0.0   VALID
APEX        Oracle Application Express              3.2.1.00.12  VALID

14 rows selected.
```

11. Check if the tables got replicated to the physical standby database.

12. In the physical standby database, check if those two tables got replicated indicating that the physical standby database is both upgraded and is in SYNC with the primary database, as follows:

```
SQL> select owner, table_name from dba_tables where table_name in
('BEFORE_UPGRADE',' AFTER_UPGRADE');

OWNER                       TABLE_NAME
--------------------        ----------------
SYS                         BEFORE_UPGRADE
SYS                         AFTER_UPGRADE
```

With this step, we can now confirm that both the primary and the physical standby database upgrades have been completed successfully. Let's move to the final step, which is to enable the broker.

Start the data guard broker process in both the primary and the physical standby database

Since both the primary and the standby database upgrade are completed, we can now start the **dataguard** broker (**dmon**) process in both the primary and the standby databases and enable the **dataguard** broker.

Run the following commands in the primary database:

1. Check the broker parameter to get the current values, as follows:

```
SQL> @/home/Oracle/rac_database_info.sql


DATABASE_HOST    DB_NAME     DATABASE_ROLE     OPEN_MODE    STARTUP_TIME
-------------    ---------   -------------     -----------  -----------
chapvm-19crac1   vicedbpr1   PRIMARY                READ WRITE   16-FEB-21
chapvm-19crac2   vicedbpr2   PRIMARY                READ WRITE   16-FEB-21

SQL> show parameter broker
NAME                       TYPE        VALUE
-------------------        --------    --------------------------
dg_broker_config_file1     string      +DATA/vicedbpr/dr1vicedbpr.dat
dg_broker_config_file2     string      +DATA/vicedbpr/dr2vicedbpr.dat
dg_broker_start            boolean     FALSE
```

2. Start the broker process as follows:

```
SQL> ALTER SYSTEM SET DG_BROKER_START=TRUE;
System altered.

SQL> show parameter broker

NAME                       TYPE        VALUE
-------------------        ---------   --------------------------
dg_broker_config_file1     string      +DATA/vicedbpr/dr1vicedbpr.dat
dg_broker_config_file2     string      +DATA/vicedbpr/dr2vicedbpr.dat
dg_broker_start            boolean     TRUE
```

Run the following commands in the physical standby database:

1. Check the broker parameter to get the current values, as follows:

```
SQL> @/home/Oracle/rac_database_info.sql
DATABASE_HOST     DB_NAME     DATABASE_ROLE     OPEN_MODE              STARTUP
-----------------  ---------  ----------------  --------------------   -----------
chapstdby-19crac1  vicedbdr1  PHYSICAL STANDBY  READ ONLY WITH APPLY   16-FEB-21
chapstdby-19crac2  vicedbdr2  PHYSICAL STANDBY  READ ONLY WITH APPLY   16-FEB-21


SQL> show parameter broker

NAME                       TYPE        VALUE
-------------------        --------    --------------------------
dg_broker_config_file1     string      +DATA/vicedbdr/dr1vicedbdr.dat|
dg_broker_config_file2     string      +DATA/vicedbdr/dr2vicedbdr.dat
dg_broker_start            boolean     FALSE
```

2. Start the broker process as follows:

```
SQL> ALTER SYSTEM SET DG_BROKER_START=TRUE;
System altered.

SQL> SHOW PARAMETER DG_BROKER

NAME                     TYPE        VALUE
--------------------     --------    -------------------------
dg_broker_config_file1   string      +DATA/vicedbdr/dr1vicedbdr.dat|
dg_broker_config_file2   string      +DATA/vicedbdr/dr2vicedbdr.dat
dg_broker_start          boolean     TRUE
```

Enable the broker configuration from the primary database, by completing the following steps:

1. Check the current **dataguard** broker configuration, as follows:

```
[oracle@chapvm-19crac1 ~]$ dgmgrl
DGMGRL for Linux: Release 19.0.0.0.0 - Production on Tue Feb 16
10:04:28 2021

Version 19.9.0.0.0

Copyright (c) 1982, 2019, Oracle and/or its affiliates.  All rights
reserved.

Welcome to DGMGRL, type "help" for information.
DGMGRL> connect sys
Password:
Connected to "vicedbpr"
Connected as SYSDBA.
DGMGRL>
DGMGRL> show configuration

Configuration - vicedbpr

  Protection Mode: MaxPerformance
  Members:
    vicedbpr - Primary database
    vicedbdr - Physical standby database
Fast-Start Failover:  Disabled
Configuration Status:
DISABLED
```

2. Enable the configuration, as follows:

```
DGMGRL> enable configuration;
Enabled.
```

3. Check the current configuration, as follows:

```
DGMGRL> show configuration
```

```
Configuration - vicedbpr
        Protection Mode: MaxPerformance
    Members:
      vicedbpr - Primary database
      vicedbdr - Physical standby database

        Fast-Start Failover:  Disabled

        Configuration Status:
    SUCCESS    (status updated 14 seconds ago)
```

Perform the final check to confirm that both the primary and the physical standby database are upgraded to Oracle 19c (19.9.0)

Check the primary database, as follows:

```
SQL>set lines 200
SQL>col HOST_NAME for a35
SQL>col banner for a99
SQL>select i.instance_name,i.host_name,v.banner
    from gv$instance i, gv$version v
    where i.inst_id=v.inst_id;


INSTANCE_NAME  HOST_NAME         BANNER

-------------  --------------    -------------------------------------
vicedbpr       chapvm-19crac1    Oracle Database 19c Enterprise
                                 Edition Release 19.0.0.0.0 - Production
vicedbpr       chapvm-19crac2    Oracle Database 19c Enterprise
                                 Edition Release 19.0.0.0.0 - Production
```

Check the physical standby database, as follows:

```
SQL>set lines 200
SQL>col HOST_NAME for a35
SQL>col banner for a99
SQL>select i.instance_name,i.host_name,v.banner
    from gv$instance i, gv$version v
    where i.inst_id=v.inst_id;

INSTANCE_NAME  HOST_NAME         BANNER
-------------  ----------------  ---------------------------------
Vicedbdr1      chapstdby-19crac1 Oracle Database 19c Enterprise
                                 Release 19.0.0.0.0 - Production
vicedbdr2      chapstdby-19crac2 Oracle Database 19c Enterprise
                                 Edition Release 19.0.0.0.0 -Production
```

This completes the upgrade of the Oracle database from version Oracle 11g (11.2.0.4) to version Oracle 19c (19.9.0). We have seen that the AutoUpgrade utility upgraded all the components including the Timezone in the primary database, and we just upgraded the physical standby database with all the upgrade redo data that it received from the primary database.

Post upgrade tasks

Please note that we did not implement these steps as we will test the downgrade using the Oracle provided scripts in the following section. We cannot downgrade if we change the compatible parameter to 19c. If you want to downgrade, skip this step and go to the next section. However, if you don't want to downgrade the database, you can follow these steps to complete the post upgrade tasks.

For the post upgrade tasks, we can complete the following steps in both the primary and the physical standby databases:

- **FRA space usage**: Until you drop the guaranteed restore point, keep checking the FRA space usage and increase the space as necessary for this process.

- **Dropping GRP**: We can also drop the restore point in both the primary and the physical standby database.

- **Database compatibility**: We can change the compatible parameter after waiting for some time as we cannot downgrade the database after changing this parameter to 19. This is a permanent change; once you change the compatible parameter to 19.9, we cannot revert.

In the primary database, execute the following commands:

```
SQL> ALTER SYSTEM SET COMPATIBLE = '19.0.0' SCOPE=SPFILE;
System altered.

[oracle@chapvm-19crac1 ~]$ srvctl stop  database -d vicedbpr
[oracle@chapvm-19crac1 ~]$ srvctl start database -d vicedbpr

[oracle@chapvm-19crac1 ~]$ srvctl status  database -d vicedbpr
Instance vicedbpr1 is running on node chapvm-19crac1
Instance vicedbpr2 is running on node chapvm-19crac2
```

In the physical standby database, execute the following commands:

```
SQL> ALTER SYSTEM SET COMPATIBLE = '19.0.0' SCOPE=SPFILE;
System altered.
```

```
[oracle@chapstdby-19crac1 dbs]$ srvctl stop  database -d vicedbdr
[oracle@chapstdby-19crac1 dbs]$ srvctl start database -d vicedbdr

[oracle@chapstdby-19crac1 dbs]$ srvctl status  database -d vicedbdr
Instance vicedbdr1 is running on node chapstdby-19crac1
Instance vicedbdr2 is running on node chapstdby-19crac2
```

With this, we have successfully upgraded both the primary and the physical standby Oracle 11g (11.2.0.4) database to Oracle 19c (19.9.0). In the following section, we will test the downgrade option using the Oracle provided scripts.

Oracle database downgrade

In this section, we will see how we can downgrade both the primary and the physical standby databases from 19c to 11.2.0.4 using the Oracle provided scripts.

Oracle database downgrade methods

Oracle provides several methods to downgrade an upgraded database to its previous version. A few methods are mentioned as follows:

1. Downgrade scripts

2. Flashback to restore point

3. Data Pump

4. Oracle GoldenGate

Among these methods, the fastest and the simplest way to downgrade the database from any upgrade version to its previous version is to flashback the database to a previously created guaranteed restore point that was created before starting the upgrade process. Since we already saw how to downgrade a database using the **FLASHBACK** method in the previous chapter, in this chapter, we will downgrade the database using the Oracle provided scripts (refer to *Figure 3.4*). We would recommend using the flashback method to downgrade the database, as it is a straight forward method. This method will also work as long as we don't change the database compatibility to the upgrade version. Please take a look at *Figure 3.4* for a pictorial representation of the same:

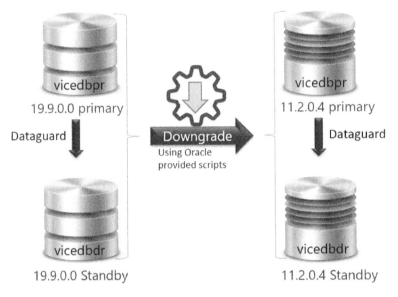

Figure 3.4: *Downgrade 19.9.0 database to 11.2.0.4 using Oracle provided scripts*

High-level steps performed as part of this downgrade activity

Let's discuss the high-level steps that are performed when downgrading the Oracle database from 19c to 11.2.0.4, as follows:

1. Perform the pre-upgrade steps on the primary database.

2. Downgrade the primary database using the Oracle provided scripts (**dbdowngrade**).

3. Perform any post upgrade steps on the primary database.

4. Downgrade the Timezone version using the Oracle provided scripts.

5. Check and make sure that the standby database is downgraded with the migrated redo data that it received from the standby database.

6. Remove and recreate the **dataguard** broker configuration.

7. Perform any post upgrade checks on the standby database.

Important note on a known bug

Let's check one important known issue before even trying this approach where we downgrade Oracle 19c (19.9.0) database to 11.2.0.4/12c using the Oracle provided scripts.

After successfully downgrading the database from 19c to 11.2.0.4 / 12c with **dbdowngrade** (shown in the following section) script, we might run into the following issue when we try to downgrade the timezone by running the script **catrelod.sql**:

```
"Database Instance might crash with

ORA-00600: internal error code, arguments: [8153], [0], [], [], [], [],
[], [], [], [], [], []

XDB SGA reset to NULL.
```

As per the following Oracle doc, this issue is caused by the bug, 23238774 which is fixed in the latest 12c versions. But it is not yet fixed in 11.2.0.4. Check Mos notes: (Doc ID 2410848.1).

This issue is mostly occurring when we are downgrading from Oracle 19c (19.9.0) to Oracle 11g (11.2.0.4). It works fine when we are downgrading the 19c to 12c versions as they have fixed the bug in the 12c versions.

If you are downgrading to 11.2.0.4, we prefer and recommend the "*Flashback the database to preupgrade guaranteed restore point*" method to downgrade the database. But if you did not create the guaranteed restore point before starting the database upgrade, and if you run into a situation where you must downgrade the database using the Oracle provided scripts, we would like to mention some of our following observations:

- The following steps (which are performed below) work fine without any issues for 12c and later downgrades.

- If you are downgrading to 11.2.0.4, you need to keep the preceding issue in mind and you can try following the workaround mentioned in the preceding **doc_id**.

Let's see how the manual downgrade using the Oracle provided scripts works.

Pre-downgrade steps/checks

The following are a few pre-downgrade steps that we can check before starting the database downgrade.

Check for incompatibilities when downgrading the Oracle Database

First, Check the Oracle database to see if the compatibility has any issues to the version that we will be downgrading to. In our case, we will downgrade to 11.2.0.4. We can downgrade the database to 11g from 19c as long as we don't change the compatible parameter to 19c.

Run the following command in the primary database:

```
SQL> Set lines 200
SQL> col name for a10
SQL> col value for a10
SQL> col DESCRIPTION for a66
SQL> set lines 200
SQL> SELECT name, value, description FROM v$parameter WHERE name =
'compatible';

NAME        VALUE        DESCRIPTION
----------  ----------   ------------------------------------------------
compatible  11.2.0.4.0   Database will be completely compatible with
                         this software version
```

As we can see, the database is compatible with 11.2.0.4, since we did not change the compatible parameter to 19c yet. We are good to downgrade.

Take a full backup of the primary database before proceeding with the downgrade

Oracle recommends to take a full database backup before we downgrade any database to its previous version. We can use RMAN to take a full backup of the database.

Disable the Oracle database vault

To check if the Oracle database vault is enabled in our database, run the following command in the primary database; if it's enabled, we need to disable it:

```
SQL> col parameter for a22
SQL> SELECT * FROM V$OPTION WHERE PARAMETER = 'Oracle Database Vault';

PARAMETER               VALUE        CON_ID
----------------------  ----------   ----------
Oracle Database Vault   FALSE        0
```

Please check the Oracle document to disable the Oracle database vault.

Downgrade Oracle Label Security

In the primary database, downgrade the Oracle Label Security if the source database is using it.

If our database uses the Oracle Label Security and if we are downgrading to 11.2 version, we need to run the following **Oracle Label Security (OLS)** preprocess downgrade script from 19c home before downgrading the database.

First, check whether the OLS parameter is enabled in our database, as follows:

```
SQL> SELECT VALUE FROM V$OPTION WHERE PARAMETER = 'Oracle Label
Security';

VALUE
----------
FALSE
```

If it's **True**, we can run the following script to downgrade the OLS. But since it's **FALSE** in our case, we don't have to run the **olspredowngrade.sql** script:

```
SQL> @ORACLE_HOME/rdbms/admin/olspredowngrade.sql
```

Purging audit trail files

If the source database has the unified auditing feature enabled, then complete the following steps to purge the audit trail:

1. First check if we have any audit records existing in our primary database, as follows:

   ```
   SQL> select count(*) from unified_audit_trail;

   COUNT(*)
   ----------
      0
   ```

2. If the preceding SQL statement returns nothing, we can skip this step. If it returns any number, then we can take a backup of the existing audit data to a table and purge the audit trail, as follows:

   ```
   SQL> create table audit_backup_tab as (select * from unified_
   audit_trail);
   ```

3. Now, we can purge the audit trail using the following statements:

   ```
   SQL> exec dbms_audit_mgmt.clean_audit_trail(audit_trail_type =>
   dbms_audit_mgmt.audit_trail_unified, use_last_arch_timestamp =>
   false);
   ```

Checking Timezone file in the primary database server

Check the Timezone version and ensure that the Timezone file is present in the 19c database home, as follows:

```
SQL> select * from v$timezone_file;

FILENAME               VERSION     CON_ID
--------------------   ----------  ----------
timezlrg_32.dat        32          0
```

This is the current timezone version of our 19c database. We can see that this file is present in the following 19c database home:

```
[oracle@chapvm-19crac1 zoneinfo]$ /u01/app/Oracle/product/19c/db_1/
oracore/zoneinfo
[oracle@chapvm-19crac1 zoneinfo]$ ls -ltr timezlrg_32.dat
-rw-r--r--. 1 Oracle oinstall 786909 Jun 19  2018 timezlrg_32.dat
[oracle@chapvm-19crac1 zoneinfo]$
```

Drop the user **sysman** if we have the OEM configured for this database, as follows:

```
DROP USER sysman CASCADE;
```

Standby lag check

Before proceeding further with the downgrade, first make sure that the physical standby database is in sync with the primary database. To do this, complete the following steps:

1. In the primary database, switch the logfiles, as follows:

   ```
   SQL> @/home/Oracle/rac_database_info.sql

   DATABASE_HOST    DB_NAME    DATABASE_ROLE   OPEN_MODE   STARTUP_TIME
   --------------   ---------  -------------   ----------  -----------
   chapvm-19crac1   vicedbpr1  PRIMARY         READ WRITE  16-FEB-21
   chapvm-19crac2   vicedbpr2  PRIMARY         READ WRITE  16-FEB-21

   SQL> archive log list;
   Database log mode               Archive Mode
   Automatic archival              Enabled
   Archive destination             USE_DB_RECOVERY_FILE_DEST
   Oldest online log sequence      195
   Next log sequence to archive    196
   Current log sequence            196
   ```

2. In the physical standby database, check if it's receiving and applying the log files, as follows:

```
SQL> @/home/Oracle/rac_database_info.sql

DATABASE_HOST     DB_NAME    DATABASE_ROLE      OPEN_MODE             STARTUP
----------------  ---------  -----------------  --------------------  -----------
chapstdby-19crac1 vicedbdr1  PHYSICAL STANDBY   READ ONLY WITH APPLY  16-FEB-21
chapstdby-19crac2 vicedbdr2  PHYSICAL STANDBY   READ ONLY WITH APPLY  16-FEB-21

INST_ID PROCESS  STATUS         THREAD#   SEQUENCE#  BLOCK#   BLOCKS
------- -------  ------------   -----     ---------  -------- ------
      1 MRP0     APPLYING_LOG      1       196          64    102400

THREAD#    ARCHIVED    APPLIED     GAP
---------- ----------  ----------  ----------
1            196         195         1
2             68          68         0
```

Shutdown the standby database

We can stop the physical standby database. If it's a single instance database, we can shut down the database using the **shutdown** command from **sqlplus**. In our case, since it's an RAC database, we can shut down the database using the **srvctl stop** command as follows:

```
[oracle@chapstdby-19crac1 dbs]$ srvctl stop database -d vicedbdr
Instance vicedbdr1 is not running on node chapstdby-19crac1
Instance vicedbdr2 is not running on node chapstdby-19crac2
```

Downgrade primary database

Starting with Oracle 19c, Oracle is providing a new downgrade utility called **dbdowngrade**. It comes as a shell command which is located in **$ORACLE_HOME/bin** of the 19c database home. We can still use the **catdwgrd.sql** script manually if we want. Here, we will downgrade the database using the **dbdowngrade** utility.

We will first downgrade the database and then downgrade the timezone.

Database downgrade

Complete the following steps to downgrade the primary database:

1. Shutdown the primary database.

   We can shut down the primary database now. If it's a single instance database, we can shut down the database using the **shutdown** command from **sqlplus**. If it's an **RAC** database, we can complete the following steps.

2. Set the **cluster_database** parameter to **FALSE** and stop the primary database, as follows:

```
SQL> alter system set cluster_database=FALSE scope=spfile sid='*';
System altered.

[oracle@chapvm-19crac1 vicedbpr]$ srvctl status database -d
vicedbpr
Instance vicedbpr1 is running on node chapvm-19crac1
Instance vicedbpr2 is running on node chapvm-19crac2

[oracle@chapvm-19crac1 vicedbpr]$ srvctl stop  database -d
vicedbpr
[oracle@chapvm-19crac1 vicedbpr]$ srvctl status  database -d
vicedbpr
Instance vicedbpr1 is not running on node chapvm-19crac1
Instance vicedbpr2 is not running on node chapvm-19crac2
```

3. Create a parameter file (**pfile**). Create a **pfile** as we need it to start the database in the downgrade mode.

   In the primary database, use the following command:

```
SQL> create pfile='/u01/app/Oracle/product/19c/db_1/dbs/downgrade_
vicedbprinit.ora' from spfile='+DATA/vicedbpr/spfilevicedbpr.ora';
```

4. Start the primary database in the downgrade mode.

   Start the primary database first instance in the downgrade mode. From the node-1 of the primary database, start the instance in the downgrade mode using the **pfile** created in the preceding step, as follows:

```
[oracle@chapvm-19crac1 dbs]$ export ORACLE_HOME=/u01/app/Oracle/
product/19c/db_1

[oracle@chapvm-19crac1 dbs]$ export PATH=$ORACLE_HOME/bin:$PATH

SQL> startup downgrade pfile='/u01/app/Oracle/product/19c/db_1/
dbs/downgrade_vicedbprinit.ora';

ORACLE instance started.
Total System Global Area 3070227080 bytes
Fixed Size                  8901256 bytes
Variable Size             805306368 bytes
Database Buffers         2248146944 bytes
Redo Buffers                7872512 bytes
Database mounted.
Database opened.
SQL>
```

5. Downgrade the database by running the **dbdowngrade** command.

   Run the **dbdowngrade** command as follows:

   ```
   [oracle@chapvm-19crac1 dbs]$ export ORACLE_HOME=/u01/app/Oracle/
   product/19c/db_1

   [oracle@chapvm-19crac1 dbs]$ export PATH=$ORACLE_HOME/bin:$PATH

   [oracle@chapvm-19crac1 dbs]$ sqlplus / as sysdba

   SQL> spool /u01/app/Oracle/product/19c/db_1/cfgtoollogs/
   downgrade/catdwgrd.log
   SQL> @/u01/app/oracle/product/19c/db_1/rdbms/admin/catdwgrd.sql
   ```

   We can open a new terminal and tail the preceding logfile, as follows:

   ```
   [oracle@chapvm-19crac1 dbs]$ tail -f /u01/app/Oracle/product/19c/
   db_1/cfgtoollogs/downgrade/catdwgrd.log

   COMP_TIMESTAMP CATDWGRD_BGN            2021-02-16 17:01:21
   DBUA_TIMESTAMP CATDWGRD_BGN   FINISHED 2021-02-16 17:01:21
   DBUA_TIMESTAMP CATDWGRD_BGN       NONE 2021-02-16 17:01:21

   Session altered.
   Session altered.
   DOC>############################################################
   DOC>############################################################

   DOC>
   DOC> If the below SQL statement raises an 'ORA-01722: invalid
   number' error
   DOC> then catdwgrd.sql has already been run on this database.
   DOC>
   DOC> Please refer to Chapter 6 of the Database Upgrade Guide,
   Downgrading

   DOC> Oracle Database to an Earlier Release" for information about
   DOC> continuing the downgrade process by running catrelod.sql
   using the
   DOC> earlier release server. If there were errors running
   catdwgrd.sql,
   DOC> recover the database, address the errors, and rerun
   catdwgrd.sql.
   DOC>

   DOC>############################################################
   DOC>############################################################
   DOC>#
   no rows selected
   PL/SQL procedure successfully completed.
   Note: Output truncated for better visibility.
   ```

6. Shutdown the database instance which is running from **19c** home, as follows:

    SQL> shutdown immediate;

7. Modify the **pfile** created in step 2.

8. We can modify the parameter file created in step 2, and remove the unnecessary hidden parameters (like for example **_unified_pga_pool_ size**) that were created in **19c**. Once modified, we can rename the **pfile** with the instance name as follows:

    ```
    [oracle@chapstdby-19crac1 dbs]$ cd /u01/app/Oracle/
    product/11.2.0.4/db_1/dbs

    [oracle@chapstdby-19crac1 dbs]$ cp /u01/app/Oracle/product/19c/
    db_1/dbs/downgrade_vicedbprinit.ora /u01/app/Oracle/
    product/11.2.0.4/db_1/dbs/

    [oracle@chapstdby-19crac1 dbs]$ mv initvicedbpr1.ora
    initvicedbpr1.ora.old
    [oracle@chapstdby-19crac1 dbs]$ mv downgrade_vicedbprinit.ora
    initvicedbpr1.ora
    ```

Downgrading the Timezone

If we upgraded the DST version during the Oracle database upgrade from 11.2.0.4 to 19.9.0 either by using **AutoUpgrade** or by manual steps, then in order to downgrade the Timezone version back to its source database version, we need to apply this patch 28125601 to the 11.2.0.4 Oracle database home. If we don't apply this patch, the **catrelod** script, which we run in the following step will error out and give the error ORA-01722. We have to apply this patch to make the **catrelod** script run without any issues. To avoid this issue, download and install the following patch for TSTZ in 11.2.0.4 home in all the nodes. Check the following known issues for more information on the error:

Patch 28125601: RDBMS - PROACTIVE DSTV32 UPDATE - TZDATA2018E

```
[oracle@chapvm-19crac1 ~]$ export ORACLE_HOME=/u01/app/Oracle/
product/11.2.0.4/db_1
[oracle@chapvm-19crac1 ~]$ export PATH=$ORACLE_HOME/bin:$PATH

[oracle@chapvm-19crac1 ~]$ $ORACLE_HOME/OPatch/opatch lspatches

28125601;    <-------
30670774;Database Patch Set Update : 11.2.0.4.200414 (30670774)
29938455;OCW Patch Set Update : 11.2.0.4.191015 (29938455)
OPatch succeeded.
```

Since the one-off patch (28125601) is applied, we can follow below steps for downgrading the timezone.

1. Start the primary database in the upgrade mode from the 11g home, as follows:

```
[oracle@chapvm-19crac1 dbs]$ export ORACLE_HOME=/u01/app/Oracle/
product/11.2.0.4/db_1
[oracle@chapvm-19crac1 dbs]$ export PATH=$ORACLE_HOME/bin:$PATH

[oracle@chapvm-19crac1 dbs]$ sqlplus / as sysdba
SQL> startup upgrade;
ORACLE instance started.
Total System Global Area 3070227080 bytes
Fixed Size                   8901256 bytes
Variable Size              805306368 bytes
Database Buffers          2248146944 bytes
Redo Buffers                 7872512 bytes
Database mounted.
Database opened.
SQL>
```

Run the script catrelod.sql in the primary database:

```
SQL> @/u01/app/Oracle/product/11.2.0.4/db_1/rdbms/admin/catrelod.
sql

TIMESTAMP
------------------------------------------------------------
COMP_TIMESTAMP RELOD__BGN 2021-02-16 17:08:28 2459328 61708

DOC>############################################################
DOC>############################################################
DOC>  The following statement will cause an "ORA-01722: invalid
number"
DOC>  error if the database server version is not 11.2.0.
DOC>  Perform "ALTER SYSTEM CHECKPOINT" prior to "SHUTDOWN
DOC>  The following statement will cause an "ORA-01722: invalid
number"
DOC>  error if the database has not been opened for MIGRATE.
DOC>
DOC>    if the old Oracle release is expecting a time zone file
ersion
DOC>    that does not exist.
DOC>    Note that 11.2.0.3 ships with time zone file version 14.
DOC>
DOC> o Action:
DOC>    Perform "ALTER SYSTEM CHECKPOINT" prior to "SHUTDOWN
BORT", and
DOC>    patch old ORACLE_HOME to the same time zone file version
as used
```

Note : Output truncated for better visibility.

2. Run the **utlrp** script to compile the invalid objects.

   Once the reload command is complete, run the script **utlrp.sql** and shutdown the primary database, as follows:

```
SQL> @$ORACLE_HOME/rdbms/admin/utlrp.sql
SQL> shutdown immediate;
```

3. Downgrade the Oracle **clusterware** database configuration of the primary database as follows:

```
[oracle@chapvm-19crac1 dbs]$ export ORACLE_HOME=/u01/app/Oracle/
product/19c/db_1
[oracle@chapvm-19crac1 dbs]$ export PATH=$ORACLE_HOME/bin:$PATH
[oracle@chapvm-19crac1 dbs]$ srvctl downgrade database -d
vicedbpr -o /u01/app/Oracle/product/11.2.0.4/db_1 -t 11.2.0.4
```

4. Recreate the server parameter (**spfile**) from the modified **pfile**, set the **cluster_database** parameter to **TRUE**, and start the database using the **srvctl** command, as follows:

```
SQL> create spfile='+DATA/vicedbpr/spfilevicedbpr.ora' from pfile='/
u01/app/Oracle/product/11.2.0.4/db_1/dbs/initvicedbpr1.ora';
File created.

[oracle@chapvm-19crac1 dbs]$srvctl start instance -d vicedbpr -n
chapvm-19crac1

[oracle@chapvm-19crac1 dbs]$sqlplus / as sysdba

SQL> alter system set cluster_database=TRUE scope=spfile sid='*';
SQL> System altered.

[oracle@chapvm-19crac1 dbs]$srvctl stop database -d vicedbpr
[oracle@chapvm-19crac1 dbs]$srvctl start database -d vicedbpr

[oracle@chapvm-19crac1 dbs]$srvctl status database -d vicedbpr
Instance vicedbpr1 is not running on node chapvm-19crac1
Instance vicedbpr2 is not running on node chapvm-19crac2
```

5. Finally, check the registry components in the primary database, as follows:

```
SQL> @/home/Oracle/rac_database_info.sql
```

DATABASE_HOST	DB_NAME	DATABASE_ROLE	OPEN_MODE	STARTUP_TIME
chapvm-19crac1	vicedbpr1	PRIMARY	READ WRITE	16-FEB-21

```
chapvm-19crac2    vicedbpr2      PRIMARY      READ WRITE   16-FEB-21

SQL>select COMP_ID,COMP_NAME,VERSION,STATUS from dba_registry;
COMP_ID     COMP_NAME                              VERSION      STATUS
----------- -------------------------------------- ------------ ------
OWB         OWB                                    11.2.0.4.0   VALID
APEX        Oracle Application Express             3.2.1.00.12  VALID
EM          Oracle Enterprise Manager              11.2.0.4.0   VALID
AMD         OLAP Catalog                           11.2.0.4.0   VALID
SDO         Spatial                                11.2.0.4.0   VALID
ORDIM       Oracle Multimedia                      11.2.0.4.0   VALID
XDB         Oracle XML Database                    11.2.0.4.0   VALID
CONTEXT     Oracle Text                            11.2.0.4.0   VALID
EXF         Oracle Expression Filter               11.2.0.4.0   VALID
RUL         Oracle Rules Manager                   11.2.0.4.0   VALID
OWM         Oracle Workspace Manager               11.2.0.4.0   VALID
ATALOG      Oracle Database Catalog Views          11.2.0.4.0   VALID
CATPROC     Oracle Database Packagesand Types      11.2.0.4.0   VALID
JAVAVM      JServer JAVA Virtual Machine           11.2.0.4.0   VALID
XML         Oracle XDK                             11.2.0.4.0   VALID
CATJAVA     Oracle Database Java Packages          11.2.0.4.0   VALID
APS         OLAP Analytic Workspace                11.2.0.4.0   VALID
XOQ         Oracle OLAP API                        11.2.0.4.0   VALID
RAC         Oracle Real Application Clusters       11.2.0.4.0   VALID
19 rows selected.
```

This completes the downgrade of the primary database from version 19.9.0 to version 11.2.0.4. Now, let's downgrade the physical standby database.

Downgrading the physical standby database to Oracle 11g (11.2.0.4)

Let's look at the following steps:

1. Create a **pfile** from the **19c spfile** and remove the unnecessary hidden **19c** parameters, as follows:

   ```
   SQL> create pfile='/u01/app/Oracle/product/11.2.0.4/db_1/
   dbs/finalinit.ora' from spfile='+data/vicedbdr/PARAMETERFILE/
   spfilevicedbdr1.ora';

   File created.
   ```

2. Modify the **init.ora** and remove the underscore parameters and recreate the **spfile**, as follows:

```
SQL> create spfile='+data/vicedbdr/PARAMETERFILE/spfilevicedbdr1.
ora' from pfile='/u01/app/Oracle/product/11.2.0.4/db_1/dbs/
finalinit.ora';
File created.
```

3. Downgrade the standby database **clusterware** configuration using the **srvctl** command as follows:

```
[oracle@chapstdby-19crac1 dbs]$  export ORACLE_HOME=/u01/app/
Oracle/product/19c/db_1
[oracle@chapstdby-19crac1 dbs]$  export PATH=$ORACLE_HOME/
bin:$PATH

[oracle@chapstdby-19crac1 dbs]$  srvctl downgrade database -d
vicedbdr  -o /u01/app/Oracle/product/11.2.0.4/db_1 -t 11.2.0.4
```

4. Also, update the **/etc/oratab** to change the database home from **19c** to 11.2.0.4, as follows:

```
[oracle@chapstdby-19crac1 dbs]$ vi /etc/oratab
```

```
[oracle@chapstdby-19crac1 dbs]$ cat /etc/oratab | grep homes
```

```
vicedbdr1:/u01/app/Oracle/product/11.2.0.4/db_1:N        [oracle@
chapstdby-19crac1 dbs]$
```

5. Start the database instance from 11.2.0.4 home in the **MOUNT** mode on node-1 from 11.2.0.4 home. If this is an **RAC** database, we can use the **srvctl** command and if this is not an **RAC** database, we can use the **sqlplus** commands to start the instance in the **mount** mode, as follows:

```
[oracle@chapstdby-19crac1 dbs]$ export ORACLE_HOME=/u01/app/
Oracle/product/11.2.0.4/db_1


[oracle@chapstdby-19crac1 dbs]$ export PATH=$ORACLE_HOME/
bin:$PATH

[oracle@chapstdby-19crac1 dbs]$ srvctl start instance -d vicedbdr
-n chapstdby-19crac1 -o mount

[oracle@chapstdby-19crac1 dbs]$  srvctl status database -d
vicedbdr
Instance vicedbdr1 is running on node chapstdby-19crac1
Instance vicedbdr2 is not running on node chapstdby-19crac2
```

The physical standby database will be downgraded with all the migrated redo logs that it received from the primary database. Wait for some time and once the physical standby database catches up with the primary database, stop it, and then we can start it in the normal mode using the **srvctl** command. If needed, you can also start the MRP to apply the redo data if it isn't applying.

6. Check the lag in the physical standby database and start it in the normal mode and start the recovery process, as follows:

```
SQL> @/home/Oracle/standby_database_lag.sql

DATABASE_HOST      DB_NAME    DATABASE_ROLE     OPEN_MODE   STARTUP_TIME
----------------   --------   ---------------   ---------   -----------
chapstdby-19crac1  vicedbdr1  PHYSICAL STANDBY  MOUNTED     16-FEB-21
chapstdby-19crac2  vicedbdr2  PHYSICAL STANDBY  MOUNTED     16-FEB-21


INST_ID   PROCESS   STATUS         THREAD# SEQUENCE#   BLOCK#   BLOCKS
--------- --------  ------------   ------  ---------   ------   ------
   1       MRP0     APPLYING_LOG   1       282         2813     102400


THREAD#      ARCHIVED     APPLIED      GAP
----------   ----------   ----------   ----------
1            282          281          0
2            74           74           0
```

7 We can now stop and start the physical standby database in the read only mode, as follows:

```
[oracle@chapstdby-19crac1 dbs]$ srvctl stop database -d vicedbdr
[oracle@chapstdby-19crac1 dbs]$ srvctl start database -d vicedbdr

[oracle@chapstdby-19crac1 dbs]$ srvctl status database -d
vicedbdr
Instance vicedbdr1 is running on node chapstdby-19crac1
Instance vicedbdr2 is running on node chapstdby-19crac2
```

8. Finally, check the registry components in the physical standby database, as follows:

```
SQL> @/home/Oracle/rac_database_info.sql


DATABASE_HOST      DB_NAME    DATABASE_ROLE     OPEN_MODE             STARTUP
----------------   --------   ---------------   --------------------  -----------
chapstdby-19crac1  vicedbdr1  PHYSICAL STANDBY  READ ONLY WITH APPLY  16-FEB-21
chapstdby-19crac2  vicedbdr2  PHYSICAL STANDBY  READ ONLY WITH APPLY  16-FEB-21


SQL>select COMP_ID,COMP_NAME,VERSION,STATUS from dba_registry;


COMP_ID      COMP_NAME                         VERSION       STATUS
----------   -----------------------------     ----------    ------
OWB          OWB                               11.2.0.4.0    VALID
APEX         Oracle Application Express        3.2.1.00.12   VALID
EM           Oracle Enterprise Manager         11.2.0.4.0    VALID
AMD          OLAP Catalog                      11.2.0.4.0    VALID
SDO          Spatial                           11.2.0.4.0    VALID
```

ORDIM	Oracle Multimedia	11.2.0.4.0	VALID
XDB	Oracle XML Database	11.2.0.4.0	VALID
CONTEXT	Oracle Text	11.2.0.4.0	VALID
EXF	Oracle Expression Filter	11.2.0.4.0	VALID
RUL	Oracle Rules Manager	11.2.0.4.0	VALID
OWM	Oracle Workspace Manager	11.2.0.4.0	VALID
ATALOG	Oracle Database Catalog Views	11.2.0.4.0	VALID
CATPROC	Oracle Database Packages and Types	11.2.0.4.0	VALID
JAVAVM	JServer JAVA Virtual Machine	11.2.0.4.0	VALID
XML	Oracle XDK	11.2.0.4.0	VALID
CATJAVA	Oracle Database Java Packages	11.2.0.4.0	VALID
APS	OLAP Analytic Workspace	11.2.0.4.0	VALID
XOQ	Oracle OLAP API	11.2.0.4.0	VALID
RAC	Oracle Real Application Clusters	11.2.0.4.0	VALID

```
19 rows selected.
```

We have now successfully downgraded both the primary and the physical standby database from version 19.9.0 to version 11.2.0.4 using the Oracle provided downgrade scripts.

Known issues

The following are a few known issues along with the possible cause of the issue and also the solutions and/or work around.

Issue-1

We have seen in a few cases, where, when we downgrade the primary database using the previously mentioned scripts, the physical standby database downgrade will fail with ORA-600 and the instance will keep terminating, as follows:

```
ORA-00600: internal error code, arguments: [ksxptid2pid1],
[0x7F15C4A1CDD8], [4], [1], [2], [], [], [], [], [], [], []
starting up 1 shared server(s) ...
USER (ospid: 24225): terminating the instance due to error 29702
Instance terminated by USER, pid = 24225
```

Cause:

Bug 31561819 - OCW: Incompatible max members at CRSD Level Causing Database Instance Not Able to Start (Doc ID 31561819.8).

Solution:

Oracle is providing a one-off patch for this bug for the versions Oracle 12c (12.1.2.0) and above. As of now, we don't have anything for version Oracle 11g (11.2.0.4). If the issue occurs for the Oracle 11g (11.2.0.4) database, we might have to rebuild the physical standby database.

Issue-2

When we downgrade timezone from Oracle 19c to the source version (11g, 12c) by running the following script, it will fail with the error mentioned as follows:

```
SQL> @/u01/app/Oracle/product/11.2.0.4/db_1/rdbms/admin/catrelod.sql

TIMESTAMP
-----------------------------------------------------------
COMP_TIMESTAMP RELOD__BGN 2021-04-23 16:57:01 2459328 61021

DOC>#######################################################################
DOC>   The following statement will cause an "ORA-01722: invalid number"
DOC>   error if the database server version is not 11.2.0.
DOC>   Perform "ALTER SYSTEM CHECKPOINT" prior to "SHUTDOWN ABORT", and
use a
DOC>   different script or a different server.

DOC>#######################################################################
no rows selected
DOC>#######################################################################
DOC>   The following query will cause:
DOC>   - An "ORA-01722: invalid number"
DOC>     if the old Oracle release is expecting a time zone file version
DOC>     that does not exist.
DOC>     Note that 11.2.0.3 ships with time zone file version 14.
DOC>
DOC>   o Action:
DOC>     Perform "ALTER SYSTEM CHECKPOINT" prior to "SHUTDOWN ABORT", and
DOC>     patch old ORACLE_HOME to the same time zone file version as used
DOC>     in the new ORACLE_HOME.
DOC>#######################################################################
SELECT TO_NUMBER('MUST_BE_SAME_TIMEZONE_FILE_VERSION')
              *
ERROR at line 1:
ORA-01722: invalid number
```

Solution:

Before we start downgrading the timezone from 19.9.0 to either 11.2.0.4 or 12c, we need apply to apply the following one-off patch:

Patch 28125601: RDBMS - PROACTIVE DSTV32 UPDATE - TZDATA2018E

Once we apply the patch, we can re-run the script **catrelod.sql** and it will run successfully without any issues.

Issue-3

When we run **AutoUpgrade** to upgrade the primary database of a **dataguard** environment either in the deploy or the upgrade mode, it can fail with the following error:

```
2021-01-12 17:48:39.319 ERROR Error running dispatcher for job 101
Cause: An error occurred while deferring Standby in Drain phase
2021-04-21 17:48:39.320 ERROR Dispatcher failed:
Error: UPG-1711
[Unexpected exception error]
Cause: An error occurred while deferring Standby in Drain phase
```

Cause:

The reason for this error is that the **dataguard** process in the **dg_broker_start** might be set to true and the standby database is already shutdown.

Solution:

To avoid this issue, once we shut down the physical standby database, we also need to set the **dg_broker_start** parameter to **FALSE** and then rerun the **AutoUpgrade** command.

Issue-4

The latest version of **AutoUpgrade** (version 21.1.3) is checking and ensuring that the TDE wallet location is specified in the parameters, **wallet_root**. If the wallet location is specified in the **sqlnet.ora** parameter **sqlnet.encryption_wallet_location**, **AutoUpgrade** will give the following error and will not proceed until we fix the issue:

```
==============
BEFORE UPGRADE
==============

REQUIRED ACTIONS

================
```

1. Verify that the AutoUpgrade configuration file contains the
    appropriate parameters to allow AutoUpgrade to locate the
    KeyStore files – especially the source_tns_admin_dir parameter.
    It is not necessary to copy the KeyStore files to the specified
    directory. Rather, update the configuration file, so they can be
    found automatically.

    The database is using TDE, but AutoUpgrade is unable to access
    the KeyStore files. Based on the AutoUpgrade configuration file,
    which results in a TNS_ADMIN environmental value of /u01/app/

```
oracle/product/12.2.0/dbhome_1/network/admin, AutoUpgrade is
searching for the files in the following directory: +DATAC1/
vicedb/wallet

If the Oracle Transparent Data Encryption (TDE) is in use,
AutoUpgrade must be able to access the files necessary to open the
KeyStore.
```

Solution:

Starting with 19c, Oracle recommends setting the wallet location in the **init** parameter, **wallet_root**. Set the wallet location in **wallet_root** and start the database upgrade using **Autoupgrade**.

For more information, refer to the following link:

https://docs.oracle.com/en/database/oracle/oracle-database/19/upgrd/autoupgrade-configuration-file-examples.html#GUID-941F8A45-C3E8-445A-A5C9-85799A285DEC

Issue-5

After the 19c database upgrade, we observed that a few users in the database had the **SYSTEM** tablespace as their local temporary **tablespace**, as follows:

```
SQL> select username,LOCAL_TEMP_TABLESPACE from dba_users where local_
temp_tablespace='SYSTEM';

USERNAME                 LOCAL_TEMP_TABLESPACE
-------------------      -------------------------------

CBMASI                   SYSTEM
CLTY_RACL                SYSTEM
CMBI_ACT                 SYSTEM
EGATE                    SYSTEM
4 rows selected.
```

Cause

This is caused by the following bug which was supposedly fixed in **18c** but came back in **19c** again:

```
Bug 23715518 - SYSTEM TABLESPACE IS MARKED AS LOCAL_TEMP_TABLESPACE
AFTER UPGRADE
```

Solution

Change the **local_temp_tablespace** to **TEMP** (or any other user defined **Temporary** tablespace). We can use the following SQL to make that change:

For single user.

```
SQL> alter user EGATE local temporary tablespace temp;
```

For multi-users. We can use below sql which when run will generate dynamic sqls for all the users which has SYSTEM as local_temporary_tablespace.

```
SQL> select 'alter user ' || username || ' local temporary tablespace
temp;' from dba_users where local_temp_tablespace='system';

alter user CBMASI local temporary tablespace temp;
alter user CBMASI local temporary tablespace temp;
alter user CLTY_RACL local temporary tablespace temp;
alter user CMBI_ACT local temporary tablespace temp;
alter user EGATE local temporary tablespace temp;
5 rows selected.
```

Execute the output to change the local temporary tablespace for each of those users.

Please note that for this issue, Oracle has provided a one-off patch (**Patch #: 30295137**) for the 18c version, and, if needed, we can request backport for the **19c** version.

Conclusion

In this chapter, we discussed about the AutoUpgrade utility and the different stages and modes it can be run in. We learned how to upgrade the version from 11.2.0.4 to version 19.9.0 using the AutoUpgrade utility. We also saw how to downgrade the version from 19.9.0 back to version 11.2.0.4 using the Oracle provided scripts. In the next chapter, we will see how we can use AutoUpgrade to upgrade the 12.1.0.2 database to 19c, and then we will convert the upgraded database from the non-container to the pluggable database using the Oracle scripts.

Multiple choice questions

1. How many modes can an AutoUpgrade utility be run in?

    a. 2

    b. 3

    c. 6

    d. 4

2. Can the AutoUpgrade configuration file contain more than one database entry in it and can the AutoUpgrade upgrade more than one database in a single command?

    a. Yes

    b. No

3. Along with the database upgrade, does the AutoUpgrade utility also upgrade the Timezone version?

    a. Yes

    b. No

4. Does the AutoUpgrade command, when run in the analyze mode, make any changes to the source database?

    a. No

    b. Yes

Answers

1. **D** (Explanation: AutoUpgrade runs in the Analyze, Fixup, Deploy, and Upgrade modes)

2. **A**

3. **A**

4. **B**

Key terms

- Bug 23715518

- 30295137 (patch in 18c and 19c to address issue "ORA-12911: permanent tablespace cannot be temporary tablespace")

- **ORA-01722:** invalid number

- 28125601 (One-off patch for timezone downgrade issue)

- 3156181 (oracle bug for database start issue, doc id 31561819.8)

- **ORA-00600:** internal error code, arguments: [ksxptid2pid1]

CHAPTER 4

Upgrading and Converting 12c Non-CDB as 19c PDB

Introduction

In this chapter, we will see how to upgrade the Oracle 12c (12.1.0.2) non-container database (both, the primary and the physical standby database) to Oracle 19c (19.9.0). We will also migrate the upgraded database from 12c to 19c as a **pluggable database (pdb)** and plug-in to the pre-existing Oracle 19c (19.9.0) **container database (cdb)**. We can either perform these two steps in a single operation using AutoUpgrade or we can first upgrade the database using AutoUpgrade and then plug-in the upgraded database as pdb. In this chapter, we will use the second method and we will check on the first method that was discussed in *Chapter 6, Upgrading and Converting 12c Non-CDB as 19c PDB (usingUsing AutoUpgrade)*. We will also see how we can reuse the datafiles of the source standby database when it's being converted as a pluggable database in the container database of the target physical standby database. This will be helpful if the size of the physical standby database is in terabytes. We will also see how to deal with the TDE wallets and keys if the source database has an encryption enabled in it.

Structure

In this chapter, we will cover the following topics:

- Discuss high level steps required for upgrading a 12.1.0.2 non-container database to 19c database using AutoUpgrade and then convert the upgraded database as pluggable database using manual method.

- Check the source and target setup environments used to demonstrate the database upgrade

- Discuss and perform all the pre-requisites steps required for the database upgrade.

- How to download AutoUpgrade utility

- Discuss and create the Configuration file required by AutoUpgrade tool for this upgrade.

- Running AutoUpgrade in 'Analyze' mode to verify the database readiness and fix any issues that can impact the database upgrade activity.

- Discuss about AutoUpgrade locations.

- Running the AutoUpgrade in 'Deploy' mode to upgrade and covert non-cdb to pluggable database.

- Discuss about Post-Upgrade checks.

- Upgrade the Physical standby database from 12.1.0.2 to 19c.

- Discuss about the Fall-back methods that can be used to downgrade the Oracle database from the upgraded version back to the source version.

- Convert the upgrade 19c database from non-container database to pluggable database.

- Discuss in detail about the concept of 'Reusing the Source Standby Database **Files When Plugging a PDB into the Primary Database of a Data Guard Configuration** when the standby database is converted to pluggable database

- How to deal with the TDE while converting a non-cdb as pdb and plug it into a new container database.

- Discuss about options for the fallback method once the database is converted from non-container database to pluggable database.

- Test RMAN restore to restore the database from the pre-upgrade backup.

- Discuss about few known issues that can occur during the database upgrade or during the database downgrade.

Objective

After reading this chapter, you will be able to upgrade oracle database to 19c using *AutoUpgrade* utility. You will also be able to convert a non-container database to a pluggable database. You will get to know about the concept of 'Reusing the Source Standby Database Files When Plugging a PDB into the Primary Database of a Data Guard Configuration 'in the standby database when it's being plugged as Pluggable database into a new container which is also residing on same servers. You will also get familiar different fallback options for downgrading an upgraded pluggable database back to non-container database and to its source version.

An overview of Database upgrade demonstrated in this chapter

Figure 4.1 shows the high-level representation of this process of upgrading a 12.1.0.2 to 19.9.0.0 using *AutoUpgrade* command and then converting upgrade database as pluggable database:

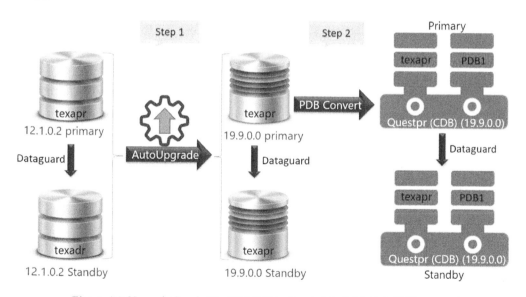

Figure 4.1: *Upgrade Oracle 12c (12.1.0.2) to Oracle 19c (19.9.0) & PDB conversion*

In the first part of this chapter, we will first upgrade both the primary and the physical standby databases from Oracle 12c (12.1.0.2) to Oracle 19c (19.9.0) using the AutoUpgrade utility and then convert it as a pluggable database. In the latter part of this chapter, we will downgrade both the primary and the physical standby database from Oracle 19c (19.9.0) back to Oracle 12c (12.1.0.2).

High-level steps that are performed as part of this upgrade and pdb conversion activity

Following are the high-level steps that are performed as part of upgrading a 12.1.0.2 database to 19c and then convert it as pluggable database and plug it into a 19c container database. This provides covers points including preupgrade, upgrade and post upgrade steps:

1. full back up of the source database.

2. Enable the flashback feature in the primary and the physical standby database.

3. Set the fast recovery area size to a higher value in both the primary and the standby databases.

4. Purge the **recyclebin** as this will save time during the database upgrade and will help in reducing the downtime needed for the database upgrade.

5. Gather the dictionary statistics to the latest as this will help for the database upgrade to run faster.

6. Run the **AutoUpgrade** script in the ANALYZE mode in the primary database and fix any required issues as identified by the AutoUpgrade tool.

7. Create a guarantee restore point in physical standby database.

8. Disable dataguard broker in both primary and physical standby database.

9. Shutdown the physical standby database.

10. Upgrade the primary database by running the AutoUpgrade script in the DEPLOY mode.

11. Perform any post-upgrade checks on the primary database.

12. Upgrade the physical standby database with the migrated redo data that it received from the primary database.

13. Enable the **dataguard** broker and perform a final check on both the primary and the standby database.

14. Migrate the upgraded non-container primary database 19c (19.9.0) as a pluggable database into an existing container database 19c (19.9.0).

15. Plug-in the non-container database 19c (19.9.0) physical standby database as a pluggable database into the pre-existing container physical standby database.

We have created two scripts which we can use to check the current database configuration and the physical standby database lag. We will be using these scripts throughout this chapter.

Script-1: The following script will pull the current database details like, the mode and the role of the database:

```
[oracle@virtual-19crac1] cat /home/oracle/rac_database_info.sql

SQL> set lines 200
SQL> col DATABASE_HOST for a30;
SQL> col HOST_NAME for a15;
SQL> col DATABASE_ROLE for a10
SQL> col OPEN_MODE for a10
SQL> col STARTUP_TIME for a20
SQL> SELECT i.HOST_NAME "DATABASE_HOST" ,i.INSTANCE_NAME "DB_NAME",
     d.DATABASE_ROLE " DATABASE_ROLE",
     d.OPEN_MODE " OPEN_MODE ", STARTUP_TIME
     from GV$DATABASE d, gv$instance I
     where i.INST_ID=d.INST_ID;
```

Script-2 This: The following script will check the current lag on the standby database and display the standby database role and mode info as well:

```
[oracle@virtual-19crac1] cat /home/oracle/standby_database_lag.sql

SQL> set lines 200
SQL> col DATABASE_HOST for a30;
SQL> col HOST_NAME for a15;
SQL> col DATABASE_ROLE for a10
SQL> col OPEN_MODE for a10
SQL> col STARTUP_TIME for a20
SQL> SELECT i.HOST_NAME "DATABASE_HOST" ,i.INSTANCE_NAME "DB_NAME",
     d.DATABASE_ROLE " DATABASE_ROLE",
     d.OPEN_MODE " OPEN_MODE ", STARTUP_TIME
     from GV$DATABASE d, gv$instance I
     where i.INST_ID=d.INST_ID;
SQL> select inst_id,process, status, thread#, sequence#, block#, blocks
     from gv$managed_standby
     where process='MRP0';
SQL> select a.thread#, (select max (sequence#) from v$archived_log where
archived='YES' and thread#=a.thread#) archived,max(a.sequence#) applied,
```

```
(select max(sequence#) from v$archived_log where archived='YES' and
thread#=a.thread#)-max(a.sequence#)gap
```

```
from v$archived_log a where a.applied='YES' group by a.thread# order by
thread#;
```

Check the configuration of the primary database and the physical standby database

For this demonstration, we have a primary database environment and a standby database environment. For the primary environment, we have Oracle 12.1.0.2 database binaries installed and patched with the April 2020 patch set update.

Setting up the Source Environment

The primary database version and the patch set is as follows:

```
RAC nodes            : virtual-19crac1
                       virtual-19crac2
OS version           : Oracle Enterprise Linux 7.1 64 bit
Oracle Home          : /u01/app/oracle/product/12c/db_1
Database Version     : 12.1.0.2 with July 2020 Database Patch Set Update
Grid Version         : 19.9.0 (Oct,2020 patch set)
```

```
[oracle@virtual-19crac1 ]$ export ORACLE_HOME=/u01/app/oracle/
product/12c/db_1
[oracle@virtual-19crac1 ]$ export PATH=$ORACLE_HOME/bin:$PATH
[oracle@virtual-19crac1 ]$ $ORACLE_HOME/OPatch/opatch lspatches
31136382;OCW PATCH SET UPDATE 12.1.0.2.200714 (31136382) 31001106;
Database Bundle Patch : 12.1.0.2.200714 (31001106)
```

The source primary database name is **texapr** and the following are its **rac** instances:

```
SQL> @/home/oracle/rac_database_info.sql
```

```
DATABASE_HOST    DB_NAME   DATABASE_ROLE   OPEN_MODE    STARTUP_TIME
---------------  -------   -------------   ----------   ------------
virtual-19crac1  texapr1   PRIMARY         READ WRITE   26-FEB-21
virtual-19crac2  texapr2   PRIMARY         READ WRITE   26-FEB-21
```

Physical standby database version and the patch set:

The physical standby database environment has a similar setup, that is, Oracle 12.1.0.2 database binaries patched with the April 2020 database release patch set.

The following is the physical standby database binary and the patch level details:

```
RAC nodes                  : virtual-dr-19crac1
                             virtual-dr-19crac2

OS version                 : Oracle Enterprise Linux 7.1 64 bit
Oracle Home                : /u01/app/oracle/product/12c/db_1
Database Version           : 12.1.0.2 with July 2020 Database Patch Set
Update
Grid Version               : 19.9.0 (Oct, 2020 patch set)

[oracle@virtual-dr-19crac1 ~]$ export ORACLE_HOME=/u01/app/oracle/
product/12c/db_1
[oracle@virtual-dr-19crac1 ~]$ export PATH=$ORACLE_HOME/bin:$PATH
[oracle@virtual-dr-19crac1 ~]$  $ORACLE_HOME/OPatch/opatch lspatches
31136382;OCW PATCH SET UPDATE 12.1.0.2.200714 (31136382) 31001106;
Database Bundle Patch : 12.1.0.2.200714 (31001106)
OPatch succeeded.
```

The physical standby database name is **texadr** and the following are its **RAC** instances:

```
SQL> @/home/oracle/rac_database_info.sql

DATABASE_HOST      DB_NAME    DATABASE_ROLE      OPEN_MODE   STARTUP_TIME
--------------     --------   ----------------   ---------   -----------
virtual-dr-19crac1 texadr1    PHYSICAL STANDBY   MOUNTED     26-FEB-21
virtual-dr-19crac2 texadr2    PHYSICAL STANDBY   MOUNTED     26-FEB-21
```

Setting up the target environment

We installed Oracle 19c (19.3.0) on both the primary and the physical standby database servers and applied the October 2020 PSU on top of the 19.3.0 binaries. If you want to use the latest patch set, you can check and download it from the MOS. We also created a CDB database with the name **questpr**. We will use this container database to plug the **texapr** once it's upgraded to the 19c (19.9.0) non-container database.

The target primary database binary version and its patch set is as follows:

```
RAC nodes                  : virtual-19crac1
                             virtual-19crac2
OS version                 : Oracle Enterprise Linux 7.1 64 bit
Oracle Home                : /u01/app/oracle/product/19c/db_1
Database Version           : 19.3.0.0 with October 2020 Database Bundle Patch
Grid Version               : 19.9.0
```

```
[oracle@virtual-19crac1 ~]$ $ORACLE_HOME/OPatch/opatch lspatches
31771877;Database Release Update : 19.9.0.0.201020 (31771877)
29585399;OCW RELEASE UPDATE 19.3.0.0.0 (29585399)
OPatch succeeded.


SQL>@rac_database_info.sql

DATABASE_HOST     DB_NAME    DATABASE_ROLE      OPEN_MODE    STARTUP_TIME
----------------  --------   --------------     ----------   ------------
virtual-19crac1   questpr1   PRIMARY            READ WRITE   26-FEB-21
virtual-19crac2   questpr2   PRIMARY            READ WRITE   26-FEB-21
```

The target physical standby database binary version and its patch set is as follows:

```
RAC nodes            : virtual-dr-19crac1
                       virtual-dr-19crac2
OS version           : Oracle Enterprise Linux 7.1 64 bit
Oracle Home          : /u01/app/oracle/product/19c/db_1
Database Version     : 19.3.0.0 with October 2020 Database Bundle Patch
Grid Version         : 19.9.0

[oracle@virtual-dr-19crac1 ~] $ORACLE_HOME/OPatch/opatch
lspatches31771877;Database Release Update : 19.9.0.0.201020 (31771877)
29585399;OCW RELEASE UPDATE 19.3.0.0.0 (29585399)
OPatch succeeded.

SQL>@/home/oracle/rac_database_info.sql

DATABASE_HOST     DB_NAME    DATABASE_ROLE     OPEN_MODE    STARTUP_TIME
----------------  --------   ----------------  ----------   ------------
virtual-dr-19crac1  questdr1  PHYSICAL STANDBY  MOUNTED      26-FEB-21
virtual-dr-19crac2  questdr2  PHYSICAL STANDBY  MOUNTED      26-FEB-21
```

As mentioned earlier, in the first step, we will upgrade the **12c** database along with its physical standby database to 19.9.0 (refer to *figure 4.2*). In the second step, we will convert the upgraded database as a pluggable database and will plug it in the pre-created 19c container database.

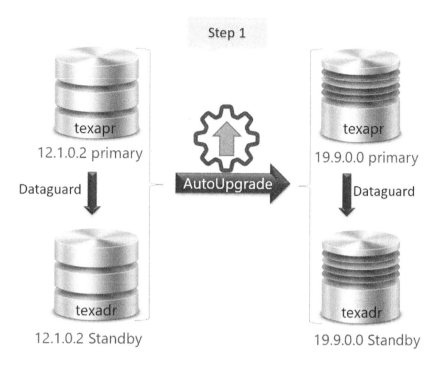

Figure 4.2: Step 1, Upgrading process Oracle 12c (12.1.0.2) to Oracle 19c (19.9.0)

In this section, we will use the AutoUpgrade utility to upgrade the Oracle 12c (12.1.0.2) database to Oracle 19c (19.9.0). In the previous chapter, we already discussed about the AutoUpgrade architecture and how it works; we will now skip that and proceed with the database upgrade.

Pre-requisites

Below are few pre-requisites and few upfront tasks that can be checked and performed before starting the database upgrade.

Perform full backup of the primary source database

Before staring any database upgrade activity, always take a **FULL** level 0 **RMAN** backup of the source database. The following is a sample **rman** script that we can use to take a Full level 0 backup of the primary source database (You can use your scripts that works for your environment.):

```
run
{
```

```
 allocate channel ch1 device type disk format '/u01/19cupgrade/DATA_
L0_%d_%Y%M%D_%s-%p-%t';
 allocate channel ch2 device type disk format '/u01/19cupgrade/DATA_
L0_%d_%Y%M%D_%s-%p-%t';
 allocate channel ch3 device type disk format '/u01/19cupgrade/DATA_
L0_%d_%Y%M%D_%s-%p-%t';
 allocate channel ch4 device type disk format '/u01/19cupgrade/DATA_
L0_%d_%Y%M%D_%s-%p-%t';
 backup incremental level 0 database plus archivelog TAG='FULL_BACKUP_
B4_UPGRADE' format  '/u01/19cupgrade/DATA_L0_%d_%Y%M%D_%s-%p-%t';
 backup tag 'CONTROL_BACKUP_B4_UPGRADE' current controlfile format '/
u01/19cupgrade/DATA_CONTROL_%d_%Y%M%D_%s-%p-%t';
 release channel ch1;
 release channel ch2;
 release channel ch3;
 release channel ch4;
}
```

Enable the flashback feature in the primary source database

Ensure that the flashback feature is enabled in both the primary and the physical standby database. When we use the AutoUpgrade utility to upgrade the Oracle database, we need to have the flashback feature enabled in the database as the AutoUpgrade utility creates a guaranteed restore point prior to the upgrade process and the upgrade process will fail in the early stages if the flashback feature is not enabled.

Login to the primary source database and enable the flashback feature using the following SQL statement:

```
SQL> alter database flashback on;
Database altered.
```

Make sure that the flashback feature is enabled successfully, using the following SQL statement:

```
SQL> select name,db_unique_name,database_role,log_mode,force_
logging,flashback_on from gv$database;
```

NAME	DB_UNIQUE_NAME	DATABASE_ROLE	LOG_MODE	FORCE_LOGGING	FLASHBACK_ON
virtual-19crac1	texapr	PRIMARY	ARCHIVELOG	YES	YES
virtual-19crac1	texapr	PRIMARY	ARCHIVELOG	YES	YES

Enable Flashback in the physical standby database

In order to enable flashback in the physical standby database, we must cancel the MRP and then enable the flashback and re-start the MRP.

Login to the physical standby database and run the following SQL statements:

```
SQL> alter database recover managed standby database cancel;
Database altered.


SQL> alter database flashback on;
Database altered.

SQL> alter database recover managed standby database using current
logfile disconnect;
Database altered.
```

Make sure that the flashback is enabled successfully using the following SQL statement in the physical standby database:

```
SQL> select name, db_unique_name, database_role, log_mode, force_
logging, flashback_on from gv$database;
```

NAME	DB_UNIQUE_NAME	DATABASE_ROLE	LOG_MODE	FORCE_LOGGING	FLASHBACK_ON
TEXAPR	texadr	PHYSICAL STANDBY	ARCHIVELOG	YES	YES
TEXAPR	Texadr	PHYSICAL STANDBY	ARCHIVELOG	YES	YES

Ensure enough space is available in Fast Recovery Area (FRA)

We must ensure that we have enough free space in the **Fast recovery area (FRA)** and set the recovery destination size to a sufficient number as we need the recovery logs until we change the compatible parameter to 19.0.0 after the upgrade. Also, the FRA will store all the flashback logs which we would need in case we have to downgrade the database back to 12.1.0.2 after the upgrade using the **flashback** method. So, please check and set **db_recovery_file_dest_size** to a higher value. We need to set this to a higher value in both the source (that is, 12.1.0.2) primary and the physical standby databases; in our case, we are setting it to 20G, as follows:

```
SQL> show parameter recovery
```

NAME	TYPE	VALUE
db_recovery_file_dest	string	+DATA1
db_recovery_file_dest_size	big integer	3G

```
recovery_parallelism                    integer      0

SQL> alter system set db_recovery_file_dest_size=20G scope=both sid='*';
System altered.

SQL> show parameter recovery
NAME                                 TYPE             VALUE
-----------------------------        -----------      ----------------------
db_recovery_file_dest                string           +DATA1
db_recovery_file_dest_size           big integer      20G
recovery_parallelism                 integer          0
```

This completes the precheck steps. Ensure that both the primary and the physical standby database are in sync with each other and that we enabled the flashback feature in both the primary and the physical standby database.

Purge recyclebin

Check the **recyclebin** and purge it; in some cases, it might take more time if we have too many objects in the **recyclebin**, so it's always a good idea to purge the **recyclebin** before starting the upgrade process as this can significantly reduce the overall time taken for the database upgrade. It might be a good idea if we can check this well ahead of time and purge the **recyclebin** in the source primary database. If the **recyclebin** is having too many objects, sometimes it might even take at least a couple of hours to get them purged, which will significantly increase the downtime required for the database upgrade.

Let's look at the following steps:

1. Check the object count in the **recyclebin**, as follows:
   ```
   SQL> select count(*) from recyclebin;
   ```

2. Purge the recycle bin using the following SQL statement:
   ```
   SQL> purge dba_recyclebin;
   DBA Recyclebin purged.
   ```

3. Re-check the object count in the **recyclebin**, as follows:
   ```
   SQL> select count(*) from recyclebin;
   ```

Gather dictionary statistics

It's always good to collect the dictionary statistics before the database upgrade process. Having good statistics on the dictionary tables and fixed objects can help the database upgrade to run faster, and thus help in reducing the overall downtime required for the database upgrade.

We can use the following SQL statement to check when the dictionary stats were last collected, as follows:

```
SQL> col OPERATION for a33
SQL> set lines 200
SQL> SELECT OPERATION,to_char(MAX(END_TIME),'DD-MON-YY hh24:mi') LATEST
     FROM dba_optstat_operations
     where OPERATION in
     ('gather_fixed_objects_stats','gather_dictionary_stats')
     group by operation;

OPERATION                            LATEST
---------------------------------    ---------------
gather_fixed_objects_stats           25-FEB-21 09:10
gather_dictionary_stats              25-FEB-21 10:25
```

We can gather the dictionary stats using the following statements:

```
SQL> EXECUTE DBMS_STATS.GATHER_DICTIONARY_STATS;
PL/SQL procedure successfully completed.

SQL> EXECUTE DBMS_STATS.GATHER_FIXED_OBJECTS_STATS;
PL/SQL procedure successfully completed.
```

Upgrade of Application Express (APEX)

If the source database has the Oracle APEX installed, we can upgrade it upfront as the APEX upgrade does not depend on the database upgrade. We can refer to the following MOS note for the APEX upgrade. We can also do this step upfront to save time during the actual upgrade process.

For more details, refer to *Master Note for Oracle Application Express (APEX) Upgrades (Doc ID 1088970.1)*

Upgrading Oracle 12c (12.1.0.2) database to oracle 18c (19.9.0)

In this section, we will upgrade both the primary and the physical standby database from the 12.1.0.2 to 19.9.0 version. Let's' start the process by completing the pre-upgrade steps.

Disable the dataguard broker

We must disable the **dataguard** broker before the database upgrade and enable it back after the upgrade. ButHowever, we must first ensure that the standby database is in sync with the primary database and then disable the **dataguard** broker.

For the primary database, execute a couple of log switches and check the current archive log list using the following SQL statements:

```
SQL> @/home/oracle/rac_database_info.sql

DATABASE_HOST      DB_NAME     DATABASE_ROLE      OPEN_MODE     STARTUP_TIME
---------------    ---------   --------------     ----------    -------------
virtual-19crac1    texapr1     PRIMARY            READ WRITE    26-FEB-21
virtual-19crac2    texapr2     PRIMARY            READ WRITE    26-FEB-21


SQL> alter system switch all logfile;
System altered.

SQL> archive log list;
Database log mode              Archive Mode
Automatic archival             Enabled
Archive destination            USE_DB_RECOVERY_FILE_DEST
Oldest online log sequence     50
Next log sequence to archive   51
Current log sequence           51
SQL>
```

In the Physical standby database, check to see if the standby database is receiving the redo logs from the primary database and if the MRP process is applying the logs to keep it in sync with the primary database. We can check this as follows:

```
SQL> @/home/oracle/standby_database_lag.sql

DATABASE_HOST         DB_NAME     DATABASE_ROLE        OPEN_MODE    STARTUP_TIME
------------------    ---------   ------------------   ---------    -----------
virtual-dr-19crac1    texadr1     PHYSICAL STANDBY     MOUNTED      26-FEB-21
virtual-dr-19crac2    texadr2     PHYSICAL STANDBY     MOUNTED      26-FEB-21


INST_ID   PROCESS   STATUS            THREAD#   SEQUENCE#   BLOCK#   BLOCKS
--------  --------  ---------------   --------  ----------  -------  ------
   1      MRP0      APPLYING_LOG      1         51          54       102400


THREAD#    ARCHIVED    APPLIED     GAP
---------- ----------  ----------  ----------
   1         51          50          1
   2         42          42          0
```

Once the physical standby database is in SYNC with the primary database, we can disable the **dataguard** broker. In the primary database, check the current configuration and disable the broker configuration as follows:

```
[oracle@virtual-19crac1]$ dgmgrl
DGMGRL for Linux: Version 12.1.0.2 - 64bit Production
```

```
Copyright (c) 2000, 2009, Oracle. All rights reserved.

Welcome to DGMGRL, type "help" for information.
DGMGRL> connect sys
Password:
Connected.
DGMGRL>

DGMGRL> show configuration

      Configuration - texapr

      Protection Mode: MaxPerformance
        Members:
        texapr - Primary database
          texadr - Physical standby database

      Fast-Start Failover: DISABLED

      Configuration Status:
      SUCCESS
DGMGRL>
```

Disable the Fast start failover (FSFO) if it's enabled

Fast start failover (FSFO) is a feature which allows the dataguard broker to failover a failed primary database to one of the configured physical standby databases. If it is enabled, we can disable it as follows:

```
DGMGRL>DISABLE FAST_START FAILOVER;
```

Disable the dataguard broker configuration

We can disable the configuration and re-verify the broker configuration. When we run the following command, it will disable the broker's active management of the databases in the Oracle dataguard configuration:

```
DGMGRL> DISABLE CONFIGURATION;
Disabled.

DGMGRL>  SHOW CONFIGURATION;

 Configuration - texapr

      Protection Mode: MaxPerformance
        Members:
        texapr - Primary database
        texadr - Physical standby database
      Fast-Start Failover: DISABLED
      Configuration Status:
   DISABLED
```

Stop the data guard broker (DMON) process in the primary database

We can disable the **dataguard** broker in the primary database by setting the **DG_BROKER_START** parameter to false. Check the following:

```
SQL> @/home/oracle/rac_database_info.sql

DATABASE_HOST        DB_NAME    DATABASE_ROLE    OPEN_MODE      STARTUP_TIME
---------------      --------   -------------    ----------     ---------------
virtual-19crac1      texapr1    PRIMARY          READ WRITE     26-FEB-21
virtual-19crac2      texapr2    PRIMARY          READ WRITE     26-FEB-21


SQL> show parameter broker

NAME                          TYPE         VALUE
--------------------------    ----------   ----------------------
dg_broker_config_file1        string       +DATA/texapr/dr1texapr.dat
dg_broker_config_file2        string       +DATA/texapr/dr2texapr.dat
dg_broker_start               boolean      TRUE
```

Stop the data guard broker process as follows:

```
SQL> ALTER SYSTEM SET DG_BROKER_START=FALSE;
System altered.

SQL> show parameter DG_BROKER_START

NAME                          TYPE         VALUE
--------------------------    ----------   ----------------------
dg_broker_config_file1        string       +DATA/texapr/dr1texapr.dat
dg_broker_config_file2        string       +DATA/texapr/dr2texapr.dat
dg_broker_start               boolean      FALSE
```

Backup the DB broker configuration files for the primary database

It's always a good idea to back up the broker configuration files. In our case, we have these files in ASM, and we will login to the ASM instance and make a copy of the broker configuration files, as follows:

```
[oracle@virtual-19crac1]$. Oraenv
ORACLE_SID = [oracle] ? +ASM1
The Oracle base has been set to /u01/app/oracle
[oracle@virtual-19crac1]$  asmcmd
ASMCMD>

ASMCMD> cp +DATA/texapr/dr1texapr.dat +DATA/texapr/dr1texapr.dat.bak
copying +DATA/texapr/dr1texapr.dat +DATA/texapr/dr1texapr.dat.bak
```

```
ASMCMD> cp +DATA/texapr/dr2texapr.dat +DATA/texapr/dr2texapr.dat.bak
copying cp +DATA/texapr/dr2texapr.dat +DATA/texapr/dr2texapr.dat.bak
```

This completes the process of disabling the data guard broker steps in the primary database, let's repeat the same process in the physical standby database.

Since we have already disabled the dataguard broker configuration from the primary database, we just need to stop the data guard broker (**DMON**) process in the physical standby database, as follows:

```
SQL> @/home/oracle/rac_database_info.sql
```

DATABASE_HOST	DB_NAME	DATABASE_ROLE	OPEN_MODE	STARTUP_TIME
virtual-dr-19crac1	texadr1	PHYSICAL STANDBY	MOUNTED	26-FEB-21
virtual-dr-19crac2	texadr2	PHYSICAL STANDBY	MOUNTED	26-FEB-21

```
SQL> show parameter dg_broker
```

NAME	TYPE	VALUE
dg_broker_config_file1	string	+DATA/texadr/dr1texadr.dat
dg_broker_config_file2	string	+DATA/texadr/dr1texadr.dat
dg_broker_start	boolean	TRUE

Stop the data guard broker process as follows:

```
SQL> alter system set dg_broker_start=false;
System altered.

SQL> SHOW PARAMETER DG_BROKER
```

NAME	TYPE	VALUE
dg_broker_config_file1	string	+DATA/vicedbdr/dr1vicedbdr.dat
dg_broker_config_file2	string	+DATA/vicedbdr/dr2vicedbdr.dat
dg_broker_start	boolean	FALSE

Backup the DB broker configuration files of the physical standby database

Backup the data guard broker configuration files of the physical standby database. Since our broker configuration files are in the ASM instance, login to the ASM instance, and copy the files as follows:

```
SQL> SHOW PARAMETER DG_BROKER
```

NAME	TYPE	VALUE
dg_broker_config_file1	string	+DATA/texadr/dr1texadr.dat

```
dg_broker_config_file2          string      +DATA/texadr/dr2texadr.dat
dg_broker_start                 boolean     FALSE
```

Login to the ASM and take a backup of the config files, as follows:

```
[oracle@virtual-dr-19crac1 ~]$. oraenv
ORACLE_SID = [oracle] ? +ASM1
The Oracle base has been set to /u01/app/oracle

[oracle@virtual-dr-19crac1 ~]$ asmcmd

ASMCMD>
ASMCMD> cp +DATA/texadr/dr1texadr.dat +DATA/texadr/dr1texadr.dat.bak
Copying +DATA/texadr/dr1texadr.dat +DATA/texadr/dr1texadr.dat.bak

ASMCMD> cp +DATA/texadr/dr2texadr.dat +DATA/texadr/dr2texadr.dat.bak
Copying +DATA/texadr/dr2texadr.dat +DATA/texadr/dr2texadr.dat.bak
```

This completes the step for disabling and stopping the data guard broker on both the primary database and the physical standby database.

Working directories

Create a staging directory with the primary database name. We will use this directory as a working directory to save all the required log files, as follows:

```
[oracle@virtual-dr-19crac1 ~]$ mkdir -p /u01/software/upgrade/texapr
```

Copy the required Oracle files from the source database Oracle 12c (12.1.0.2) to Oracle 19c (19.9.0) database home.

Network files

For the network related files, complete the following steps:

1. Add the source database TNS entry in the **tnsnames.ora** file of the Oracle 19c (19.9.0) database home.

2. Take a backup of the current **tnsnames.ora** file in Oracle 19c (19.9.0) database home, as follows:

    ```
    [oracle@virtual-dr-19crac1 ~]$. cd /u01/app/oracle/product/19c/
    db_1/network/admin
    [oracle@virtual-dr-19crac1 admin ~]$. cp tnsnames.ora tnsnames.
    ora.Feb26
    ```

3. Add the primary and the physical standby database entries to the Oracle 19c (19.9.0) **tnsnames.ora** file, as follows:

    ```
    [oracle@virtual-dr-19crac1 admin ~]$. vi tnsnames.ora
    ```

```
texapr =
 (DESCRIPTION =
   (ADDRESS = (PROTOCOL = TCP)(HOST = virtual-19crac-scan)(PORT =
1521))
   (CONNECT_DATA =
     (SERVER = DEDICATED)
     (SERVICE_NAME = texapr)     )
   )
 )

texadr =
 (DESCRIPTION =
   (ADDRESS = (PROTOCOL = TCP)(HOST = virtual-dr-19crac-scan)
(PORT = 1521))
     (CONNECT_DATA =
     (SERVER = DEDICATED)
     (SERVICE_NAME = texadr)   )
   )
 )
```

Primary database initialization parameter (pfile/spfile) files

Copy the primary database initialization parameter files (**pfile** and **spfile**) from theOracle 12c (12.1.0.2) to Oracle 19c (19.9.0) home:

```
[oracle@virtual-19crac1 ~] cp /u01/app/oracle/product/12c/db_1/
dbs/*start*ora  /u01/app/oracle/product/19c/db_1/dbs/
```

Password files

The password file is in the **dbs** folder; we can copy it to theOracle 19c (19.9.0) **dbs** folder, as follows:

```
[oracle@virtual-19crac1 ~] cp /u01/app/oracle/product/12c/db_1/
dbs/*orapwstar* /u01/app/oracle/product/19c/db_1/dbs/
```

Check the INVALID objects' counts in the primary database

It's always a good idea to take a snapshot of the invalid objects' count before starting the database upgrade process.

For the primary database, complete the following steps:

1. First run the **utlrp** script to compile any **INVALID** objects and then take a count of the invalid objects, so that we can compare the count after the database upgrade, as follows:

   ```
   SQL > @$ORACLE_HOME/rdbms/admin/utlrp

   SQL> select count(*) from dba_objects where status='INVALID';
   ```

2. Let's take the count of the invalid objects in the **SYS** and **SYSTEM** schemas, as follows:

   ```
   SQL> spool /u01/software/upgrade/texapr/pre-upgrade_SYS_SYSTEM_
   invalid_Objects.log

   SQL> col owner for a25
   SQL> set lines 200
   SQL> set pages 200
   SQL> col object_type for a30;
   SQL> set lines 200
   SQL> SELECT i.HOST_NAME "DATABASE_HOST" ,
           i.INSTANCE_NAME "DB_NAME", d.DATABASE_ROLE
           " DATABASE_ROLE", d.OPEN_MODE " OPEN_MODE ", STARTUP_TIME
          from GV$DATABASE d, gv$instance i
          where i.INST_ID=d.INST_ID;

   SQL> select owner,object_name,object_type,status
          from dba_objects
          where status='INVALID' and owner in ('SYS','SYSTEM')
          order by owner ;

   spool off;
   ```

3. Next, we can take the invalid object count for the non-sys and non-system schemas, as follows:

   ```
   SQL> spool /u01/software/upgrade/texapr/pre-upgrade_non-SYS_
   invalid_objects.log

   SQL> col owner for a25
   SQL> set lines 200
   SQL> set pages 200
   SQL> col object_type for a30;
   SQL> set lines 200

   SQL> SELECT i.HOST_NAME "DATABASE_HOST" ,
           i.INSTANCE_NAME "DB_NAME", d.DATABASE_ROLE
           " DATABASE_ROLE", d.OPEN_MODE " OPEN_MODE ", STARTUP_TIME
          from GV$DATABASE d, gv$instance i
          where i.INST_ID=d.INST_ID;

   SQL> select count(*)
   ```

```
        from dba_objects
        where status='INVALID' and owner not in ('SYS','SYSTEM');
SQL> select owner,object_type,count(*)
        from dba_objects
        where status='INVALID' and owner not in ('SYS','SYSTEM')
        group by owner,object_type order by owner ;

SQL> select owner,object_name,object_type,status
        from dba_objects
        where status='INVALID' and owner not in ('SYS','SYSTEM')
        order by owner ;

spool off;
```

4. Check if the spool files got created. We can use this information to compare with the post-upgrade invalid object count that we will be taking after the database upgrade, as follows:

```
oracle@virtual-19crac1 admin]$ cd /u01/software/upgrade/texapr

[oracle@virtual-19crac1 texapr]$ ls -ltr

total 8

-rw-r--r-- 1 oracle oinstall 1650 Feb 27 08:50 pre-upgrade_SYS_
SYSTEM_invalid_Objects.log

-rw-r--r-- 1 oracle oinstall 2383 Feb 27 08:50 pre-upgrade_non-
SYS_invalid_objects.log
```

For testing purposes, in the primary database, let's create a test table called **before_upgrade**, just to crosscheck after the upgrade to see if it comes to the standby database confirming that the upgrade is successful.

Login to the primary database and create the test table as follows:

```
SQL> Create table BEFORE_UPGRADE (NAME Varchar(30));
Table created.

SQL> insert into BEFORE_UPGRADE values ('Table Before Upgrade');
1 row created.

SQl > commit;
Commit complete.
```

Download the latest AutoUpgrade tool

As mentioned earlier, Oracle strongly recommends downloading the latest version and using it instead of the default one that comes with Oracle 19c. We can download the latest AutoUpgrade tool from the following My Oracle support (MOS) *Doc ID 2485457.1*

Once downloaded, we can stage it in the following location and then from here, you can copy it to the 19c database home.

```
[oracle@virtual-dr-19crac1 ~]$. cd /u01/software/
[oracle@virtual-dr-19crac1 software]$ ls -ltr autoupgrade.jar
-rwxrwxr-x. 1 oracle oinstall 2868558 Jan 18 10:53 autoupgrade.jar
```

Now, copy it to the **19c** database home, as follows:

```
[oracle@virtual-dr-19crac1 ~]$. cd /u01/software/
[oracle@virtual-dr-19crac1 software]$  ls -ltr  /u01/app/oracle/
product/19c/db_1/rdbms/admin/autoupgrade.jar

[oracle@virtual-dr-19crac1 software]$  mv /u01/app/oracle/product/19c/
db_1/rdbms/admin/autoupgrade.jar /u01/app/oracle/product/19c/db_1/rdbms/
admin/autoupgrade.jar.default

[oracle@virtual-dr-19crac1 software]$. cp /u01/software/autoupgrade.jar
/u01/app/oracle/product/19c/db_1/rdbms/admin/
```

Configuration file creation for AutoUpgrade

The AutoUpgrade utility requires a configuration file which it uses for performing the pre-upgrade and the actual upgrade of the database. The configuration file will contain information like the source database version, target database version, **log** directory location, and so on. We can manually create the file, or we can create a sample config file using **autoupgrade.jar** and modify it to include the source and target database details.

We must create the sample file from the Oracle 19c home belowand later we can modify as per the requirement, as follows:

```
[oracle@virtual-dr-19crac1 ~]$. cd /u01/software/upgrade/texapr
[oracle@virtual-dr-19crac1 texapr ~]$. export ORACLE_HOME=/u01/app/
oracle/product/19c/db_1
[oracle@virtual-dr-19crac1 texapr ~]$. export PATH=$ORACLE_HOME/bin:PATH

[oracle@virtual-dr-19crac1 texapr ~]$.  /u01/app/oracle/product/19c/
db_1/jdk/bin/java -jar $ORACLE_HOME/rdbms/admin/autoupgrade.jar -create_
sample_file config
```

This will create a sample configuration file in the current directory (**/u01/software/ upgrade/texapr/sample_config.cfg**) and you can modify and use it for the upgrade, as follows:

```
[oracle@virtual-19crac1 texapr]$ ls -ltr
```

```
-rw-r--r-- 1 oracle oinstall 1650 Feb 27 08:50 pre-upgrade_SYS_SYSTEM_
invalid_Objects.log
```

```
-rw-r--r-- 1 oracle oinstall 2383 Feb 27 08:50 pre-upgrade_non-SYS_
invalid_objects.log
-rw-r--r-- 1 oracle oinstall 5885 Feb 27 08:53 sample_config.cfg
```

Modify the configuration file for this upgrade

We made a copy of the sample config file and modified the copied file as follows:

```
[oracle@virtual-19crac1 texapr]$ cd /u01/software/upgrade/texapr
[oracle@virtual-19crac1 texapr]$ cp sample_config.cfg texapr_config.cfg

[oracle@virtual-19crac1 texapr]$ cat texapr_19c.cfg

global.autoupg_log_dir=/u01/software/upgrade/texapr
upg1.log_dir=/u01/software/upgrade/texapr
upg1.sid=texapr1
upg1.source_home=/u01/app/oracle/product/12c/db_1
upg1.target_home=/u01/app/oracle/product/19c/db_1
upg1.start_time=NOW
upg1.upgrade_node=virtual-19crac1
upg1.run_utlrp=yes
upg1.timezone_upg=yes
upg1.target_version=19
#upg1.defer_standby_log_shipping=yes              # AutoUpgrade can
defer the log-      shipping to configured standby databases
```

We already discussed about the parameters that were included in this configuration file in the previous chapter.

Running AutoUpgrade in Analyze mode

We know all the modes; so, let's run the AutoUpgrade in the analyze mode for our upgrade. As mentioned earlier, this mode will only read the source database and check if the database is ready for the upgrade. Please note that this mode will not make any changes to the source database.

Export the ORACLE_HOME to the to 19c home directory and run the AutoUpgrade command as shown here:

```
[oracle@virtual-19crac1 texapr]$ ORACLE_HOME=/u01/app/oracle/
product/19c/db_1
[oracle@virtual-19crac1 texapr]$ export PATH=$ORACLE_HOME/bin:$PATH
[oracle@virtual-19crac1 texapr]$ cd /u01/software/upgrade/texapr

$ORACLE_HOME/jdk/bin/java -jar $ORACLE_HOME/rdbms/admin/autoupgrade.jar
-config texapr_upgrade.cfg -mode ANALYZE
```

If the preceding command runs successfully, it will start reading the source database for the upgrade and generate not only a bunch of the log files, but also create the preupgrade and post-upgrade fixup scripts. FollowingThe following is part of the output for the preceding command:

```
[oracle@virtual-19crac1 texapr]$ $ORACLE_HOME/jdk/bin/java -jar $ORACLE_
HOME/rdbms/admin/AutoUpgrade.jar -config texapr_upgrade.cfg -mode ANALYZE

autoupgrade tool launched with default options
Processing config file ...
+-------------------------------+
| Starting AutoUpgrade execution |
+-------------------------------+
1 databases will be analyzed
Type 'help' to list console commands
upg> Job 100 completed
------------------ Final Summary --------------------
Number of databases        [1]
Jobs finished              [1]
Jobs failed                [0]
Jobs pending               [0]
```

Please check the summary report at the following links:

/u01/software/upgrade/texapr/cfgtoollogs/upgrade/auto/status/status.html

/u01/software/upgrade/texapr/cfgtoollogs/upgrade/auto/status/status.log

While it's' still running, we can use the following commands to check the status of the job and monitor/manage/control the jobs from the AutoUpgrade:

- **lsj**: To list the jobs.

- **status**: To show the job status.

- **Tasks:** To show the tasks executing

- **abort**: To abort a specific job.

- **resume**: To resume a specific job which might have been stopped. We can use **job_id** for resuming a job.

As mentioned, the AutoUpgrade utility creates multiple subdirectories in the log location defined in the config file. Each time we run AutoUpgrade in either the Analyze mode or the **Deploy** mode, it creates a sub directory with a naming convention like 100,101…etc.

In our case, You can check the various directories/logs in **/u01/software/upgrade/texapr**

```
[oracle@virtual-19crac1 ~]$ cd /u01/software/upgrade/texapr
[oracle@virtual-19crac1 texapr]$ ls -ltr
total 12
-rwx------ 1 oracle oinstall 1650 Feb 27 08:50 pre-upgrade_SYS_SYSTEM_
invalid_Objects.log
-rwx------ 1 oracle oinstall 2383 Feb 27 08:50 pre-upgrade_non-SYS_
invalid_objects.log
-rwx------ 1 oracle oinstall 1281 Feb 27 08:57 texapr_upgrade.cfg
drwx------ 3 oracle oinstall   21 Feb 27 09:29 cfgtoollogs
drwx------ 4 oracle oinstall   29 Feb 27 09:29 texapr1
[oracle@virtual-19crac1 texapr]$ cd texapr1
[oracle@virtual-19crac1 texapr1]$ ls -ltr
total 0
drwx------ 2 oracle oinstall 125 Feb 27 09:29 temp
drwx------ 3 oracle oinstall 119 Feb 27 09:29 100
[oracle@virtual-19crac1 texapr1]$ cd 100
[oracle@virtual-19crac1 100]$ ls -trl
total 160
-rwx------ 1 oracle oinstall      0 Feb 27 09:29 autoupgrade_err.log
-rwx------ 1 oracle oinstall    300 Feb 27 09:29 autoupgrade_20210227_
user.log
drwx------ 2 oracle oinstall   4096 Feb 27 09:29 prechecks
-rwx------ 1 oracle oinstall 152851 Feb 27 09:29 autoupgrade_20210227.
log

[oracle@virtual-19crac1 100]$ ls -ltr
total 160
-rwx------ 1 oracle oinstall      0 Feb 27 09:29 autoupgrade_err.log
-rwx------ 1 oracle oinstall    300 Feb 27 09:29 autoupgrade_20210227_
user.log
drwx------ 2 oracle oinstall   4096 Feb 27 09:29 prechecks
-rwx------ 1 oracle oinstall 152851 Feb 27 09:29 autoupgrade_20210227.
log
[oracle@virtual-19crac1 100]$
```

Among these log files, the log file with **dbname_preupgrade.log** (example, in this case, **texapr_preupgrade.log**) is one of the important logfiles to check. This logfile will have all the pre-upgrade checks/post upgrade recommendations and the information on the fixup scripts. It will also list all the issues that need to be addressed.

The following is the sample output of **texapr_preupgrade.log**:

```
[oracle@virtual-19crac1 prechecks]$ cat texapr_preupgrade.log
Report generated by AutoUpgrade 21.1.1 (#8ee6880) on 2021-02-27 09:29:32
Upgrade-To version: 19.0.0.0.0
```

```
========================================
Status of the database prior to upgrade
========================================
          Database Name:  texapr1
         Container Name:  texapr1
           Container ID:  0
                Version:  12.1.0.2.0
         DB Patch Level:  No Patch Bundle applied
             Compatible:  12.1.0.2.0
              Blocksize:  8192
               Platform:  Linux x86 64-bit
          Timezone File:  18
      Database log mode:  ARCHIVELOG
               Readonly:  false
                Edition:  EE

Oracle Component                        Upgrade Action     Current Status
----------------                        --------------     --------------
Oracle Workspace Manager                [to be upgraded]   VALID
OLAP Analytic Workspace                 [to be upgraded]   VALID
Oracle Text                             [to be upgraded]   VALID
Oracle Database Vault                   [to be upgraded]   VALID
Oracle Server                           [to be upgraded]   VALID
Real Application Clusters               [to be upgraded]   VALID
Oracle Java Packages                    [to be upgraded]   VALID
Oracle XDK for Java                     [to be upgraded]   VALID
Oracle Label Security                   [to be upgraded]   VALID
Oracle XML Database                     [to be upgraded]   VALID
Oracle Multimedia                       [to be upgraded]   VALID
Oracle OLAP API                         [to be upgraded]   VALID
JServer JAVA Virtual Machine            [to be upgraded]   VALID
Oracle Spatial                          [to be upgraded]   VALID

==============
BEFORE UPGRADE
==============
  REQUIRED ACTIONS
  ================
```

1. (AUTOFIXUP) Empty the RECYCLEBIN immediately before the database
    upgrade.

    The database contains two objects in the recycle bin.

    The recycle bin must be completely empty before the database
    upgrade.

```
  RECOMMENDED ACTIONS

  ===================
```

2. Upgrade the Oracle Application Express (APEX) manually before or after the database upgrade.

   The database contains APEX version 4.2.5.00.08, which is not supported on the target version 19.0.0.0.0. APEX must be upgraded to at least version 18.2.0.00.12 either before or after the database is upgraded.

   Starting with Oracle Database Release 18, APEX is not upgraded automatically as part of the database upgrade. Refer to My Oracle Support

   Note 1088970.1 for information about the APEX installation and upgrades. Refer to MOS Note 1344948.1 for the minimum APEX version supported for your target database release. The unsupported versions of APEX will be in an INVALID state when its database dependencies are not in sync with the upgraded database.

INFORMATION ONLY
================

3. (AUTOFIXUP) Mandatory changes are applied automatically in the during_upgrade_pfile_dbname.ora file. Some of these changes may be present in the after_upgrade_pfile_dbname.ora file. The during_ upgrade_pfile_dbname.ora is used to start the database in the upgrade mode. The after_upgrade_pfile_dbname.ora is used to start the database once the upgrade has been completed successfully.

   Parameter
   ----
   cluster_database='FALSE'

   Mandatory changes are required to perform the upgrade. These changes are implemented in the during_ and after_upgrade_pfile_ dbname.ora files.

4. Check the Oracle Backup and Recovery User's Guide for information on how to manage an RMAN recovery catalog schema.

   If you are using a version of the recovery catalog schema that is older than what is required by the RMAN client version, then you must upgrade the catalog schema.

   It is a good practice to have the catalog schema as the same or higher version than the RMAN client version you are using.

5. To help you keep track of your tablespace allocations, the following AUTOEXTEND tablespaces are expected to successfully EXTEND during the upgrade process:

   | | | Min Size |
Tablespace	Size	For Upgrade

SYSTEM	780 MB	1019 MB
TEMP	60 MB	240 MB
UNDOTBS1	265 MB	401 MB
SYSAUX	660 MB	867 MB

Minimum tablespace sizes for the upgrade are estimates.

6. Follow the instructions in the Oracle Multimedia README.txt
file in <19 ORACLE_HOME>/ord/im/admin/README.txt, or MOS note
2555923.1 to determine if Oracle Multimedia is being used. If
Oracle Multimedia is being used, refer to MOS note 2347372.1 for
suggestions on replacing the Oracle Multimedia.

Oracle Multimedia component (ORDIM) is installed.

Starting with release 19c, Oracle Multimedia is desupported. The
object types still exist, but the methods and procedures will
raise an exception. Refer to the 19 Oracle Database Upgrade
Guide, the Oracle Multimedia README.txt file in <19 ORACLE_
HOME>/ord/im/admin/README.txt, or MOS note 2555923.1 for more
information.

```
=============
AFTER UPGRADE
=============
  REQUIRED ACTIONS
  ================
  None

  RECOMMENDED ACTIONS

  ===================
```

7. (AUTOFIXUP) Upgrade the database time zone file using the DBMS_DST

package.

The database is using the time zone file version 18 and the target
19 release ships with the time zone file version 32.

Oracle recommends upgrading to the desired (latest) version of
the time zone file. For more information, refer to "Upgrading
the Time Zone File and Timestamp with Time Zone Data" in the 19
Oracle Database Globalization Support Guide.

8. (AUTOFIXUP) Recompile the objects with the timestamp mismatch.
Please refer to MOS note 781959.1 for more details.

There are objects whose timestamp are mismatched with its parent
objects.

Timestamp of the dependent objects must coincide with the
timestamp of parent objects.

9. (AUTOFIXUP) Gather the dictionary statistics after the upgrade using the following command:

    EXECUTE DBMS_STATS.GATHER_DICTIONARY_STATS;

    Oracle recommends gathering the dictionary statistics after the upgrade.

    The dictionary statistics provide essential information to the Oracle optimizer to help it find the efficient SQL execution plans. After a database upgrade, the statistics need to be re-gathered as there can now be tables that have significantly changed during the upgrade or new tables that do not have the statistics gathered yet.

10. Gather the statistics on fixed objects after the upgrade and when there is a representative workload on the system, using the following command:

    EXECUTE DBMS_STATS.GATHER_FIXED_OBJECTS_STATS;

    Oracle recommends gathering the fixed object statistics after the upgrade. This recommendation is given for all the preupgrade runs.

    Fixed object statistics provide essential information to the Oracle optimizer to help it find the efficient SQL execution plans. Those statistics are specific to the Oracle Database release that generates them, and can be stale upon the database upgrade.

    For information on managing optimizer statistics, refer to the 12.1.0.2 Oracle Database SQL Tuning Guide.

11. (AUTOFIXUP) Run @?/rdbms/admin/utlrp.sql in order to recompile any invalid objects.

    There are invalid objects in the database after the upgrade.

    The invalid database objects need to be recompiled after the upgrade.

It is mandatory to fix any reported issues in the preceding section and then proceed with the next steps.

Creating GRP in the physical standby database

Since we will downgrade the database using the flashback method, we must create the guaranteed restore points for this purpose. In the primary database, the AutoUpgrade process will create the guaranteed restore points before it starts the database upgrade, but in the physical standby database, we need to create the guaranteed restore point manually. As mentioned in the first chapter, it is very important that we create a guaranteed restore point in the physical standby database.

So, before starting the upgrade process in primary database, if we do not create the restore point in the physical standby database first, we might encounter issues while downgrading the physical standby database and we might end up rebuilding the physical standby database after downgrading the primary database; so, ensure that you create the guaranteed restore point in the physical standby database first.

Before creating the guaranteed restore point, ensure that both the primary database and the physical standby databases are in sync. Once they are in the sync state, we can stop the log shipping from the primary database to the physical standby database. We can defer the log shipping on the primary database using either the SQL command or by using the data guard broker environment.

If you are not using the data guard broker, then we can cancel the log shipping and the managed recover process on the physical standby database using the following SQL commands.

On the primary database, defer the log shipping as follows:

```
SQL> alter system set log_archive_dest_state_2='DEFER' scope=both
sid='*';
System altered.
```

On the physical standby database, cancel the MRP process as follows:

```
SQL> Alter database recover managed standby database cancel;
Database altered.
```

Once the managed recovery process is cancelled, we can create the guaranteed restore point, as follows:

```
SQL> create restore point standby_before_19c_upgrade guarantee flashback
database;
Restore point created.
```

Enable the log shipping back in the primary and start the MRP in the standby databasegiven. On the primary database, enable the log shipping as follows:

```
SQL> alter system set log_archive_dest_state_2='ENABLE' scope=both
sid='*';
System altered.
```

On standby database, start the MRP process follows:

```
SQL> alter database recover managed standby database disconnect from
session;
Database altered.
```

Shutdown the physical standby database

We can now stop the physical standby database. If this is an RAC database, we can use the server control utility to check the status and stop the physical standby database by completing the following steps:

1. Check the current status of the physical standby database using the **srvctl** command, as follows:

   ```
   [oracle@virtual-dr-19crac1 admin]$ srvctl status database -d
   texadr
   Instance texadr1 is running on node virtual-dr-19crac1
   Instance texadr2 is running on node virtual-dr-19crac2
   ```

2. Stop the physical standby database using the **srvctl** command, as follows:

   ```
   [oracle@virtual-dr-19crac1 admin]$ srvctl stop database -d texadr
   ```

3. Check the current status using the **srvctl** command again, as follows:

   ```
   [oracle@virtual-dr-19crac1 admin]$ srvctl status database -d
   texadr
   Instance texadr1 is not running on node virtual-dr-19crac1
   Instance texadr2 is not running on node virtual-dr-19crac2
   ```

Upgrade the primary database using AutoUpgrade

Run the AutoUpgrade command in the **DEPLOY** mode to upgrade the database. We need to run this from the Oracle 19c home. So, let's export the Oracle home to point to Oracle 19c first and then run the AutoUpgrade command as follows:

```
[oracle@virtual-19crac1 texapr]$ export ORACLE_HOME=/u01/app/oracle/
product/19c/db_1
[oracle@virtual-19crac1 texapr]$ export PATH=$PATH:$ORACLE_HOME/
bin:$PATH
[oracle@virtual-19crac1 texapr]$ echo $ORACLE_HOME
/u01/app/oracle/product/19c/db_1

[oracle@virtual-19crac1 texapr]$ cd /u01/software/upgrade/texapr
```

Run the AutoUpgrade command in the **DEPLOY** mode to upgrade the database, as follows:

```
[oracle@virtual-19crac1 texapr]$ $ORACLE_HOME/jdk/bin/java -jar $ORACLE_
HOME/rdbms/admin/AutoUpgrade.jar -config texapr_upgrade.cfg -mode DEPLOY
```

The following is part of the output when the preceding command is run successfully:

```
[oracle@virtual-19crac1 texapr]$ $ORACLE_HOME/jdk/bin/java -jar $ORACLE_
HOME/rdbms/admin/autoupgrade.jar -config texapr_upgrade.cfg -mode DEPLOY

AutoUpgrade tool launched with default options

Processing config file ...
+--------------------------------+
| Starting AutoUpgrade execution |
+--------------------------------+
1 databases will be processed
Type 'help' to list console commands
upg> lsj
+----+-------+---------+---------+-------+-------------+--------+----
|Job#|DB_NAME|STAGE|OPERATION|STATUS|START_TIME|UPDATED|     MESSAGE|
+-------+---------+---------+-------+-------------+--------+---------
101|texapr1|PREFIXUPS|EXECUTING|RUNNING|21/02/27 10:57|10:57:22|Loading
database information|
--+-------+---------+---------+-------+-------------+--------+-------
Total jobs 1 upg> lsj
+----+-------+-----+---------+-------+-------------+--------+------+
|Job#|DB_NAME|STAGE|OPERATION| STATUS|START_TIME| UPDATED|MESSAGE|
+----+-------+-----+---------+-------+-------------+--------+------+
| 101|texapr1|DRAIN|PREPARING|RUNNING|21/02/27 10:57|10:57:28|       |
+----+-------+-----+---------+-------+-------------+--------+------+
Total jobs 1upg> lsj
+----+-------+---------+---------+-------+-------------+--------+----
|Job#|DB_NAME|STAGE|OPERATION| STATUS|START_TIME| UPDATED|MESSAGE|
+----+-------+---------+---------+-------+-------------+--------+----
| 101|texapr1|DBUPGRADE|EXECUTING|RUNNING|21/02/27
10:57|11:08:56|49%Upgraded |
+----+-------+---------+---------+-------+-------------+--------+----
Total jobs 1 upg> lsj
+----+-------+---------+---------+-------+-------------+--------+----
|Job#|DB_NAME|STAGE|OPERATION| STATUS|START_TIME| UPDATED|MESSAGE|
+----+-------+---------+---------+-------+-------------+--------+----
| 101|texapr1|DBUPGRADE|EXECUTING|RUNNING|21/02/27
0:57|11:17:57|91%Upgraded |
+----+-------+---------+---------+-------+-------------+--------+----
Total jobs 1
upg> Job 101 completed
------------------ Final Summary --------------------
Number of databases         [ 1 ]
Jobs finished               [1]
Jobs failed                 [0]
Jobs pending                [0]
---- Drop GRP at your convenience once you consider it is no longer needed ----
```

```
Drop GRP from texapr1: drop restore point AUTOUPGRADE_9212_TEXAPR1121020
```

```
Please check the summary report at the following links:
```

```
/u01/software/upgrade/texapr/cfgtoollogs/upgrade/auto/status/status.html
/u01/software/upgrade/texapr/cfgtoollogs/upgrade/auto/status/status.log
```

You can open a new terminal and check the different directories that the AutoUpgrade tool creates for the various logs, including the prefix/postfix directories; please see the following:

```
[oracle@virtual-19crac1 ~]$ cd /u01/software/upgrade/texapr

[oracle@virtual-19crac1 texapr]$ ls -ltr
total 12
-rwx------ 1 oracle oinstall 1650 Feb 27 08:50 pre-upgrade_SYS_SYSTEM_
invalid_Objects.log
-rwx------ 1 oracle oinstall 2383 Feb 27 08:50 pre-upgrade_non-SYS_
invalid_objects.log
-rwx------ 1 oracle oinstall 1281 Feb 27 08:57 texapr_upgrade.cfg
drwx------ 3 oracle oinstall   21 Feb 27 09:29 cfgtoollogs
drwx------ 4 oracle oinstall   29 Feb 27 09:29 texapr1
[oracle@virtual-19crac1 texapr]$ cd texapr1
[oracle@virtual-19crac1 texapr1]$ ls -ltr
total 0
drwx------ 2 oracle oinstall  125 Feb 27 09:29 temp
drwx------ 3 oracle oinstall  119 Feb 27 09:29 100
drwx------ 4 oracle oinstall 4096 Feb 27 11:26 101

[oracle@virtual-19crac1 texapr1]$ cd 101
[oracle@virtual-19crac1 101]$ ls -ltr
total 716
drwx------ 2 oracle oinstall     28 Feb 27 11:16 preupgrade
drwx------ 2 oracle oinstall   4096 Feb 27 11:16 prechecks
drwx------ 2 oracle oinstall    135 Feb 27 11:16 prefixups
drwx------ 2 oracle oinstall     31 Feb 27 11:20 drain
drwx------ 2 oracle oinstall   4096 Feb 27 11:24 dbupgrade
drwx------ 2 oracle oinstall   4096 Feb 27 11:25 postchecks
drwx------ 2 oracle oinstall     88 Feb 27 11:25 postfixups
-rwx------ 1 oracle oinstall  12448 Feb 27 11:35 autoupgrade_20210227_
user.log
drwx------ 2 oracle oinstall     29 Feb 27 11:25 postupgrade
-rwx------ 1 oracle oinstall   6883 Feb 27 11:26 autoupgrade_err.log
-rwx------ 1 oracle oinstall 693521 Feb 27 11:26 autoupgrade_20210227.
log
```

In this case, the directory **/u01/software/upgrade/texapr/texapr1/100** was created when we ran AutoUpgrade with the **ANALYZE** mode, whereas the directory

/u01/software/upgrade/texapr/texapr1/101 was created when we ran AutoUpgrade with the **DEPLOY** mode.

Go to the directory **/u01/software/upgrade/texapr/texapr1/101** and monitor the following logfile:

```
[oracle@virtual-19crac1 ~]$ cd /u01/software/upgrade/texapr/texapr1/101
[oracle@virtual-19crac1 101]$ tail -f autoupgrade_20210227_user.log
2021-02-27 10:57:26.007 INFO Analyzing texapr1, 87 checks will run using
2 threads
2021-02-27 10:58:20.061 INFO Defer redo log shipping to standby database
2021-02-27 10:59:26.586 INFO Password file /u01/app/oracle/product/12c/
db_1/dbs/orapwtexapr1
2021-02-27 10:59:26.838 INFO [virtual-19crac2] Password file /u01/app/
oracle/product/12c/db_1/dbs/orapwtexapr2 is not found on remote host
2021-02-27 10:59:49.527 INFO Total Number of upgrade phases is 108
2021-02-27 10:59:49.530 INFO Begin Upgrade on Database [texapr]
2021-02-27 10:59:54.699 INFO 0%Upgraded
2021-02-27 11:02:56.581 INFO 14%Upgraded
2021-02-27 11:05:56.758 INFO 23%Upgraded
2021-02-27 11:08:56.949 INFO 49%Upgraded
2021-02-27 11:11:57.155 INFO 49%Upgraded
2021-02-27 11:14:57.319 INFO 70%Upgraded
2021-02-27 11:17:57.433 INFO 91%Upgraded
2021-02-27 11:20:57.710 INFO 91%Upgraded
2021-02-27 11:23:57.948 INFO 93%Upgraded
2021-02-27 11:25:21.745 INFO SUCCESSFULLY UPGRADED [texapr]
2021-02-27 11:25:21.745 INFO End Upgrade on Database [texapr]
2021-02-27 11:25:24.011 INFO SUCCESSFULLY UPGRADED [texapr]
2021-02-27 11:25:24.024 INFO texapr Return status is SUCCESS
2021-02-27 11:25:48.112 INFO Analyzing texapr1, 14 checks will run using
2 threads
2021-02-27 11:25:49.208 INFO Using /u01/software/upgrade/texapr/
texapr1/101/prechecks/texapr_checklist.cfg to identify required fixups

2021-02-27 11:25:49.209 INFO Content of the checklist /u01/software/
upgrade/texapr/texapr1/101/prechecks/texapr_checklist.cfg is:
```

While the upgrade is still running, you can also check if the other **RAC** instances are down, and tail the alert log and the upgrade log. Another log that we can check is **upg_summary.log** in the location **/u01/software/upgrade/texapr/texapr1/101/dbupgrade**, as follows:

```
[oracle@virtual-19crac1 dbupgrade]$ cat upg_summary.log

Oracle Database Release 19 Post-Upgrade Status Tool     02-27-2021
11:24:1

Database Name: TEXAPR
```

```
Component                          Current    Full          Elapsed Time
Name                               Status     Version       HH:MM:SS
Oracle Server                      UPGRADED   19.9.0.0.0    00:08:37
JServer JAVA Virtual Machine       UPGRADED   19.9.0.0.0    00:02:24
Oracle XDK                         UPGRADED   19.9.0.0.0    00:00:43
Oracle Database Java Packages      UPGRADED   19.9.0.0.0    00:00:07
OLAP Analytic Workspace            UPGRADED   19.9.0.0.0    00:00:07
Oracle Label Security              UPGRADED   19.9.0.0.0    00:00:04
Oracle Database Vault              UPGRADED   19.9.0.0.0    00:00:21
Oracle Text                        UPGRADED   19.9.0.0.0    00:00:21
Oracle Workspace Manager           UPGRADED   19.9.0.0.0    00:00:19
Oracle Real Application ClustersUPGRADED      19.9.0.0.0    00:00:00
Oracle XML Database                UPGRADED   19.9.0.0.0    00:00:50
Oracle Multimedia                  UPGRADED   19.9.0.0.0    00:00:38
Spatial                            LOADING    19.9.0.0.0    00:02:55
Oracle OLAP API                    INVALID    19.9.0.0.0    00:00:08
Datapatch                                                   00:05:06
Final Actions                                               00:05:35
Post Upgrade                                                00:00:16
Total Upgrade Time: 00:23:37

Grand Total Upgrade Time:    [0d:0h:25m:57s]
```

Once the primary database upgrade is completed, let's verify a few checks, as follows:

1. First, check the **/etc/oratab** entries in all the nodes to see if the **autoupgrade** process updated the database entry to point to the new Oracle **19c** home, as follows:

```
[oracle@virtual-19crac1 ~]$ cat /etc/oratab | grep texapr1
texapr1:/u01/app/oracle/product/19c/db_1:N

[oracle@virtual-19crac2 ~]$ cat /etc/oratab | grep texapr
texapr2:/u01/app/oracle/product/19c/db_1:N
```

Check the cluster configuration of the database to see if the autoupgrade has upgraded the configuration.

```
oracle@virtual-19crac1 ~]$ srvctl config database -d texapr
Database unique name: texapr
Database name: texapr
Oracle home: /u01/app/oracle/product/19c/db_1
Oracle user: oracle
Spfile: +DATA/texapr/spfiletexapr.ora
Password file:
Domain:
Start options: open
```

```
Stop options: immediate
Database role: PRIMARY
Management policy: AUTOMATIC
Server pools:
Disk Groups: DATA
Mount point paths:
Services:
Type: RAC
Start concurrency:
Stop concurrency:
OSDBA group: oinstall
OSOPER group: oinstall
Database instances: texapr1,texapr2
Configured nodes: virtual-19crac1,virtual-dr-19crac2
CSS critical: no
CPU count: 0
Memory target: 0
Maximum memory: 0
Default network number for database services:
Database is administrator managed
```

2. Check if the AutoUpgrade utility has created the guaranteed restore point in the primary database, as follows:

```
SQL> set lines 200
SQL> col name for a40
SQL> col GUARANTEE_FLASHBACK_DATABASE for a20
SQL> col TIME for a60
SQL> set lines 190
SQL> select NAME,GUARANTEE_FLASHBACK_DATABASE,TIME from
V$restore_point;

NAME                           GUARANTEE_FLASHBACK  TIME
------------------------------ -------------------  ------------
AUTOUPGRADE_9212_TEXAPR1121020 YES                  27-FEB-21
                                                    10.57.12.000000 AM
```

3. Run the **utlrp** script in the primary database and check the registry to see if all the components are upgraded and are in the valid state, as follows:

```
SQL> @/home/oracle/rac_database_info.sql

DATABASE_HOST    DB_NAME  DATABASE_ROLE  OPEN_MODE   STARTUP_TIME
---------------  -------  -------------  ----------  ----------
virtual-19crac1  texapr1  PRIMARY        READ WRITE  27-FEB-21
virtual-19crac2  texapr2  PRIMARY        READ WRITE  27-FEB-21
```

4. Run the following **utlrp** script:

```
SQL> @$ORACLE_HOME/rdbms/admin/utlrp
```

5. Now, check the componentscomponents' status in the **dba** registry, as follows:

```
SQL> select COMP_ID,COMP_NAME,VERSION,STATUS from dba_registry;

COMP_ID      COMP_NAME                           VERSION      STATUS
----------   --------------------------------    ----------   ------
CATALOG      Oracle Database Catalog Views       19.0.0.0.0   VALID
CATPROC      Oracle Database Packages and Types  19.0.0.0.0   VALID
JAVAVM       JServer JAVA Virtual Machine         19.0.0.0.0   VALID
XML          Oracle XDK                          19.0.0.0.0   VALID
CATJAVA      Oracle Database Java Packages       19.0.0.0.0   VALID
APS          OLAP Analytic Workspace             19.0.0.0.0   VALID
RAC          Oracle Real Application Clusters    19.0.0.0.0   VALID
XDB          Oracle XML Database                 19.0.0.0.0   VALID
OWM          Oracle Workspace Manager            19.0.0.0.0   VALID
CONTEXT      Oracle Text                         19.0.0.0.0   VALID
ORDIM        Oracle Multimedia                   19.0.0.0.0   VALID
SDO          Spatial                             19.0.0.0.0   VALID
XOQ          Oracle OLAP API                     19.0.0.0.0   VALID
OLS          Oracle Label Security               19.0.0.0.0   VALID
APEX         Oracle Application Express          4.2.5.00.08  VALID
DV           Oracle Database Vault               19.0.0.0.0   VALID

16 rows selected.
```

6. Check the timezone version to ensure that the AutoUpgrade has upgraded its version to 32 (19c Timezone version)., as follows:

```
SQL > SELECT version FROM v$timezone_file;

VERSION
---------
32
1 row selected.
```

7. If this is the **RAC** database, we can check if the database is up in all the nodes. If it's' not up in the other nodes of the cluster, we can start them, as follows:

```
SQL> alter system set cluster_database=true scope=spfile sid='*';
System altered.

[oracle@virtual-19crac1 ~]$ srvctl stop  database -d texapr
[oracle@virtual-19crac1 ~]$ srvctl start database -d texapr
```

```
[oracle@virtual-19crac1 ~]$ srvctl status database -d texapr
Instance texapr1 is running on node virtual-19crac1
Instance texapr2 is running on node virtual-19crac2
```

Check for the post upgrade invalid objects

It's' always a good idea to take a snapshot of the invalid objects' count after the database upgrade, as we can compare it with the pre-upgrade invalid count to make sure that they both are the same. On the primary database, first run the **utlrp** script to compile any **INVALID** objects and then take a count of Invalidthe objects, so that we can compare the counts after the database upgrade., as follows:

1. First take the count of the invalid objects in the **SYS** and **SYSTEM** schemas, as follows:

```
SQL> spool /u01/software/upgrade/texapr/texapr_postupgrade/
texapr_post-upgrade_SYS_SYSTEM_invalid_Objects.log

SQL> col owner for a25
SQL> set lines 200
SQL> SELECT i.HOST_NAME "DATABASE_HOST" ,
        i.INSTANCE_NAME "DB_NAME", d.DATABASE_ROLE " DATABASE_ROLE",
        d.OPEN_MODE " OPEN_MODE ", STARTUP_TIME
        from GV$DATABASE d, gv$instance i
        where i.INST_ID=d.INST_ID;
SQL> select owner,object_name,object_type,status
      from dba_objects
      where status='INVALID' and owner in ('SYS','SYSTEM')
    order by owner ;
spool off;
```

2. Next, take the invalid object count for the other schemas, as follows:

```
SQL> spool /u01/software/upgrade/texapr/texapr_postupgrade/
texapr_post-upgrade_non-SYS_invalid_objects.log

SQL> col owner for a25
SQL> set lines 200
SQL> set pages 200
SQL> col object_type for a30;
SQL> col DATABASE_HOST for a40;
SQL>SELECT i.HOST_NAME "DATABASE_HOST" ,
        i.INSTANCE_NAME "DB_NAME", d.DATABASE_ROLE " DATABASE_ROLE",
        d.OPEN_MODE " OPEN_MODE ", STARTUP_TIME
        from GV$DATABASE d, gv$instance i
        where i.INST_ID=d.INST_ID;
SQL> select count(*)
      from dba_objects
```

```
          where status='INVALID' and owner not in ('SYS','SYSTEM');
SQL> select owner,object_type,count(*)
     from dba_objects
     where status='INVALID' and owner not in ('SYS','SYSTEM')
     group by owner,object_type order by owner ;
SQL> select owner,object_name,object_type,status
     from dba_objects
     where status='INVALID' and owner not in ('SYS','SYSTEM')
     order by owner ;
spool off;
```

Next, we will **createc** a second **TEST** table in the primary database.

CreateC a second test table just to crosscheck and see if it is coming to the physical standby database through the logs without any issues, as follows:

```
SQL> Create table AFTER_UPGRADE (NAME Varchar(30));
Table created.

SQL> insert into AFTER_UPGRADE values ('Table AFTER Upgrade');
1 row created.
```

```
SQL> commit;
Commit complete.
SQL> alter system switch all logfile;
System altered.
```

With this step, the primary database upgrade is completed. Now, let's upgrade the physical standby database.

Upgrading physical standby database to Oracle 19c (19.9.0)

By now, the primary database is upgraded to Oracle 19c; now let's upgrade the physical standby database. The physical standby database upgrade will happen with the migrating redo logs that it receives from the primary database. As of now, the physical standby database is down. Let's upgrade its configuration file first and then start the database using the server control utility. But first, let's take a look at a few pre-checks and ensure that they are completed, as follows:

1. First copy the password files/parameter files and database **tnsnames.ora** entry from the Oracle 11g to Oracle 19c home. We need to do this step in all the nodes of the cluster, as follows:

```
@Physical Standby database server

[oracle@virtual-dr-19crac1 ~]$ cp /u01/app/oracle/
product/12.1.0.2/db_1/dbs/* texadr*

/u01/app/oracle/product/19c/db_1/dbs

[oracle@virtual-dr-19crac1 ~]$ cp /u01/app/oracle/
product/12.1.0.2/network/admin/* texadr* /u01/app/oracle/
product/19c/db_1/network/admin/
```

2. Modify the database entry in **/etc/oratab** to point to the Oracle 19c (19.3.0) home. We need to do this step in all the nodes of the cluster, as follows:

```
[oracle@virtual-dr-19crac1 ~]$ ~]$  cat /etc/oratab | grep texadr

viceprdr:/u01/app/oracle/product/19c/db_1:N
viceprdr1:/u01/app/oracle/product/19c/db_1
```

3. Upgrade the cluster configuration information of the physical standby database using the **srvctl upgrade** command, as follows:

```
[oracle@virtual-dr-19crac1 ~]$ export ORACLE_HOME=/u01/app/
oracle/product/19c/db_1
[oracle@virtual-dr-19crac1 ~]$ export PATH=$ORACLE_HOME/bin:$PATH

[oracle@virtual-dr-19crac1 ~]$ srvctl upgrade database -db texadr
-o /u01/app/oracle/product/19c/db_1

[oracle@virtual-dr-19crac1 ~]$ srvctl config database -d texadr
Database unique name: texadr
Database name:
Oracle home: /u01/app/oracle/product/19c/db_1
Oracle user: oracle
Spfile: +data/texadr/PARAMETERFILE/spfiletexadr1.ora
Password file:
Domain:
Start options: mount
Stop options: immediate
Database role: PHYSICAL_STANDBY
Management policy: AUTOMATIC
Server pools:
Disk Groups: DATA
Mount point paths:
Services:
Type: RAC
Start concurrency:
Stop concurrency:
OSDBA group: oinstall
OSOPER group: oinstall
```

```
Database instances: texadr1,texadr2
Configured nodes: virtual-dr-19crac1,virtual-dr-19crac2
CSS critical: no
CPU count: 0
Memory target: 0
Maximum memory: 0
Default network number for database services:
Database is administrator managed
```

4. Start the physical standby database in the **MOUNT** mode. From the node-1 of the physical standby database server, start the physical standby database in the mount stage, as follows:

```
[oracle@virtual-dr-19crac1 ~]$  srvctl start database -d texadr
-o mount
```

5. Enable the log shipping on the primary database, as follows:

```
SQL> ALTER SYSTEM SET log_archive_dest_state 2=enable SCOPE=BOTH
sid='*';
System altered.
```

The primary database will start shipping all the redo logs to the physical standby database.

6. Start the managed recovery process in the physical standby database, as follows:

```
SQL> ALTER DATABASE RECOVER managed standby database using
current logfile disconnect;
Database altered.
```

For the physical standby database, thet MRP will now start applying all the logs that it has received from the primary database. This might take some time depending upon the number of archive log files that the primary database has generated during its upgrade. The physical standby database will be upgraded with all the migrated redo data that it received from the primary database.

We can check the alert log and wait for some time for the physical standby database to sync with the primary database, as follows:

```
Alert Log of standby database:
-------------------------------
MRP0 (PID:10412): Media Recovery Log +DATA/TEXADR/
ARCHIVELOG/2021_02_27/thread_2_seq_53.418.1065622623
```

```
2021-02-27T14:20:46.552632-06:00
MRP0 (PID:10412): Media Recovery Log +DATA/TEXADR/
ARCHIVELOG/2021_02_27/thread_1_seq_183.526.1065622641

2021-02-27T14:20:46.568486-06:00
MRP0 (PID:10412): Media Recovery Log +DATA/TEXADR/
ARCHIVELOG/2021_02_27/thread_2_seq_54.419.1065622623
2021-02-27T14:20:46.606384-06:00
MRP0 (PID:10412): Media Recovery Log +DATA/TEXADR/
ARCHIVELOG/2021_02_27/thread_1_seq_184.527.1065622641
2021-02-27T14:20:46.733400-06:00
MRP0 (PID:10412): Media Recovery Waiting for T-1.S-185 (in
transit)
2021-02-27T14:20:46.738255-06:00
Recovery of Online Redo Log: Thread 1 Group 6 Seq 185 Reading mem
0
  Mem# 0: +DATA/TEXADR/ONLINELOG/group_6.279.1065559227
  Mem# 1: +DATA/TEXADR/ONLINELOG/group_6.280.1065559227
MRP0 (PID:10412): Media Recovery Waiting for T-2.S-55 (in
transit)
2021-02-27T14:20:46.746418-06:00Recovery of Online Redo Log:
Thread 2 Group 9 Seq 55 Reading mem 0
  Mem# 0: +DATA/TEXADR/ONLINELOG/group_9.285.1065559227
  Mem# 1: +DATA/TEXADR/ONLINELOG/group_9.286.1065559227

Resize operation completed for file# 3, old size 808960K, new size
819200K
```

7. Stop the database and start it by using the **srvctl** command.

8. Wait until the standby database catches up with the primary and we can then modify the standby database configuration start option to **READ ONLY**, and then stop the database and start it by using the **SRVCTL** command as follows:

```
[oracle@virtual-dr-19crac1 ~]$ srvctl modify database -d texadr
-startoption  "READ ONLY"

[oracle@virtual-dr-19crac1 ~]$ srvctl stop  database -d texadr
[oracle@virtual-dr-19crac1 ~]$ srvctl start  database -d texadr

[oracle@virtual-dr-19crac1 ~]$ srvctl status database -d texadr
Instance texadr1 is running on node virtual-dr-19crac1
Instance texadr2 is running on node virtual-dr-19crac2
```

Start the MRP and check the lag, as follows:

```
SQL> ALTER DATABASE RECOVER managed standby database using
current logfile disconnect;
Database altered.
```

9. Check the components' status in the standby database, as follows:

```
SQL> col OPEN_MODE for a10

SQL> col STARTUP_TIME for a20
SQL> col OBJECT_NAME for a30
SQL> SELECT i.HOST_NAME "DATABASE_HOST" ,
        i.INSTANCE_NAME "DB_NAME",
        d.DATABASE_ROLE "DATABASE_ROLE",
        d.OPEN_MODE " OPEN_MODE ", STARTUP_TIME
      from GV$DATABASE d, gv$instance i
      where i.INST_ID=d.INST_ID;

DATABASE_HOST       DB_NAME   DATABASE_ROLE     OPEN_MODE     STARTUP_TIME
------------------- --------- ----------------- ------------- --------
virtual-dr-19crac1  texadr1   PHYSICAL STANDBY  READ ONLY WITH APPLY 27-FEB-21
virtual-dr-19crac1  texadr1   PHYSICAL STANDBY  READ ONLY WITH APPLY 27-FEB-21
```

10. Now, check the components' status in the **dba** registry, as follows:

```
SQL> col COMP_ID for a10
SQL> col COMP_NAME for a40
SQL> col VERSION for a15
SQL> set lines 180
SQL> set pages 999
SQL> select COMP_ID,COMP_NAME,VERSION,STATUS from dba_registry;

COMP_ID    COMP_NAME                                VERSION     STATUS
---------- ---------------------------------------- ---------- ------
CATALOG    Oracle Database Catalog Views            19.0.0.0.0  VALID
CATPROC    Oracle Database Packages and Types       19.0.0.0.0  VALID
JAVAVM     JServer JAVA Virtual Machine             19.0.0.0.0  VALID
XML        Oracle XDK                               19.0.0.0.0  VALID
CATJAVA    Oracle Database Java Packages            19.0.0.0.0  VALID
APS        OLAP Analytic Workspace                  19.0.0.0.0  VALID
RAC        Oracle Real Application Clusters         19.0.0.0.0  VALID
XDB        Oracle XML Database                      19.0.0.0.0  VALID
OWM        Oracle Workspace Manager                 19.0.0.0.0  VALID
CONTEXT    Oracle Text                              19.0.0.0.0  VALID
ORDIM      Oracle Multimedia                        19.0.0.0.0  VALID
SDO        Spatial                                  19.0.0.0.0  VALID
XOQ        Oracle OLAP API                          19.0.0.0.0  VALID
OLS        Oracle Label Security                    19.0.0.0.0  VALID
APEX       Oracle Application Express               4.2.5.00.08 VALID
DV         Oracle Database Vault                    19.0.0.0.0  VALID
16 rows selected.
```

11. Check if the tables got replicated to the physical standby database. Check if those two tables got replicated indicating that the standby database is both upgraded and in **SYNC** with the primary database, as follows:

```
SQL> select owner, table_name from dba_tables where table_name in
('BEFORE_UPGRADE',' AFTER_UPGRADE);
OWNER                    TABLE_NAME
------------------       -----------------
SYS                      BEFORE_UPGRADE
SYS                      AFTER_UPGRADE
```

With this step, we have successfully completed upgrading the primary and the physical standby database; now let's enable the data guard broker.

Start the data guard broker process in both the primary and the standby databases

Login to the Primary and standby databases and start the dataguard broker dmon process and enable the dataguard configuration as shown in the following steps:

1. In the Primary database, **set the dg_broker_start to true.**:

    ```
    SQL> ALTER SYSTEM SET DG_BROKER_START=TRUE;
    System altered.
    ```

2. In the Physical standby database, **set the dg_broker_start to true.**:

    ```
    SQL> ALTER SYSTEM SET DG_BROKER_START=TRUE;
    System altered.
    ```

3. Enable the broker configuration from the primary database, as follows:

    ```
    [oracle@chopvm-19crac1 ~]$ dgmgrl
    DGMGRL for Linux: Release 19.0.0.0.0 - Production on Tue Feb 27
    5:04:28 2021
    Version 19.9.0.0.0
    Copyright (c) 1982, 2019, Oracle and/or its affiliates.  All rights
    reserved.

    Welcome to DGMGRL, type "help" for information.
    DGMGRL> connect sys
    Password:
    Connected to "texapr"
    Connected as SYSDBA.
    DGMGRL>
    ```

4. Check the current configuration, as follows:

    ```
    DGMGRL> show configuration
    Configuration - texapr

      Protection Mode: MaxPerformance
    ```

```
    Members:
    texapr - Primary database
      texadr - Physical standby database
        Fast-Start Failover:  Disabled

Configuration Status:
DISABLED
```

5. Enable the configuration, as follows:

```
DGMGRL> enable configuration;
Enabled.
```

6. Re-check the current configuration, as follows:

```
DGMGRL>  show configuration;

Configuration - texapr

  Protection Mode: MaxPerformance
  Members:
  texapr - Primary database
    texadr - Physical standby database

Fast-Start Failover:  Disabled

Configuration Status:
SUCCESS (status updated 16 seconds ago)
```

7. Perform the final check to confirm that both the primary and the standby databases are upgraded to 19.9.0, as follows:

Check in the Primary database:

```
SQL>set lines 200
SQL>col HOST_NAME for a35
SQL>col banner for a99
SQL>select i.instance_name,i.host_name,v.banner
    from gv$instance i, gv$version v
    where i.inst_id=v.inst_id;


INSTANCE_NAME  HOST_NAME         BANNER
-------------  -------------     --------------------------------
texapr1        virtual-19crac1   Oracle Database 19c
                                 Enterprise Edition
                                 Release 19.0.0.0.0: Production
texapr2        virtual-19crac2   Oracle Database 19c
                                 Enterprise Edition
                                 Release 19.0.0.0.0 - Production
```

Check in the Physical standby database:

```
SQL>set lines 200
SQL>col HOST_NAME for a35
SQL>col banner for a99
SQL>select i.instance_name,i.host_name,v.banner
    from gv$instance i, gv$version v
    where i.inst_id=v.inst_id;

INSTANCE_NAME   HOST_NAME          BANNER
-------------   -------------      ------------------------------
texadr1         virtual-dr-19crac1 Oracle Database 19c
                                   Enterprise Edition
                                   Release 19.0.0.0.0: Production
texadr2         virtual-dr-19crac2 Oracle Database 19c
                                   Enterprise Edition
                                   Release 19.0.0.0.0: Production
```

This completes the upgrade of the Oracle database from Oracle 12c (12.1.0.2) to Oracle 19c (19.9.0). We saw that the AutoUpgrade utility has upgraded all the components including the Timezone in the primary database and we just upgraded the physical standby database with all the upgrade redo data that it received from the primary database.

Fallback method

At this stage, if you want to downgrade both the primary and the physical standby database, you can skip the post-upgrade tasks and downgrade the database by using either the flashback method or the Oracle provided downgrade scripts described in the previous chapters.

But ifif you want to continue with converting this database as a pluggable database, we can complete the post-upgrade steps mentioned in the following section.

Post upgrade tasks

For the post upgrade tasks, we can complete the following steps in both the primary and the standby databases:

- **FRA space usage**: Until you drop the restore point, keep checking the FRA space usage and increase the space as necessary.

- **Dropping GRP**: We can also drop the restore point in both the primary and the standby databases.

- **Database compatibility**: We can change the compatible parameter after waiting for one week as we cannot downgrade the database after changing this parameter to 19. Since this is a permanent change, once you change the compatible parameter to 19.9, we cannot revert, so please wait for one week and then change it.

In the **In the** Primary database, **change the compatible as below and bounce the database.**use the following command:

```
SQL> ALTER SYSTEM SET COMPATIBLE = '19.0.0' SCOPE=SPFILE;
System altered.

[oracle@virtual-19crac1 ~]$ srvctl stop  database -d texapr
[oracle@virtual-19crac1 ~]$ srvctl start database -d texapr
[oracle@virtual-19crac1 ~]$ srvctl status  database -d texapr
Instance texapr1 is running on node virtual-19crac1
Instance texapr2 is running on node virtual-19crac2
```

In the **In the** Physical standby database, **change the compatible as below and bounce the database.**use the following command:

```
SQL> ALTER SYSTEM SET COMPATIBLE = '19.0.0' SCOPE=SPFILE;
System altered.

[oracle@virtual-dr-19crac1 dbs]$ srvctl stop  database -d texadr

[oracle@virtual-dr-19crac1 dbs]$ srvctl start database -d texadr
[oracle@virtual-dr-19crac1 dbs]$ srvctl status  database -d texadr
Instance texadr1 is running on node virtual-dr-19crac1
Instance texadr2 is running on node virtual-dr-19crac2
```

With this, we have successfully upgraded both the primary and the physical standby database from the Oracle 12c (12.1.0.2) database to Oracle 19c (19.9.0). In the following section, we will work on converting this database as a pluggable database and we will plug-in into an existing container database as **questpr**.

> As mentioned at the beginning of this chapter, we can upgrade and convert an Oracle 12c (12.1.0.2) database to Oracle 19c using a single command. We will check this option in *Chapter 6, Upgrading and Converting 12c non-CDB as 19c PDB (using AutoUpgrade)*. For now, we will convert the database as a pluggable database with the Oracle provided scripts.

Conversion of non-CDB as a pluggable database (PDB)

In this section, we will see how to convert both the primary database (**texapr**) and the physical standby database (**texadr**) as a pluggable database and plug-in into the

Oracle 19c (19.9.0) container database (**questpr**), as shown in *figure* 4.3. The *figure* 4.3 shows high level representation of this non-cdb to pdb conversion:

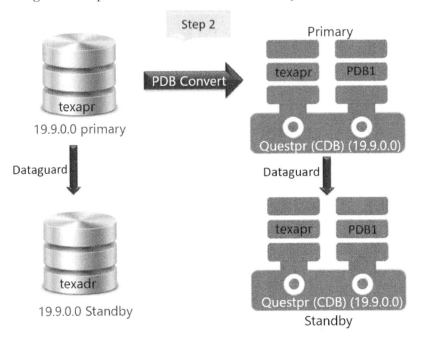

Figure 4.3: Converting Non container database (non-cdb) as a pluggable database (PDB)

Now, we will see how we can convert the non-cdb database (**texapr**) and plug-in as a pluggable database into a pre-exiting Oracle 19c (19.9.0) container database, **questpr**.

The target container primary database and the physical standby database environment are as follows:

```
SQL>@rac_database_info.sql
```

DATABASE_HOST	DB_NAME	DATABASE_ROLE	OPEN_MODE	STARTUP_TIME
virtual-19crac1	questpr1	PRIMARY	READ WRITE	27-FEB-21
virtual-19crac2	questpr2	PRIMARY	READ WRITE	27-FEB-21

The target container physical standby database binary version and its patch set is as follows:

```
SQL>@/home/oracle/rac_database_info.sql
```

DATABASE_HOST	DB_NAME	DATABASE_ROLE	OPEN_MODE	STARTUP_TIME
virtual-dr-19crac1	questdr1	PHYSICAL STANDBY	MOUNTED	27-FEB-21
virtual-dr-19crac2	questdr2	PHYSICAL STANDBY	MOUNTED	27-FEB-21

Reusing datafiles in the Standby datafiles during PDB conversion

Generally, when we add a new pluggable database to a primary container database, which is part of the multitenant dataguard environment, we would need to restore the pluggable database in the physical standby container database, so that the container physical standby database can continue to be in sync with the primary database. We must do this even if the pluggable database and the container database are on the same servers. This would work fine for the smaller databases but if the size of the pluggable database is in terabytes, restoring the pluggable database will take time. For the larger databases, we can use the concept of reusing the physical standby pluggable database's datafiles. This works only if both the new pluggable physical standby database and the container physical standby database are on the same servers.

For more details on this method, refer to MOS.

Reusing the Source Standby Database Files When Plugging a PDB into the Primary Database of a Data Guard Configuration (Doc ID 2273829.1).

In this section, we will follow this approach and reuse the source physical standby database's datafiles when we plug-in **texapr** into the primary container database, **questpr**. In this method, we will create aliases for all the source physical standby database's datafiles, and when we plug-in the **pdb** in the primary container database, the MRP process running in the container physical standby process will recognize all the source physical standby database's datafiles because of all the aliases, and it will sync the container physical standby database. Let's see the following steps to understand how this will work:

Standby lag check

1. Ensure that both the non-cdb physical standby database (**texadr**) and the cdb physical standby database (**questdr**) are in sync with their respective primary databases, as follows:

   a. Check if the non-container primary(*texapr*) **database** and physical standby(*texadr)* database are in sync.

   For the non-container primary database (**texapr**), run the following command:

   ```
   SQL> @/home/oracle/rac_database_info.sql
   ```

DATABASE_HOST	DB_NAME	DATABASE_ROLE	OPEN_MODE	STARTUP_TIME
virtual-19crac1	texapr1	PRIMARY	READ WRITE	27-FEB-21

```
virtual-19crac2  texapr2    PRIMARY       READ WRITE  27-FEB-21

SQL> alter system switch all logfile;
System altered.

SQL> archive log list;
Database log mode              Archive Mode
Automatic archival             Enabled
Archive destination            USE_DB_RECOVERY_FILE_DEST
Oldest online log sequence     142
Next log sequence to archive   143
Current log sequence           143
```

For the non-container physical standby database (**texadr**), run the following command:

```
SQL> @/home/oracle/standby_database_lag.sql
```

DATABASE_HOST	DB_NAME	DATABASE_ROLE	OPEN_MODE	STARTUP_T
virtual-dr-19crac1	texadr1	PHYSICAL STANDBY	MOUNTED	27-FEB-21
virtual-dr-19crac2	texadr2	PHYSICAL STANDBY	MOUNTED	27-FEB-21

INST_ID	PROCESS	STATUS	THREAD#	SEQUENCE#	BLOCK#	BLOCKS
1	MRP0	APPLYING_LOG	1	143	4	102400

THREAD#	ARCHIVED	APPLIED	GAP
1	143	142	1
2	66	66	0

b. Check if the container primary database*(questpr)* and the physical standby *(questdr)* database are in sync, as follows:

For the container primary database (**questpr**), run the following command:

```
SQL> @/home/oracle/rac_database_info.sql
```

DATABASE_HOST	DB_NAME	DATABASE_ROLE	OPEN_MODE	STARTUP_TIME
virtual-19crac1	questpr1	PRIMARY	READ WRITE	27-FEB-21
virtual-19crac2	questpr2	RIMARY	READ WRITE	27-FEB-21

```
SQL> alter system switch all logfile;
System altered.

SQL> archive log list;
```

```
Database log mode              Archive Mode
Automatic archival             Enabled
Archive destination            USE_DB_RECOVERY_FILE_DEST
Oldest online log sequence     17
Next log sequence to archive   18
Current log sequence           18
SQL>
```

For the container physical standby database (**questdr**), run the following command:

```
SQL> @/home/oracle/standby_database_lag.sql
```

```
DATABASE_HOST      DB_NAME  DATABASE_ROLE    OPEN_MODE   STARTUP_T
----------------   -------- ---------------  ----------  ---------
virtual-dr-19crac1 questdr1 PHYSICAL STANDBY MOUNTED     27-FEB-21
virtual-dr-19crac2 questdr2 PHYSICAL STANDBY MOUNTED     27-FEB-21


INST_ID PROCESS STATUS       THREAD# SEQUENCE# BLOCK# BLOCKS
------  ------- -----------  ------- --------- ------ ------
     1  MRP0    APPLYING_LOG  1           15     87   102400


THREAD#    ARCHIVED    APPLIED    GAP
---------- ---------- ---------- ----------
   1          17         17         0
   2          10         10         0
```

As we can see, both the non-cdb and the cdb physical standby databases are in sync with their databases; so, let's move to the next step.

Obtain the GUID of the from texapr (non-cdb primary database(texapr)

We need to get the guide of the source primary database; we will use this info in one of our scripts, as follows:

```
SQL> @/home/oracle/rac_database_info.sql
DATABASE_HOST     DB_NAME    DATABASE_ROLE   OPEN_MODE   STARTUP_TIME
----------------  ---------  ------------    ---------   ----------
virtual-19crac1   texapr1    PRIMARY         READ WRITE  27-FEB-21
virtual-19crac2   texapr2    PRIMARY         READ WRITE  27-FEB-21

SQL> select guid from v$containers;
GUID
```

```
--------------------------------
BC47838E9CFF0F34E053011478C051BB
```

The physical standby database system, and the location of the datafiles of both the non-cdb physical standby database and the cdb physical standby database will be in different directories in ASM.

This is just like in our case.

The following is location of the datafiles of the non-cdb standby database, **TEXADR:** **'+DATA/TEXADR/DATAFILE**'

The following is location of the datafiles of the cdb standby database, **QUESTDR:** **'+DATA/QUESTDR/DATAFILE**'.

Now, once we plug-in the non-cdb primary database (**texapr**) into the cdb primary database (**questpr**), all the datafiles of the non-cdb physical standby database (**testdr**) must have the aliases created in the container physical standby database datafiles directory for the redo apply (MRP) process to find them. If we don't create the aliases, the redo apply process won't be able to apply the redo data and the physical standby database will be out of sync. So, we need to create the aliases for all the non-cdb physical standby database datafiles in the container physical standby database datafile directory, as below. shown in the following section.

Creating aliases for the non-cdb standby database (texadr) datafiles

For this step, first we need to create a script (**build_alias_for_noncdb_stby.** **sql**), which when run in the non-cdb physical standby database, will generate a dynamic SQL (**create_non-cdb_aliases.sql**) as the output. When we run the **create_non-cdb_aliases.sql** in the ASM of the standby server, it will create all the required aliases.

So first, let's create the **build_alias_for_noncdb_stby.sql** as follows:

```
[oracle@virtual-dr-19crac1 dbs]$ cd /u01/software/migration/texapr/
[oracle@virtual-dr-19crac1 dbs]$ vi build_alias_for_noncdb_stby.sql

SQL> set feedback off
SQL> set heading off
SQL> set echo off
SQL> set space 0
SQL> set tab off
SQL> set newpage 0
SQL> set linesize 999
```

```
SQL> set pagesize 0
SQL> set trimspool on
SQL> set ver off
SQL> spool create_non-cdb_aliases.sql
SQL> prompt set echo on
SQL> select 'alter diskgroup &&diskgrp_name_without_plus_sign add
directory '||''''||'+&&diskgrp_name_without_plus_sign/&&cdb_database_
name_in_UPPER_CASE/'||guid||''''||';' from v$containers;

SQL> select 'alter diskgroup &&diskgrp_name_without_plus_sign add
directory '||''''||'+&&diskgrp_name_without_plus_sign/&&cdb_database_
name_in_UPPER_CASE/'||guid||'/datafile'||''''||';' from v$containers;

SQL> select 'alter diskgroup &&diskgrp_name_without_plus_sign add alias
'||''''||replace(replace(replace(name,'.','_'),'/&non_cdb_database_name_
in_UPPER_CASE','/&&cdb_database_name_in_UPPER_CASE'),'datafile',guid||'/
datafile')||''''||' for '||''''||name||''''||';' from v$datafile df,
(select guid from v$containers) con;
Exit
```

We need to run the preceding SQL in the non-cdb standby database. When we run it, it will ask for the following inputs:

```
Disk group name           : DATA
cdb standby database name : QUESTDR
non-cdb standby database  : TEXADR
```

Let's run the preceding script in the non-cdb physical standby database, as follows:

```
SQL>@/home/oracle/standby_database_lag.sql

DATABASE_HOST        DB_NAME     DATABASE_ROLE       OPEN_MODE    STARTUP_TIME
------------------   ----------  ----------------    -----------  ------------
virtual-dr-19crac1   texadr1     PHYSICAL STANDBY    MOUNTED      27-FEB-21
virtual-dr-19crac2   texadr2     PHYSICAL STANDBY    MOUNTED      27-FEB-21

SQL> @build_stdby_aliases.sql

set echo on
Enter value for diskgrp_name_without_plus_sign: DATA
Enter value for cdb_database_name_in_upper_case: QUESTDR
alter diskgroup DATA add directory '+DATA/QUESTDR/
BC8580629CA16FDDE053011478C09928';
alter diskgroup DATA add directory '+DATA/QUESTDR/
BC8580629CA16FDDE053011478C09928/datafile';
```

```
Enter value for non_cdb_database_name_in_upper_case: TEXADR
```

```
alter diskgroup DATA add alias '+DATA/QUESTDR/DATAFILE/
system_257_1066128787' for '+DATA/TEXADR/DATAFILE/
system.257.1066128787';
alter diskgroup DATA add alias '+DATA/QUESTDR/DATAFILE/
sysaux_256_1066128795' for '+DATA/TEXADR/DATAFILE/
sysaux.256.1066128795';
alter diskgroup DATA add alias '+DATA/QUESTDR/DATAFILE/
undotbs1_288_1066128797' for '+DATA/TEXADR/DATAFILE/
undotbs1.288.1066128797';
alter diskgroup DATA add alias '+DATA/QUESTDR/DATAFILE/
undotbs2_287_1066128799' for '+DATA/TEXADR/DATAFILE/
undotbs2.287.1066128799';
alter diskgroup DATA add alias '+DATA/QUESTDR/DATAFILE/
users_286_1066128799' for '+DATA/TEXADR/DATAFILE/users.286.1066128799';
```

```
Disconnected from Oracle Database 19c Enterprise Edition Release
19.0.0.0.0: Production
Version 19.9.0.0.0
```

Running the preceding script will generate **create_non-cdb_aliases.sq**l. Check the following SQL statement once, before we run it in the next step:

```
[oracle@virtual-dr-19crac1 texapr]$ ls -ltr
-rw-r--r-- 1 oracle oinstall  906 Feb 27 14:16 build_stdby_aliases.sql
-rw-r--r-- 1 oracle oinstall 1012 Feb 27 14:17 create_non-cdb_aliases.
sql
```

Execute the preceding generated script (**create_non-cdb_aliases.sql**) in the physical standby ASM as the **sysasm** user, as follows:

```
[oracle@virtual-dr-19crac1 texapr]$ . oraenv
ORACLE_SID = [texadr1] ? +ASM1
The Oracle base remains unchanged with value /u01/app/oracle
```

```
[oracle@virtual-dr-19crac1 texapr]$ sqlplus / as sysasm
```

```
SQL*Plus: Release 19.0.0.0.0 - Production on Thu Feb 27 14:19:57 2021
Version 19.9.0.0.0
Copyright (c) 1982, 2019, Oracle.  All rights reserved.
Connected to:
Oracle Database 19c Enterprise Edition Release 19.0.0.0.0 - Production
Version 19.9.0.0.0
```

```
SQL> @create_non-cdb_aliases.sql
```

```
SQL> Enter value for diskgrp_name_without_plus_sign: DATA
```

```
SQL> Enter value for cdb_database_name_in_upper_case: QUESTDR
```

```
SQL> alter diskgroup DATA add directory '+DATA/QUESTDR/
BC8580629CA16FDDE053011478C09928';
Diskgroup altered.

SQL> alter diskgroup DATA add directory '+DATA/QUESTDR/
BC8580629CA16FDDE053011478C09928/datafile';
Diskgroup altered.

SQL> Enter value for non_cdb_database_name_in_upper_case: TEXADR

SQL> alter diskgroup DATA add alias '+DATA/QUESTDR/
DATAFILE/system_257_1066128787' for '+DATA/TEXADR/DATAFILE/
system.257.1066128787';
Diskgroup altered.

SQL> alter diskgroup DATA add alias '+DATA/QUESTDR/DATAFILE/
sysaux_256_1066128795' for +DATA/TEXADR/DATAFILE/sysaux.256.1066128795';
Diskgroup altered.

SQL> alter diskgroup DATA add alias '+DATA/QUESTDR/DATAFILE/
undotbs1_288_1066128797' for '+DATA/TEXADR/DATAFILE/
undotbs1.288.1066128797';
Diskgroup altered.

SQL> alter diskgroup DATA add alias '+DATA/QUESTDR/DATAFILE/
undotbs2_287_1066128799' for '+DATA/TEXADR/DATAFILE/
undotbs2.287.1066128799';
Diskgroup altered.

SQL> alter diskgroup DATA add alias '+DATA/QUESTDR/DATAFILE/
users_286_1066128799' for '+DATA/TEXADR/DATAFILE/users.286.1066128799';
Diskgroup altered.

SQL>
```

Since we have all the aliases in place, when the non-cdb primary database **texapr** is plugged into the cdb primary database **questpr**, the physical standby database of the cdb physical standby database **questdr** will apply the redo logs without any issues.

Export of TDE keys

Since we have **Transparent Data Encryption** (**TDE**) enabled in the source database, we need to take the export of the TDE keys of the non-container primary database and import them into the container primary database keystore after we plug the non-cdb primary as a pluggable database. Let's look at the following steps:

1. Log in to the non-cdb primary database, **texapr** and export the keys as follows:

```
SQL> ADMINISTER KEY MANAGEMENT EXPORT ENCRYPTION KEYS WITH SECRET
"mySecret" TO '/u01/software/keystore/texapr_keystore_export_for_
upgrade/texapr_export.p12' FORCE KEYSTORE IDENTIFIED BY Welcome1;

Keystore altered.
```

2. Stop the non-cdb physical standby database (**texadr**) and restart it on one instance in the **mount** mode and cancel the MRP, as follows:

```
[oracle@virtual-dr-19crac1 ~]$ srvctl status database -d texadr
Instance texadr1 is running on node virtual-dr-19crac1
Instance texadr2 is running on node virtual-dr-19crac2

[oracle@virtual-dr-19crac1 ~]$ srvctl stop  database -d texadr

[oracle@virtual-dr-19crac1 ~]$ srvctl start instance -d texadr -n
virtual-dr-19crac1 -o mount

[oracle@virtual-dr-19crac1 ~]$ srvctl status database -d texadr
Instance texadr1 is running on node virtual-dr-19crac1
Instance texadr2 is not running on node virtual-dr-19crac2
```

3. Check and start the MRP process of the non-cdb physical standby database, **texadr**:

```
SQ> ALTER DATABASE RECOVER managed standby database using current
logfile disconnect;
Database altered.
```

4. Shutdown the non-cdb primary database.

    At this time, we can stop the non-cdb primary database, **texapr**, and start only one instance in the mount mode, as follows:

```
[oracle@virtual-19crac1 ~]$ srvctl status database -d texapr
Instance texapr1 is running on node virtual-19crac1
Instance texapr2 is running on node virtual-19crac2

[oracle@virtual-19crac1 ~]$ srvctl stop database -d texapr

[oracle@virtual-19crac1 ~]$ srvctl start instance -d texapr -n
virtual-19crac1 -o mount

[oracle@virtual-19crac1 ~]$ srvctl status database -d texapr
Instance texapr1 is running on node virtual-19crac1
Instance texapr2 is not running on node virtual-19crac2

[oracle@virtual-19crac1 ~]$
```

5. Flush the redo data in the non-cdb primary database (**texapr**). Before we plug-in the non-cdb database as a pdb database, flush the redo on the primary and then open the database in the **READ ONLY** mode. This will ensure

that no changes can be made to the non-cdb primary database, as follows:

```
SQL> @/home/oracle/rac_database_info.sql

DATABASE_HOST    DB_NAME   DATABASE_ROLE    OPEN_MODE   STARTUP_TIME
---------------  --------  --------------   ----------- ------------
virtual-19crac1  texapr1   PRIMARY                      MOUNTED  27-FEB-21

SQL> alter system flush redo to texadr no confirm apply;
System altered.

SQL> alter database open read only;
Database altered.
```

6. Check the nonn-cdb databases standby database lag. Ensure that the non-primary and non-cdb physical standby databases are in sync with each other for the last time before we convert them as PDBs.

   In the non-cdb primary database, **texapr**, get the **checkpoint_change#** of the system data file for the non-cdb primary database (**texapr**):

```
SQL> @/home/oracle/rac_database_info.sql

DATABASE_HOST    DB_NAME   DATABASE_ROLE    OPEN_MODE   STARTUP_TIME
---------------  -------   --------------   ----------- ------------
virtual-19crac1  texapr1   PRIMARY          MOUNTED     27-FEB-21


SQL> select file#, CHECKPOINT_CHANGE# from v$datafile_header where
file#=1;
FILE#       CHECKPOINT_CHANGE#
----------  ------------------
      1     3025387
```

Now, sync the non-cdb physical standby database, **texadr** until the preceding **checkpoint_change# number** as shown below:

```
SQL> @/home/oracle/rac_database_info.sql

DATABASE_HOST       DB_NAME   DATABASE_ROLE    OPEN_MODE   STARTUP_TIME
------------------  -------   ----------------  ---------  ------------
virtual-dr-19crac1  texadr1   PHYSICAL STANDBY MOUNTED     27-FEB-21


SQL> alter database recover managed standby database until change
3025387;
Database altered.
```

Once the physical standby database is in sync with the primary, you can check the **checkpoint_change#** in the physical standby database; it will be the same as that in the primary database, as follows:

```
SQL> select file#, CHECKPOINT_CHANGE# from v$datafile_header where file#=1;
FILE#      CHECKPOINT_CHANGE#
---------  ------------------
       1   3025387
```

Creation of Manifest file

For the non-cdb primary database (**texapr**), we must create the manifest file which will have the metadata of the database. We will use this XML file to plug-in to the **19c** container database (**questpr**), as follows:

```
SQL> exec dbms_pdb.describe('/u01/software/migration/texapr/texapr_pdb_
mig.xml');
PL/SQL procedure successfully completed.
```

Shutdown the non-cdb primary and standby databases

We can now shutdown both the non-cdb primary and the standby databases.

Stop the non-cdb primary database, as follows:

```
[oracle@virtual-19crac1 texapr]$ srvctl stop database -d texapr
```

```
[oracle@virtual-19crac1 texapr]$ srvctl status database -d texapr
Instance texapr1 is not running on node virtual-19crac1
Instance texapr2 is not running on node virtual-19crac2
```

Stop the non-cdb physical standby database, as follows:

```
[oracle@virtual-dr-19crac1 ~]$ srvctl stop database -d texadr
```

```
[oracle@virtual-dr-19crac1 ~]$ srvctl status database -d texadr
Instance texadr1 is not running on node virtual-dr-19crac1
Instance texadr2 is not running on node virtual-dr-19crac2
```

All the activities in the source databases are now completed; let's move on to the next step.

Plug the non-cdb primary database into the 19.9.0 container database

We will now plug the non-primary database, **texapr** into the 19.9.0 container database, **questpr**. We will use the manifest file which has all the required metadata in it to plug the database into a container database., as shown in *Figure 4.4* represents the pictorial representation of the PDB conversion:

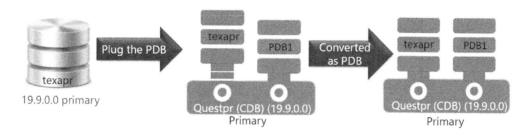

Figure 4.4: Plugging non-cdb as pdb

We need to first plug the database and then run the **noncdb_to_pdb** script which converts the non-cdb to a pluggable database. Now, let's take two typical cases which we see in our real-world environments.

For the non-dataguard environments and with the TDE enabled:

For the databases that has the TDE enabled and with no standby databases configured, we just need to plug the database and import the TDE keys into the container database and we are all set.

For the dataguard environments and with the TDE enabled:

For the databases which has the TDE enabled and have the standby databases, we need to stop the cdb standby database first, and then plug the PDB in the primary database, and then run the non-cdb to the pdb conversion scripts. The reason for stopping the standby database is that the redo apply will keep on failing until we import the TDE keys for the non-cdb primary database and copy the keys to the cdb standby database.

Since ours is the second case, that is, the environment where the TDE is enabled, let's stop the standby first and continue with the rest of the steps as follows:

Stop the cdb Physical Standby database (questdr)

We can now stop the standby database. Since this a rac database, we can use srvctl stop command to stop the database.

```
[oracle@virtual-dr-19crac1 ~]$ srvctl stop database -d questdr
[oracle@virtual-dr-19crac1 ~]$ srvctl status database -d questdr
Instance questdr1 is not running on node virtual-dr-19crac1
Instance questdr2 is not running on node virtual-dr-19crac2
```

Create the pluggable database

We can now create the pdb database, **texapr** in the primary cdb database, **questpr**. For this we will use the manifest file that we created in step 11, as follows:

```
SQL> @/home/oracle/rac_database_info.sql


DATABASE_HOST      DB_NAME    DATABASE_ROLE   OPEN_MODE    STARTUP_TIME
-----------------  --------   -------------   ----------   ------------
virtual-19crac1    questpr1   PRIMARY         READ WRITE   27-FEB-21
virtual-19crac2    questpr2   PRIMARY         READ WRITE   27-FEB-21

SQL> create pluggable database texapr USING '/u01/software/migration/
texapr/texapr_pdb_mig.xml' tempfile reuse NOCOPY;
Pluggable database created.


SQL> show pdbs
CON_ID      CON_NAME     OPEN MODE    RESTRICTED
----------  ----------   ---------    -----------
        2   PDB$SEED     READ ONLY    NO
        3   TEXAPR       MOUNTED
```

As you can see, we are using **nocopy** as we don't want the pdb creation process to create another copy of the datafiles. Once we create the new **pdb** database, it will be in the restrict mode initially and we cannot open the new **pdb** database yet, as we still have a few steps to complete before we can open it.

Check the PDB violations

At this stage, we can check for the violation in the container database, **questpr**. It will report multiple violations for the newly created pluggable database, but don't worry on those, as they will go away once we run the pdb conversion script in the next step, as follows:

```
SQL> @/home/oracle/rac_database_info.sql


DATABASE_HOST      DB_NAME    DATABASE_ROLE   OPEN_MODE    STARTUP_TIME
-----------------  --------   -------------   ----------   ------------
virtual-19crac1    questpr1   PRIMARY         READ WRITE   27-FEB-21
virtual-19crac2    questpr2   PRIMARY         READ WRITE   27-FEB-21

SQL> set pages 200
SQL> column message format 60
SQL> column status format a9
SQL> column type format a9
SQL> column con_id format 9
```

```
SQL> select con_id, name, type, message, status
     from PDB_PLUG_IN_VIOLATIONS
     where name ='TESTPR' and status<>'RESOLVED'
     order by name,time;
CON_ID TYPE      MESSAGE                                      STATUS
------ --------- ----------- --------------------------       ---------
3      WARNING   CDB parameter processes mismatch:
                 Previous 800 Current 200                     PENDING
3      WARNING   CDB parameter cpu_count mismatch:
                 Previous 12 Current 24                       PENDING
3      WARNING   CDB parameter use_large_pages mismatch:
                 Previous 'ONLY' Current 'AUTO_ONLY'          PENDING
3      WARNING   CDB parameter shared_pool_size mismatch:
                 Previous  1792M Current 0                    PENDING
3      WARNING   CDB parameter streams_pool_size mismatch:
                 Previous 256M Current 0                      PENDING
3      WARNING   CDB parameter resource_manager_cpu_allocation
                 mismatch: Previous 12 Current 0              PENDING
3      WARNING   CDB parameter archive_lag_target mismatch:
                     Previous 1800 Current 0                  PENDING
3      WARNING   CDB parameter cluster_database mismatch:
                 Previous FALSE Current TRUE                  PENDING
3      WARNING   CDB parameter parallel_force_local mismatch:
                 Previous TRUE Current FALSE                  PENDING
3      WARNING   CDB parameter parallel_servers_target mismatch:

                 Previous 96 Current 100                      PENDING
3      WARNING   CDB parameter optimizer_adaptive_plans mismatch:
                 Previous FALSE Current TRUE                  PENDING
3      WARNING   CDB parameter enable_ddl_logging mismatch:
                 Previous TRUE Current FALSE                  PENDING
12 rows selected.
```

Pluggable database conversion

After creating the pluggable database from the non-cdb database, we must run the script **noncdb_to_pdb.sql** to convert it from the non-cdb to pdb.

Connect to the **pdb** database, **texapr** and run the following script:

```
SQL> alter session set container=texapr;
Session altered.

SQL> @$ORACLE_HOME/rdbms/admin/noncdb_to_pdb.sql
```

The following is part of the output that we will get once we execute the preceding command; please note that the output is truncated for better visibility:

```
SQL> SET FEEDBACK 1
```

```
SQL> SET NUMWIDTH 10
SQL> SET LINESIZE 80
DOC>########################################################################
####
DOC>########################################################################
DOC>    The following statement will cause an "ORA-01403: no data found"
DOC>    error if we're not in a PDB.
DOC>    This script is intended to be run right after plugin of a PDB,
DOC>    while inside the PDB.
DOC>########################################################################
DOC>########################################################################
DOC>#
SQL>
SQL> VARIABLE cdbname VARCHAR2(128)
SQL> VARIABLE pdbname VARCHAR2(128)
SQL> BEGIN
  2    SELECT sys_context('USERENV', 'CDB_NAME')
  3      INTO :cdbname
  4      FROM dual
  5      WHERE sys_context('USERENV', 'CDB_NAME') is not null;
  6    SELECT sys_context('USERENV', 'CON_NAME')
  7      INTO :pdbname
  8      FROM dual
  9      WHERE sys_context('USERENV', 'CON_NAME') <> 'CDB$ROOT';
 10  END;
 11  /
PL/SQL procedure successfully completed.
SQL>
SQL> @@?/rdbms/admin/loc_to_common0.sql
SQL> Rem
SQL> Rem $Header: rdbms/admin/loc_to_common0.sql /main/9 2018/07/25
3:49:55 surman Exp $
SQL> Rem loc_to_common0.sql
SQL> Rem Copyright (c) 2015, 2018, Oracle and/or its affiliates.
SQL> Rem All rights reserved.
SQL> alter session set container = "&pdbname";
Session altered.
SQL>
SQL> alter session set "_enable_view_pdb"=false;
Session altered.
SQL>
SQL> -- leave the PDB in the same state it was when we started
SQL> BEGIN
2    execute immediate '&open_sql &restricted_state';
  3  EXCEPTION
  4    WHEN OTHERS THEN
  5      BEGIN
```

```
 6      IF (sqlcode <> -900) THEN
 7        RAISE;
 8      END IF;
 9    END;
10  END;
11  /
PL/SQL procedure successfully completed.
SQL>
SQL> WHENEVER SQLERROR CONTINUE;
SQL>
```

Re-check the PDB violations

The preceding step will convert the **non-cdb** database to the **pdb** database. Now, if we check for the violations in the container database, **questpr**, it will report only the violation this time and that's for the TDE keys, as follows:

```
SQL> @/home/oracle/rac_database_info.sql
```

DATABASE_HOST	DB_NAME	DATABASE_ROLE	OPEN_MODE	STARTUP_TIME
virtual-19crac1	questpr1	PRIMARY	READ WRITE	27-FEB-21
virtual-19crac2	questpr2	PRIMARY	READ WRITE	27-FEB-21

```
SQL> set pages 200
SQL> column message format 60
SQL> column status format a9
SQL> clumn type format a9
SQL> column con_id format 9
SQL> column name format a8
SQL> select con_id, name, type, message, status
     from PDB_PLUG_IN_VIOLATIONS
     where name ='TESTPR' and status<>'RESOLVED'
     order by name,time;
```

CON_ID	TYPE	MESSAGE	STATUS
3	ERROR	PDB needs to import keys from source.	PENDING

We can now open the **pdb** database and import the TDE keys. Connect to the primary container database, **questpr** and open the **pdb** database, **texapr**. It will open in the restricted mode because its TDE keys have not yet been imported, as follows:

```
SQL> @/home/oracle/rac_database_info.sql
```

DATABASE_HOST	DB_NAME	DATABASE_ROLE	OPEN_MODE	STARTUP_TIME

```
virtual-19crac1    questpr1   PRIMARY              READ WRITE   27-FEB-21
virtual-19crac2    questpr2   PRIMARY              READ WRITE   27-FEB-21

SQL> show pdbs
CON_ID      CON_NAME       OPEN MODE    RESTRICTED
----------  ----------     ---------    -----------
        2 PDB$SEED       READ ONLY    NO
        3 TEXAPR         MOUNTED

SQL> alter pluggable database TEXAPR open;
    Warning: PDB altered with errors.

SQL> show pdbs

CON_ID      CON_NAME       OPEN MODE    RESTRICTED
----------  ----------     ---------    -----------
        2 PDB$SEED       READ ONLY    NO
        3 TEXAPR         READ WRITE   YES
```

Importing the TDE keys into the Pluggable database, texapr

For the Primary database, we will import the TDE keys using below few steps. Whereas for the standby database, we will copy the TDE keys from primary database to standby database server.

1. **Handling TDE keys in the Primary database**

   Connect to the **TEXAPR PDB** in the primary CDB to prepare importing the keys. If you have **autologin** enabled for the **tde** wallet, you will need to use the force option as shown in the following section. If you have the password base wallet, you don't have to use the force option. In our case, we have **autologin** enabled for the **tde** wallet, so we are using the force option while importing the **pdb** keys, as follows:

   ```
   SQL> alter session set container=TEXAPR;
   Session altered.

   SQL> show con_name;
   CON_NAME
   --------
   TEXAPR

   SQL> ADMINISTER KEY MANAGEMENT IMPORT ENCRYPTION KEYS WITH SECRET
   "mySecret" FROM '/u01/software/keystore/texapr_keystore_export_
   for_upgrade/texapr_export.p12' FORCE KEYSTORE IDENTIFIED BY
   Welcome1 with backup;

   keystore altered.
   ```

Once the TDE keys have been imported, If you check the activation key for the imported keys, it will show the original activation time of the pluggable database, as follows:

```
SQL> select key_id, activation_time from v$encryption_keys order by
activation_time;

KEY_ID                                                    ACTIVATION_TIME
-------------------------------------------------------   -----------------
AXS+MnPTak9iv4OiqAq6rhQAAAAAAAAAAAAAAAAAAAAAAAAAAAAAAAA    24-FEB-21
                                                          10.37.06.68018
                                                          PM +00:00

1 row selected.
```

The activation time here is from the time the key was activated in the non-cdb **texapr** to when **tde** was enabled in the database. We need to activate the keys after it has been imported into any new database. But as the PDB is still in the restricted mode, we must open it in the normal mode for activating the key that was just imported, as follows:

```
SQL> show con_name;

CON_NAME
----------
TEXAPR


SQL> shutdown immediate;
Pluggable Database closed.

SQL> startup;
Pluggable Database opened.

SQL> show pdbs
CON_ID CON_NAME      OPEN MODE    RESTRICTED
---------- -----     ----------   -----------
        3 TEXAPR     READ WRITE   NO
```

We can now activateNow, import the key as follows:

```
SQL> ADMINISTER KEY MANAGEMENT USE KEY
'AXS+MnPTak9iv4OiqAq6rhQAAAAAAAAAAAAAAAAAAAAAAAAAAAAAAAA' FORCE
KEYSTORE IDENTIFIED BY Welcome1 with backup using 'keystore';
keystore altered.
```

Next, we will have to check to see if theValidate that the **TDE** key is active, and that the activation time is the current date/time, as follows:

```
SQL> select key_id, activation_time from v$encryption_keys order
by activation_time;
KEY_ID                                                    ACTIVATION_TIME
-------------------------------------------------------   ----------------
```

```
AXS+MnPTak9iv4OiqAq6rhQAAAAAAAAAAAAAAAAAAAAAAAAAAAA    27-Feb-2021
                                                       14.36.12.023327
                                                       PM +00:00
```

```
1 row selected.
```

Notice, the activation time has changed. This completes all the steps in the primary database. We have successfully upgraded and migrated the 12.1.0.2 non-cdb database, **texapr** to the 19.9.0 pluggable database. Now, let's take care of the 19.9.0 container standby database to make sure that it starts the database sync with the primary database.

2. **Handling TDE keys in Standby database:**

    As of now, the **19c** standby database is down. Let's copy the entire content of the **TDE** keystore from the cdb primary location to the cdb standby location. Depending on the version and the **TDE** configuration, the location can be found in either the **sqlnet.ora ENCRYPTION_WALLET_LOCATION** entry or the **spfile** using the **WALLET_ROOT** parameter setting.

    To copy the TDE keys from the primary to the standby database, we can use any of the following methods:

    -   Copy the contents using the **cp/scp** commands.

    -   Export the keys to the local file system in the primary database, **scp** them to the physical standby database, and then in the physical standby database, use the 'administer key management **MERGE** keystore' command to merge the new keys to the existing keystore.

    -   Copy the **TDE** keys in the standby database by using the **dbms_file_transfer.copy_file** package. We can check this package.

For our case, we went with the first method, where we copied the entire content of the wallet files from the primary to the standby database server as follows:

First, for the primary database, first copy the contents from ASM to the local file system, as follows:

```
[oracle@virtual-19crac1 new_keystore]$ asmcmd

ASMCMD> cd +DATA/QUESTPR/WALLET

ASMCMD> cp * /u01/software/migration/TEXAPR_migration/new_keystore/

copying +DATA/QUESTPR/WALLET/ewallet.p12 -> /u01/software/migration/
TEXAPR_migration/new_keystore//ewallet.p12

copying +DATA/QUESTPR/WALLET/ewallet_2021022817531509.p12
-> /u01/software/migration/TEXAPR_migration/new_keystore//
ewallet_2021022817531509.p12
```

```
copying +DATA/QUESTPR/WALLET/cwallet.sso.bak -> /u01/software/migration/
TEXAPR_migration/new_keystore//cwallet.sso.bak

copying +DATA/QUESTPR/WALLET/cwallet.sso -> /u01/software/migration/
TEXAPR_migration/new_keystore//cwallet.sso

copying +DATA/QUESTPR/WALLET/ewallet_2021022820272947.p12
-> /u01/software/migration/TEXAPR_migration/new_keystore//
ewallet_2021022820272947.p12

copying +DATA/QUESTPR/WALLET/ewallet_2021022820334986_keystore.
p12 -> /u01/software/migration/TEXAPR_migration/new_keystore//
ewallet_2021022820334986_keystore.p12

ASMCMD> exit
```

Next, we can copy the wallet files from the primary database to the physical standby database server using the scp command, as follows:

```
[oracle@virtual-19crac1 new_keystore]$ scp command* oracle@virtual-
dr-19crac1.localdomain:/u01/software/migration/TEXAPR_migration/new_
keystore/
```

Once the wallet files copied to Physical standby database server, in the Standby database server we have to copy the wallet keys from the local file system to ASM, as follows:

```
[oracle@virtual-dr-19crac1~] asmcmd

ASMCMD> cp /u01/software/migration/QUESTPR_newkeystore/* .

copying /u01/software/migration/QUESTPR_newkeystore/cwallet.sso ->
+DATA/QUESTDR/WALLET/cwallet.sso

copying /u01/software/migration/QUESTPR_newkeystore/cwallet.sso.bak ->
+DATA/QUESTDR/WALLET/cwallet.sso.bak

copying /u01/software/migration/QUESTPR_newkeystore/ewallet.p12 ->
+DATA/QUESTDR/WALLET/ewallet.p12

copying /u01/software/migration/QUESTPR_newkeystore/
ewallet_2021022817531509.p12 -> +DATA/QUESTDR/WALLET/
ewallet_2021022817531509.p12

copying /u01/software/migration/QUESTPR_newkeystore/
ewallet_2021022820272947.p12 -> +DATA/QUESTDR/WALLET/
ewallet_2021022820272947.p12

copying /u01/software/migration/QUESTPR_newkeystore/
ewallet_2021022820334986_keystore.p12 -> +DATA/QUESTDR/WALLET/
ewallet_2021022820334986_keystore.p12

ASMCMD>
```

Once the keystore is copied, we have to restart the standby container standby, **questpr**, as follows:

```
[oracle@virtual-dr-19crac1 dbs]$ srvctl status database -d questdr
Instance questdr1 is not running on node virtual-dr-19crac1
Instance questdr2 is not running on node virtual-dr-19crac2

[oracle@virtual-dr-19crac1 dbs]$ srvctl start database -d questdr
[oracle@virtual-dr-19crac1 dbs]$ srvctl status database -d questdr
Instance questdr1 is running on node virtual-dr-19crac1
Instance questdr2 is running on node virtual-dr-19crac2

SQL>@/home/oracle/rac_database_info.sql

DATABASE_HOST        DB_NAME    DATABASE_ROLE     OPEN_MODE   STARTUP_TIME
------------------   ---------  ----------------  ----------  -----------
virtual-dr-19crac1   questdr1   PHYSICAL STANDBY  MOUNTED     27-FEB-21
virtual-dr-19crac2   questdr2   PHYSICAL STANDBY  MOUNTED     27-FEB-21
```

If the **dataguard** broker is already enabled by this time, it will start applying the redo logs in the standby database. We can also monitor the alert log at the container standby database, **questdr** and we can see the messages for the **pdb** database, **texadr**. You will see the lines for each file as the tablespaces are processed, as follows:

```
TEXAPR(4):Recovery scanning directory +DATA/QUESTDR/
BC47838E9CFF0F34E053011478C051BB/DATAFILE for any matching files

TEXAPR(4):Recovery created file +DATA/QUESTDR/
BC47838E9CFF0F34E053011478C051BB/DATAFILE/system.257.1066128787

TEXAPR(4):Datafile 15 added to flashback set

TEXAPR(4):Successfully added datafile 15 to media recovery

TEXAPR(4):Datafile #15: '+DATA/QUESTDR/BC47838E9CFF0F34E053011478C051BB/
DATAFILE/system.257.1066128787'

TEXAPR(4):Recovery created file +DATA/QUESTDR/
BC47838E9CFF0F34E053011478C051BB/DATAFILE/sysaux.256.1066128795

TEXAPR(4):Datafile 16 added to flashback set

TEXAPR(4):Successfully added datafile 16 to media recovery

TEXAPR(4):Datafile #16: '+DATA/QUESTDR/BC47838E9CFF0F34E053011478C051BB/
DATAFILE/sysaux.256.1066128795'
```

After the process is completed, and once the standby database gets in sync with the primary database, we can verify that there are no errors or missing data files, as follows:

First, in the **Container primary database**, check the datafiles information.:

```
SQL>@/home/oracle/rac_database_info.sql

DATABASE_HOST      DB_NAME    DATABASE_ROLE     OPEN_MODE     STARTUP_TIME
----------------   --------   ---------------   ----------    ------------
virtual-19crac1    questpr1   PRIMARY           READ WRITE    27-FEB-21
virtual-19crac2    questpr2   PRIMARY           READ WRITE    27-FEB-21


SQL> show pdbs

CON_ID      CON_NAME     OPEN MODE     RESTRICTED
---------   ---------    ----------    ------------
      2     PDB$SEED     READ ONLY     NO
      3     TEXAPR       READ WRITE    NO

SQL> alter session set container=TEXAPR;
Session altered.

SQL> select file_name from dba_data_files;
-----------------------------------------------
+DATA/TEXADR/DATAFILE/sysaux.256.1066128795
+DATA/TEXADR/DATAFILE/undotbs2.287.1066128799
+DATA/TEXADR/DATAFILE/undotbs1.288.1066128797
+DATA/TEXAPR/DATAFILE/users.286.1066128799
+DATA/TEXADR/DATAFILE/system.257.1066128787
5 rows selected.
```

In the **Container physical standby database**, check the datafiles information and compare it with the primary datafiles info.:

We can open the physical standby database in the **READ ONLY** mode and we must open the pluggable database (**texapr**) in the **READ ONLY** mode as follows:

```
SQL>@/home/oracle/rac_database_info.sql

DATABASE_HOST       DB_NAME    OPEN_MODE                                     STARTUP_TIME
----------------    --------   ------------------------------------------   ------------
virtual-dr-19crac1  questdr1   PHYSICAL STANDBY READ ONLY WITH APPLY 27-FEB-21
virtual-dr-19crac2  questdr2   PHYSICAL STANDBY READ ONLY WITH APPLY 27-FEB-21


SQL> show pdbs
CON_ID CON_NAME              OPEN MODE    RESTRICTED
---------  ----------------  ----------   ------------
      2 PDB$SEED             READ ONLY    NO
      3 TEXAPR               MOUNTED

SQL> alter pluggable database all open read only;
Pluggable database altered.
```

```
SQL>  show pdbs

CON_ID CON_NAME          OPEN MODE  RESTRICTED
--------- -------------   ----------  ------------
        2 PDB$SEED        READ ONLY  NO
        3 TEXAPR          READ ONLY
SQL> select file_name from dba_data_files;

FILE_NAME
-----------------------------------------------------------------------
+DATA/QUESTDR/BC47838E9CFF0F34E053011478C051BB/DATAFILE/
users.286.1066128799
+DATA/QUESTDR/BC47838E9CFF0F34E053011478C051BB/DATAFILE/
undotbs2.287.1066128799
+DATA/QUESTDR/BC47838E9CFF0F34E053011478C051BB/DATAFILE/
undotbs1.288.1066128797
+DATA/QUESTDR/BC47838E9CFF0F34E053011478C051BB/DATAFILE/
sysaux.256.1066128795
+DATA/QUESTDR/BC47838E9CFF0F34E053011478C051BB/DATAFILE/
system.257.1066128787
5 rows selected.
```

From the preceding output, you can see the directory that we created with the **guide** name in it. The standby database uses this directory and with all the aliases that we have created in our earlier step, it keeps the standby database in sync with the primary database.

Let's perform a quick test. Let's create a table in the primary pluggable database, **texapr** and see if it's being replicated to the standby pluggable database.

Login to the **Container primary database** and connect to the pluggable database, texapr and create a table as follows:

```
SQL> show pdbs

CON_ID CON_NAME          OPEN MODE   RESTRICTED
---------- -------        ---------   ----------
        2 PDB$SEED        READ ONLY   NO
        3 TEXAPR          READ WRITE  NO

SQL> alter session set container=TEXAPR;
Session altered.

SQL> create table post_upgrade (name varchar(100)) tablespace TBS_NAME;

SQL> insert into post_upgrade values  ('Successfully upgraded 121
database to 19c and plugged into 19c Container');
1 row created.
```

```
SQL> commit;
Commit complete.

SQL> alter session set container=CDB$ROOT;
Session altered.

SQL> alter system switch all logfile;
System altered.
```

Now login to container **physical standby database** and connect the pluggable database, texapr and check if the table got replicated.

SQL>@/home/oracle/rac_database_info.sql

```
DATABASE_HOST        DB_NAME   OPEN_MODE                               STARTUP_TIME
-----------------    --------  ------------------------------------    ---------
virtual-dr-19crac1   questdr1  PHYSICAL STANDBY READ ONLY WITH APPLY   27-FEB-21
virtual-dr-19crac2   questdr2  PHYSICAL STANDBY READ ONLY WITH APPLY   27-FEB-21

SQL> alter session set container=TEXAPR;
Session altered.


SQL> select * from post_upgrade;
NAME
----------------------------------------------------------------------
Successfully upgraded 121 database to 19c and plugged into 19c Container
```

As we can see from the above output that the table is replicated from the primary pdb to the standby pdb proving that the standby container database is in sync with the primary container database.

Fallback method

As mentioned earlier in this chapter, for fallback, we just need to drop the 19c (19.9) pluggable database and restore the non-cdb from 12.1 home. At the high level, you can complete the following steps:

1. Drop the pluggable database, **texapr**.

2. We can connect to the **Container** database, **questpr** and stop the **pdb** database, **texapr** and then drop it. We must do the same thing for the standby **pdb** database as well, as follows:

    ```
    SQL> alter pluggable database texapr close instances=all;
      Pluggable database altered
    ```

    ```
    SQL> drop pluggable database texapr including datafiles;
    Pluggable database dropped.
    ```

3. Restore the database from the 12.1 home.

    We can restore the backup that we took from before starting the upgrade activity. In our case, we can use the following **RMAN** command from the 12.1 home, and it will restore the database with the backup which we took before starting the upgrade (If you have any **RMAN** restore commands that you have already tested in your environment, you can use those scripts too.):

```
RMAN>
run
{
startup nomount;
RESTORE CONTROLFILE FROM /u01/app/software/19cupgrade/texapr_
upgrade/backup_before_upgrade/DATA_CONTROL_%d_%Y%M%D_%s-%p-%t'";
alter database mount;
restore database;
set until time="to_date('26022021 12:56:00','ddmmyyyy
hh24:mi:ss')"; (use appropriate backup time)
recover database;

}
```

Once the restore completes, you must open the database reset logs, as follows:

```
RMAN> alter database open resetlogs;
Statement processed
```

Once we restore the primary database, we will also have to rebuild the 12.1.0.2 physical standby database from the 12.1.0.2 primary database.

Known issues

Issue-1

We have upgraded the Oracle 12c (12.1.0.2) non-container database to Oracle 19c (19.10.0) as a pluggable database in the container database with the TDE enabled. The Oracle 19c (19.10.0) container databases crashes with corruption with the error code **ORA-00600: internal error code, arguments: [kcbb_prepare_4], [3]**. We were not able to start the Oracle 19c (19.10.0) container database as it kept on crashing. This issue happened on Oracle Exadata (Oracle Linux flavor).

The following is the information from the database alert log:

```
""kcbb_prepare: encryption detected corruption that cannot be online
repaired (error code 3). Crashing the instance to avoid corrupting the
database.
Errors in file /u01/app/oracle/diag/rdbms/GREETCDB/GREETCDB2/trace/
GREETCDB2_dbw1_238621.trc (incident=269081) (PDBNAME=CDB$ROOT):
```

```
ORA-00600: internal error code, arguments: [kcbb_prepare_4], [3], [],
[], [], [], [], [], [], [], [], []
```

The incident details are at the following location:

```
/u01/app/oracle/diag/rdbms/GREETCDB/GREETCDB2/incident/incdir_269081/
GREETCDB2_dbw1_238621_i269081.trc"
```

Cause

Oracle confirmed that this is a new bug and the Oracle development team logged this following bug and created a new one-off patch for 19.10 version:

32103427; DBWN GETS ORA-00600 [KCBB_PREPARE_4] AFTER CRASH/MEDIA RECOVERY.

Solution

We have downloaded the following one-off patch and once we applied it, we were able to start the Oracle 19c (19.10.0) multitenant database without any issues. As of now, Oracle has released this one-off patch for Oracle Linux Server. This issue is fixed in 23.1 version.

Patch: **p32103427_1910000DBRU_Linux-x86-64.zip**

Issue-2

After the **19c** database upgrade, we started seeing the **ORA-28365: wallet is not open** error randomly in our **RAC** database. We have set the following parameters in the **os** profile which we will run before starting the Oracle **rac** database:

```
[oracle@virtual-19crac1 ~]$ cat /u01/app/oracle/profiles/profile.questpr

export ORACLE_UNQNAME=questpr
export TNS_ADMIN=/u01/app/oracle/product/12c/db_1/network/admin
export ORACLE_SID=questpr1
export ORACLE_BASE=/u01/app/oracle
export ORACLE_HOME=/u01/app/oracle/product/12c/db_1
export PATH=/bin:/usr/sbin:/usr/bin:/usr/ucb/:/usr/bin/X11:/usr/local/
bin:$ORACLE_HOME/bin:$ORACLE_BASE/jre/bin:$ORACLE_HOME/OPatch:.
[oracle@virtual-19crac1 ~]$

Note : In above example, questpr is the database name
'/u01/app/oracle/product/19.3.0/dbhome_1' is the database home
```

Cause

Even though we have set these parameters in the **os** parameter, we still need to set the same parameters in **srvctl** using the **srvctl setenv** command.

Solution

If we have the **TDE** setup for the **RAC** database, we have to setup the following parameters in **srvctl** and bounce the database for the **TDE** to work without any issues:

```
srvctl setenv database -d questpr -T «ORACLE_BASE=/u01/app/oracle»
srvctl setenv database -d questpr -T «ORACLE_HOME=/u01/app/oracle/
roduct/19.3.0/dbhome_1»
srvctl setenv database -d questpr -t «TNS_ADMIN=/u01/app/oracle/
product/19.3.0/dbhome_1/network/admin»
srvctl setenv database -d questpr -T «ORACLE_UNQNAME=QUESTPR»

Note : In above example, questpr is the database name
'/u01/app/oracle/product/19.3.0/dbhome_1' is the database home
```

Conclusion

In this chapter, we successfully upgraded the 12.1 non cdb primary database and its non-cdb physical standby database to 19.9.0. We also successfully downgraded the 19.9.0 non-cdb primary and its non-cdb physical standby database back to 12.1 using the Oracle provided scripts. We also saw how to handle the physical standby database, in case the size of the non-cdb physical standby database is big (size in TBs). We also saw how to handle the TDE keys when we migrate the non-cdb database as the pluggable database.

We did the exercise of upgrading and converting a non-cdb database as the **pdb** database in two steps. We can upgrade and convert the database to **pdb** in one step by using the **AutoUpgrade** command. The main advantage of doing this two-step process in one is that we can upgrade the database to 19c, and if at this stage for some reason, we decide to downgrade the database back to the source version, we will be able to that by just doing the flashback or the Oracle provided scripts. If everything looks good, we can then convert the database as **pdb**. But if we are upgrading and converting the database as **pdb** using a single step (which we will see in *Chapter 6, Upgrading and Converting 12c Non-CDB as 19c PDB (usingUsing AutoUpgrade)*), the only way to downgrade the database is to drop the database and restore the database using the source version database back. That being said, if you have hundreds of databases to upgrade and migrate as a pluggable database, you can use the single **AutoUpgrade** command to upgrade and convert the database as this will save a lot of time. In the next chapter '*Upgrading Oracle Multitenant Database from 12c/18c to 19c*', we will see how we can upgrade a multitenant container database along with one or all of its pluggable databases to 19c. .

Multiple choice questions

1. Do we have to upgrade the database first and then convert it to a pluggable database?

    a. Yes

    b. No

    c. May be

2. Oracle 19c comes with a default autoupgrade.jar file; is it good to use this or download the latest autoupgrade from mos?

    a. We can use it, but Oracle strongly recommends downloading the latest autoupgradeAU utility.

    b. No, we cannot use it.

3. When we migrate the non-cdb database as a pdb database, do we need to copy its TDE keys to the container database wallet location, even if they both are on the same servers?

    a. Yes

    b. No

    c. Not sure

Answers

1. b

2. a

3. a

Key terms

- 32103427; DBWN GETS ORA-00600 [KCBB_PREPARE_4] AFTER CRASH/MEDIA RECOVERY.

- Reusing the Source Standby Database Files When Plugging a PDB into the Primary Database of a Data Guard Configuration (Doc ID 2273829.1)

- "ORA-28365: wallet is not open"

CHAPTER 5

Upgrading Oracle Multitenant Database From 12c/18c to 19c

Introduction

In this chapter, we will see how we can upgrade the Oracle multitenant container database along with one or all of its pluggable databases from Oracle 12c (12.1.0.2) to Oracle 19c (19.9.0). In this chapter, we will demonstrate two scenarios. In the first scenario, we will upgrade an Oracle 12c (12.1.0.2) multitenant container database along with all of its pluggable databases to Oracle 19c (19.9.0), whereas, in the second scenario, we will upgrade just an Oracle 18c (18.3.0.0) pluggable database to Oracle 19c (19.9.0) without upgrading the 18c container database.

If you are not licensed for the Oracle Multitenant architecture, then you may have up to three **pluggable databases (PDBs)** in each container database at any given time. If you have a license for the Oracle Multitenant architecture, you can have up to 4096 pluggable databases.

Structure

In this chapter, we will cover the following topics:

- The high-level steps for scenario 1, where we will upgrade a 12.1.0.2 container database along with all of its pluggable databases to the 19c database using AutoUpgrade.

- Checking of the source and target setup environments used to demonstrate the database upgrade.

- Discussion and completion of all the pre-requisites steps required for the database upgrade.

- How to download the AutoUpgrade utility?

- Discussion and creation of the configuration file required by the AutoUpgrade tool for this upgrade.

- Running AutoUpgrade in the 'Analyze' mode to verify the database readiness and fixing any issues that can impact the database upgrade activity.

- Discussion on the AutoUpgrade log locations.

- Running the AutoUpgrade in the 'Deploy' mode to upgrade the 12.1.0.2 container database along with all its pluggable databases to 19c.

- Discussion on the post-upgrade checks.

- Upgrading of the physical standby database from 12.1.0.2 to 19c.

- Discussion and performance of the fall-back operation to downgrade the database back to its source version.

- Conversion of the upgraded 19c database from the non-container database to the pluggable database.

- Discussion on the steps for Scenario 2 to upgrade the 18c pluggable database to 19c.

- Checking of the target environment setup for this scenario.

- Running AutoUpgrade in the 'Analyze' mode to verify if the source pluggable database is ready to be upgraded.

- Discussion on the AutoUpgrade log locations.

- Running the AutoUpgrade in the 'Deploy' mode to upgrade the 18c pluggable database and plug it in the 19c container database.

- Discussion on a few known issues that can occur during the database upgrade or the database downgrade.

Objective

After studying this chapter, you will be able to upgrade the Oracle container database along with its pluggable databases to 19c using the AutoUpgrade utility. You will also be able to upgrade a single pluggable database from an 18c container database to a 19c container database. You will also get familiar with the different fallback options for downgrading an upgraded container database and an upgraded pluggable database back to its source version.

Scenarios demonstrated in this chapter

In this chapter, we will be testing the following two scenarios:

- **Scenario 1**: Upgrading the container database along with all the pluggable databases to the Oracle 19c container database.

- **Scenario 2**: Upgrading a single pluggable database from the source container database to target the Oracle 19c container database.

Scenario-1: Upgrading the container database along with all the pluggable databases to the Oracle 19c container database

For this scenario, we will upgrade a two-node RAC multitenant database along with one of its pluggable databases from version Oracle 12c (12.1.0.2) to Oracle 19c (19.9.0) using the AutoUpgrade utility (refer to *Figure 5.1*). We will also upgrade its physical standby database using the redo logs. We will also see how to handle the **transparent data encryption (TDE)** keys if the source database has the transparent data encryption enabled, as shown in *Figure 5.1*:

Figure 5.1: *Upgrading the 12.1.0.2 container database to 19.9.0 container database*

High-level steps that are performed as part of this upgrade activity

The following are the high-level steps that are performed as part of upgrading a 12.1.0.2 container database along with its pluggable databases to 19c:

1. Take a full back-up of the primary database.

2. Enable the flashback feature in the primary and the physical standby database.

3. Set the fast recovery area size to a higher value in both the primary and the physical standby database.

4. Purge the **recyclebin** as this will save time during the database upgrade and will help in reducing the downtime needed for the database upgrade.

5. Gather the dictionary statistics to the latest, as this will help the database upgrade to run faster.

6. Create a guaranteed restore point in the physical standby database.

7. Ensure that the physical standby database is in sync with the primary database before starting the database upgrade activity.

8. Disable the **dataguard** broker in both the primary and the physical standby database.

9. Shutdown the physical standby database.

10. Run the **AutoUpgrade** script in the **ANALYZE** mode in the primary and fix any required issues as identified by the AutoUpgrade tool.

11. Upgrade the primary database by running the AutoUpgrade tool in the **DEPLOY** mode.

12. Perform any post upgrade checks on the primary database.

13. Upgrade the physical standby database with the migrated redo data that it received from the primary database.

14. Enable the **dataguard** broker and perform a final check on both the primary and the physical standby database.

15. Perform any post upgrade steps for the physical standby database.

We created two scripts which we can use to check the current database configuration and the standby database lag. We will be using these following scripts throughout this chapter:

Script-1: The following script will pull the current database details like, the mode and the role of the database:

```
[oracle@virtual-19crac1] cat /home/oracle/rac_database_info.sql

SQL> set lines 200
SQL> col DATABASE_HOST for a30;
SQL> col HOST_NAME for a15;
SQL> col DATABASE_ROLE for a10
SQL> col OPEN_MODE for a10
SQL> col STARTUP_TIME for a20
SQL> SELECT i.HOST_NAME "DATABASE_HOST"  ,i.INSTANCE_NAME "DB_NAME",
     d.DATABASE_ROLE " DATABASE_ROLE",
     d.OPEN_MODE " OPEN_MODE ", STARTUP_TIME
     from GV$DATABASE d, gv$instance I
     where i.INST_ID=d.INST_ID;
```

Script-2: The following script will check the current lag on the standby database and display the standby database role and mode info as well:

```
[oracle@virtual-19crac1] cat /home/oracle/standby_database_lag.sql

SQL> set lines 200
SQL> col DATABASE_HOST for a30;
SQL> col HOST_NAME for a15;
SQL> col DATABASE_ROLE for a10
SQL> col OPEN_MODE for a10
SQL> col STARTUP_TIME for a20
SQL> SELECT i.HOST_NAME "DATABASE_HOST"  ,i.INSTANCE_NAME "DB_NAME",
     d.DATABASE_ROLE " DATABASE_ROLE",
     d.OPEN_MODE " OPEN_MODE ", STARTUP_TIME
     from GV$DATABASE d, gv$instance I
     where i.INST_ID=d.INST_ID;
SQL>select inst_id,process, status, thread#, sequence#, block#, blocks
from gv$managed_standby
where process='MRP0';

SQL>select a.thread#, (select max (sequence#)
    from v$archived_log
    where archived='YES' and thread#=a.thread#) archived,
    max(a. sequence#) applied, (select max(sequence#)
    from v$archived_log
    where archived='YES' and thread#=a.thread#)-max(a.sequence#)gap
    from v$archived_log a where a.applied='YES'
    group by a.thread# order by thread#;
```

Check the configuration of the primary database and the physical standby database

For this demonstration, we have the primary database environment and the standby database environment. For the primary environment, we have the Oracle 12.1.0.2 database binaries installed and patched with the April 2020 patch set update.

Setting up the source environment

The following are the source primary and the standby database versions along with the patch set information:

The source primary database version is as follows:

```
RAC nodes           : virtual-19crac1
                      virtual-19crac2
OS version          : Oracle Enterprise Linux 7.1 64 bit
Oracle Home         : /u01/app/oracle/product/12c/db_1
Database Version    : 12.1.0.2 with July 2020 Database Bundle Patch
Grid Version        : 19.9.0
[oracle@virtual-19crac1 admin]$ $ORACLE_HOME/OPatch/opatch lspatches
27487279;
28125601;
31136382;OCW PATCH SET UPDATE 12.1.0.2.200714 (31136382)
31001106;Database Bundle Patch : 12.1.0.2.200714 (31001106)
```

The primary database with the CDB and PDB information is as follows:

```
SQL> @/home/oracle/rac_database_info.sql
DATABASE_HOST      DB_NAME      DATABASE_ROLE    OPEN_MODE    STARTUP_TIME
-----------------  ----------   --------------   ----------   -------------
virtual-19crac2    tee12cdb1    PRIMARY          READ WRITE   15-MAR-21
virtual-19crac2    tee12cdb1    PRIMARY          READ WRITE   15-MAR-21

SQL> show pdbs
CON_ID CON_NAME        OPEN MODE   RESTRICTED
---------- --------    ----------  -----------
         2 PDB$SEED     READ ONLY   NO
         3 TRENDPDB     READ WRITE  NO
```

The source physical standby database version is as follows:

The physical standby database environment setup is the same as the source primary database. The following is our physical standby database configuration:

```
Cluster nodes        : virtual-dr-19crac1
                       virtual-dr-19crac2
OS version           : Oracle Enterprise Linux 7.1 64 bit
Oracle Home          : /u01/app/oracle/product/12c/db_1
Database Version     : 12.1.0.2 with July 2020 Database Bundle Patch
Grid Version         : 19.9.0
[oracle@virtual-19crac1 admin]$ $ORACLE_HOME/OPatch/opatch lspatches
27487279;
28125601;
31136382;OCW PATCH SET UPDATE 12.1.0.2.200714 (31136382)
31001106;Database Bundle Patch : 12.1.0.2.200714 (31001106)
```

The physical standby database with the CDB and PDB information is as follows:

```
SQL> @/home/oracle/rac_database_info.sql


DATABASE_HOST       DB_NAME       DATABASE_ROLE      OPEN_MODE   STARTUP_TIME
-----------------   -----------   ----------------   ---------   ------------
virtual-dr-19crac1  tee12cdr1     PHYSICAL STANDBY   MOUNTED     15-MAR-21
virtual-dr-19crac2  tee12cdr2     PHYSICAL STANDBY   MOUNTED     15-MAR-21

SQL> show pdbs

CON_ID CON_NAME         OPEN MODE   RESTRICTED
---------- --------     ---------   -----------
     2 PDB$SEED         MOUNTED
     3 TRENDPDB         MOUNTED
```

In the source database, we also have TDE enabled at the CDB and PDB level.

The following is the TDE information from the **container** database, **tee12cdb**:

```
SQL> select tablespace_name,encrypted from dba_tablespaces where
encrypted='YES' ;

TABLESPACE_NAME    ENCRYPTED
---------------    -----------
ENCRYPTED_TS       YES

SQL> select owner,table_name,TABLESPACE_NAME from dba_tables where
table_name='ENCRYPT';

OWNER   TABLE_NAME TABLESPACE_NAME
------  ---------- ---------------
SYS     ENCRYPT    ENCRYPTED_TS

SQL> select * from ENCRYPT;

NAME
------------------------------------------------------------------
```

This is from the encrypted tablespaces in the TEE12CDB CDB database

The following is the encrypted tablespace information from the pluggable database, **trendpdb**. We need to login to the container database and connect the pluggable database, as follows:

```
SQL> alter session set container=TRENDPDB;
Session altered.

SQL> show con_name;

CON_NAME
----------
TRENDPDB

SQL> select tablespace_name,encrypted from dba_tablespaces where
encrypted='YES' ;
TABLESPACE_NAME    ENCRYPTED
---------------    ---------
ENCRYPTED_TS       YES

SQL> select owner,table_name,TABLESPACE_NAME from dba_tables where
table_name='ENCRYPT';

OWNER       TABLE_NAME  TABLESPACE_NAME
----------  ----------  ---------------
SYS         ENCRYPT     ENCRYPTED_TS

SQL> select * from ENCRYPT;

NAME
------------------------------------------------------------------
```

This is from the encrypted tablespaces in the TRENDPDB pluggable database.

Setting up the target environment

We have installed Oracle 19c (19.3.0) on both the primary and the physical standby database servers and applied the October 2020 PSU on top of the 19.3.0 binaries. The following is the target primary database binary version and its patch set:

```
Cluster nodes     : virtual-19crac1
                    virtual-19crac2
OS version        : Oracle Enterprise Linux 7.1 64 bit
Oracle Home       : /u01/app/oracle/product/19c/db_1
Database Version  : 19.3.0.0 with October 2020 Database Bundle Patch
Grid Version      : 19.9.0
```

```
[oracle@virtual-19crac1 ~]$ $ORACLE_HOME/OPatch/opatch lspatches
31771877;Database Release Update : 19.9.0.0.201020 (31771877)
29585399;OCW RELEASE UPDATE 19.3.0.0.0 (29585399)
OPatch succeeded.
```

The following is the target physical standby database binary version and its patch set:

```
Cluster nodes        : virtual-dr-19crac1
                       virtual-dr-19crac2
OS version           : Oracle Enterprise Linux 7.1 64 bit
Oracle Home          : /u01/app/oracle/product/19c/db_1
Database Version     : 19.3.0.0 with October 2020 Database Bundle Patch
Grid Version         : 19.9.0
[oracle@virtual-dr-19crac1 ~]    $ORACLE_HOME/OPatch/opatch lspatches
31771877;Database Release Update : 19.9.0.0.201020 (31771877)
29585399;OCW RELEASE UPDATE 19.3.0.0.0 (29585399)
OPatch succeeded.
```

Pre-requisites

Check some of the pre-requisites and also a few upfront tasks that we can perform for the database upgrade.

Perform full backup of the primary source database

Before staring any database upgrade activity, always take a **FULL** level 0 **RMAN** backup of the source database. The following is a sample **rman** script that we can use to take the full level 0 backup of the primary source database (You can use your scripts that works for your environment.):

```
RMAN >
run
{
allocate channel ch1 device type disk format '/u01/19cupgrade/DATA_
L0_%d_%Y%M%D_%s-%p-%t';
allocate channel ch2 device type disk format '/u01/19cupgrade/DATA_
L0_%d_%Y%M%D_%s-%p-%t';
allocate channel ch3 device type disk format '/u01/19cupgrade/DATA_
L0_%d_%Y%M%D_%s-%p-%t';
allocate channel ch4 device type disk format '/u01/19cupgrade/DATA_
L0_%d_%Y%M%D_%s-%p-%t';
backup incremental level 0 database plus archivelog TAG='FULL_BACKUP_B4_
UPGRADE' format '/u01/19cupgrade/DATA_L0_%d_%Y%M%D_%s-%p-%t';
```

```
backup tag 'CONTROL_BACKUP_B4_UPGRADE' current controlfile format '/
u01/19cupgrade/DATA_CONTROL_%d_%Y%M%D_%s-%p-%t';
release channel ch1;
release channel ch2;
release channel ch3;
release channel ch4;
}
```

Enable the flashback feature in the primary source database

Ensure that the flashback is enabled in both the primary and the physical standby database. When we use the **AutoUpgrade** utility to upgrade the Oracle database, we need to have the flashback feature enabled in the database as the AutoUpgrade utility creates a guaranteed restore point before completing the upgrade process and the upgrade process will fail in the early stages if the flashback feature is not enabled.

Login to the primary source database and enable the flashback feature using the following SQL statement:

```
SQL> alter database flashback on;
Database altered.
```

Make sure that the flashback feature is enabled successfully, using the following SQL statement:

```
SQL> select name,db_unique_name,database_role,log_mode,force_
logging,flashback_on from gv$database;
```

NAME	DB_UNIQUE_NAME	DATABASE_ROLE	LOG_MODE	FORCE_LOGGING	FLASHBACK_ON
TEE12CDB	tee12cdb	PRIMARY	ARCHIVELOG	YES	YES
TEE12CDB	tee12cdb	PRIMARY	ARCHIVELOG	YES	YES

Enable the flashback feature in the source physical standby database

In order to enable the flashback feature in the physical standby database, we have to cancel the **managed recovery process** (**MRP**) and then enable the flashback and re-start the MRP. Login to the source physical standby database and run the following SQL statements:

```
SQL> alter database recover managed standby database cancel;
Database altered.

SQL> alter database flashback on;
Database altered.
```

```
SQL> alter database recover managed standby database using current
logfile disconnect;
Database altered.
```

Make sure that the flashback feature is enabled successfully using the following SQL statement in the source physical standby database:

```
SQL> select name,db_unique_name,database_role,log_mode,force_
logging,flashback_on from gv$database;
```

```
NAME       DB_UNIQUE_NAME  DATABASE_ROLE     LOG_MODE    FORCE_LOGGING  FLASHBACK_ON
---------  --------------  ----------------  ----------  -----------    -----------
TEE12CDB   tee12cdr        PHYSICAL STANDBY  ARCHIVELOG  YES            YES
TEE12CDB   tee12cdr        PHYSICAL STANDBY  ARCHIVELOG  YES            YES
```

Ensure enough space is available in Fast Recovery Area (FRA)

Ensure that we have enough free space in the fast recovery area, and that we the set recovery destination size to a sufficient number as we need the recovery logs until we change the compatible parameter to 19.0.0 after the upgrade. Also, the FRA will store all the flashback logs which we would need in case we have to downgrade the Oracle database back to Oracle 12c (12.1.0.2) after the upgrade using the **flashback** method. Check and set the **db_recovery_file_dest_size** parameter to a higher value. We need to set this parameter with a higher value in both the primary and the physical standby database (that is, **12c** databases). In our case, we are setting this parameter value to 20G, as follows:

```
SQL> show parameter recovery
NAME                                TYPE         VALUE
----------------------------------- -----------  --------------------
db_recovery_file_dest               string       +DATA1
db_recovery_file_dest_size          big integer  4506M
recovery_parallelism                integer      0
```

```
SQL> alter system set db_recovery_file_dest_size=20G scope=both sid='*';
System altered.
```

```
SQL> show parameter recovery
NAME                                TYPE         VALUE
----------------------------------- -----------  --------------
db_recovery_file_dest               string       +DATA1
db_recovery_file_dest_size          big integer  20G
recovery_parallelism                integer      0
```

Purge recyclebin

Check the **recyclebin** and purge it; in some cases, it might take more time if we have too many objects in the **recyclebin**. So, it's always a good idea to purge the recycle bin before starting the upgrade process as this can significantly reduce the overall time taken for the database upgrade. It might be a good idea if we can check this well ahead of time and purge the **recyclebin** in the source primary database. If the **recyclebin** is having too many objects, sometimes it might even take a minimum of two hours to get them purged, which will significantly increase the downtime required for the database upgrade.

Let's look at the following steps:

1. Check the object count in the **recyclebin**, as follows:

```
SQL> select count(*)  from recyclebin;
```

2. Purge the recycle bin using the following SQL statement:

```
SQL> purge dba_recyclebin;
DBA Recyclebin purged.
```

3. Re-check the object count in the **recyclebin**, as follows:

```
SQL> select count(*)  from recyclebin;
```

Gather the dictionary statistics

It's always good to collect the dictionary statistics before starting the database upgrade process. Having good statistics on the dictionary tables and fixed objects can help the database upgrade to run faster, and thus help in reducing the overall downtime required for the database upgrade.

We can use the following SQL statement to check when the dictionary stats were last collected:

```
SQL> SELECT OPERATION, to_char(MAX(END_TIME),'DD-MON-YY hh24:mi') LATEST
     FROM dba_optstat_operations
     where OPERATION
     in ('gather_fixed_objects_stats','gather_dictionary_stats')
     group by operation;


OPERATION                             LATEST
------------------------------------- ---------------
gather_fixed_objects_stats            14-MAR-21 10:10
gather_dictionary_stats               15-MAR-21 08:34
```

We can gather the dictionary statistics using the following statements:

```
SQL> EXECUTE DBMS_STATS.GATHER_DICTIONARY_STATS;
```

```
PL/SQL procedure successfully completed.

SQL> EXECUTE DBMS_STATS.GATHER_FIXED_OBJECTS_STATS;
PL/SQL procedure successfully completed.
```

Creating GRP in physical standby database

Since we will downgrade the database using the **flashback** method, we must create the guaranteed restore points for this purpose. In the primary database, the **AutoUpgrade** process will create the guaranteed restore point before it starts the database upgrade, but in the physical standby database, we need to create the guaranteed restore point manually. As mentioned in the earlier chapters, it is very important that we create a guaranteed restore point in the physical standby database. However, before starting the upgrade process in the primary database, if we do not create the restore point in physical standby database first, we might encounter issues while downgrading the physical standby database and we might end up rebuilding the physical standby database after downgrading the primary database; so, ensure that you create the guaranteed restore point in the physical standby database first.

Before creating the guaranteed restore point, ensure that both the primary database and the physical standby databases are in sync. Once they are in the sync state, we can stop the log shipping from the primary database to the physical standby database. We can defer the log shipping on the primary database using either the SQL command or the data guard broker environment.

If you are not using the data guard broker, then we can cancel the log shipping and the managed recover process on the physical standby database using the following SQL commands:

On the primary database, defer the log shipping as follows:

```
SQL> alter system set log_archive_dest_state_2='DEFER' scope=both
sid='*';
System altered.
```

On the physical standby database, cancel the MRP process as follows:

```
SQL> Alter database recover managed standby database cancel;
Database altered.
```

If we have the data guard broker set up in the primary database, we can disable the log shipping and redo applying by completing the following steps:

1. Login to the primary database, as follows:

   ```
   SQL> ALTER SYSTEM SET DG_BROKER_START=TRUE;
   System altered.
   ```

2. Login to the **dataguard** broker of the primary database, as follows:

```
[oracle@virtual-19crac1 prechecks]$

dgmgrl
DGMGRL for Linux: Version 12.1.0.2.0 - 64bit Production
Copyright (c) 2000, 2009, Oracle. All rights reserved.
Welcome to DGMGRL, type "help" for information.
DGMGRL> connect sys
Password:
Connected.
DGMGRL>
```

3. Enable the configuration as it has been disabled previously, as follows:

```
DGMGRL> enable configuration
Enabled.
```

4. Disable the log shipping on the primary database and log applying on the standby database as follows:

```
DGMGRL> edit database tee12cdb set state = 'TRANSPORT-OFF';
Succeeded.
```

```
DGMGRL> edit database tee12cdr set state = 'APPLY-OFF';
Succeeded.
```

Once the MRP is cancelled, we can create the guaranteed restore point as follows:

```
SQL> create restore point standby_before_19c_upgrade guarantee flashback
database;
Restore point created.
```

Enable the log shipping back in the primary and start the MRP in the physical standby database, as follows.

On the primary database, enable the log shipping as follows:

```
SQL> alter system set log_archive_dest_state_2='ENABLE' scope=both
sid='*';
System altered.
```

On the physical standby database, start the MRP process as follows:

```
SQL> alter database recover managed standby database disconnect from
session;
Database altered.
```

If we have the dataguard broker configured in the primary database, we can enable the log shipping on the primary database and start the redo apply process on the physical standby database as follows:

1. Login to the primary database as follows:

```
SQL> ALTER SYSTEM SET DG_BROKER_START=TRUE;
```

```
System altered.
```

2. Login to the **dataguard** broker of the primary database, as follows:

```
[oracle@virtual-19crac1 prechecks]$

dgmgrl
DGMGRL for Linux: Version 12.1.0.2.0 - 64bit Production
Copyright (c) 2000, 2009, Oracle. All rights reserved.
Welcome to DGMGRL, type "help" for information.
DGMGRL> connect sys
Password:
Connected.

DGMGRL> edit database tee12cdb set state = 'TRANSPORT-ON';
Succeeded.

DGMGRL> edit database tee12cdr set state = 'APPLY-ON';
Succeeded.
```

Upgrading the Application Express (APEX)

If the source database has the Oracle Application Express (APEX) installed, we can upgrade it upfront, as the APEX upgrade does not depend on the database upgrade. We can refer to the following MOS note for the APEX upgrade. We can also complete this step upfront to save time during the actual upgrade process.

For more details, refer to *Master Note for Oracle Application Express (APEX) Upgrades (Doc ID 1088970.1)*.

Upgrading the database Oracle 12c (12.1.0.2) to Oracle 19c (19.9.0)

In this section, we will upgrade both the primary database along with all of its pluggable database from 12.1.0.2 to 19.9.0 version. We will also upgrade the standby database. Let's start the process by completing the pre-upgrade steps.

Disable the dataguard broker

We have to disable the **dataguard** broker before the database upgrade and enable it after the upgrade is complete. Ensure that the physical standby database is in sync with the primary database and then disable the **dataguard** broker.

For the source primary database, ensure that the physical standby database is in sync. In the primary database, switch the logfiles and take a snapshot of the current archive log files information, as follows:

```
SQL> @/home/oracle/rac_database_info.sql
DATABASE_HOST       DB_NAME    DATABASE_ROLE   OPEN_MODE   STARTUP_TIME
-----------------   ---------- --------------- ----------  ------------
virtual-19crac2     tee12cdb1  PRIMARY         READ WRITE  15-MAR-21
virtual-19crac2     tee12cdb1  PRIMARY         READ WRITE  15-MAR-21
SQL> alter system switch all logfile;
System altered.
SQL> alter system switch all logfile;
System altered.

SQL> archive log list;
Database log mode              Archive Mode
Automatic archival             Enabled
Archive destination            USE_DB_RECOVERY_FILE_DEST
Oldest online log sequence     29
Next log sequence to archive   30
Current log sequence           30
SQL>
```

For the source physical standby database, check whether the physical standby database is receiving the redo logs from the primary database and whether the MRP process is applying the logs to keep it in sync with the primary database. We can check this by using the following SQL statements:

```
SQL> @/home/oracle/rac_database_info.sql

DATABASE_HOST       DB_NAME    DATABASE_ROLE     OPEN_MODE  STARTUP_TIME
-----------------   ---------- ---------------   --------   ------------
virtual-dr-19crac1  tee12cdr1  PHYSICAL STANDBY  MOUNTED    15-MAR-21
virtual-dr-19crac2  tee12cdr2  PHYSICAL STANDBY  MOUNTED    15-MAR-21

INST_ID  PROCESS  STATUS        THREAD#  SEQUENCE#   BLOCK#  BLOCKS
-------  -------- ------------- -------- ----------  ------  --------
    1    MRP0     APPLYING_LOG  1        33          6154    102400

THREAD#   ARCHIVED    APPLIED     GAP
--------- ----------  ----------  ----------
    1       33          32          1
    2       14          14          0
```

As we can see, the physical standby database is in sync with the primary database.

Disable the dataguard broker configuration.

We can check the current configuration and disable the broker configuration, as follows:

```
[oracle@virtual-19crac1]$ dgmgrl
```

```
DGMGRL for Linux: Version 12.1.0.2.0 - 64bit Production
Copyright (c) 2000, 2009, Oracle. All rights reserved.
Welcome to DGMGRL, type "help" for information.
DGMGRL> connect sys
Password:
Connected.
DGMGRL>

DGMGRL> show configuration
       Configuration - tee12cdb_bg
         Protection Mode: MaxPerformance
         Members:
         tee12cdb - Primary database
           tee12cdr - Physical standby database
       Fast-Start Failover: DISABLED
       Configuration Status:
       SUCCESS   (status updated 9 seconds ago)
DGMGRL>
```

Disable the Fast start failover if it is enabled

Fast start failover (**FSFO**) is a feature which allows the **dataguard** broker to failover a failed primary database to one of the configured physical standby database. If it is enabled, we can disable it as follows:

```
DGMGRL>DISABLE FAST_START FAILOVER;
```

We can now disable the configuration and re-verify the broker configuration. When we run the following command, it will disable the broker's active management of the databases in the Oracle data guard configuration:

```
DGMGRL> DISABLE CONFIGURATION;
Disabled.
DGMGRL> SHOW CONFIGURATION;
 Configuration - tee12cdb_bg
       Protection Mode: MaxPerformance
       Members:
       tee12cdb - Primary database
         tee12cdr - Physical standby database
     Fast-Start Failover: DISABLED
     Configuration Status:
 DISABLED
```

Stop the data guard broker (DMON) process in the primary database

We can disable the **dataguard** broker in the primary database by setting the **DG_BROKER_START** parameter to false. Check the following:

```
SQL> @/home/oracle/rac_database_info.sql
DATABASE_HOST      DB_NAME      DATABASE_ROLE   OPEN_MODE    STARTUP_TIME
-----------------  -----------  --------------  -----------  ------------
virtual-19crac2    tee12cdb1    PRIMARY         READ WRITE   15-MAR-21
virtual-19crac2    tee12cdb1    PRIMARY         READ WRITE   15-MAR-21

SQL> show parameter broker
NAME                         TYPE         VALUE
-----------------------      -----------  -------------------------------
dg_broker_config_file1       string       +DATAC1/tee12cdb/dr1tee12cdb.dat
dg_broker_config_file2       string       +DATAC1/tee12cdb/dr2tee12cdb.dat
dg_broker_start              boolean      TRUE
```

Stop the data guard broker process as follows:

```
SQL> ALTER SYSTEM SET DG_BROKER_START=FALSE;
System altered.

SQL> show parameter DG_BROKER_START

NAME                         TYPE         VALUE
-----------------------      -----------  -------------------------------
dg_broker_config_file1       string       +DATAC1/tee12cdb/dr1tee12cdb.dat
dg_broker_config_file2       string       +DATAC1/tee12cdb/dr2tee12cdb.dat
dg_broker_start              boolean      FALSE
```

Backup DB broker configuration files for primary database

It's always a good idea to back up the broker configuration files. In our case, we have these files in ASM; we will login to the ASM instance and make a copy of the broker configuration files, as follows:

```
[oracle@virtual-19crac1]$. oraenv
ORACLE_SID = [oracle] ? +ASM1
The Oracle base has been set to /u01/app/oracle
[oracle@virtual-19crac1]$ asmcmd
ASMCMD>

ASMCMD> cp +DATAC1/tee12cdb/dr1tee12cdb.dat +DATAC1/tee12cdb/
dr1tee12cdb.dat.bak
Copying +DATAC1/tee12cdb/dr1tee12cdb.dat +DATAC1/tee12cdb/dr1tee12cdb.
```

```
dat.bak
ASMCMD> cp +DATAC1/tee12cdb/dr2tee12cdb.dat +DATAC1/tee12cdb/
dr2tee12cdb.dat.bak

Copying +DATAC1/tee12cdb/dr2tee12cdb.dat +DATAC1/tee12cdb/dr2tee12cdb.
dat.bak
```

This completes the steps for disabling the broker on the source primary database. Let's do the same in the physical standby database, and since we have already disabled the **dataguard** broker configuration from the primary database, we just need to stop the data guard broker (**DMON**) process in the physical standby database, as follows:

```
SQL> @/home/oracle/rac_database_info.sql


DATABASE_HOST       DB_NAME     DATABASE_ROLE      OPEN_MODE   STARTUP_TIME
---------------     ---------   ----------------   ---------   -----------
virtual-dr-19crac1  tee12cdr1   PHYSICAL STANDBY   MOUNTED     15-MAR-21
virtual-dr-19crac2  tee12cdr2   PHYSICAL STANDBY   MOUNTED     15-MAR-21


SQL> SHOW PARAMETER DG_BROKER

NAME                      TYPE          VALUE
----------------------    -----------   -------------------------------
dg_broker_config_file1    string        +DATAC1/TEE12CDR/dr1tee12cdr.dat
dg_broker_config_file2    string        +DATAC1/TEE12CDR/dr2tee12cdr.dat
dg_broker_start           boolean       TRUE
```

Stop the data guard broker process as follows:

```
SQL> ALTER SYSTEM SET DG_BROKER_START=FALSE;
System altered.

SQL> SHOW PARAMETER DG_BROKER

NAME                      TYPE          VALUE
----------------------    -----------   -------------------------------
dg_broker_config_file1    string        +DATAC1/TEE12CDR/dr1tee12cdr.dat
dg_broker_config_file2    string        +DATAC1/TEE12CDR/dr2tee12cdr.dat
dg_broker_start           boolean       FALSE
```

Backup the dataguard configuration files of the physical standby database

Backup the data guard broker configuration files of the physical standby database. Since our broker configuration files are in ASM, login to the **asm** instance and copy the files and take a backup of the config files, as follows:

```
[oracle@virtual-dr-19crac1 ~]$ . oraenv
```

```
ORACLE_SID = [oracle] ? +ASM1
The Oracle base has been set to /u01/app/oracle
[oracle@virtual-dr-19crac1 ~]$ asmcmd

ASMCMD> cp +DATAC1/TEE12CDR/dr1tee12cdr.dat +DATAC1/TEE12CDR/
dr1tee12cdr.dat.bak
Copying +DATAC1/TEE12CDR/dr1tee12cdr.dat +DATAC1/TEE12CDR/dr1tee12cdr.
dat.bak

ASMCMD> cp +DATAC1/TEE12CDR/dr2tee12cdr.dat +DATAC1/TEE12CDR/
dr2tee12cdr.dat.bak
Copying +DATAC1/TEE12CDR/dr2tee12cdr.dat +DATAC1/TEE12CDR/dr2tee12cdr.
dat.bak
```

This completes the step for disabling and stopping the data guard broker on both the primary and the physical standby database.

Working directories

Create a staging directory with the primary database name and we will use this directory as the working directory to save all the required log files, as follows:

```
mkdir -p /u01/software/upgrade/tee12cdb
```

Copy the required Oracle database configuration files

We have to copy the Oracle configuration files from the source primary database Oracle 12c (12.1.0.2) to Oracle 19c (19.9.0) database home.

Network files

For the network related files, complete the following steps:

1. Add the source database TNS entry in the **tnsnames.ora** file of the Oracle 19c (19.9.0) database home.

2. Take a backup of the current **tnsnames.ora** file in the **19c** database home, as follows:

    ```
    [oracle@virtual-19crac1 ~]$ cd /u01/app/oracle/product/19c/db_1/
    network/admin
    [oracle@virtual-19crac1 ~]$ cp tnsnames.ora tnsnames.ora.March16
    ```

    Now, add the primary and the standby database entry to the 19c tnsnames.ora file, as follows:

    ```
    [oracle@virtual-19crac1 ~]$ vi tnsnames.ora

    TEE12CDB =
      (DESCRIPTION =
    ```

```
      (ADDRESS = (PROTOCOL = TCP)(HOST = virtual-19crac-scan)(PORT
  = 1521))
    (CONNECT_DATA =
      (SERVER = DEDICATED)
      (SERVICE_NAME = tee12cdb)
    )
  )

TEE12CDR =
  (DESCRIPTION =
    (ADDRESS = (PROTOCOL = TCP)(HOST = virtual-dr-19crac-scan)
(PORT = 1521))
    (CONNECT_DATA =
      (SERVER = DEDICATED)
      (SERVICE_NAME = tee12cdr)
    )
  )
```

Checking sqlnet.ora file entries

Since we have the encryption enabled in the source primary database, we also need to check whether the **sqlnet.ora** file in the 19.9.0 has the correct wallet location. If the 19c home doesn't have it, we can create it. We need to do this in all the nodes of the primary and the physical standby database, as follows:

```
vi /u01/app/oracle/product/19c/db_1/network/admin/sqlnet.ora

ENCRYPTION_WALLET_LOCATION=
  (SOURCE=
    (METHOD=FILE)
    (METHOD_DATA=
    (DIRECTORY=+DATAC1/$ORACLE_UNQNAME/WALLET)
  )
)
```

Primary database initialization parameter (pfile/spfile) files

Copy the primary database **pfile** and **spfile** files from the 12.1.0.2 to the 19c DB home. We have to complete this step in all the nodes of the primary and the standby database clusters, as follows:

```
[oracle@virtual-19crac1 ~]$ cp /u01/app/oracle/product/12c/db_1/
dbs/*tee12*ora  /u01/app/oracle/product/19c/db_1/dbs/
```

Password files

The password file is in the **dbs** folder; we can copy it to the Oracle 19c (19.9.0) **dbs** folder, as follows:

```
[oracle@virtual-19crac1 ~]$ cp /u01/app/oracle/product/12c/db_1/
dbs/*orapw*tee12*  /u01/app/oracle/product/19c/db_1/dbs/
```

Check the INVALID objects' counts in the primary database

It's always a good idea to take a snapshot of the invalid objects' count before starting the database upgrade process.

For the source primary database, complete the following steps:

1. First run the **utlrp** script to compile any **INVALID** objects and then take a count of the invalid objects, so that we can compare the count after the database upgrade, as follows:

   ```
   SQL> @$ORACLE_HOME/rdbms/admin/utlrp
   ```

   ```
   SQL> select count(*) from dba_objects where status='INVALID';
   ```

2. Let's take the count of the invalid objects in the **SYS** and **SYSTEM** schemas, as follows:

   ```
   SQL> spool /u01/software/upgrade/tee12cdb/pre-upgrade_SYS_SYSTEM_
   invalid_Objects.log
   ```

   ```
   SQL> SELECT i.HOST_NAME "DATABASE_HOST" ,
        i.INSTANCE_NAME "DB_NAME", d.DATABASE_ROLE " DATABASE_ROLE",
        d.OPEN_MODE " OPEN_MODE ", STARTUP_TIME
        from GV$DATABASE d, gv$instance i
        where i.INST_ID=d.INST_ID;
   ```

   ```
   SQL> select owner,object_name,object_type,status
        from dba_objects
        where status='INVALID' and owner in ('SYS','SYSTEM')
        order by owner;
   spool off;
   ```

3. Next, we can take the invalid object count for the non-sys and the non-system schemas, as follows:

   ```
   SQL> spool /u01/software/upgrade/tee12cdb/pre-upgrade_non-SYS_
   invalid_objects.log
   ```

   ```
   SQL> SELECT i.HOST_NAME "DATABASE_HOST" ,
   ```

```
        i.INSTANCE_NAME "DB_NAME", d.DATABASE_ROLE " DATABASE_ROLE",
        d.OPEN_MODE " OPEN_MODE ", STARTUP_TIME
        from GV$DATABASE d, gv$instance i
        where i.INST_ID=d.INST_ID;
SQL> select count(*) from dba_objects
     where status='INVALID' and owner not in ('SYS','SYSTEM');
SQL> select owner,object_type,count(*)
     from dba_objects
     where status='INVALID' and owner not in ('SYS','SYSTEM')
     group by owner,object_type order by owner;

SQL> select owner,object_name,object_type,status
     from dba_objects
     where status='INVALID' and owner not in ('SYS','SYSTEM')
     order by owner ;
spool off;
```

4. Check if the spool files got created. We can use this information to compare it with the post-upgrade invalid object count that we will be taking after the database upgrade, as follows:

```
[oracle@virtual-19crac1 tee12cdb]$      ls -ltr
total 12
-rw-r--r-- 1 oracle oinstall  323 Mar 16 13:02 preupgrade_
invalid_object_count.log
-rw-r--r-- 1 oracle oinstall 1656 Mar 16 13:02 pre-upgrade_SYS_
SYSTEM_invalid_Objects.log
-rw-r--r-- 1 oracle oinstall 2383 Mar 16 13:02 pre-upgrade_non-
SYS_invalid_objects.log
[oracle@virtual-19crac1 tee12cdb]$ pwd
/u01/software/upgrade/tee12cdb
```

For testing purposes, in the primary database, let's create a table called **before_upgrade** just to crosscheck after the upgrade to see if it comes to the physical standby database confirming that the upgrade is successful.

Login to the primary database and create the test table as follows:

```
SQL> Create table BEFORE_UPGRADE (NAME Varchar(30));
Table created.

SQL> insert into BEFORE_UPGRADE values ('Table Before Upgrade');
1 row created.

SQL> commit;
Commit complete.
```

Download the latest AutoUpgrade tool

As mentioned earlier, Oracle strongly recommends downloading the latest version and using it instead of the default one that comes with Oracle 19c. We can download the latest AutoUpgrade tool from the MOS Doc ID 2485457.1:

Once downloaded, we can stage it in the following location and you can copy it to the 19c database home, as follows:

```
[oracle@virtual-19crac1]$  cp /u01/software/upgrade/tee12cdb/
autoupgrade.jar /u01/app/oracle/product/19c/db_1/rdbms/admin/
[oracle@virtual-19crac1]$ ls -ltr  /u01/app/oracle/product/19c/db_1/
rdbms/admin/autoupgrade.jar
-rwxr-x--- 1 oracle oinstall 2868558 Mar 16 13:15 /u01/app/oracle/
product/19c/db_1/rdbms/admin/autoupgrade.jar
```

Configuration file creation for AutoUpgrade

The AutoUpgrade utility requires a config file which it uses for performing the pre-upgrade and the actual upgrade of the database. The config file is a simple file that will contain information like the source database version, target database version, **log** directory location, and so on. We can manually create the file, or we can create the sample config file using **autoupgrade.jar** and modify it to include the source and the target database details.

We already saw how to create the sample config file in our previous chapters; we did the same and created the sample file from the Oracle 19c home and modified it, as follows:

```
[oracle@virtual-19crac1 tee12cdb]$ cat tee12cdb_upgrade_config.cfg

global.autoupg_log_dir=/u01/software/upgrade/tee12cdb
upg1.log_dir=/u01/software/upgrade/tee12cdb  # Path of the log directory
upg1.sid=tee12cdb1                    # ORACLE_SID of the source DB
upg1.source_home=/u01/app/oracle/product/12c/db_1
upg1.target_home=/u01/app/oracle/product/19c/db_1
upg1.start_time=NOW                   # Optional Start time
upg1.upgrade_node=virtual-19crac1     # Optional hostname
upg1.run_utlrp=yes                    # run utlrp after upgrade
upg1.timezone_upg=yes                 # For Timezone upgrade
upg1.target_version=19                # Target ORACLE_HOME
upg1.defer_standby_log_shipping=yes   # Defer log-shipping standby db
```

In the preceding config file, we mentioned the log directory, the source and target database home locations, and also, set the **timezone_upg** value to **yes**, which will upgrade the Timezone (**tstz**) data. The config file also has the parameter **defer_**

standby_log_shipping value set to **yes** which should defer the log shipping to the physical standby database of the primary database.

Running AutoUpgrade in Analyze mode

We know all the modes; let's run the AutoUpgrade in the Analyze mode for our upgrade. As mentioned earlier, this mode will only will read the source database and check if the database is ready for the upgrade.

 This mode will not make any changes to the source database.

Export the Oracle home to **19c** database home, as follows:

```
[oracle@virtual-19crac1 tee12cdb]$ export ORACLE_HOME=/u01/app/oracle/
product/19c/db_1
[oracle@virtual-19crac1 tee12cdb]$ export PATH=$ORACLE_HOME/bin:$PATH
```

Now, run the AutoUpgrade in the **ANALYZE** mode as follows:

```
[oracle@virtual-19crac1 tee12cdb]$ $ORACLE_HOME/jdk/bin/java -jar
$ORACLE_HOME/rdbms/admin/autoupgrade.jar -config tee12cdb_upgrade_config.
cfg -mode ANALYZE
```

This command reads the source database for the upgrade and generates not only a bunch of the log files, but also creates the preupgrade and the post-upgrade fixup scripts and it typically runs very fast.

The following is part of the output for the preceding command:

```
[oracle@virtual-19crac1 tee12cdb]$ $ORACLE_HOME/jdk/bin/java -jar
$ORACLE_HOME/rdbms/admin/autoupgrade.jar -config tee12cdb_upgrade_config.
cfg -mode ANALYZE
AutoUpgrade tool launched with default options
Processing config file ...
+------------------------------+
| Starting AutoUpgrade execution |
+------------------------------+
1 databases will be analyzed
Type 'help' to list console commands

upg> lsj
--+---------+---------+-------+-------------+--------+--------------
|Job#|DB_NAME|STAGE|OPERATION| STATUS|START_TIME| UPDATED|MESSAGE|
+---------+---------+-------+-------------+--------+---------------+
| 104|tee12cdb1|PRECHECKS|PREPARING|RUNNING|21/03/16
17:37|17:37:32|Remaining 59/215|
-+---------+---------+-------+-------------+--------+---------------+
```

```
Total jobs 1
upg> lsj
--+---------+---------+-------+-------------+--------+---------------+
|Job#|DB_NAME|STAGE|OPERATION| STATUS|START_TIME| UPDATED|MESSAGE|
-+---------+---------+-------+-------------+--------+---------------+
| 104|tee12cdb1|PRECHECKS|PREPARING|RUNNING|21/03/16
17:37|17:37:38|Remaining 22/215|
+----+---------+---------+---------+-------+-------------+--------+---
Total jobs 1

upg> Job 104 completed
------------------ Final Summary --------------------
Number of databases         [1]

Jobs finished               [1]
Jobs failed                 [0]
Jobs pending                [0]
```

Please check the summary report at the following links:

/u01/software/upgrade/tee12cdb/cfgtoollogs/upgrade/auto/status/status.
html
/u01/software/upgrade/tee12cdb/cfgtoollogs/upgrade/auto/status/status.
log

Log files of AutoUpgrade

The AutoUpgrade utility creates multiple sub directories in the log location defined in the configuration file. Each time we run the AutoUpgrade utility in either the **Analyze** mode or the **Deploy** mode, it creates a subdirectory with the naming conventions like 100,101…etc.

You can check the various directories/logs in **/u01/software/upgrade/tee12cdb** in our case, as follows:

```
oracle@virtual-19crac1 prechecks]$ cd /u01/software/upgrade/tee12cdb/
[oracle@virtual-19crac1 tee12cdb]$ ls -ltr
total 2828
-rwx------ 1 oracle oinstall     323 Mar 16 13:02 preupgrade_invalid_
object_count.log
-rwx------ 1 oracle oinstall    1656 Mar 16 13:02 pre-upgrade_SYS_
SYSTEM_invalid_Objects.log
-rwx------ 1 oracle oinstall    2383 Mar 16 13:02 pre-upgrade_non-SYS_
invalid_objects.log
-rwx------ 1 oracle oinstall 2868558 Mar 16 13:13 autoupgrade.jar
-rwx------ 1 oracle oinstall    5874 Mar 16 13:20 sample_config.cfg
-rwx------ 1 oracle oinstall    1406 Mar 16 13:34 tee12cdb_upgrade_
config.cfg
```

```
drwx------ 3 oracle oinstall      21 Mar 16 20:24 cfgtoollogs
drwx------ 5 oracle oinstall      40 Mar 16 20:26 tee12cdb1

[oracle@virtual-19crac1 tee12cdb]$ cd tee12cdb1/
[oracle@virtual-19crac1 tee12cdb1]$ ls -ltr
total 8
drwx------  3 oracle oinstall  119 Mar 16 20:25 100
drwx------  2 oracle oinstall 4096 Mar 16 21:54 temp

[oracle@virtual-19crac1 tee12cdb1]$ cd 100
[oracle@virtual-19crac1 100]$ ls -ltr
total 384
-rwx------ 1 oracle oinstall      0 Mar 16 20:24 autoupgrade_err.log
-rwx------ 1 oracle oinstall    303 Mar 16 20:24 autoupgrade_20210316_
user.log
-rwx------ 1 oracle oinstall 384536 Mar 16 20:25 autoupgrade_20210316.
log
drwx------ 2 oracle oinstall   4096 Mar 16 20:25 prechecks

[oracle@virtual-19crac1 100]$ cd prechecks/
[oracle@virtual-19crac1 prechecks]$ ls -ltr
total 628
-rwx------ 1 oracle oinstall 165229 Mar 16 20:24 prechecks_cdb_root.log
-rwx------ 1 oracle oinstall 145112 Mar 16 20:24 prechecks_pdb_seed.log
-rwx------ 1 oracle oinstall 145106 Mar 16 20:25 prechecks_trendpdb.log
-rwx------ 1 oracle oinstall  24569 Mar 16 20:25 tee12cdb_checklist.xml
-rwx------ 1 oracle oinstall  25925 Mar 16 20:25 tee12cdb_checklist.json
-rwx------ 1 oracle oinstall   7271 Mar 16 20:25 tee12cdb_checklist.cfg
-rwx------ 1 oracle oinstall  49228 Mar 16 20:25 tee12cdb_preupgrade.
html
-rwx------ 1 oracle oinstall  36258 Mar 16 20:25 upgrade.xml
-rwx------ 1 oracle oinstall  24627 Mar 16 20:25 tee12cdb_preupgrade.log
ß Important log
[oracle@virtual-19crac1 prechecks]$
```

Among these log files, the log file with **dbname_preupgrade.log** (example, in this case, **tee12cdb_preupgrade.log**) is one of the most important logfiles to check. This logfile will have all the pre-upgrade checks/post upgrade recommendations and the fixup scripts' information. It will also list all the issues that need to be addressed.

Check the following output of **tee12cdb_preupgrade.log**. Please note that since this is a multitenant database with one or more pluggable databases in it, this log file will have the preupgrade summary for each of the container database. Like in this case, you can first see the action items for the **CDB$ROOT** container and then the second section of the preupgrade log has the action items for the **PDB** database, **TRENDPDB** database, as follows:

```
[oracle@virtual-19crac1 104]$ cd /u01/software/upgrade/tee12cdb/
tee12cdb1/104/prechecks
[oracle@virtual-19crac1 prechecks]$ ls -ltr
total 620
-rwx------ 1 oracle oinstall 165225 Mar 16 17:37 prechecks_cdb_root.log
-rwx------ 1 oracle oinstall 145112 Mar 16 17:37 prechecks_pdb_seed.log

-rwx------ 1 oracle oinstall 145106 Mar 16 17:37 prechecks_trendpdb.log
-rwx------ 1 oracle oinstall  23622 Mar 16 17:37 tee12cdb_checklist.xml
-rwx------ 1 oracle oinstall  24941 Mar 16 17:37 tee12cdb_checklist.json
-rwx------ 1 oracle oinstall   7064 Mar 16 17:37 tee12cdb_checklist.cfg
-rwx------ 1 oracle oinstall  48105 Mar 16 17:37 tee12cdb_preupgrade.
html
-rwx------ 1 oracle oinstall  36056 Mar 16 17:37 upgrade.xml
-rwx------ 1 oracle oinstall  23844 Mar 16 17:37 tee12cdb_preupgrade.log
```

Start of the START OF and TRENDPDB(PDB) Preupgrade log

```
[oracle@virtual-19crac1 prechecks]$ cat tee12cdb_preupgrade.log
Report generated by AutoUpgrade 21.1.1 (#8ee6880) on 2021-03-16 17:37:41

Upgrade-To version: 19.0.0.0.0

==========================================
Status of the database prior to upgrade
==========================================
        Database Name:  tee12cdb1
       Container Name:  CDB$ROOT
         Container ID:  1
              Version:  12.1.0.2.0
       DB Patch Level:  No Patch Bundle applied
           Compatible:  12.1.0.2.0
            Blocksize:  8192
             Platform:  Linux x86 64-bit
        Timezone File:  18
    Database log mode:  ARCHIVELOG
             Readonly:  false
              Edition:  EE

Oracle Component                         Upgrade Action    Current Status
----------------                         --------------    --------------
Oracle Workspace Manager                 [to be upgraded]  VALID
OLAP Analytic Workspace                  [to be upgraded]  VALID
Oracle Text                              [to be upgraded]  VALID
Oracle Database Vault                    [to be upgraded]  VALID
Oracle Server                            [to be upgraded]  VALID
```

```
Real Application Clusters            [to be upgraded]   VALID
Oracle Java Packages                 [to be upgraded]   VALID
Oracle XDK for Java                  [to be upgraded]   VALID
Oracle Label Security                [to be upgraded]   VALID
Oracle XML Database                  [to be upgraded]   VALID
Oracle Multimedia                    [to be upgraded]   VALID
Oracle OLAP API                      [to be upgraded]   VALID
JServer JAVA Virtual Machine         [to be upgraded]   VALID
Oracle Spatial                       [to be upgraded]   VALID

==============
BEFORE UPGRADE
==============

  REQUIRED ACTIONS

  ================
```

1. (AUTOFIXUP) Empty the RECYCLEBIN immediately before the database upgrade.

   The database contains 1 object in the recycle bin.

   The recycle bin must be completely empty before the database upgrade.

      RECOMMENDED ACTIONS

      ===================

2. Upgrade the Oracle Application Express (APEX) manually before or after the database upgrade.

   The database contains the APEX version 4.2.5.00.08, which is not supported on the target version 19.0.0.0.0. APEX must be upgraded to at least version 18.2.0.00.12 either before or after the database is upgraded.

   Starting with Oracle Database Release 18, APEX is not upgraded automatically as part of the database upgrade. Refer to My Oracle Support Note 1088970.1 for information about the APEX installation and upgrades. Refer to MOS Note 1344948.1 for the minimum APEX version supported for your target database release. The unsupported versions of APEX will be in an INVALID state when its database dependencies are not in sync with the upgraded database.

3. Turn on LOCAL UNDO by executing the following command, "ALTER DATABASE LOCAL UNDO ON", from CDB$ROOT. The database must be in the upgrade mode in order to successfully execute this command. This can be executed prior to the upgrade if the source database version is 12.2 or higher. Otherwise, the command must be executed after the upgrade. If AutoUpgrade is being used to upgrade the database, this can be done automatically by setting

the enable_local_undo configuration parameter to YES.

Database tee12cdb1 has LOCAL UNDO turned off.

It is recommended to turn the LOCAL UNDO on in any database that uses the CDB architecture.

```
INFORMATION ONLY
================
```

4. No action needed.

   Using the default parallel upgrade options, this CDB with 2 PDBs will first upgrade the CDB$ROOT, and then upgrade at most 1 PDBs at a time using two parallel processes per PDB.

   The number of PDBs upgraded in parallel and the number of parallel

   processes per PDB can be adjusted as described in the Database Upgrade Guide.

5. (AUTOFIXUP) Mandatory changes are applied automatically in the during_upgrade_pfile_dbname.ora file. Some of these changes maybe present   in the after_upgrade_pfile_dbname.ora file. The during_upgrade_pfile_dbname.ora is used to start the database in the upgrade mode. The after_upgrade_pfile_dbname.ora is used to start the database once the upgrade is completed successfully.

   ```
   Parameter
   ---------
   cluster_database='FALSE'
   ```

   Mandatory changes are required to perform the upgrade. These changes are implemented in the during_ and after_upgrade_pfile_dbname.ora files.

6. Check the Oracle Backup and Recovery User's Guide for information on how to manage an RMAN recovery catalog schema.

   If you are using a version of the recovery catalog schema that is older than that required by the RMAN client version, then you must upgrade the catalog schema.

   It is a good practice to have the catalog schema as the same or higher version than the RMAN client version you are using.

7. To help you keep track of your tablespace allocations, the following AUTOEXTEND tablespaces are expected to successfully EXTEND during the upgrade process:

   ```
                                           Min Size
   Tablespace                      Size    For Upgrade
   ```

```
----------                      ----------  -----------
SYSTEM                            790 MB      1023 MB
TEMP                               60 MB       240 MB
UNDOTBS1                          375 MB       401 MB
SYSAUX                            780 MB       980 MB
```

The minimum tablespace sizes for upgrade are estimates.

8. Follow the instructions in the Oracle Multimedia README.txt file in <19 ORACLE_HOME>/ord/im/admin/README.txt, or MOS note 2555923.1 to determine if Oracle Multimedia is being used. If Oracle Multimedia is being used, refer to MOS note 2347372.1 for suggestions on replacing Oracle Multimedia.

Oracle Multimedia component (ORDIM) is installed.

Starting with release 19c, Oracle Multimedia is desupported. The object types still exist, but the methods and procedures will raise an exception. Refer to the 19 Oracle Database Upgrade Guide, the Oracle Multimedia README.txt file in <19 ORACLE_HOME>/ord/im/admin/README.txt, or MOS note 2555923.1 for more information.

```
=============
AFTER UPGRADE
=============
   REQUIRED ACTIONS
   ================
   None

   RECOMMENDED ACTIONS

   ===================
```

9. (AUTOFIXUP) Upgrade the database time zone file using the DBMS_DST package.

The database is using the time zone file version 18 and the target 19 release ships with the time zone file version 32.

Oracle recommends upgrading to the desired (latest) version of the time zone file. For more information, refer to "Upgrading the Time Zone File and Timestamp with Time Zone Data" in the 19 Oracle Database Globalization Support Guide.

10. (AUTOFIXUP) Recompile the objects with the timestamp mismatch. Please refer to MOS note 781959.1 for more details.

There are objects whose timestamp are mismatched with its parent objects.

Timestamp of the dependent objects must coincide with the

timestamp of parent objects.

11. (AUTOFIXUP) Gather the dictionary statistics after the upgrade using the following command:

EXECUTE DBMS_STATS.GATHER_DICTIONARY_STATS;

Oracle recommends gathering the dictionary statistics after the upgrade.

The dictionary statistics provide essential information to the Oracle optimizer to help it find the efficient SQL execution plans. After a database upgrade, the statistics need to be re-gathered as there can now be tables that have significantly changed during the upgrade or new tables that do not have the statistics gathered yet.

12. Gather the statistics on fixed objects after the upgrade and when there is a representative workload on the system using the following command:

EXECUTE DBMS_STATS.GATHER_FIXED_OBJECTS_STATS;

Oracle recommends gathering the fixed object statistics after the upgrade. This recommendation is given for all the preupgrade runs.

The fixed object statistics provide essential information to the Oracle optimizer to help it find the efficient SQL execution plans. Those statistics are specific to the Oracle Database release that generates them, and can be stale upon the database upgrade.

For information on managing optimizer statistics, refer to the 12.1.0.2 Oracle Database SQL Tuning Guide.

13. (AUTOFIXUP) Run @?/rdbms/admin/utlrp.sql in order to recompile any invalid objects.

There are invalid objects in the database after the upgrade.

Invalid database objects need to be recompiled after the upgrade.

Report generated by AutoUpgrade 21.1.1 (#8ee6880) on 2021-03-16 17:37:41.

Upgrade-To version: 19.0.0.0.0
======================================
Status of the database prior to the upgrade
======================================
    Database Name: tee12cdb1

```
      Container Name:  PDB$SEED              ß Seed PDB database summary
        Container ID:  2
             Version:  12.1.0.2.0
      DB Patch Level:  No Patch Bundle applied
          Compatible:  12.1.0.2.0
           Blocksize:  8192
            Platform:  Linux x86 64-bit
       Timezone File:  18

   Database log mode:  ARCHIVELOG
            Readonly:  false
             Edition:  EE
   Oracle Component                      Upgrade Action        Current Status
   ----------------                      --------------        ------------
   Oracle Workspace Manager              [to be upgraded]      VALID
   OLAP Analytic Workspace               [to be upgraded]      VALID
   Oracle Text                           [to be upgraded]      VALID
   Oracle Database Vault                 [to be upgraded]      VALID
   Oracle Server                         [to be upgraded]      VALID
   Real Application Clusters             [to be upgraded]      VALID
   Oracle Java Packages                  [to be upgraded]      VALID
   Oracle XDK for Java                   [to be upgraded]      VALID
   Oracle Label Security                 [to be upgraded]      VALID
   Oracle XML Database                   [to be upgraded]      VALID
   Oracle Multimedia                     [to be upgraded]      VALID
   Oracle OLAP API                       [to be upgraded]      VALID
   JServer JAVA Virtual Machine          [to be upgraded]      VALID
   Oracle Spatial                        [to be upgraded]      VALID

===============
BEFORE UPGRADE
===============

  REQUIRED ACTIONS
  ================
  None

  RECOMMENDED ACTIONS

  ====================

  1.  Upgrade Oracle Application Express (APEX) manually before or after
      the database upgrade.

      The database contains APEX version 4.2.5.00.08, which is not
      supported on the target version 19.0.0.0.0. APEX must be upgraded
      to at least version 18.2.0.00.12 either before or after the
      database is upgraded.

      Starting with Oracle Database Release 18, APEX is not upgraded
      automatically as part of the database upgrade. Refer to My
      Oracle Support Note 1088970.1 for information about the APEX
```

installation and upgrades. Refer to MOS Note 1344948.1 for the minimum APEX version supported for your target database release. The unsupported versions of APEX will be in an INVALID state when its database dependencies are not in sync with the upgraded database.

2. (AUTOFIXUP) Gather the statistics on the fixed objects prior to the upgrade.

   None of the fixed object tables have had the stats collected.

   Gathering the statistics on fixed objects, if none have been gathered yet. This is recommended prior to upgrading.

   For information on managing optimizer statistics, refer to the 12.1.0.2. Oracle Database SQL Tuning Guide.

   INFORMATION ONLY

   =================

3. Synchronize your standby databases before the database upgrade.

   The standby database is not currently synchronized with its associated primary database.

   To keep the data in the source primary database synchronized with its associated standby databases, all the standby databases must be synchronized before the database upgrade. See My Oracle Support Note 2064281.1 for details.

4. To help you keep track of your tablespace allocations, the following AUTOEXTEND tablespaces are expected to successfully EXTEND during the upgrade process:

Tablespace	Size	Min Size For Upgrade
SYSTEM	250 MB	486 MB
TEMP	20 MB	240 MB
SYSAUX	490 MB	720 MB

   The minimum tablespace sizes for the upgrade are estimates.

5. Follow the instructions in the Oracle Multimedia README.txt file in <19 ORACLE_HOME>/ord/im/admin/README.txt, or MOS note 2555923.1 to determine if Oracle Multimedia is being used. If Oracle Multimedia is being used, refer to MOS note 2347372.1 for suggestions on replacing Oracle Multimedia.

   The Oracle Multimedia component (ORDIM) is installed.

Starting with release 19c, Oracle Multimedia is desupported. The object types still exist, but the methods and procedures will raise an exception. Refer to the 19 Oracle Database Upgrade Guide, the Oracle Multimedia README.txt file in <19 ORACLE_HOME>/ord/im/admin/README.txt, or MOS note 2555923.1 for more information.

```
=============

AFTER UPGRADE

=============
REQUIRED ACTIONS
===============
   None
   RECOMMENDED ACTIONS

   ===================
```

6. (AUTOFIXUP) Upgrade the database time zone file using the DBMS_DST package.

    The database is using the time zone file version 18 and the target 19 release ships with the time zone file version 32.

    Oracle recommends upgrading to the desired (latest) version of the time zone file. For more information, refer to "Upgrading the Time Zone File and Timestamp with Time Zone Data" in the 19 Oracle Database Globalization Support Guide.

7. (AUTOFIXUP) Recompile the objects with the timestamp mismatch. Please refer to MOS note 781959.1 for more details.

    There are objects whose timestamp are mismatched with its parent objects.

    Timestamp of the dependent objects must coincide with the timestamp of parent objects.

8. (AUTOFIXUP) Gather the dictionary statistics after the upgrade using the following command:

     EXECUTE DBMS_STATS.GATHER_DICTIONARY_STATS;

    Oracle recommends gathering the dictionary statistics after the upgrade.

    The dictionary statistics provide essential information to the Oracle optimizer to help it find the efficient SQL execution plans. After a database upgrade, the statistics need to be re-gathered as there can now be tables that have significantly changed during the upgrade or new tables that do not have the statistics gathered yet.

9. Gather the statistics on fixed objects after the upgrade and when there is a representative workload on the system using the following command:

   EXECUTE DBMS_STATS.GATHER_FIXED_OBJECTS_STATS;

   Oracle recommends gathering the fixed object statistics after the upgrade. This recommendation is given for all the preupgrade runs.

   The fixed object statistics provide essential information to the Oracle optimizer to help it find the efficient SQL execution plans. Those statistics are specific to the Oracle Database release that generates them, and can be stale upon the database upgrade.

   For information on managing optimizer statistics, refer to the 12.1.0.2 Oracle Database SQL Tuning Guide.

10. (AUTOFIXUP) Run @?/rdbms/admin/utlrp.sql in order to recompile any invalid objects.

    There are invalid objects in the database after the upgrade.

    The invalid database objects need to be recompiled after the upgrade.

Report generated by AutoUpgrade 21.1.1 (#8ee6880) on 2021-03-16 17:37:42.

Upgrade-To version: 19.0.0.0.0
=======================================
Status of the database prior to the upgrade
=======================================
```
       Database Name:  tee12cdb1
      Container Name:  TRENDPDB   ß Application Pluggable database summary
        Container ID:  3
             Version:  12.1.0.2.0
      DB Patch Level:  No Patch Bundle applied
          Compatible:  12.1.0.2.0
           Blocksize:  8192
            Platform:  Linux x86 64-bit
       Timezone File:  18
   Database log mode:  ARCHIVELOG
            Readonly:  false
             Edition:  EE
```

Oracle Component	Upgrade Action	Current Status
Oracle Workspace Manager	[to be upgraded]	VALID
OLAP Analytic Workspace	[to be upgraded]	VALID
Oracle Text	[to be upgraded]	VALID

```
Oracle Database Vault                     [to be upgraded]  VALID
Oracle Server                             [to be upgraded]  VALID
Real Application Clusters                 [to be upgraded]  VALID
Oracle Java Packages                      [to be upgraded]  VALID
Oracle XDK for Java                       [to be upgraded]  VALID
Oracle Label Security                     [to be upgraded]  VALID
Oracle XML Database                       [to be upgraded]  VALID
Oracle Multimedia                         [to be upgraded]  VALID
Oracle OLAP API                           [to be upgraded]  VALID
JServer JAVA Virtual Machine              [to be upgraded]  VALID
Oracle Spatial                            [to be upgraded]  VALID


==============
BEFORE UPGRADE
==============

  REQUIRED ACTIONS
  ================

  1.  (AUTOFIXUP) Empty the RECYCLEBIN immediately before the database
      upgrade.

      The database contains 1 object in the recycle bin.

      The recycle bin must be completely empty before the database
      upgrade.

        RECOMMENDED ACTIONS
        ===================

  2.  Upgrade the Oracle Application Express (APEX) manually before or
      after the database upgrade.

      The database contains the APEX version 4.2.5.00.08, which is not
      supported on the target version 19.0.0.0.0. APEX must be upgraded
      to at least version 18.2.0.00.12 either before or after the
      database is upgraded.

      Starting with Oracle Database Release 18, APEX is not upgraded
      automatically as part of the database upgrade. Refer to My
      Oracle Support Note 1088970.1 for information about the APEX
      installation and upgrades. Refer  to MOS Note 1344948.1 for the
      minimum APEX version supported for your target database release.
      The unsupported versions of APEX will be in an INVALID state
      when its database dependencies are not in sync with the upgraded
      database.

        INFORMATION ONLY

        ================
```

3. Synchronize your standby databases before the database upgrade.

   The standby database is not currently synchronized with its associated primary database.

   To keep the data in the source primary database synchronized with its associated standby databases, all the standby databases must be synchronized before the database upgrade. See My Oracle Support Note 2064281.1 for details.

4. To help you keep track of your tablespace allocations, the following AUTOEXTEND tablespaces are expected to successfully EXTEND during the upgrade process:

   ```
                                           Min Size
   Tablespace                  Size        For Upgrade
   ----------                  ----------  -----------
   SYSTEM                      260 MB      492 MB
   TEMP                        20 MB       240 MB
   SYSAUX                      520 MB      730 MB
   ```

   The minimum tablespace sizes for the upgrade are estimates.

5. Follow the instructions in the Oracle Multimedia README.txt file in <19 ORACLE_HOME>/ord/im/admin/README.txt, or MOS note 2555923.1 to determine if Oracle Multimedia is being used. If Oracle Multimedia is being used, refer to MOS note 2347372.1 for suggestions on replacing Oracle Multimedia.

   The Oracle Multimedia component (ORDIM) is installed.

   Starting with release 19c, Oracle Multimedia is desupported. The object types still exist, but the methods and procedures will raise an exception. Refer to the 19 Oracle Database Upgrade Guide, the Oracle Multimedia README.txt file in <19 ORACLE_HOME>/ord/im/admin/README.txt, or MOS note 2555923.1 for more information.

   ```
   =============
   AFTER UPGRADE
   =============
      REQUIRED ACTIONS
      ================
      None

      RECOMMENDED ACTIONS

      ===================
   ```

6. (AUTOFIXUP) Upgrade the database time zone file using the DBMS_DST package.

The database is using the time zone file version 18 and the target 19 release ships with the time zone file version 32.

Oracle recommends upgrading to the desired (latest) version of the time zone file. For more information, refer to "Upgrading the Time Zone File and Timestamp with Time Zone Data" in the 19 Oracle Database Globalization Support Guide.

7. (AUTOFIXUP) Recompile the objects with the timestamp mismatch. Please refer to MOS note 781959.1 for more details.

There are objects whose timestamp are mismatched with its parent objects.

Timestamp of the dependent objects must coincide with the timestamp of parent objects.

8. (AUTOFIXUP) Gather the dictionary statistics after the upgrade using the following command:

```
EXECUTE DBMS_STATS.GATHER_DICTIONARY_STATS;
```

Oracle recommends gathering the dictionary statistics after the upgrade.

The dictionary statistics provide essential information to the Oracle optimizer to help it find the efficient SQL execution plans. After a database upgrade, the statistics need to be re-gathered as there can now be tables that have significantly changed during the upgrade or new tables that do not have the statistics gathered yet.

9. Gather the statistics on fixed objects after the upgrade and when there is a representative workload on the system using the following command:

```
EXECUTE DBMS_STATS.GATHER_FIXED_OBJECTS_STATS;
```

Oracle recommends gathering the fixed object statistics after the upgrade. This recommendation is given for all the preupgrade runs.

The fixed object statistics provide essential information to the Oracle optimizer to help it find the efficient SQL execution plans. Those statistics are specific to the Oracle Database release that generates them, and can be stale upon the database upgrade.

For information on managing optimizer statistics, refer to the 12.1.0.2 Oracle Database SQL Tuning Guide.

10. (AUTOFIXUP) Run @?/rdbms/admin/utlrp.sql in order to recompile any invalid objects.

```
There are invalid objects in the database after the upgrade.
The invalid database objects need to be recompiled after the
upgrade.
[oracle@virtual-19crac1 prechecks]$
```

Check the above logfile thoroughly and make sure to address the issues if the preupgrade log reports any.

Shutdown the physical standby database

We can now stop the physical standby database. If this is an **RAC** database, we can use the server control utility to check the status and stop the physical standby database, mentioned as follows:

1. Check the current status of the physical standby database using the **srvctl** command, as follows:

```
[oracle@virtual-dr-19crac1 ~]$ srvctl status database -d tee12cdr
Instance tee12cdr1 is running on node virtual-dr-19crac1
Instance tee12cdr2 is running on node virtual-dr-19crac2
```

2. Stop the physical standby database using the **srvctl** command, as follows:

```
[oracle@virtual-dr-19crac1 ~]$ srvctl stop database -d tee12cdr
```

3. Check the current status using the **srvctl** command again, as follows:

```
[oracle@virtual-dr-19crac1 ~]$ srvctl status database -d tee12cdr
Instance tee12cdr1 is not running on node virtual-dr-19crac1
Instance tee12cdr2 is not running on node virtual-dr-19crac2
```

Upgrade the primary database using AutoUpgrade

Run the **AutoUpgrade** command in the **DEPLOY** mode to upgrade the database. We need to run this from the Oracle 19c home. So, lets export the Oracle home to point to Oracle 19c first and then run the **AutoUpgrade** command as shown in the following section.

Export the Oracle home to 19c database home, as follows:

```
[oracle@virtual-19crac1 tee12cdb]$ export ORACLE_HOME=/u01/app/oracle/
product/19c/db_1
[oracle@virtual-19crac1 tee12cdb]$ export PATH=$ORACLE_HOME/bin:$PATH
```

Now, run the AutoUpgrade in the **DEPLOY** mode as follows:

```
[oracle@virtual-19crac1 tee12cdb]$ $ORACLE_HOME/jdk/bin/java -jar
$ORACLE_HOME/rdbms/admin/AutoUpgrade.jar -config tee12cdb_upgrade_config.
cfg -mode DEPLOY
```

The following is part of the output when the preceding command is run successfully:

```
[oracle@virtual-19crac1 tee12cdb]$ $ORACLE_HOME/jdk/bin/java -jar
$ORACLE_HOME/rdbms/admin/autoupgrade.jar -config tee12cdb_upgrade_config.
cfg -mode DEPLOY

AutoUpgrade tool launched with default options
Processing config file ...

+-------------------------------+
| Starting AutoUpgrade execution |
+-------------------------------+
1 databases will be processed
Type 'help' to list console commands

upg> lsj

+----+---------+---------+---------+-------+--------------+--------+-
|Job#|DB_NAME|STAGE|OPERATION|STATUS|START_TIME| UPDATED|
MESSAGE|
+----+---------+---------+---------+-------+--------------+--------+-
| 101|tee12cdb1|PRECHECKS|PREPARING|RUNNING|21/03/16
20:26|20:26:20|Remaining 191/215|
+----+---------+---------+---------+-------+--------------+--------+--
Total jobs 1 upg> lsj
+----+---------+---------+---------+-------+--------------+--------+--
|Job#|DB_NAME|STAGE|OPERATION|STATUS|START_TIME|UPDATED|     MESSAGE|
+---+---------+---------+---------+-------+--------------+--------+---
| 101|tee12cdb1|PRECHECKS|PREPARING|RUNNING|21/03/16
20:26|20:26:27|Generating Reports|
+----+---------+---------+---------+-------+--------------+--------+--
Total jobs 1 upg> lsj
+----+---------+---------+---------+-------+--------------+--------+--
|Job#|DB_NAME|STAGE|OPERATION|STATUS|START_TIME| UPDATED|     MESSAGE|
+----+---------+---------+---------+-------+.   ---------+--------+--
| 101|tee12cdb1|DBUPGRADE|EXECUTING|RUNNING|21/03/16
20:26|20:34:40|0%Upgraded CDB$ROOT|
+----+---------+---------+---------+-------+--------------+--------+--
Total jobs 1 upg> lsj
+----------+---------+---------+-------+--------------+--------+------
|Job#|DB_NAME|STAGE|OPERATION|STATUS|START_TIME|UPDATED|     MESSAGE|
+----+---------+---------+---------+-------+--------------+--------+--
| 101|tee12cdb1|DBUPGRADE|EXECUTING|RUNNING|21/03/16
```

```
20:26|20:46:41|49%Upgraded CDB$ROOT|
+----+---------+---------+---------+-------+-------------+--------+--

Total jobs 1
```

While the **AutoUpgrade** process is running, we can open a new terminal and check the different directories that the AutoUpgrade tool creates for the various logs:

```
[oracle@virtual-19crac1 tee12cdb1]$ cd 101
[oracle@virtual-19crac1 101]$ ls -ltr
total 856
-rwx------ 1 oracle oinstall      0 Mar 16 20:26 autoupgrade_20210316.
log.lck
-rwx------ 1 oracle oinstall      0 Mar 16 20:26 autoupgrade_err.log.lck
-rwx------ 1 oracle oinstall      0 Mar 16 20:26 autoupgrade_err.log
-rwx------ 1 oracle oinstall      0 Mar 16 20:26 autoupgrade_20210316_
user.log.lck
drwx------ 2 oracle oinstall     28 Mar 16 20:26 preupgrade
drwx------ 2 oracle oinstall   4096 Mar 16 20:26 prechecks
drwx------ 2 oracle oinstall   4096 Mar 16 20:29 prefixups
drwx------ 2 oracle oinstall     33 Mar 16 20:32 drain
-rwx------ 1 oracle oinstall   9811 Mar 16 20:43 autoupgrade_20210316_
user.log
-rwx------ 1 oracle oinstall 813940 Mar 16 20:43 autoupgrade_20210316.
log
drwx------ 2 oracle oinstall   4096 Mar 16 20:44 dbupgrade
```

Check the following log file and you can see the upgrade status for the **CDB$ROOT** container upgrade info at first. Once the **AutoUpgrade** upgrades the root container, it will pick the next container database and start upgrading it. In our case, it will upgrade **trendpdb** next, mentioned as follows:

```
[oracle@virtual-19crac1 101]$ cd /u01/software/upgrade/tee12cdb/
tee12cdb1/101

[oracle@virtual-19crac1 101]$ tail -f autoupgrade_20210316_user.log
2021-03-16 20:30:54.515 INFO Disable Dataguard Broker2021-03-16
20:30:54.685 INFO Generating dataguard disable file /u01/software/
upgrade/tee12cdb/tee12cdb1/temp/dg_broker_disable_tee12cdb1
2021-03-16 20:32:00.305 INFO Password file /u01/app/oracle/product/12c/
db_1/dbs/orapwtee12cdb1 is not found Post Upgrade is continuing
2021-03-16 20:32:00.600 INFO [virtual-19crac2] Password file /u01/app
oracle/product/12c/db_1/dbs/orapwtee12cdb2 is not found on remote host
2021-03-16 20:34:34.948 INFO Total Number of upgrade phases is 108
2021-03-16 20:34:34.952 INFO Begin Upgrade on Database [tee12cdb-
CDB$ROOT]
2021-03-16 20:34:40.415 INFO 0%Upgraded CDB$ROOT
2021-03-16 20:37:41.179 INFO 12%Upgraded CDB$ROOT
```

```
2021-03-16 20:40:41.560 INFO 23%Upgraded CDB$ROOT
2021-03-16 20:43:41.716 INFO 39%Upgraded CDB$ROOT
2021-03-16 20:52:42.350 INFO 81%Upgraded CDB$ROOT
2021-03-16 20:55:42.655 INFO 91%Upgraded CDB$ROOT
```

If you check the following logfile, you can see that the AutoUpgrade utility upgrades the **container** database and then the PDBs:

```
[oracle@virtual-19crac1 101]$ tail -f autoupgrade_20210316_user.log

2021-03-16 20:58:44.521 INFO 92%Upgraded CDB$ROOT
2021-03-16 21:01:45.835 INFO 97%Upgraded CDB$ROOT
2021-03-16 21:02:07.011 INFO SUCCESSFULLY UPGRADED [tee12cdb-CDB$ROOT]
2021-03-16 21:02:07.012 INFO End Upgrade on Database [tee12cdb-CDB$ROOT]
2021-03-16 21:02:11.038 INFO Total Number of upgrade phases is 108
2021-03-16 21:02:11.044 INFO Total Number of upgrade phases is 108
2021-03-16 21:02:12.609 INFO Begin Upgrade on Database [tee12cdb-
PDB$SEED]
2021-03-16 21:02:12.894 INFO Begin Upgrade on Database [tee12cdb-
TRENDPDB]
2021-03-16 21:02:16.452 INFO 0%Upgraded PDB$SEED
2021-03-16 21:02:16.479 INFO 0%Upgraded TRENDPDB
2021-03-16 21:05:17.545 INFO 5%Upgraded PDB$SEED
2021-03-16 21:05:17.553 INFO 5%Upgraded TRENDPDB
2021-03-16 21:08:18.624 INFO 18%Upgraded PDB$SEED
2021-03-16 21:08:18.657 INFO 18%Upgraded TRENDPDB
2021-03-16 21:11:19.029 INFO 21%Upgraded PDB$SEED
2021-03-16 21:38:23.697 INFO 91%Upgraded PDB$SEED
2021-03-16 21:41:24.283 INFO 91%Upgraded PDB$SEED
2021-03-16 21:41:24.292 INFO 91%Upgraded TRENDPDB
2021-03-16 21:44:24.614 INFO 92%Upgraded PDB$SEED
2021-03-16 21:44:24.620 INFO 92%Upgraded TRENDPDB
2021-03-16 21:45:56.077 INFO SUCCESSFULLY UPGRADED [tee12cdb-TRENDPDB]
2021-03-16 21:45:56.077 INFO End Upgrade on Database [tee12cdb-TRENDPDB]
```

Once the primary database upgrade is complete, let's verify a few things, as follows:

1. First, check the **/etc/oratab** in all the nodes to see if **AutoUpgrade** updated the **db** entry to point to the new **19c** home, as follows:

    Node1:

    ```
    [oracle@virtual-19crac1 101]$ cat /etc/oratab | grep tee12cdb
    tee12cdb1:/u01/app/oracle/product/19c/db_1:N Node2:
    ```

    ```
    [oracle@virtual-19crac2]$ cat /etc/oratab | grep tee12cdb
    ```

    ```
    tee12cdb2:/u01/app/oracle/product/19c/db_1:N
    ```

Let's now check if the AutoUpgrade has upgraded the cluster configuration information, as follows:

```
[oracle@virtual-19crac2 admin]$ srvctl status database -d
tee12cdb
Instance tee12cdb1 is running on node virtual-19crac1
Instance tee12cdb2 is running on node virtual-19crac2


[oracle@virtual-19crac2 admin]$ srvctl config database -d tee12cdb
Database unique name: tee12cdb
Database name: tee12cdb
Oracle home: /u01/app/oracle/product/19c/db_1
Oracle user: oracle
Spfile: +DATAC1/TEE12CDB/PARAMETERFILE/spfiletee12cdb.ora
Password file: +DATAC1/TEE12CDB/PASSWORD/
wdtee12cdb.588.1067369185
Domain:
Start options: open
Stop options: immediate
Database role: PRIMARY
Management policy: AUTOMATIC
Server pools:
Disk Groups: DATAC1
Mount point paths:
Services:
Type: RAC
Start concurrency:
Stop concurrency:
OSDBA group: oinstall
OSOPER group: oinstall
Database instances: tee12cdb1,tee12cdb2
Configured nodes: virtual-19crac1,virtual-19crac2
CSS critical: no
CPU count: 0
Memory target: 0
Maximum memory: 0
Default network number for database services:
Database is administrator managed
```

2. Check if the AutoUpgrade utility has created the guaranteed restore point in the primary database, as follows:

```
SQL>select NAME, GUARANTEE_FLASHBACK_DATABASE, TIME from
V$restore_point;

NAME                                GUARANTEE_F    TIME
--------------------------------    ----------     ---------
```

```
AUTOUPGRADE_9212_TEE12CDB1121020   YES        16-MAR-21
                                              08.26.04.0000 PM
```

3. Run the **utlrp** script in the primary database and check the registry to see whether all the components are upgraded and whether they are in a valid state, as follows:

```
SQL> @/home/oracle/rac_database_info.sql

DATABASE_HOST   DB_NAME     DATABASE_ROLE  OPEN_MODE   STARTUP_TIME
--------------  ---------   -------------  ----------  ------------
virtual-19crac2 tee12cdb1   PRIMARY        READ WRITE  16-MAR-21
virtual-19crac2 tee12cdb1   PRIMARY        READ WRITE  16-MAR-21
```

4. Run the **utlrp** script, as follows:

```
SQL> @$ORACLE_HOME/rdbms/admin/utlrp
```

5. Now, check the components' status in the **dba** registry, as follows:

```
SQL> select COMP_ID,COMP_NAME,VERSION,STATUS from dba_registry;

COMP_ID    COMP_NAME                              VERSION      STATUS
--------   ------------------------------------   ---------    ------
CATALOG    Oracle Database Catalog Views          19.0.0.0.0   VALID
CATPROC    Oracle Database Packages and Types     19.0.0.0.0   VALID
JAVAVM     JServer JAVA Virtual Machine           19.0.0.0.0   VALID
XML        Oracle XDK                             19.0.0.0.0   VALID
CATJAVA    Oracle Database Java Packages          19.0.0.0.0   VALID
APS        OLAP Analytic Workspace                19.0.0.0.0   VALID
RAC        Oracle Real Application Clusters       19.0.0.0.0   VALID
XDB        Oracle XML Database                    19.0.0.0.0   VALID
OWM        Oracle Workspace Manager               19.0.0.0.0   VALID
CONTEXT    Oracle Text                            19.0.0.0.0   VALID
ORDIM      Oracle Multimedia                      19.0.0.0.0   VALID
SDO        Spatial                                19.0.0.0.0   VALID
XOQ        Oracle OLAP API                        19.0.0.0.0   VALID
OLS        Oracle Label Security                  19.0.0.0.0   VALID
APEX       Oracle Application Express             4.2.5.00.08  VALID
DV         Oracle Database Vault                  19.0.0.0.0   VALID

16 rows selected.
```

6. Check the timezone version to ensure that the **AutoUpgrade** has upgraded its version to that of the **19c**, as follows:

```
SQL > SELECT version FROM v$timezone_file;

VERSION
```

```
---------
32
```

```
1 row selected.
```

7. If this is the **RAC** database, we can check if the database is up in all the nodes. If it's not up in the other nodes of the cluster, we can start them.

8. Set the **cluster_database** parameter to true and start the database by using the **srvctl** command, as follows:

```
SQL> alter system set cluster_database=true scope=spfile sid='*';
System altered.
```

```
[oracle@virtual-19crac1 admin]$ srvctl stop database -d tee12cdb
oracle@virtual-19cra1 admin]$ srvctl start database -d tee12cdb
Instance tee12cdb1 is running on node virtual-19crac1
Instance tee12cdb2 is running on node virtual-19crac2
```

Check for the post upgrade invalid objects

It's always a good idea to take a snapshot of the invalid objects' count after the database upgrade, as we can compare it with the pre-upgrade invalid count to make sure that they are both the same. On the primary database, first run the **utlrp** script to compile any **INVALID** objects and then take a count of the invalid objects, so that we can compare the count after the database upgrade; to do this, complete the following steps:

1. First take the count of the invalid objects in the **SYS** and **SYSTEM** schemas, as follows:

```
SQL> spool /u01/software/upgrade/tee12cdb/tee12cdb_postupgrade/
tee12cdb_post-upgrade_SYS_SYSTEM_invalid_Objects.log
```

```
SQL> SELECT i.HOST_NAME "DATABASE_HOST" ,
     i.INSTANCE_NAME "DB_NAME", d.DATABASE_ROLE " DATABASE_ROLE",
     d.OPEN_MODE " OPEN_MODE ", STARTUP_TIME
     from GV$DATABASE d, gv$instance i
     where i.INST_ID=d.INST_ID;
```

```
SQL> select owner,object_name,object_type,status
     from dba_objects
     where status='INVALID' and owner in ('SYS','SYSTEM')
     order by owner;
spool off;
```

2. Next, take the invalid object count for the other schemas, as follows:

```
SQL> spool /u01/software/upgrade/tee12cdb/tee12cdb_postupgrade/
tee12cdb_post-upgrade_non-SYS_invalid_objects.log
SQL> SELECT i.HOST_NAME "DATABASE_HOST" ,
     i.INSTANCE_NAME "DB_NAME", d.DATABASE_ROLE " DATABASE_ROLE",
     d.OPEN_MODE " OPEN_MODE ", STARTUP_TIME
     from GV$DATABASE d, gv$instance i
     where i.INST_ID=d.INST_ID;

SQL> select count(*) from dba_objects
     where status='INVALID' and owner not in ('SYS','SYSTEM');
SQL> select owner,object_type,count(*)
     from dba_objects
     where status='INVALID' and owner not in ('SYS','SYSTEM')
     group by owner,object_type order by owner;
SQL> select owner,object_name,object_type,status
     from dba_objects
     where status='INVALID' and owner not in ('SYS','SYSTEM')
     order by owner;
spool off;
```

With this step, the primary database upgrade is completed. Let's upgrade the physical standby database now.

Upgrading the physical standby database to Oracle 19c (19.9.0)

The primary database is upgraded to Oracle 19c. Now, let's upgrade the physical standby database. The physical standby database upgrade will happen with the migration of redo logs that it received from the primary database. As of now, the physical standby database is down. Let's upgrade its configuration file first and start the database using the server control utility. But first, let's take a look at a few pre-checks and ensure that they are completed. Let's look at the following steps:

1. **Copy the Oracle configuration files**: Copy the password files/parameter files and database **tnsnames.ora** entry from Oracle 12c to Oracle 19c home. We need to do this step in all the nodes of the cluster, as follows:

@Physical standby database server:

```
[oracle@virtual-dr-19crac1 ~]$ cp /u01/app/oracle/product/12c/
db_1/dbs/*tee12cd*
/u01/app/oracle/product/19c/db_1/dbs
```

2. Modify the database entry in **/etc/oratab** to point to the Oracle 19c (19.3.0) home. We need to do this step in all the nodes of the cluster, as follows:

```
[oracle@virtual-dr-19crac1 ~]$ cat /etc/oratab | grep viceprdr
tee19cdr:/u01/app/oracle/product/19c/db_1:N
tee19cdr1:/u01/app/oracle/product/19c/db_1
```

3. Upgrade the cluster configuration information of standby database using the **srvctl upgrade** command, as follows:

```
[oracle@virtual-dr-19crac1 ~]$ export ORACLE_HOME=/u01/app/
oracle/product/12c/db_1
[oracle@virtual-dr-19crac1 ~]$ export PATH=$ORACLE_HOME/bin:$PATH

[oracle@virtual-dr-19crac1 ~]$ srvctl upgrade database -db
tee19cdr -o /u01/app/oracle/product/19c/db_1

[oracle@virtual-dr-19crac1 dbs]$ srvctl config database -d
tee12cdr
Database unique name: tee12cdr
Database name: tee12cdr
Oracle home: /u01/app/oracle/product/19c/db_1
Oracle user: oracle
Spfile: +datac1/TEE12CDR/PARAMETERFILE/spfiletee12cdr1.ora
Password file:
Domain:
Start options: mount
Stop options: immediate
Database role: PHYSICAL_STANDBY
Management policy: AUTOMATIC
Server pools:
Disk Groups: DATAC1
Mount point paths:
services:
Type: RAC
Start concurrency:
Stop concurrency:
OSDBA group: oinstall
OSOPER group: oinstall
Database instances: tee12cdr1,tee12cdr2
Configured nodes: virtual-dr-19crac1,virtual-dr-19crac2
CSS critical: no
CPU count: 0
Memory target: 0
Maximum memory: 0
Default network number for database services:
Database is administrator managed
```

4. Start the physical standby database in the **MOUNT** mode. From node 1 of the physical standby database server, start the physical standby database in the **mount** stage, as follows:

```
[oracle@virtual-dr-19crac1 dbs]$ srvctl start database -d
tee12cdr -o mount
```

5. Enable the log shipping on the primary database, as follows:

```
SQL> ALTER SYSTEM SET log_archive_dest_state_2=enable SCOPE=BOTH
sid='*';
System altered.
```

The primary database will now start shipping all the redo logs to the physical standby database.

6. Start the recovery process in the physical standby database, as follows:

```
SQL> ALTER DATABASE RECOVER managed standby database using
current logfile disconnect;
Database altered.
```

For the physical standby database, the MRP will now start applying all the logs that it has received from the primary database. This might take some time depending upon the number of archive log files that the primary database has generated during its upgrade. The physical standby database will be upgraded with all the migrated redo data that it received from the primary database. If needed, you can defer and enable the log shipping a few times and make sure that the primary database is sending the logs to the standby database.

We can check the alert log and wait for some time for the physical standby database to sync with the primary database. You can also check to see if the physical standby database has received and applied the logs and if it is in sync with the primary database, as follows:

```
SQL> @/home/oracle/rac_database_info.sql
```

DATABASE_HOST	DB_NAME	DATABASE_ROLE	OPEN_MODE	STARTUP_TIME
virtual-dr-19crac1	tee12cdr1	PHYSICAL STANDBY	MOUNTED	16-MAR-21
virtual-dr-19crac2	tee12cdr2	PHYSICAL STANDBY	MOUNTED	16-MAR-21

INST_ID	PROCESS	STATUS	THREAD#	SEQUENCE#	BLOCK#	BLOCKS
1	MRP0	APPLYING_LOG	2	85	874	102400

```
THREAD#      ARCHIVED      APPLIED     GAP
----------   ----------    ----------  ----------
   1           120           118        2
   2            87            84        3
```

At this time, we can modify the standby database configuration to open in the **READ ONLY** mode and bounce the database once and restart the MRP process and check if the standby database is in sync, as follows:

```
[oracle@virtual-dr-19crac1 dbs]$ srvctl modify database -d
tee12cdr -startoption "READ ONLY"

[oracle@virtual-dr-19crac1 dbs]$ srvctl stop database -d tee12cdr

[oracle@virtual-dr-19crac1 dbs]$ srvctl start database -d
tee12cdr

[oracle@virtual-dr-19crac1 dbs]$ srvctl status database -d
tee12cdr
Instance tee12cdr1 is running on node virtual-dr-19crac1
Instance tee12cdr2 is running on node virtual-dr-19crac2
```

7. Start the MRP and check the lag, as follows:

```
SQL> ALTER DATABASE RECOVER managed standby database using
current logfile disconnect; Database altered.

SQL> @/home/oracle/standby_database_lag.sql

DATABASE_HOST     DB_NAME   DATABASE_ROLE     OPEN_MODE            STARTUP_T
----------------- --------- ---------------   -----------------    --------
virtual-dr-19crac1 tee12cdr1 PHYSICAL STANDBY READ ONLY WITH APPLY 16-MAR-21
virtual-dr-19crac2 tee12cdr2 PHYSICAL STANDBY READ ONLY WITH APPLY 16-MAR-21

INST_ID    PROCESS  STATUS        THREAD#  SEQUENCE#  BLOCK#  BLOCKS
---------- -------  -----------   -------  ---------- ------- -----
   1       MRP0     APPLYING_LOG  1          120       1021    102400

THREAD#      ARCHIVED      APPLIED     GAP
----------   ----------    ----------  ----------
   1           120           120        0
   2            89            89        0
```

8. Check the components' status in the physical standby database, as follows:

```
SQL> @/home/oracle/rac_database_info.sql

DATABASE_HOST     DB_NAME   DATABASE_ROLE     OPEN_MODE          STARTUP_TIME
----------------- --------- ---------------   ---------------    ------
```

```
virtual-dr-19crac1 tee12cdr1 PHYSICAL STANDBY READ ONLY WITH APPLY  16-MAR-21
virtual-dr-19crac2 tee12cdr2 PHYSICAL STANDBY READ ONLY WITH APPLY  16-MAR-21

SQL> select COMP_ID,COMP_NAME,VERSION,STATUS from dba_registry;

COMP_ID   COMP_NAME                              VERSION      STATUS
-------   ------------------------------------   ----------   -------

CATALOG   Oracle Database Catalog Views          19.0.0.0.0   VALID
CATPROC   Oracle Database Packages and Types     19.0.0.0.0   VALID
JAVAVM    JServer JAVA Virtual Machine           19.0.0.0.0   VALID
XML       Oracle XDK                             19.0.0.0.0   VALID
CATJAVA   Oracle Database Java Packages          19.0.0.0.0   VALID
APS       OLAP Analytic Workspace                19.0.0.0.0   VALID
RAC       Oracle Real Application Clusters       19.0.0.0.0   VALID
XDB       Oracle XML Database                    19.0.0.0.0   VALID
OWM       Oracle Workspace Manager               19.0.0.0.0   VALID
CONTEXT   Oracle Text                            19.0.0.0.0   VALID
ORDIM     Oracle Multimedia                      19.0.0.0.0   VALID
SDO       Spatial                                19.0.0.0.0   VALID
XOQ       Oracle OLAP API                        19.0.0.0.0   VALID
OLS       Oracle Label Security                  19.0.0.0.0   VALID
APEX      Oracle Application Express             4.2.5.00.08  VALID
DV        Oracle Database Vault                  19.0.0.0.0   VALID

16 rows selected.
```

9. Check if the tables got replicated to the physical standby database:

For the physical standby database, check if the table got replicated, indicating that the physical standby database is both upgraded and in **SYNC** with the primary database, as follows:

```
SQL> select * from BEFORE_UPGRADE;
NAME
------------------------------
Table Before Upgrade
```

With this step, the upgrading of the standby database is now successfully completed. Let's enable the broker now.

10. Check if the encrypted tablespace looks fine in the primary database:

For the primary database, we can check the encrypted tablespaces and see no issues while accessing the encrypted data. You might need to export **ORACE_UNQNAME** to point to the **cdb** database name, as follows:

```
[oracle@virtual-19crac1 admin]$ export ORACLE_UNQNAME=TEE12CDB
SQL> @/home/oracle/rac_database_info.sql
```

```
DATABASE_HOST      DB_NAME    DATABASE_ROLE   OPEN_MODE   STARTUP_TIME
-------------      ---------  -------------   ----------  ----------
virtual-19crac2    tee12cdb1  PRIMARY         READ WRITE  16-MAR-21
virtual-19crac2    tee12cdb1  PRIMARY         READ WRITE  16-MAR-21

SQL> select tablespace_name,encrypted from dba_tablespaces where
encrypted='YES' ;

TABLESPACE_NAME    ENCRYPTED
---------------    ----------
ENCRYPTED_TS       YES

SQL> select owner,table_name,TABLESPACE_NAME from dba_tables
where table_name='ENCRYPT';
OWNER   TABLE_NAME TABLESPACE_NAME
------  ---------- ---------------
SYS     ENCRYPT    ENCRYPTED_TS
```

Login to the pluggable database and query the encrypted table, as follows:

```
SQL> alter session set container=TRENDPDB;
Session altered.
SQL> show con_name;
CON_NAME
-----------
TRENDPDB

SQL> select * from ENCRYPT;
NAME
------------------------------------------------------------------
This is from Encrypted tablespaces in TRENDPDB Pluggable database
```

Start the broker in both primary and standby databases

We can start the dataguard broker in both the primary and the standby databases, by completing the following steps:

1. Check and start the data guard broker if it is not started in both the primary database and the standby database.

   For the primary database, run the following:

   ```
   SQL> @/home/oracle/rac_database_info.sql
   ```

   ```
   DATABASE_HOST      DB_NAME    DATABASE_ROLE   OPEN_MODE   STARTUP_TIME
   -------------      ---------  -------------   ----------  ----------
   virtual-19crac2    tee12cdb1  PRIMARY         READ WRITE  16-MAR-21
   ```

```
virtual-19crac2  tee12cdb1  PRIMARY        READ WRITE  16-MAR-21

SQL> show parameter broker

NAME                      TYPE     VALUE
--------------------      -------  --------------------------
dg_broker_config_file1    string   +DATAC1/tee12cdb/dr1tee12cdb.dat
dg_broker_config_file2    string   +DATAC1/tee12cdb/dr2tee12cdb.dat
dg_broker_start           boolean  FALSE
```

Stop the data guard broker process as follows:

```
SQL> ALTER SYSTEM SET DG_BROKER_START=TRUE;
System altered.


SQL> show parameter DG_BROKER_START

NAME                      TYPE     VALUE
--------------------      -------  --------------------------
dg_broker_config_file1    string   +DATAC1/tee12cdb/dr1tee12cdb.dat
dg_broker_config_file2    string   +DATAC1/tee12cdb/dr2tee12cdb.dat
dg_broker_start           boolean  FALSE
```

For the physical standby database, run the following:

```
SQL> @/home/oracle/rac_database_info.sql

DATABASE_HOST       DB_NAME   DATABASE_ROLE      OPEN_MODE  STARTUP_T
------------------  --------  -----------------  --------   ---------
virtual-dr-19crac1  tee12cdr1  PHYSICAL STANDBY  MOUNTED    16-MAR-21
virtual-dr-19crac2  tee12cdr2  PHYSICAL STANDBY  MOUNTED    16-MAR-21


SQL> SHOW PARAMETER DG_BROKER

NAME                      TYPE     VALUE
--------------------      -------  --------------------------
dg_broker_config_file1    string   +DATAC1/TEE12CDR/dr1tee12cdr.dat
dg_broker_config_file2    string   +DATAC1/TEE12CDR/dr2tee12cdr.dat
dg_broker_start           boolean  FALSE
```

Stop the data guard broker process as follows:

```
SQL> ALTER SYSTEM SET DG_BROKER_START=TRUE;
System altered.

NAME                      TYPE     VALUE
--------------------      -------  --------------------------
dg_broker_config_file1    string   +DATAC1/TEE12CDR/dr1tee12cdr.dat
dg_broker_config_file2    string   +DATAC1/TEE12CDR/dr2tee12cdr.dat
```

```
dg_broker_start            boolean    TRUE
```

2. Enable the broker configuration from the primary database.

3. Check and enable the data guard broker configuration if it is disabled in the primary database, as follows:

```
[oracle@virtual-19crac1 admin]$ dgmgrl
DGMGRL for Linux: Release 19.0.0.0.0 - Production on Thu Mar 16
20:56:42 2021
Version 19.9.0.0.0

Copyright (c) 1982, 2019, Oracle and/or its affiliates.  All rights
reserved.

Welcome to DGMGRL, type "help" for information.
DGMGRL> connect sys
Password:
Connected to "tee12cdb"
Connected as SYSDBA.
DGMGRL>
```

4. Check the current configuration, as follows:

```
 DGMGRL> show configuration;
Configuration - tee12cdb_bg
        Protection Mode: MaxPerformance
        Members:
        tee12cdb - Primary database
          tee12cdr - Physical standby database
      Fast-Start Failover:  Disabled
Configuration Status:
DISABLED
```

5. Enable the configuration, as follows:

```
DGMGRL> enable configuration;
Enabled.
```

6. Re-check the current configuration, as follows:

```
DGMGRL> show configuration;
Configuration - tee12cdb_bg
        Protection Mode: MaxPerformance
        Members:
        tee12cdb - Primary database
          tee12cdr - Physical standby database
      Fast-Start Failover:  Disabled
      Configuration Status:
```

```
WARNING     (status updated 23 seconds ago)

DGMGRL>
```

If we see any issues in the broker configuration, we can remove and recreate the configuration. We have seen in a few cases where the **dataguard** broker doesn't work after the database upgrades, and we ended up removing and recreating the broker configuration.

Post upgrade tasks

Please note that we did not implement these steps as we will test the downgrade in the following section. We cannot downgrade if we change the compatible parameter to **19c**. If you want to downgrade, skip this step and go to the next section. However, if you don't want to downgrade the database, you can perform the following steps to complete the post upgrade tasks.

For the post upgrade tasks, we can complete the following steps both for the primary and the physical standby databases:

- **FRA space usage**: Until we drop the restore point, keep checking the FRA space usage and increase the space as necessary.

- **Dropping GRP**: We can also drop the restore point in both the primary and the standby databases, as follows:

  ```
  SQL>DROP RESTORE POINT AUTOUPGRADE_9212_TEE12CDB1121020;
  ```

- **Database compatibility**: We can change the compatible parameter after waiting for one week as we cannot downgrade the database after changing this parameter to 19. Since this is a permanent change, once we change the compatible parameter to 19.9, we CANNOT revert, so please wait for one week and then change it, as follows:

  ```
  SQL > ALTER SYSTEM SET COMPATIBLE = '19.0.0' SCOPE=SPFILE
  sid='*';
  ```

With this step, we have successfully upgraded both the primary and the physical standby 12.1.0.2 multi-tenant database along with its pluggable database to 19.9.0. Let us now see how we can downgrade both the container and the pluggable database back to 12.1.0.2.

Fallback using Flashback to GRP

In this section, we will downgrade both the primary and the physical standby container databases along with their pluggable database from 19.9.0 back to 12.1.0.2 by flashbacking them to the guaranteed restore points that were created before the database upgrade. The best and the fastest way to downgrade the database from any upgraded version to its previous version is to **Flashback** the database to a previously created guaranteed restore point. As discussed earlier, this method will work as long as we don't change the database compatibility to the upgraded version.

In the **dataguard** environment, for this strategy to work, **FLASHBACK** must be enabled in both the primary and the physical standby databases, and we should create a guaranteed restore point in the physical standby database. However, before we start the database upgrade task, we need to make sure that the **db_recovery_dest_size** parameter is set to a bigger value in both the primary and the physical standby database. We did create a guaranteed restore point in the physical standby database manually first, so we should be able to downgrade the physical standby database without any issues.

Let's test it out. We will now downgrade both the primary database (**tee12cdb**) and the standby database (**tee12cdr**) from 19.9 to 12.1.0.2, as shown in *Figure 5.2*:

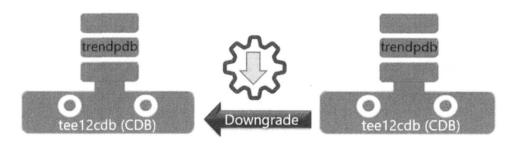

Figure 5.2: Downgrading from Oracle 19c (19.9.0) container database to Oracle 12c (12.1.0.2)

Downgrade using the Flashback method

Stop the log shipping on the primary and redo applying on the physical standby database. If we have the **dataguard** broker configured, we can disable the log shipping and log applying as follows:

@Primary database:

```
DGMGRL> edit database tee12cdb set state = 'TRANSPORT-OFF';
DGMGRL> edit database tee12cdr set state = 'APPLY-OFF';
```

However, if we don't have the **dataguard** broker configured, we can disable the log shipping on the primary and cancel the recovery on the standby database, as follows:

@Primary database:

```
SQL> alter system set log_archive_dest_state_2='defer' scope=both sid='*';
```

```
System altered.
```

@Physical standby database:

```
SQL> alter database recover managed standby database cancel;
Database altered.
```

Downgrading the primary database

Shutdown the primary database running from 19c home and start only one instance in the mount state. If this is an **RAC** database, you can use the **srvctl** command for this, and if this is not an **RAC** database, you can use the **sqlplus** command to start the database, as follows:

1. Check the current status of the primary database, as follows:

   ```
   [oracle@virtual-19crac1 admin]$ srvctl status database -d
   tee12cdb
   Instance tee12cdb1 is running on node virtual-19crac1
   Instance tee12cdb2 is running on node virtual-19crac2
   ```

2. Stop the database, as follows:

   ```
    [oracle@virtual-19crac1 admin]$ srvctl stop database -d tee12cdb
   ```

3. Check the status of the database, as follows:

   ```
   [oracle@virtual-19crac1 admin]$ srvctl status database -d
   tee12cdb
   Instance tee12cdb1 is not running on node virtual-19crac1
   Instance tee12cdb2 is not running on node virtual-19crac2
   ```

4. Start the first instance of the database on **node1**, as follows:

   ```
   [oracle@virtual-19crac1 admin]$ srvctl start instance -d tee12cdb
   -n virtual-19crac1 -o mount
   ```

5. Check the status of the database, as follows:

   ```
   [oracle@virtual-19crac1 admin]$ srvctl status database -d
   tee12cdb
   Instance tee12cdb1 is running on node virtual-19crac1
   Instance tee12cdb2 is not running on node virtual-19crac2
   [oracle@virtual-19crac1 admin]$
   ```

6. Check the restore point that we created in the primary database before we started the database and let's flashback the primary database to that restore point, as follows:

   @Primary database:

```
SQL> @/home/oracle/rac_database_info.sql

DATABASE_HOST    DB_NAME    DATABASE_ROLE    OPEN_MODE    STARTUP_TIME
---------------  ---------  -------------    ----------   ------------
virtual-19crac1  tee12cdb1  PRIMARY          MOUNTED      17-MAR-21


SQL> select NAME,GUARANTEE_FLASHBACK_DATABASE,TIME from
V$restore_point;

NAME                              GUARANTEE_FLA   TIME
--------------------------------  -------------   --------------------
AUTOUPGRADE_9212_TEE12CDB1121020  YES             16-MAR-21
                                                  08.26.04.000000000 PM
```

7. Flashback the primary database to the preceding guaranteed restore point, as follows:

```
SQL> flashback database to RESTORE POINT AUTOUPGRADE_9212_
TEE12CDB1121020;
Flashback complete.
```

8. Create a new parameter file **pfile** in the primary database from the current **spfile** and remove all the hidden parameters as they are from 19c and then recreate the **spfile** from the modified **pfile**, as follows:

```
SQL> show parameter spfile

NAME        TYPE      VALUE
---------   ------    ----------------- ----------- --------------
spfile      string    +DATAC1/TEE12CDB/PARAMETERFILE/
                      spfiletee12cdb.ora


SQL> create pfile='/u01/app/oracle/product/12c/db_1/dbs/after_
downgrade.ora' from spfile='+DATAC1/TEE12CDB/PARAMETERFILE/
spfiletee12cdb.ora';
File created.
```

9. Modify the **pfile** (**/u01/app/oracle/product/12c/db_1/dbs/after_ downgrade.ora**) and remove all the hidden parameters from it. Once we modify the parameter file **pfile**, we can shut down the primary database which is running from 19c home and create the **spfile** from the modified **pfile**, as follows:

```
[oracle@virtual-19crac1 admin]$srvctl stop database -d tee12cdb

SQL>create spfile='+DATAC1/TEE12CDB/PARAMETERFILE/spfiletee12cdb.
ora' from pfile='/u01/app/oracle/product/12c/db_1/dbs/after_
downgrade.ora';
File created.
```

10. Downgrade the Oracle clusterware database configuration. We now need to downgrade the cluster configuration of the primary database from the 19c home as follows:

```
[oracle@virtual-19crac1 admin]$ export ORACLE_HOME=/u01/app/
oracle/product/19c/db_1

[oracle@virtual-19crac1 admin]$ export PATH=$ORACLE_HOME/
bin:$PATH

[oracle@virtual-19crac1 admin]$ srvctl downgrade database -d
tee12cdb  -o /u01/app/oracle/product/12c/db_1 -t 12.1.0.2
```

11. Also, update the configuration file **/etc/oratab** to change the database home from 19c to 12.1.0.2, as follows:

```
[oracle@virtual-19crac1 dbs]$ vi /etc/oratab

[oracle@virtual-19crac1 ~]$ cat /etc/oratab   | grep tee19cdb1
tee19cdb1:/u01/app/oracle/product/12c/db_1
[oracle@virtual-19crac1 dbs]$
```

12. Start the database instance from 12.1.0.2 home in the mount mode on node 1 from 12.1.0.2 home. If this is an **RAC** database, we can use the **srvctl** command and if this is not an **RAC** database, then we can use the **sqlplus** commands to start the instance in the **mount** mode, as follows:

```
[oracle@virtual-19crac1 dbs]$ export ORACLE_HOME=/u01/app/oracle/
product/12c/db_1

[oracle@virtual-19crac1 dbs]$ export PATH=$ORACLE_HOME/bin:$PATH

[oracle@virtual-19crac1 admin]$ srvctl start instance -d tee12cdb
-n virtual-19crac1 -o mount

[oracle@virtual-19crac1 dbs]$ srvctl status database -d tee12cdb
Instance tee12cdb1 is running on node virtual-19crac1
Instance tee12cdb2 is not running on node virtual-19crac2
```

13. Open the database in the reset logs. Once the database is open in the **mount** mode, we can open the database with the resetlogs as we have downgraded the database, as follows:

```
[oracle@virtual-19crac1 ~]$ sqlplus / as sysdba

SQL*Plus: Release 12.1.0.2.0 Production on Wed Mar 17 10:56:03
2021
Copyright (c) 1982, 2014, Oracle.  All rights reserved.
Connected to:
Oracle Database 12c Enterprise Edition Release 12.1.0.2.0 - 64bit
```

```
Production
With the Partitioning, Real Application Clusters, Automatic
Storage Management, OLAP,Advanced Analytics and Real Application
Testing options

SQL> @/home/oracle/rac_database_info.sql

DATABASE_HOST    DB_NAME    DATABASE_ROLE   OPEN_MODE   STARTUP_TIME
---------------- ---------- -----------     ---------   -----------
virtual-19crac1  tee12cdb1  PRIMARY         MOUNTED     17-MAR-21

SQL> alter database open resetlogs;
Database altered.
```

14. Stop the primary database and start it in the normal mode, as follows:

```
[oracle@virtual-19crac1 admin]$srvctl stop database -d tee12cdb

[oracle@virtual-19crac1 admin]$srvctl start database -d tee12cdb

[oracle@virtual-19crac1 admin]$srvctl status database -d tee12cdb
Instance tee12cdb1 is running on node virtual-19crac1
Instance tee12cdb2 is running on node virtual-19crac2
```

15. Check the registry components to see if they have been successfully downgraded to 12.1.0.2, as follows:

```
SQL> @/home/oracle/rac_database_info.sql

DATABASE_HOST    DB_NAME    DATABASE_ROLE OPEN_MODE   STARTUP_TIME
---------------- ---------- ------------- ----------  -----------
virtual-19crac2  tee12cdb1  PRIMARY       READ WRITE  17-MAR-21
virtual-19crac2  tee12cdb1  PRIMARY       READ WRITE  17-MAR-21

SQL> select COMP_ID,COMP_NAME,VERSION,STATUS from dba_registry;

COMP_ID    COMP_NAME                            VERSION        STATUS
---------- ------------------------------       ------------   ---------
DV         Oracle Database Vault                12.1.0.2.0     VALID
APEX       Oracle Application Express           4.2.5.00.08    VALID
OLS        Oracle Label Security                12.1.0.2.0     VALID
SDO        Spatial                              12.1.0.2.0     VALID
ORDIM      Oracle Multimedia                    12.1.0.2.0     VALID
CONTEXT    Oracle Text                          12.1.0.2.0     VALID
OWM        Oracle Workspace Manager             12.1.0.2.0     VALID
XDB        Oracle XML Database                  12.1.0.2.0     VALID
CATALOG    Oracle Database Catalog Views        12.1.0.2.0     VALID
CATPROC    Oracle Database Packages and Types   12.1.0.2.0     VALID
JAVAVM     JServer JAVA Virtual Machine         12.1.0.2.0     VALID
```

```
XML        Oracle XDK                         12.1.0.2.0        VALID
CATJAVA    Oracle Database Java Packages      12.1.0.2.0        VALID
APS        OLAP Analytic Workspace            12.1.0.2.0        VALID
XOQ        Oracle OLAP API                    12.1.0.2.0        VALID
RAC        Oracle Real Application Clusters 12.1.0.2.0          VALID
16 rows selected.
```

16. Now, check the Timezone version, as follows:

```
SQL> SELECT version FROM v$timezone_file;

VERSION
----------
       18
```

This completes the steps to downgrade the primary database using the flashback to restore point method. Now, let's downgrade the standby database using the same method.

Downgrading the physical standby database

For downgrading the physical standby database using the flashback to restore point method, we will be using the restore point that we created before starting the database upgrade to 19.9.0, as follows:

1. Shutdown the physical standby database from the current home (**19c**) and start only one instance in the **mount** mode, as follows:

```
[oracle@virtual-dr-19crac1 dbs]$ srvctl stop  database -d
tee12cdr

[oracle@virtual-dr-19crac1 dbs]$ srvctl start instance -d
tee12cdr -n virtual-dr-19crac1 -o mount

[oracle@virtual-dr-19crac1 dbs]$ srvctl status database -d
tee12cdr
Instance tee12cdr1 is running on node virtual-dr-19crac1
Instance tee12cdr2 is not running on node virtual-dr-19crac2
```

2. Check the restore point that we created in the standby database before starting the upgrade activity, as follows:

```
SQL> @/home/oracle/rac_database_info.sql

DATABASE_HOST       DB_NAME    DATABASE_ROLE     OPEN_MODE   STARTUP_TIME
-----------------   ---------  ---------------   ----------  ------------
virtual-dr-19crac1 tee12cdr1   PHYSICAL STANDBY  MOUNTED     17-MAR-21
```

```
SQL> select NAME,GUARANTEE_FLASHBACK_DATABASE,TIME from
V$restore_point;

NAME                         GUARANTEE_FLASHBACK  TIME
--------------------------   -------------------  ---------------
STANDBY_BEFORE_19C_UPGRADE   YES                  16-MAR-21
                                                  08.21.51.000000000 PM
```

Please note that in the restore point creation of the physical standby database, the timestamp is before the primary database restore point creation time. The restore point time in the physical standby database must always be before that of its primary database.

3. On the physical standby database, first cancel the manager recovery process using the following SQL statement:

```
SQL> alter database recover managed standby database cancel;
Database altered.
```

4. On the physical standby database, flashback the physical standby database to the preceding restore point, and this will downgrade the database back to 12.1.0.2, as follows:

```
SQL> flashback database to RESTORE POINT STANDBY_BEFORE_19C_
UPGRADE;
Flashback complete.
```

5. Create a temporary **pfile** from the current **spfile**. On the physical standby database, create **pfile** and remove all the hidden parameters as they are from 19c and recreate the **spfile**, as follows:

```
SQL> show parameter spfile

NAME       TYPE         VALUE
---------- -----------  -------------------------------
spfile     string       +DATAC1/TEE12CDR/PARAMETERFILE/
                        spfiletee12cdr1.ora
SQL> create pfile='/u01/app/oracle/product/12c/db_1/dbs/after_
downgrade.ora' from spfile='+DATAC1/TEE12CDR/PARAMETERFILE/
spfiletee12cdr1.ora';

File created.
```

6. Shutdown the physical standby database and modify the **pfile** created in the preceding step and remove all the underscore parameters which belongs to the **19c** database from it, as follows:

```
[oracle@virtual-dr-19crac1 dbs]$ srvctl stop database -d tee12cdr
```

7. Now, create the **spfile** from the modified **pfile**, as follows:

```
SQL> create spfile='+DATAC1/TEE12CDR/PARAMETERFILE/spfiletee12cdr1.
ora' from pfile='/u01/app/oracle/product/12c/db_1/dbs/after_
downgrade.ora';
File created.
```

8. Downgrade the physical standby database's clusterware configuration and start the database in the **mount** mode from the 12.1.0.2 home using the **srvctl** command, as follows:

```
[oracle@virtual-dr-19crac1 dbs]$ export ORACLE_HOME=/u01/app/
oracle/product/19c/db_1
```

```
[oracle@virtual-dr-19crac1 dbs]$ export PATH=$ORACLE_HOME/
bin:$PATH
```

```
[oracle@virtual-dr-19crac1 dbs]$ srvctl downgrade database -d
tee12cdr -o /u01/app/oracle/product/12c/db_1 -t 12.1.0.2
```

9. Next, change the configuration file **/etc/oratab** entry for the physical standby database to point to 12.1.0.2 home, as follows:

```
[oracle@virtual-dr-19crac1 dbs]$ vi /etc/oratab
```

10. Start the first database instance in the **mount** mode from the 12.1.0.2 home, as follows:

```
[oracle@virtual-dr-19crac1 ~]$ export ORACLE_HOME=/u01/app/
oracle/product/12c/db_1
[oracle@virtual-dr-19crac1 ~]$ export PATH=$ORACLE_HOME/bin:$PATH
```

```
[oracle@virtual-dr-19crac1 ~]$ srvctl start instance -d tee12cdr
-n virtual-dr-19crac1 -o mount
```

```
[oracle@virtual-dr-19crac1 ~]$ srvctl status database -d tee12cdr
Instance tee12cdr1 is running on node virtual-dr-19crac1
Instance tee12cdr2 is not running on node virtual-dr-19crac2
```

We can start the MRP process and the log shipping in the primary database and let the physical standby database sync up with the primary database. Once it catches up, we can stop and start the physical standby databases on both the nodes and restart the MRP process. This completes the step of downgrading the physical standby database.

Recreate the data guard broker configuration

Since we have downgraded the database, we will need to recreate the dataguard broker configuration. Ensure that the broker is started in both the primary and the physical standby database. If it's not started, we can start it by using the following command:

@Primary database:

```
SQL> ALTER SYSTEM SET DG_BROKER_START=TRUE;
System altered.
```

@Physcial standby database:

```
SQL> ALTER SYSTEM SET DG_BROKER_START=TRUE;
System altered.
```

Remove the existing configuration and re-create the new configuration as follows:

```
[oracle@virtual-19crac1 dbs]$ dgmgrl
DGMGRL for Linux: Version 12.1.0.2.0 - 64bit Production
Copyright (c) 2000, 2009, Oracle. All rights reserved.
Welcome to DGMGRL, type "help" for information.
DGMGRL> connect sys
Password:
Connected.

DGMGRL> show configuration;
Configuration details cannot be determined by DGMGRL
```

As we can see, it's not able to determine the old configuration. Let's remove the old configuration and create a new configuration as follows:

```
DGMGRL> remove configuration;
Removed configuration
```

Create the new data guard broker configuration, as follows:

```
DGMGRL> create configuration tee12cdb as primary database is 'tee12cdb'
connect identifier is 'tee12cdb';
DGMGRL> add database 'tee12cdr' as connect identifier is 'tee12cdr';
```

Enable the new dataguard broker configuration, as follows:

```
DGMGRL> enable configuration;
Enabled.

DGMGRL> show configuration;

Configuration - tee12cdb

  Protection Mode: MaxPerformance
  Members:
  tee12cdb - Primary database
    tee12cdr - Physical standby database

Fast-Start Failover: DISABLED
Configuration Status:
SUCCESS (status updated 73 seconds ago)
```

Once we enable the broker configuration, we can see that the primary database starts shipping all the redo data that was generated by the primary database while it got upgraded to the physical standby database, and the MRP process, which is started by the broker, will start applying the downgraded migrate redo data to the physical standby database. At this time, we can keep checking the physical standby database alert log. We will see that the MRP process will start applying all the log files, including the logs containing the downgraded redo data.

In case we don't have the dataguard broker configured, we can enable the log shipping on the primary and start the recovery on the physical standby database, as follows:

@Primary database:

```
SQL> alter system set log_archive_dest_state_2='ENABLE' scope=sid='*';
System altered.
```

@Physical standby database:

```
SQL> ALTER DATABASE RECOVER managed standby database using current logfile disconnect;
Database altered.
```

Once the MRP applies all the redo data to the physical standby database, we can stop and start the standby database in the **READ ONLY** mode and check the registry components' status and the timezone version to see if they have downgraded successfully.

Set the **cluster_database** parameter value to **TRUE** and bounce the database, as follows:

```
SQL> alter system set cluster_database=TRUE scope=spfile  sid='*';
System altered.
```

 Stop the database with the following command:

```
[oracle@virtual-dr-19crac1 dbs]$s srvctl stop database -d tee12cdr
```

Start the database in the **READ ONLY** mode, as follows:

```
[oracle@virtual-dr-19crac1 dbs]$ srvctl start  database -d tee12cdr   -o
'READ ONLY'
[oracle@virtual-dr-19crac1 dbs]$ srvctl status database -d tee12cdr
Instance tee12cdr1 is running on node virtual-dr-19crac1
Instance tee12cdr2 is running on node virtual-dr-19crac2
```

Next, check the registry component status in the physical standby database, as follows:

```
SQL> @/home/oracle/rac_database_info.sql
```

```
DATABASE_HOST       DB_NAME    DATABASE_ROLE    OPEN_MODE              STARTUP_TIME
-----------------   --------   ---------------- -------------------    -----------
virtual-dr-19crac1  tee12cdr1  PHYSICAL STANDBY READ ONLY WITH APPLY   17-MAR-21
virtual-dr-19crac2  tee12cdr2  PHYSICAL STANDBY READ ONLY WITH APPLY   17-MAR-21


SQL> select COMP_ID, COMP_NAME, VERSION, STATUS from dba_registry;


COMP_ID     COMP_NAME                             VERSION       STATUS
----------  ------------------------------------  ----------    -------------
DV          Oracle Database Vault                 12.1.0.2.0    VALID
APEX        Oracle Application Express            4.2.5.00.08   VALID
OLS         Oracle Label Security                 12.1.0.2.0    VALID
SDO         Spatial                               12.1.0.2.0    VALID
ORDIM       Oracle Multimedia                     12.1.0.2.0    VALID
CONTEXT     Oracle Text                           12.1.0.2.0    VALID
OWM         Oracle Workspace Manager              12.1.0.2.0    VALID
XDB         Oracle XML Database                   12.1.0.2.0    VALID
CATALOG     Oracle Database Catalog Views         12.1.0.2.0    VALID
CATPROC     Oracle Database Packages and Types    12.1.0.2.0    VALID
JAVAVM      JServer JAVA Virtual Machine          12.1.0.2.0    VALID
XML         Oracle XDK                            12.1.0.2.0    VALID
CATJAVA     Oracle Database Java Packages         12.1.0.2.0    VALID
APS         OLAP Analytic Workspace               12.1.0.2.0    VALID
XOQ         Oracle OLAP API                       12.1.0.2.0    VALID
RAC         Oracle Real Application Clusters      12.1.0.2.0    VALID

16 rows selected.
```

Now, check the Timezone version in the physical standby database, as follows:

```
SQL> SELECT version FROM v$timezone_file;
 VERSION
---------
       18
```

Timezone has been successfully downgraded from 32(19c) to 18(12c). We can also check the encrypted tablespaces and make sure that they are accessible after the downgrade, as follows:

```
[oracle@virtual-19crac1 dbs]$ export ORACLE_UNQNAME=TEE12CDB


SQL> @/home/oracle/rac_database_info.sql


DATABASE_HOST       DB_NAME     DATABASE_ROLE   OPEN_MODE    STARTUP_TIME
-----------------   ----------  --------------- ----------   -------------
virtual-19crac2     tee12cdb1   PRIMARY         READ WRITE   17-MAR-21
virtual-19crac2     tee12cdb1   PRIMARY         READ WRITE   17-MAR-21

SQL> select * from ENCRYPT;
```

```
NAME
----------------------------------------------------------------
This is from the encrypted tablespaces in the TEE12CDB CDB database.
```

Login to the pluggable database and query the encrypted table, as follows:

```
SQL> alter session set container=TRENDPDB;
Session altered.

SQL> show con_name;

CON_NAME
----------
TRENDPDB

SQL> select * from ENCRYPT;
NAME
----------------------------------------------------------------
This is from the encrypted tablespaces in the TRENDPDB Pluggable
database.
```

As you can see, the encryption tables look fine. We are good with it as well and with this check, we have completed all the steps with Scenario 1.

In this first scenario, we saw how to upgrade an Oracle **12c** (12.1.0.2) multitenant database along with its pluggable databases to **19c**. We also saw how we can downgrade both the primary and its physical standby database back to **12c** using the flashback approach.

Now, let's discuss how to upgrade just one pluggable database of an **18c** Multitenant container database to 19c without upgrading the whole container database. In the real time environments, we will often have this requirement where we just need to upgrade one or more pluggable databases from the lower version to the **19c** Multitenant database. In those cases, we will not upgrade the whole container database, but we will upgrade just the individual pluggable database. We will test this as Scenario 2.

Scenario-2: Upgrading a single pluggable database from the source container database to the target Oracle 19c container database

In the previous scenario, we saw how we can use AutoUpgrade to upgrade the Oracle multitenant container database along with its pluggable databases from

Oracle 12c (12.1.0.2) to Oracle 19c (19.9.0). In the following section, we will see how we can upgrade an individual pluggable database from Oracle 18c (18.3.0) to Oracle 19c (19.9.0) without upgrading the whole container database, as shown in *Figure 5.3*:

Figure 5.3: *Upgrading 18c pluggable database to 19c*
pluggable database using a single AutoUpgrade command

We have an **18c container** database with name, **riskcdb** and it has one pluggable database with the name **scanpdb**. We will upgrade this pluggable database to **19c** and plug it into the 19c container database, **questpr**.

For this exercise, we will use the Oracle 18c container database as our source database version and upgrade one of the pluggable databases from 18c to 19c.

The high-level steps performed as part of this upgrade activity

The following are the high-level steps that are performed as part of upgrading the pluggable database, **scanpdb** from 18c to 19c:

1. Check the source and target environment setup.

2. Check the configuration file required by AutoUpgrade for this particular upgrade.

3. Run the AutoUpgrade in the **Analyze** mode.

4. Verify the logs created from the **Analyze** mode.

5. Run the AutoUpgrade in the **Deploy** mode to upgrade the pluggable database, **scanpdb**.

6. Perform the post database upgrade steps.

Check the configuration of the primary database and the physical standby database

For this demonstration, we have a primary database environment and the standby database environments. For the primary environment, we have the Oracle 12.1.0.2 database binaries installed and patched with the April 2020 patch set update.

Setting up the source environment

The following is the source primary and standby database versions along with the patch set information:

The source primary database version is as follows:

```
RAC nodes           : virtual-19crac1
                      virtual-19crac2
OS version          : Oracle Enterprise Linux 7.1 64 bit
Oracle Home         : /u01/app/oracle/product/18c
Database Version    : 18.3.0.0 with April 2021 Database Bundle Patch
Grid Version        : 19.9.0

[oracle@virtual-19crac1 admin]$ $ORACLE_HOME/OPatch/opatch lspatches
32552752;OJVM RELEASE UPDATE: 18.14.0.0.210420 (32552752)
32524155;Database Release Update : 18.14.0.0.210420 (32524155)
28090553;OCW RELEASE UPDATE 18.3.0.0.0 (28090553)
OPatch succeeded.
```

The source database with the CDB and PDB information is as follows:

```
SQL> @/home/oracle/rac_database_info.sql

DATABASE_HOST      DB_NAME     DATABASE_ROLE   OPEN_MODE    STARTUP_TIME
-----------------  ----------  --------------- ----------   -------------
virtual-19crac2    riskcdb1    PRIMARY         READ WRITE   14-JUN-21
virtual-19crac2    riskcdb2    PRIMARY         READ WRITE   14-JUN-21

SQL> show pdbs

CON_ID CON_NAME       OPEN MODE   RESTRICTED
---------- --------   ---------   -----------
        2 PDB$SEED    READ ONLY   NO
        3 SCANPDB     READ WRITE  NO
```

The status of the source **pdb dba_registry** components are as follows:

```
SQL> alter session set container=scanpdb;
Session altered.


SQL> select COMP_ID,COMP_NAME,VERSION,STATUS from dba_registry;

COMP_ID      COMP_NAME                          VERSION      STATUS
----------   --------------------------------   ----------   -----------
CATALOG      Oracle Database Catalog Views      18.0.0.0.0   VALID
CATPROC      Oracle Database Packages and Types 18.0.0.0.0   VALID
RAC          Oracle Real Application Clusters   18.0.0.0.0   VALID
JAVAVM       JServer JAVA Virtual Machine        18.0.0.0.0   VALID
XML          Oracle XDK                         18.0.0.0.0   VALID
CATJAVA      Oracle Database Java Packages      18.0.0.0.0   VALID
APS          OLAP Analytic Workspace            18.0.0.0.0   VALID
XDB          Oracle XML Database                18.0.0.0.0   VALID
OWM          Oracle Workspace Manager           18.0.0.0.0   VALID
CONTEXT      Oracle Text                        18.0.0.0.0   VALID
ORDIM        Oracle Multimedia                  18.0.0.0.0   VALID
SDO          Spatial                            18.0.0.0.0   VALID
XOQ          Oracle OLAP API                    18.0.0.0.0   VALID
OLS          Oracle Label Security              18.0.0.0.0   VALID
DV           Oracle Database Vault              18.0.0.0.0   VALID

15 rows selected.
```

We will unplug/upgrade the preceding Oracle 18c pluggable database, **scanpdb** and plug it into the following Oracle 19c multitenant database (**questpr**).

Setting up the target database environment

For the target database setup, we have installed Oracle 19c (19.3.0) on the database servers and applied the Oct 2020 **patch set update** (**PSU**). We also created a container database with the name **questpr** and we will use this container database to plug the **scanpdb** once it is upgraded to Oracle 19c (19.9.0).

The target database container database along with its binary version and the patch set update is as follows:

```
RAC nodes          : virtual-19crac1
                     virtual-19crac2
OS version         : Oracle Enterprise Linux 7.1 64 bit
Oracle Home        : /u01/app/oracle/product/19c/db_1
Database Version   : 19.3.0.0 with October 2020 Database Bundle Patch
Grid Version       : 19.9.0

[oracle@virtual-19crac1 ~]$ $ORACLE_HOME/OPatch/opatch lspatches
```

```
31771877;Database Release Update : 19.9.0.0.201020 (31771877)
29585399;OCW RELEASE UPDATE 19.3.0.0.0 (29585399)
OPatch succeeded.

SQL>@rac_database_info.sql

DATABASE_HOST    DB_NAME    DATABASE_ROLE    OPEN_MODE    STARTUP_TIME
--------------   --------   -------------    ----------   -------------
virtual-19crac1  questpr1   PRIMARY          READ WRITE   14-JUN-21
virtual-19crac2  questpr2   PRIMARY          READ WRITE   14-JUN-21
```

Working directories

Create a staging directory with the primary database name and use this directory as the working directory to save all the required log files, as follows:

```
mkdir -p /u01/software/upgrade/riskcdb
```

As we did in the other upgrade exercises, we can perform all the prechecks including the purging of **dba_recyclebin**, gathering the dictionary stats, etc.

Configuration file

As mentioned earlier, always use the latest version of the AutoUpgrade tool. For this upgrade, we will use the following config file:

```
[oracle@virtual-19crac1 riskcdb]$ cat scanpdb_config.cfg

global.autoupg_log_dir=/u01/software/upgrade/riskcdb

upg1.log_dir=/u01/software/upgrade/riskcdb
upg1.source_home=/u01/app/oracle/product/18c
upg1.target_home=/u01/app/oracle/product/19c/db_1
upg1.sid=riskcdb1                        # ORACLE_SID of the source DB/CDB
upg1.pdbs=scanpdb                        # PDB that's being unplugged/upgraded
upg1.target_cdb=questpr1                 # Target Container database(cdb)
upg1.start_time=NOW                      # Upgrade start time
upg1.upgrade_node=virtual-19crac1        # Upgrade hostname
upg1.run_utlrp=yes                       # option to run utlrp after upgrade
upg1.timezone_upg=yes                    # Option to upgrade the timezone
upg1.target_version=19                   # Oracle versi of target ORACLE_HOME
```

As we can see, in the preceding configuration file, we included the Oracle 18c source container database (**riskcdb**), the Oracle 18c source pluggable database (**scanpdb**), and the target Oracle 19c container database (**questpr**), into which the source **pdb** will be plugged and upgraded to Oracle **19c**.

Running AutoUpgrade in the Analyze mode

Let's run AutoUpgrade in the **Analyze** mode for our upgrade. As mentioned earlier, this mode will only read the source database and check if the database is ready for the upgrade. Let's look at the following steps:

1. Export the Oracle home to **19c** database home, as follows:

```
[oracle@virtual-19crac1 riskcdb]$ export ORACLE_HOME=/u01/app/
oracle/product/19c/db_1
[oracle@virtual-19crac1 riskcdb]$ export PATH=$ORACLE_HOME/
bin:$PATH
```

2. Now, run the AutoUpgrade in the **ANALYZE** mode as follows:

```
[oracle@virtual-19crac1 riskcdb]$ $ORACLE_HOME/jdk/bin/java -jar
$ORACLE_HOME/rdbms/admin/autoupgrade.jar -config scanpdb_config.cfg
-mode ANALYZE
```

3. The following is the output for the preceding command:

```
[oracle@virtual-19crac1 riskcdb]$ export ORACLE_HOME=/u01/app/
oracle/product/19c/db_1

[oracle@virtual-19crac1 riskcdb]$ export PATH=$ORACLE_HOME/
bin:$PATH

[oracle@virtual-19crac1 riskcdb]$ $ORACLE_HOME/jdk/bin/java -jar
$ORACLE_HOME/rdbms/admin/autoupgrade.jar -config scanpdb_config.cfg
-mode ANALYZE

AutoUpgrade tool launched with default options
Processing config file ...
+-------------------------------+
| Starting AutoUpgrade execution |
+-------------------------------+
1 databases will be analyzed
Type 'help' to list console commands
upg> lsj
+----+--------+--------+---------+-------+------------+--------+-------
|Job#|DB_NAME|STAGE|OPERATION| STATUS|START_TIME|UPDATED|MESSAGE|
+----+--------+--------+---------+-------+------------+--------+-------
| 100|riskcdb1|PRECHECKS|PREPARING|RUNNING|21/06/14
09:02|09:02:35|Loading database information|
+----+--------+--------+---------+-------+------------+--------+-------
Total jobs 1
upg> lsj
+----+--------+--------+---------+-------+------------+--------+------
|Job#|DB_NAME|STAGE|OPERATION|STATUS|START_TIME|UPDATED|MESSAGE|
```

```
+----+--------+---------+---------+-------+-------------+------
| 100|riskcdb1|PRECHECKS|PREPARING|RUNNING|21/06/14
09:02|09:03:01|Remaining 1/74|
+----+--------+---------+---------+-------+-------------+------
Total jobs 1
upg> lsj
+----+--------+---------+---------+-------+-------------+------
|Job#|DB_NAME|STAGE|OPERATION|STATUS|START_TIME|UPDATED| MESSAGE
+----+--------+---------+---------+-------+-------------+-------
| 100|riskcdb1|PRECHECKS|PREPARING|RUNNING|21/06/14
09:02|09:03:01|Remaining 1/74|
+----+--------+---------+---------+-------+-------------+-------
Total jobs 1
upg> Job 100 completed
------------------ Final Summary -------------------
Number of databases        [1]
Jobs finished              [1]
Jobs failed                [0]
Jobs pending               [0]
```

Please check the summary report at the following links:

/u01/software/upgrade/riskcdb/cfgtoollogs/upgrade/auto/status/
status.html
/u01/software/upgrade/riskcdb/cfgtoollogs/upgrade/auto/status/
status.log
[oracle@virtual-19crac1 riskcdb]$

Database upgrade log files

For this run, the AutoUpgrade utility created various logs in **/u01/software/
upgrade/riskcdb/riskcdb1**; in our case, as follows:

```
[oracle@virtual-19crac1 riskcdb]$ cd riskcdb1/100/prechecks/
[oracle@virtual-19crac1 prechecks]$ ls -ltr
total 260
-rwx------ 1 oracle oinstall 175093 Jun 14 09:03 prechecks_scanpdb.log
-rwx------ 1 oracle oinstall   7325 Jun 14 09:03 riskcdb_checklist.xml
-rwx------ 1 oracle oinstall   7817 Jun 14 09:03 riskcdb_checklist.json
-rwx------ 1 oracle oinstall   2573 Jun 14 09:03 riskcdb_checklist.cfg
-rwx------ 1 oracle oinstall  27565 Jun 14 09:03 riskcdb_preupgrade.html
-rwx------ 1 oracle oinstall  28409 Jun 14 09:03 upgrade.xml
-rwx------ 1 oracle oinstall  10393 Jun 14 09:03 riskcdb_preupgrade.log
ß Important log

[oracle@virtual-19crac1 prechecks]$
```

Let's check the preupgrade log file to see if the source pluggable database (**scanpdb**) is good to be upgraded to the 19c pluggable database, as follows:

```
[oracle@virtual-19crac1 prechecks]$ cat riskcdb_preupgrade.log
Report generated by AutoUpgrade 21.1.3 (#57ab246) on 2021-06-14 09:03:53
Upgrade-To version: 19.0.0.0.0
=======================================
Status of the database prior to upgrade
=======================================
      Database Name:  riskcdb1
     Container Name:  SCANPDB
       Container ID:  3
            Version:  18.3.0.0.0
     DB Patch Level:  Database Release Update : 18.3.0.0.180717
28090523)
         Compatible:  18.0.0
          Blocksize:  8192
           Platform:  Linux x86 64-bit
      Timezone File:  31
  Database log mode:  ARCHIVELOG
           Readonly:  false
            Edition:  EE

  Oracle Component                          Upgrade Action     Current Status
  ----------------                          --------------     --------------
  OLAP Analytic Workspace                   [to be upgraded]   VALID
  Oracle Server                             [to be upgraded]   VALID
  Oracle Java Packages                      [to be upgraded]   VALID
  Oracle Text                               [to be upgraded]   VALID
  Oracle Database Vault                     [to be upgraded]   VALID
  JServer JAVA Virtual Machine              [to be upgraded]   VALID
  Oracle Label Security                     [to be upgraded]   VALID
  Oracle Multimedia                         [to be upgraded]   VALID
  Oracle Workspace Manager                  [to be upgraded]   VALID
  Real Application Clusters                 [to be upgraded]   VALID
  Oracle Spatial                            [to be upgraded]   VALID
  Oracle XML Database                       [to be upgraded]   VALID
  Oracle XDK for Java                       [to be upgraded]   VALID
  Oracle OLAP API                           [to be upgraded]   VALID

  *

  * ALL Components in This Database Registry:

  *

  Component   Current     Current      Original     Previous
Component
```

CID	Version	Status	Version	Version	Schema
APS	18.3.0.0.0	VALID	18.1.0.0.0		SYS
CATALOG	18.3.0.0.0	VALID	18.1.0.0.0		SYS
CATJAVA	18.3.0.0.0	VALID	18.1.0.0.0		SYS
CATPROC	18.3.0.0.0	VALID	18.1.0.0.0		SYS
CONTEXT	18.3.0.0.0	VALID	18.1.0.0.0		CTXSYS
DV	18.3.0.0.0	VALID	18.1.0.0.0		DVSYS
JAVAVM	18.3.0.0.0	VALID	18.1.0.0.0		SYS
OLS	18.3.0.0.0	VALID	18.1.0.0.0		LBACSYS
ORDIM	18.3.0.0.0	VALID	18.1.0.0.0		ORDSYS
OWM	18.3.0.0.0	VALID	18.1.0.0.0		WMSYS
RAC	18.3.0.0.0	VALID	18.1.0.0.0		SYS
SDO	18.3.0.0.0	VALID	18.1.0.0.0		MDSYS
XDB	18.3.0.0.0	VALID	18.1.0.0.0		XDB
XML	18.3.0.0.0	VALID	18.1.0.0.0		SYS
XOQ	18.3.0.0.0	VALID	18.1.0.0.0		OLAPSYS

```
==============
BEFORE UPGRADE
==============

REQUIRED ACTIONS
================
None
RECOMMENDED ACTIONS

===================
```

1. To prevent any unexpected data loss, consider using another backup strategy.

    The Guaranteed Restore Point (GRP) is not available as a backup strategy for this upgrade type in AutoUpgrade.

    An UnplugPlug Upgrade will occur on the database SCANPDB from the source CDB riskcdb1 to CDB questpr1.

2. (AUTOFIXUP) Gather the statistics on fixed objects prior to the upgrade using the following command:

    ```
    EXECUTE DBMS_STATS.GATHER_FIXED_OBJECTS_STATS;
    ```

    None of the fixed object tables have had the stats collected.

    Gathering the statistics on fixed objects, if none have been gathered yet, is recommended prior to upgrading.

    For information on managing optimizer statistics, refer to the 18.0.0.0 Oracle Database Upgrade Guide.

INFORMATION ONLY

=================

3. To help you keep track of your tablespace allocations, the following AUTOEXTEND tablespaces are expected to successfully EXTEND during theupgrade process:

Tablespace	Size	Min Size For Upgrade
SYSTEM	270 MB	501 MB
TEMP	62 MB	240 MB
UNDOTBS1	100 MB	400 MB
SYSAUX	370 MB	591 MB

The minimum tablespace sizes for the upgrade are estimates.

4. Follow the instructions in the Oracle Multimedia README.txt file in <19 ORACLE_HOME>/ord/im/admin/README.txt, or MOS note 2555923.1 to determine if Oracle Multimedia is being used. If Oracle Multimedia is being used, refer to MOS note 2347372.1 for suggestions on replacing Oracle Multimedia.

The Oracle Multimedia component (ORDIM) is installed.

Starting with release 19c, Oracle Multimedia is desupported. The object types still exist, but the methods and procedures will raise an exception. Refer to the 19 Oracle Database Upgrade Guide, the Oracle Multimedia README.txt file in <19 ORACLE_HOME>/ord/im/admin/README.txt, or MOS note 2555923.1 for more information.

5. The following are ALL the components in this database registry:

Component CID	Current Version	Current Status	Original Version	Previous Version	Component Schema
APS	18.3.0.0.0	VALID	18.1.0.0.0		SYS
CATALOG	18.3.0.0.0	VALID	18.1.0.0.0		SYS
CATJAVA	18.3.0.0.0	VALID	18.1.0.0.0		SYS
CATPROC	18.3.0.0.0	VALID	18.1.0.0.0		SYS
CONTEXT	18.3.0.0.0	VALID	18.1.0.0.0		CTXSYS
DV	18.3.0.0.0	VALID	18.1.0.0.0		DVSYS
JAVAVM	18.3.0.0.0	VALID	18.1.0.0.0		SYS
OLS	18.3.0.0.0	VALID	18.1.0.0.0		LBACSYS
ORDIM	18.3.0.0.0	VALID	18.1.0.0.0		ORDSYS
OWM	18.3.0.0.0	VALID	18.1.0.0.0		WMSYS

```
RAC     18.3.0.0.0   VALID     18.1.0.0.0           SYS
SDO     18.3.0.0.0   VALID     18.1.0.0.0           MDSYS
XDB     18.3.0.0.0   VALID     18.1.0.0.0           XDB
XML     18.3.0.0.0   VALID     18.1.0.0.0           SYS
XOQ     18.3.0.0.0   VALID     18.1.0.0.0           OLAPSYS
```

Review the information before upgrading.

6. The following is a count of the invalid objects by the Oracle-
   maintained users:

   Oracle-Maintained User Name   Number of INVALID Objects
   --------------------------   --------------------------
   None   None

   Review the information before upgrading.

7. The following is a count of the invalid objects by the Application
   users:

   Application User Name   Number of INVALID Objects
   --------------------------   --------------------------
   None   None

   Review the information before upgrading.

```
=============
AFTER UPGRADE
=============
 REQUIRED ACTIONS
 ================
  None

 RECOMMENDED ACTIONS

 ==================
```

8. (AUTOFIXUP) Upgrade the database time zone file using the DBMS_DST
   package.

   The database is using the time zone file version 31 and the target
   19 release ships with the time zone file version 32.

   Oracle recommends upgrading to the desired (latest) version of
   the time zone file. For more information, refer to "Upgrading
   the Time Zone File and Timestamp with Time Zone Data" in the 19
   Oracle Database Globalization Support Guide.

9. (AUTOFIXUP) Recompile the objects with timestamp mismatch. Please
   refer to MOS note 781959.1 for more details.

   There are objects whose timestamp are mismatched with its parent
   objects.

Timestamp of the dependent objects must coincide with the timestamp of parent objects.

10. (AUTOFIXUP) Gather the dictionary statistics after the upgrade using the following command:

    EXECUTE DBMS_STATS.GATHER_DICTIONARY_STATS;

    Oracle recommends gathering the dictionary statistics after the upgrade.

    The dictionary statistics provide essential information to the Oracle optimizer to help it find the efficient SQL execution plans. After a database upgrade, the statistics need to be re-gathered as there can now be tables that have significantly changed during the upgrade or new tables that do not have the statistics gathered yet.

11. Gather the statistics on fixed objects after the upgrade and when there is a representative workload on the system using the following command:

    EXECUTE DBMS_STATS.GATHER_FIXED_OBJECTS_STATS;

    Oracle recommends gathering the fixed object statistics after the upgrade. This recommendation is given for all the preupgrade runs.

    The fixed object statistics provide essential information to the Oracle optimizer to help it find the efficient SQL execution plans. Those statistics are specific to the Oracle Database release that generates them, and can be stale upon the database upgrade.

    For information on managing optimizer statistics, refer to the 18.0.0.0 Oracle Database Upgrade Guide.

12. (AUTOFIXUP) Run @?/rdbms/admin/utlrp.sql in order to recompile any invalid objects.

    There are invalid objects in the database after the upgrade.

    The invalid database objects need to be recompiled after the upgrade.

    [oracle@virtual-19crac1 prechecks]$

As we can see, the preupgrade check looks good; we can now upgrade the pluggable database, **scanpdb** to **19c**.

Run the AutoUpgrade command in the DEPLOY mode to upgrade the database

We need to run this from the Oracle 19c home. So, lets export the Oracle home to point to Oracle 19c first and then run the AutoUpgrade command as follows:

1. Export the Oracle home to **19c** database home, as follows:

    ```
    [oracle@virtual-19crac1 riskcdb]$ export ORACLE_HOME=/u01/app/
    oracle/product/19c/db_1
    ```

    ```
    [oracle@virtual-19crac1 riskcdb]$ export PATH=$ORACLE_HOME/
    bin:$PATH
    ```

2. Now, run the AutoUpgrade in the **DEPLOY** mode as follows:

    ```
    [oracle@virtual-19crac1 riskcdb]$ $ORACLE_HOME/jdk/bin/java -jar
    $ORACLE_HOME/rdbms/admin/autoupgrade.jar -config scanpdb_config.cfg
    -mode DEPLOY
    ```

3. The following is part of the output when the preceding command is run successfully:

    ```
    [oracle@virtual-19crac1 riskcdb]$ $ORACLE_HOME/jdk/bin/java -jar
    $ORACLE_HOME/rdbms/admin/autoupgrade.jar -config scanpdb_config.cfg
    -mode DEPLOY

    AutoUpgrade tool launched with default options

    Processing config file ...

    +-------------------------------+
    | Starting AutoUpgrade execution |
    +-------------------------------+
    1 databases will be processed
    Type 'help' to list console commands
    upg> lsj

    +----+-----------+---------+---------+-------+--------------+--------+---
    |Job#|DB_NAME|STAGE|OPERATION|STATUS|START_TIME|UPDATED|MESSAGE|
    +----+-----------+---------+---------+-------+--------------+--------+---
    | 101|riskcdb1|PRECHECKS|PREPARING|RUNNING|21/06/14
    09:12|09:12:41|Loading database information|
    +----+-----------+---------+---------+-------+--------------+--------+-----
    Total jobs 1
    upg> lsj
    +----+----+---------+---------+-------+--------------+--------+--
    |Job#|DB_NAME|STAGE|OPERATION|STATUS|START_TIME|UPDATED|MESSAGE|
    +----+----+---------+---------+-------+--------------+--------+--
    | 101|riskcdb1|PREFIXUPS|EXECUTING|RUNNING|21/06/14
    ```

```
09:12|09:14:34|Remaining 2/2|
+----+----+---------+---------+-------+--------------+-------+--
Total jobs 1
upg> lsj
+----+---------+---------+---------+-------+--------------+-------
|Job#| DB_NAME|STAGE|OPERATION|STATUS|START_TIME|PUDATED|MESSAGE|
+----+---------+---------+---------+-------+--------------+-------
| 101|riskcdb1|DBUPGRADE|EXECUTING|RUNNING|21/06/14
09:12|09:21:58|Running|
+----+---------+---------+---------+-------+--------------+-------
Total jobs 1
upg> lsj
+-----+---------+---------+-------+--------------+--------+-----
|Job#|DB_NAME|STAGE|OPERATION|STATUS|START_TIME|UPDATED|MESSAGE|
+----+---------+---------+---------+-------+--------------+-------+------
| 101|riskcdb1|DBUPGRADE|EXECUTING|RUNNING|21/06/14
09:12|09:22:29|0%Upgraded SCANPDB|
+-----+---------+---------+-------+--------------+--------+-----
Total jobs 1
upg> lsj
+----+---------+---------+---------+-------+--------------+------
|Job#|DB_NAME|STAGE|OPERATION|STATUS|START_TIME|UPDATED| MESSAGE|
+----+---------+---------+---------+-------+--------------+------
| 101|riskcdb1|DBUPGRADE|EXECUTING|RUNNING|21/06/14
9:12|09:40:31|91%Upgraded SCANPDB|
+----+---------+---------+---------+-------+--------------+------
Total jobs 1
upg> Job 101 completed
------------------- Final Summary --------------------

Number of databases        [1]
Jobs finished              [1]
Jobs failed                [0]
Jobs pending               [0]
```

Please check the summary report at the following links:

```
/u01/software/upgrade/riskcdb/cfgtoollogs/upgrade/auto/status/
status.html
/u01/software/upgrade/riskcdb/cfgtoollogs/upgrade/auto/status/
status.log

[oracle@virtual-19crac1 riskcdb]$
```

While the upgrade is still running, you can also check the **19c** target **cdb** database, **questpr** and we can see that the source **pdb** is plugged and getting upgraded, as follows:

```
SQL>@rac_database_info.sql
```

```
DATABASE_HOST      DB_NAME    DATABASE_ROLE    OPEN_MODE    STARTUP_TIME
---------------    --------   -------------    ----------   --------
virtual-19crac1    questpr1   PRIMARY          READ WRITE   14-JUN-21
virtual-19crac2    questpr2   PRIMARY          READ WRITE   14-JUN-21

SQL> show pdbs

    CON_ID CON_NAME      OPEN MODE   RESTRICTED
---------- ----------    ----------  ----------
         2 PDB$SEED      READ ONLY   NO
         3 SCANPDB       MIGRATE     YES
```

While the **AutoUpgrade** process is still running, we can open a new terminal and check the different directories that the **AutoUpgrade** tool creates for the various logs, as follows:

```
[oracle@virtual-19crac1]$ cd /u01/software/upgrade/riskcdb/riskcdb1/101

[oracle@virtual-19crac1 101]$ ls -ltr
drwx------ 2 oracle oinstall     28 Jun 14 09:12 preupgrade
drwx------ 2 oracle oinstall   4096 Jun 14 09:20 prechecks
drwx------ 2 oracle oinstall     85 Jun 14 09:21 prefixups
drwx------ 2 oracle oinstall     88 Jun 14 09:21 drain
drwx------ 2 oracle oinstall   4096 Jun 14 09:41 dbupgrade
drwx------ 2 oracle oinstall     39 Jun 14 09:41 noncdbtopdb
drwx------ 2 oracle oinstall   4096 Jun 14 09:41 postchecks
-rwx------ 1 oracle oinstall   1412 Jun 14 09:41 autoupgrade_err.log
drwx------ 2 oracle oinstall     88 Jun 14 09:41 postfixups
drwx------ 2 oracle oinstall     29 Jun 14 09:42 postupgrade
-rwx------ 1 oracle oinstall   8641 Jun 14 09:42 autoupgrade_20210614_
user.log
-rwx------ 1 oracle oinstall 981917 Jun 14 09:42 autoupgrade_20210614.
log
drwx------ 2 oracle oinstall     28 Jun 14 09:42 sysupdates
[oracle@virtual-19crac1 101]$
```

We can keep tail the **autoupgrade_20210614_user.log** file for the upgrade status, as follows:

```
[oracle@virtual-19crac1 101]$ tail -f autoupgrade_20210614_user.log

2021-06-14 09:14:33.479 INFO Adding fixup PURGE_RECYCLEBIN PRECHECKS YES
true ERROR to execution queue of SCANPDB
2021-06-14 09:22:15.456 INFO Begin Upgrade on Database [riskcdb-SCANPDB]
2021-06-14 09:22:29.183 INFO 0%Upgraded SCANPDB
2021-06-14 09:25:29.466 INFO 21%Upgraded SCANPDB
2021-06-14 09:28:29.669 INFO 23%Upgraded SCANPDB
2021-06-14 09:31:30.319 INFO 49%Upgraded SCANPDB
```

```
2021-06-14 09:34:30.517 INFO 60%Upgraded SCANPDB
2021-06-14 09:37:30.817 INFO 91%Upgraded SCANPDB
2021-06-14 09:40:31.345 INFO 91%Upgraded SCANPDB
2021-06-14 09:41:35.166 INFO SUCCESSFULLY UPGRADED [riskcdb-SCANPDB]
2021-06-14 09:41:35.166 INFO End Upgrade on Database [riskcdb-SCANPDB]
2021-06-14 09:41:36.362 INFO SCANPDB has been successfully upgraded
skipping the resume
2021-06-14 09:41:36.362 INFO SUCCESSFULLY UPGRADED [riskcdb]
2021-06-14 09:41:36.362 INFO End Upgrade on Database [riskcdb]
2021-06-14 09:41:36.364 INFO SUCCESSFULLY UPGRADED [riskcdb]
2021-06-14 09:41:36.381 INFO riskcdb Return status is SUCCESS
2021-06-14 09:41:56.755 INFO Analyzing riskcdb1, 12 checks will run
using 2 threads
2021-06-14 09:42:00.603 INFO The pdb(s) created in database riskcdb1
were successfully restarted
2021-06-14 09:42:00.740 INFO Return status is SUCCESS
2021-06-14 09:42:00.747 INFO Database State
        Resetting the database's state: [SUCCESS] [None]
Restart of pdb(s) created in database [riskcdb]
        [SUCCESS] [None]
```

Post upgrade steps

Once the pluggable database upgrade completes, we can login the **19c** container database, **questpr** and switch to the pluggable database, **scanpdb** and run the **utlrp** to compile the invalid objects, as follows:

```
[oracle@virtual-19crac1 ~]$ sqlplus / as sysdba

SQL*Plus: Release 19.0.0.0.0 - Production on Mon Jun 14 09:53:01 2021
Version 19.9.0.0.0
Copyright (c) 1982, 2019, Oracle.  All rights reserved.
Connected to:
Oracle Database 19c Enterprise Edition Release 19.0.0.0.0 - Production
Version 19.9.0.0.0

SQL> show pdbs

    CON_ID CON_NAME                            OPEN MODE  RESTRICTED
---------- ------------------------------- ---------- ----------
         2 PDB$SEED                            READ ONLY  NO
         3 SCANPDB                             READ WRITE NO
SQL> alter session set container=scanpdb;
Session altered.

SQL> show con_name;

CON_NAME
```

```
--------------------------------
SCANPDB

SQL> @$ORACLE_HOME/rdbms/admin/utlrp;
```

As a final step, check the status of all the components in the registry and also check the timezone version, as follows:

```
SQL> select COMP_ID,COMP_NAME,VERSION,STATUS from dba_registry;

COMP_ID      COMP_NAME                               VERSION        STATUS
----------   --------------------------------------  -------------  ---
CATALOG      Oracle Database Catalog Views           19.0.0.0.0     VALID
CATPROC      Oracle Database Packages and Types      19.0.0.0.0     VALID
RAC          Oracle Real Application Clusters        19.0.0.0.0     VALID
JAVAVM       JServer JAVA Virtual Machine            19.0.0.0.0     VALID
XML          Oracle XDK                              19.0.0.0.0     VALID
CATJAVA      Oracle Database Java Packages           19.0.0.0.0     VALID
APS          OLAP Analytic Workspace                 19.0.0.0.0     VALID
XDB          Oracle XML Database                     19.0.0.0.0     VALID
OWM          Oracle Workspace Manager                19.0.0.0.0     VALID
CONTEXT      Oracle Text                             19.0.0.0.0     VALID
ORDIM        Oracle Multimedia                       19.0.0.0.0     VALID
SDO          Spatial                                 19.0.0.0.0     VALID
XOQ          Oracle OLAP API                         19.0.0.0.0     VALID
OLS          Oracle Label Security                   19.0.0.0.0     VALID
DV           Oracle Database Vault                   19.0.0.0.0     VALID
15 rows selected.

SQL> SELECT version FROM v$timezone_file;

   VERSION
----------
        32
```

We have successfully tested the upgrading of a single pluggable database from 18c to 19c. As we saw, the AutoUpgrade utility can not only upgrade the whole container database along with all of its pluggable database from the earlier versions to Oracle 19c, it can also upgrade the individual pluggable database to the Oracle 19c container database.

Known issues

The following is a known issue along with the possible solution:

Issue-1

If we are using the AutoUpgrade utility version, 21.1.3, we can run into the following issue when we run the AutoUpgrade in the **Analyze** or the **Deploy** mode and we cannot proceed with the database upgrade, as follows:

AutoUpgrade version.

```
[oracle@virtual-19crac1 ]$ $ORACLE_HOME/jdk/bin/java -jar $ORACLE_HOME/
rdbms/admin/autoupgrade.jar -version
build.hash 57ab246
build.version 21.1.3
build.date 2021/04/21 13:32:13 <-----------
build.max_target_version 21
build.supported_target_versions 12.2,18,19,21
build.type production
```

Issue:
==============
BEFORE UPGRADE
==============

REQUIRED ACTIONS

================

1. Verify that the AutoUpgrade configuration file contains the appropriate parameters to allow AutoUpgrade to locate the KeyStore files – especially the source_tns_admin_dir parameter. It is not necessary to copy the KeyStore files to the specified directory. Rather, update the configuration file, so that they can be found automatically.

    The database is using TDE, but AutoUpgrade is unable to access the KeyStore files. Based on the AutoUpgrade configuration file which results in a TNS_ADMIN environmental value of /u01/app/oracle/product/12c/db_1/network/admin, AutoUpgrade is searching for the files in the following directory:

    +DATAC1/skzr12c/WALLET

    If Oracle **Transparent Data Encryption (TDE)** is in use, AutoUpgrade must be able to access the files necessary to open the KeyStore.

    Solution:

    Until we fix this issue, we can use the older version of the AutoUpgrade tool which we can download from Oracle. Oracle is working with the AutoUpgrade team to fix the issue and as a workaround.

Conclusion

In this chapter, we tested two scenarios. In the first scenario, we upgraded the 12.1.0.2 container database along with its pluggable database to the 19.9.0 container database. Later, we also tested downgrading the 12.1.0.2 container database with the pluggable database to the 19.9.0 container database using the flashback method. In the second scenario, we saw how to upgrade just one pluggable database from the 18c multitenant container database to 19c.

In the next chapter, we will see how we can upgrade and convert a 12c non-container database to a 19c pluggable database using a single **AutoUpgrade** command.

Multiple choice questions

1. **Do we need to give the pdb details in the AutoUpgrade configuration file when we upgrade a multitenant database?**

   a. Yes

   b. No

2. **When we are upgrading the database to 19c, which network-related file do we need to copy from the source database home to the target database home, in case we have the encrypted tablespaces in the source database?**

   a. tnsnames.ora

   b. sqlnet.ora

   c. both tnsnames.ora & sqlnet.ora

Answers

1. b

2. b

Key terms

- autoupgrade.jar -version
- upg1.target_cdb
- non-cdb to pdb

CHAPTER 6
Upgrading and Converting 12c Non-CDB as 19c PDB (Using AutoUpgrade)

Introduction

In *Chapter 4, Upgrading and Converting 12c Non-CDB as 19c PDB*, we saw how we can upgrade a 12c non-cdb as a 19c non-cdb and then convert it as a **pluggable database (pdb)**. As you see, that was a two-step process, as in the first step, we upgraded the Oracle database from 12c to 19c using the AutoUpgrade tool, and in the next step, we converted it as a pluggable database and plugged it into one of the pre-existing container databases. In this chapter, we will do the same but we will only perform one step, that is, using one `AutoUpgrade` command.

Structure

In this chapter, we will cover the following topics:

- The high-level steps required for upgrading and converting a 12.1.0.2 non-container database to 19c pluggable database using a single AutoUpgrade command

- Checking the source and target setup environments used to demonstrate the database upgrade

- The pre-requisites steps required for the database upgrade

- How to download the AutoUpgrade utility

- The configuration file required by the AutoUpgrade tool

- Running AutoUpgrade in the '**Analyze**' mode to verify the database readiness and fixing any issues that can impact the database upgrade activity

- The AutoUpgrade log locations

- Running the AutoUpgrade in the '**Deploy**' mode to upgrade and covert non-cdb to a pluggable database

- The post-upgrade checks

- Validating the database upgrade

- The fall-back methods that can be used to downgrade the Oracle database from the upgraded version back to the source version

- Test RMAN restoration to restore the database from the pre-upgrade backup

- A few known issues that can occur during the database upgrade or the database downgrade

Objective

After studying this chapter, you will get familiar with upgrading and converting a non-container database to 19c pluggable database using a single **AutoUpgrade** command. You will also see how we can downgrade the database back to the source database version by restoring the **RMAN** backup that was taken before starting the database upgrade.

An overview of the database upgrade

In the previous chapters, we already discussed about the AutoUpgrade architecture and how it works; so, in this chapter, we will skip that part and proceed with the database upgrade. In this section, we will test how we can upgrade an Oracle 12c (12.1.0.2) non-container database as the Oracle 19c (19.9.0) pluggable database using one single **AutoUpgrade** command.

Figure 6.1 shows the high-level representation of this process of upgrading and converting a 12.1.0.2 non-cdb to as 19.9.0.0 pluggable database using a single **AutoUpgrade** command, as follows:

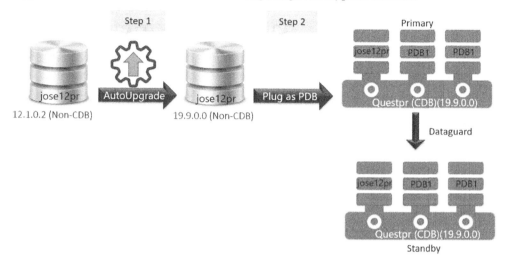

Figure 6.1: Upgrading and converting 12c non-cdb as pdb using single command

We have created the following script which we can use to check the current database configuration of the RAC database; we will be using this script throughout this chapter.

Script -1: The following script will pull the current database details like, the mode and the role of the database:

```
[oracle@virtual-19crac1] cat /home/oracle/rac_database_info.sql


SQL> set lines 200
SQL> col DATABASE_HOST for a30;
SQL> col HOST_NAME for a15;
SQL> col DATABASE_ROLE for a10
SQL> col OPEN_MODE for a10
SQL> col STARTUP_TIME for a20
SQL> SELECT i.HOST_NAME "DATABASE_HOST" ,i.INSTANCE_NAME "DB_NAME",
     d.DATABASE_ROLE " DATABASE_ROLE", d.OPEN_MODE " OPEN_MODE ",
     STARTUP_TIME
     from GV$DATABASE d, gv$instance i
     where i.INST_ID=d.INST_ID;
```

Environments used for the upgrade

The following are the source and target database environments that are used to demonstrate the database upgrade.

Setting up the source database environment

Since we already saw how we can upgrade the physical standby database in all of our previous chapters, we will skip those steps in this chapter. For this exercise, we will upgrade a 2-node Oracle 12c (12.1.0.2) RAC database. We have the Oracle 12c (12.1.0.2) database binaries installed and patched with the July 2020 **patch set update (PSU)**.

The source database version and the patch set is as follows:

```
RAC nodes          : virtual-19crac1
                     virtual-19crac2
OS version         : Oracle Enterprise Linux 7.1 64 bit
Oracle Home        : /u01/app/oracle/product/12c/db_1
Database Version   : 12.1.0.2 with July 2020 Database Bundle Patch
Grid Version       : 19.9.0

[oracle@virtual-19crac1 admin]$ $ORACLE_HOME/OPatch/opatch lspatches
27487279;
28125601;
31136382;OCW PATCH SET UPDATE 12.1.0.2.200714 (31136382)
31001106;Database Bundle Patch : 12.1.0.2.200714 (31001106)
```

The source primary database name is **jose12pr** and the following are its **RAC** instances:

```
SQL> @/home/oracle/rac_database_info.sql

DATABASE_HOST     DB_NAME     DATABASE_ROLE     OPEN_MODE     STARTUP_TIME
---------------   ---------   ---------------   ----------    ------------
virtual-19crac1   jose12pr1   PRIMARY           READ WRITE    17-MAR-21
virtual-19crac1   jose12pr1   PRIMARY           READ WRITE    17-MAR-21
```

Setting up the target environment

For the target database setup, we have installed Oracle 19c (19.3.0) on the database servers and applied the October 2020 PSU. We also created a container database with the name **questpr**, and we will use this container database to plug the **jose12pr** once it's upgraded to Oracle 19c (19.9.0). The target primary **RAC Container** database along with its binary version and the patch set update, is shown as follows:

```
RAC nodes              : virtual-19crac1
                         virtual-19crac2
OS version             : Oracle Enterprise Linux 7.1 64 bit
Oracle Home            : /u01/app/oracle/product/19c/db_1
Database Version       : 19.3.0.0 with October 2020 Database Bundle Patch
Grid Version           : 19.9.0

[oracle@virtual-19crac1 ~]$ $ORACLE_HOME/OPatch/opatch lspatches
31771877;Database Release Update : 19.9.0.0.201020 (31771877)
29585399;OCW RELEASE UPDATE 19.3.0.0.0 (29585399)
OPatch succeeded.

SQL>@rac_database_info.sql

DATABASE_HOST    DB_NAME    DATABASE_ROLE    OPEN_MODE    STARTUP_TIME
---------------  ---------  -------------    ----------   -----------
virtual-19crac1  questpr1   PRIMARY          READ WRITE   17-MAR-21
virtual-19crac2  questpr2   PRIMARY          READ WRITE   17-MAR-21
```

Pre-requisites of database upgrade

In the following section, check some of the pre-requisites and a few upfront tasks that we can perform before planning and starting the database upgrade.

Perform full backup of the primary source database

Always take a **FULL** level 0 backup of the source database before we upgrade it. Normally, if we upgrade the database to a newer version, we can simply create a guaranteed restore point before starting the database upgrade and we can just flashback the database to this restore point in case we want to downgrade it later. But in this case, since we are not only upgrading the database from 12.1 to 19.9, but also converting it as a PDB database using one command, we can't use the flashback method to downgrade the database from PDB to non-CDB.

If we really want to downgrade the upgraded/migrated PDB database back as 12.1 non-cdb, the only way we know is to drop the 19.9 PDB database and then use the backup of our source that we take before starting the upgrade process and restoring it in 12.1 home. We are not testing that here, as it is a pretty standard method which is just a regular backup/restore to rebuild the database.

The following is a sample script that we can use to take a Full level 0 backup of the primary database (You can use any scripts that work for your environment.):

```
RMAN >
run
{
 allocate channel ch1 device type disk format '/u01/19cupgrade/DATA_
L0_%d_%Y%M%D_%s-%p-%t';
 allocate channel ch2 device type disk format '/u01/19cupgrade/DATA_
L0_%d_%Y%M%D_%s-%p-%t';
 allocate channel ch3 device type disk format '/u01/19cupgrade/DATA_
L0_%d_%Y%M%D_%s-%p-%t';
 allocate channel ch4 device type disk format '/u01/19cupgrade/DATA_
L0_%d_%Y%M%D_%s-%p-%t';
 backup incremental level 0 database plus archivelog TAG='FULL_BACKUP_
B4_UPGRADE' format '/u01/19cupgrade/DATA_L0_%d_%Y%M%D_%s-%p-%t';
 backup tag 'CONTROL_BACKUP_B4_UPGRADE' current controlfile format '/
u01/19cupgrade/DATA_CONTROL_%d_%Y%M%D_%s-%p-%t';
 release channel ch1;
 release channel ch2;
 release channel ch3;
 release channel ch4;
}
```

The output for the preceding command is as follows:

```
[oracle@virtual-19crac1 ~]$ rman target /

Recovery Manager: Release 12.1.0.2.0 - Production on Sun May 2 16:58:31
2021
Copyright (c) 1982, 2014, Oracle and/or its affiliates.  All rights
reserved.
connected to target database: JOSE12PR (DBID=1173972737, not open)

RMAN> run
{
 allocate channel ch1 device type disk format '/u01/19cupgrade/DATA_
L0_%d_%Y%M%D_%s-%p-%t';
 allocate channel ch2 device type disk format '/u01/19cupgrade/DATA_
L0_%d_%Y%M%D_%s-%p-%t';
 allocate channel ch3 device type disk format '/u01/19cupgrade/DATA_
L0_%d_%Y%M%D_%s-%p-%t';
 allocate channel ch4 device type disk format '/u01/19cupgrade/DATA_
L0_%d_%Y%M%D_%s-%p-%t';
 backup incremental level 0 database plus archivelog TAG='FULL_BACKUP_
B4_UPGRADE' format  '/u01/19cupgrade/DATA_L0_%d_%Y%M%D_%s-%p-%t';
 backup tag 'CONTROL_BACKUP_B4_UPGRADE' current controlfile format '/
u01/19cupgrade/DATA_CONTROL_%d_%Y%M%D_%s-%p-%t';
 release channel ch1;
 release channel ch2;
```

```
 release channel ch3;
 release channel ch4;
}
2> 3> 4> 5> 6> 7> 8> 9> 10> 11> 12> 13>

using target database control file instead of recovery catalog
allocated channel: ch1
channel ch1: SID=43 instance=jose12pr1 device type=DISK

allocated channel: ch2
channel ch2: SID=44 instance=jose12pr1 device type=DISK

allocated channel: ch3
channel ch3: SID=45 instance=jose12pr1 device type=DISK

allocated channel: ch4
channel ch4: SID=46 instance=jose12pr1 device type=DISK

Starting backup at 02-MAY-21
channel ch1: starting archived log backup set
channel ch1: specifying archived log(s) in backup set
input archived log thread=2 sequence=1 RECID=1 STAMP=1071506982
input archived log thread=1 sequence=12 RECID=3 STAMP=1071507020
channel ch1: starting piece 1 at 02-MAY-21
channel ch2: starting archived log backup set
cchannel ch3: specifying datafile(s) in backup set
input datafile file number=00004 name=+DATAC1/JOSE12PR/DATAFILE/
undotbs1.989.1071506765

input datafile file number=00005 name=+DATAC1/JOSE12PR/DATAFILE/
undotbs2.971.1071506845

Finished backup at 02-MAY-21
channel ch1: backup set complete, elapsed time: 00:00:01
Finished backup at 02-MAY-21
released channel: ch1
released channel: ch2
released channel: ch3
released channel: ch4
RMAN>
```

Note: Above Output truncated for better visibility.

Enabling flashback in the source database

We should ensure that the flashback is enabled in our source database, **jose12pr**. When we use the AutoUpgrade utility to upgrade the Oracle database, we need to have the flashback enabled in the database as the AutoUpgrade utility creates a guaranteed restore point during the upgrade process and the upgrade process will fail in the early stages if the flashback is not enabled.

Let's look at the following steps:

1. Login to the source database and enable the flashback using the following SQL statement:

```
SQL> alter database flashback on;
Database altered.
```

2. Check to make sure that the flashback is enabled successfully as follows:

```
SQL> select name, db_unique_name, database_role, log_mode, force_
logging, flashback_on from gv$database;
```

```
NAME             DB_UNIQUE_NAME   DATABASE_ROLE LOG_MODE FORCE_LOGGING FSHBACK
---------------  --------------   ------------- ---------- --------- ----
virtual-19crac1  jose12pr         PRIMARY       ARCHIVELOG YES          YES
virtual-19crac1  jode12pr         PRIMARY       ARCHIVELOG YES          YES
```

3. Check to make sure that we have enough space in the **Fast Recovery Area (FRA)**.

   We must ensure that we have enough free space in the Fast recovery area as the **AutoUpgrade** utility will create the restore point and save the recovery logs. So, please check and set **db_recovery_file_dest_size** to a higher value. Let's set it to 20GB, as follows:

```
SQL> alter system set db_recovery_file_dest_size=20G scope=both
sid='*';
System altered.
```

Purge recyclebin

Please check the **recyclebin** and purge it; in some cases, it might take more time if we have too many objects in the **recyclebin**. So, it's always a good idea to purge the recycle bin before starting the upgrade, as this can significantly reduce the overall time taken for the database upgrade. It might be a good idea if we can check this well in advance and purge the **recyclebin**. If the **recyclebin** is having too many objects, sometimes it might even take at least a couple of hours to get them purged, which will significantly increase the downtime required for the database upgrade. So, please check ahead and take care of this, by completing the following steps:

1. Check the object count in the **recyclebin**, as follows:

```
SQL> select count(*)  from recyclebin;
```

2. Purge the recycle bin using the following SQL statement:

```
SQL> purge dba_recyclebin;
DBA Recyclebin purged.
```

3. Re-check the object count in the **recyclebin**, as follows:
   ```
   SQL> select count(*)  from recyclebin;
   ```

Gather the dictionary statistics

It's always good to collect the dictionary stats before the database upgrade. Having good stats on the dictionary tables and fixed objects can help the database upgrade to run faster, and thus it can help in reducing the overall downtime required for the database upgrade.

We can use the following SQL statement to check when the dictionary statistics were last collected:

```
SQL> SELECT OPERATION,to_char(MAX(END_TIME),'DD-MON-YY hh24:mi') LATEST
     FROM dba_optstat_operations
     where OPERATION in ('gather_fixed_objects_stats','gather_dictionary_
stats') group by operation;


OPERATION                          LATEST
---------------------------------- ----------------
gather_fixed_objects_stats         17-MAR-21 06:23
gather_dictionary_stats            17-MAR-21 07:28
```

We can gather the dictionary stats using the following statements:

```
SQL> EXECUTE DBMS_STATS.GATHER_DICTIONARY_STATS;
PL/SQL procedure successfully completed.

SQL> EXECUTE DBMS_STATS.GATHER_FIXED_OBJECTS_STATS;
PL/SQL procedure successfully completed.
```

Working directories

Please create a staging directory with the primary database name. We will use this directory as a working directory to save all the required log files, as follows:

```
[oracle@virtual-19crac1 ~] mkdir -p /u01/software/upgrade/jose12pr/
```

Copy the required Oracle files from the source database home (12.1.0.2) to 19c database home, as follows:

1. Network files: For the network related files, add the source database TNS entry in the **tnsnames.ora** file of **19c** home, shown as follows:

   ```
   [oracle@virtual-19crac1 ~] cd /u01/app/oracle/product/19c/db_1/
   network/admin
   [oracle@virtual-19crac1 admin ~]$. cp tnsnames.ora tnsnames.ora.
   March17
   ```

```
[oracle@virtual-19crac1 admin ~]$. vi tnsnames.ora


JOSE12PR =
  (DESCRIPTION =(ADDRESS = (PROTOCOL = TCP)(HOST = virtual-
19crac-scan)(PORT = 1521))
(CONNECT_DATA =
     (SERVER = DEDICATED)
     (SERVICE_NAME = jose12pr)
   )
  )
```

2. **Primary database initialization parameter (pfiles / spfiles) files**: Copy the primary database **pfile** and **spfile** files from **11g** to **19c** DB home, as follows:

```
[oracle@virtual-19crac1 ~]ls -ltr /u01/app/oracle/product/12c/
db_1/dbs/*jose12pr*ora
-rw-r----- 1 oracle oinstall 45 Mar 17 21:13 /u01/app/oracle/
product/12c/db_1/dbs/initjose12pr1.ora

[oracle@virtual-19crac1 ~]cp /u01/app/oracle/product/12c/db_1/
dbs/*jose12pr*ora  /u01/app/oracle/product/19c/db_1/dbs/


[oracle@virtual-19crac1 ~] ls -ltr /u01/app/oracle/product/19c/
db_1/dbs/*jose12pr*ora
-rw-r----- 1 oracle oinstall 45 Mar 18 20:29 /u01/app/oracle/
product/19c/db_1/dbs/initjose12pr1.ora
```

3. **Password files**: The password file in the **dbs** folder; we can copy it to the **19c dbs** home, as follows:

```
[oracle@virtual-19crac1 ~] cp /u01/app/oracle/product/12c/db_1/
dbs/*orapwjose* /u01/app/oracle/product/19c/db_1/dbs/
```

4. **Check the INVALID objects' counts in the primary database**: It's always a good idea to take a snapshot of the invalid objects' count before starting the database upgrade. On the primary database, first run the **utlrp** to compile any **INVALID** objects and then take a count of the invalid objects, so that we can compare the count after the database upgrade, as follows:

```
SQL > @$ORACLE_HOME/rdbms/admin/utlrp

SQL> select count(*) from dba_objects where status='INVALID';
```

5. First take the count of the invalid objects in the **SYS** and **SYSTEM** schemas, as follows:

```
SQL> spool /u01/software/upgrade/jose12pr/pre-upgrade_SYS_SYSTEM_
invalid_Objects.log
```

```
SQL> SELECT i.HOST_NAME "DATABASE_HOST" ,
        i.INSTANCE_NAME "DB_NAME", d.DATABASE_ROLE
        " DATABASE_ROLE", d.OPEN_MODE " OPEN_MODE ", STARTUP_TIME
     from GV$DATABASE d, gv$instance i
     where i.INST_ID=d.INST_ID;

SQL> select owner,object_name,object_type,status
     from dba_objects
     where status='INVALID' and owner in ('SYS','SYSTEM')
     order by owner ;
spool off;
```

6. Next, take the invalid object count for the non-sys and non-system schemas, as follows:

```
SQL> spool /u01/software/upgrade/jose12pr/pre-upgrade_non-SYS_
invalid_objects.log

SQL> SELECT i.HOST_NAME "DATABASE_HOST" ,
        i.INSTANCE_NAME "DB_NAME", d.DATABASE_ROLE
        " DATABASE_ROLE", d.OPEN_MODE " OPEN_MODE ", STARTUP_TIME
     from GV$DATABASE d, gv$instance i
     where i.INST_ID=d.INST_ID;

SQL> select count(*)
     from dba_objects
     where status='INVALID' and owner not in ('SYS','SYSTEM');

SQL> select owner,object_type,count(*)
     from dba_objects
     where status='INVALID' and owner not in ('SYS','SYSTEM')
     group by owner,object_type order by owner ;

SQL> select owner,object_name,object_type,status
       from dba_objects
     where status='INVALID' and owner not in ('SYS','SYSTEM')
     order by owner ;
spool off;
```

7. Check if the spool files got created, as follows:

```
[oracle@virtual-19crac1 jose12pr]$ ls -ltr

total 24

-rw-r--r-- 1 oracle oinstall  683 Mar 18 20:32 preupgrade_
invalid_object_count.log

-rw-r--r-- 1 oracle oinstall 1656 Mar 18 20:32 pre-pgrade_SYS_
SYSTEM_invalid_Objects.log
-rw-r--r-- 1 oracle oinstall 2383 Mar 18 20:32 pre-upgrade_non-
```

```
SYS_invalid_objects.log
```

8. **TEST Case**: For verification purposes, let's create a **TEST** table in our source database, and we can crosscheck this table after the upgrade and migration completes.

In the **jose12pr** database, run the following query:

```
SQL> Create table BEFORE_UPGRADE (NAME Varchar(30));
Table created.

SQL> insert into BEFORE_UPGRADE values ('Table Before Upgrade');
1 row created.

SQL> commit;
Commit complete.
```

Download the latest AutoUpgrade tool

As mentioned earlier, Oracle strongly recommends downloading the latest version and using it instead of the default one. We can download the latest AutoUpgrade tool from the following note:

Please refer to MOS - AutoUpgrade Tool (Doc ID 2485457.1)

Download the latest **autoupgrade.jar file** and copy it to **19c** home, as follows:

```
[oracle@virtual-19crac1 jose12pr]$ cd /u01/software/upgrade/jose12pr/

[oracle@virtual-19crac1 jose12pr]$ ls -ltr AutoUpgrade*
-rwxr-x--- 1 oracle oinstall 2868558 Mar 18 20:37 autoupgrade.jar

[oracle@virtual-19crac1 jose12pr]$  cp /u01/software/upgrade/jose12pr/
autoupgrade.jar /u01/app/oracle/product/19c/db_1/rdbms/admin/

[oracle@virtual-19crac1 jose12pr]$ ls -ltr  /u01/app/oracle/product/19c/
db_1/rdbms/admin/autoupgrade.jar

-rwxr-x--- 1 oracle oinstall 2868558 Mar 18 20:37 /u01/app/oracle/
product/19c/db_1/rdbms/admin/autoupgrade.jar
```

AutoUpgrade Configuration file

We can create a sample configuration file by running the **AutoUpgrade** jar file. You can also manually create the file or you can create a sample config file using **autoupgrade.jar** and modify it to include the source and target database details. First, let's create the sample config file. For this, we need the source **19c** binaries and create the config file as follows:

```
[oracle@virtual-19crac1 ~]$ cd /u01/software/upgrade/jose12pr
[oracle@virtual-19crac1 ~]$ export ORACLE_HOME=/u01/app/oracle/
product/19c/db_1
[oracle@virtual-19crac1 ~]$ export PATH=$ORACLE_HOME/bin:$PATH

[oracle@virtual-19crac1 ~]$ /u01/app/oracle/product/19c/db_1/jdk/bin/
java -jar $ORACLE_HOME/rdbms/admin/autoupgrade.jar -create_sample_file
config
```

Create the sample configuration file **/u01/software/upgrade/jose12pr/sample_config.cfg**. Modify the config file and add the following details for our source and target databases:

```
[oracle@virtual-19crac1 jose12pr]$ cd /u01/software/upgrade/jose12pr
[oracle@virtual-19crac1 jose12pr]$ cp sample_config.cfg jose12pr_config.
cfg
[oracle@virtual-19crac1 jose12pr]$ vi jose12pr_config.cfg

[oracle@virtual-19crac1 jose12pr]$ cat jose12pr_upgrade_config.cfg

global.autoupg_log_dir=/u01/software/upgrade/jose12pr  # global log
location
upg1.log_dir=/u01/software/upgrade/jose12pr    # log dir for upgrade job
upg1.sid=jose12pr1                             # SID of the source DB/CDB
upg1.source_home=/u01/app/oracle/product/12c/db_1  # Source ORACLE_HOME
upg1.target_home=/u01/app/oracle/product/19c/db_1  # Target ORACLE_HOME
upg1.start_time=NOW                        # Start time of the upgrade
upg1.upgrade_node=virtual-19crac1          # Optional. Localhost name
upg1.run_utlrp=yes                         # Parameter to run utlrp.
upg1.timezone_upg=yes                      # Upgrade timezone
upg1.target_version=19                     # target ORACLE_HOME version
upg1.target_cdb=questpr1                   # Target Container database
```

Please note the preceding parameter (**target_cdb**); it is this parameter which tells AutoUpgrade to use this database to plug the **jose12pr** once it is upgraded to 19.9.0.

Upgrading database Oracle 12c (12.1.0.2) to Oracle 19c (19.9.0)

In this section, we will upgrade **jose12pr** from the 12.1.0.2 to the 19.9.0 version

Running AutoUpgrade in the Analyze mode

As you now know the modes, let's run the AutoUpgrade in the **Analyze** mode for our upgrade. As mentioned earlier, this mode will only read the source database and check if the database is ready for the upgrade. Please note that, this mode will not make any changes to the source database. We need to run this from **19c** home, so set the database home to **19c** and run the command.

We need to export **ORACLE_HOME** to a new home (**19c** in this case) and then run the command as follows:

```
[oracle@virtual-19crac1 jose12pr]$ export ORACLE_HOME=/u01/app/oracle/
product/19c/db_1
[oracle@virtual-19crac1 jose12pr]$ export PATH=$ORACLE_HOME/bin:$PATH

[oracle@virtual-19crac1 jose12pr]$ cd /u01/software/upgrade/jose12pr
[oracle@virtual-19crac1 jose12pr]$ $ORACLE_HOME/jdk/bin/java -jar
$ORACLE_HOME/rdbms/admin/autoupgrade.jar -config jose12pr_upgrade_config.
cfg -mode ANALYZE
```

When we initially ran the **analyze** command, we found that prechecks were failing because our source non-cdb database **jose12pr** had the **APEX** component installed in it, whereas the target CDB database, **questpr** did not have **APEX** installed in it. The following is the error from the prechecks logfile from the first **ANALYZE** run:

```
/u01/software/upgrade/jose12pr/jose12pr1/101/prechecks
[oracle@virtual-19crac1 prechecks]$ cat jose12pr_preupgrade.log


" The following plugin violations were found:

JOSE12PR 1 ERROR PENDING APEX mismatch: PDB has installed common APEX.
CDB has not installed APEX.

Before plugging in the database jose12pr1 as a PDB of CDB questpr1,
there should not be any plugin violations that have an ERROR type."
```

As you can see, it requested to fix the APEX issue before we start the upgrade process.

So, we went ahead and installed **APEX** in the target database, **questpr**. After installing the APEX, we re-ran the **AutoUpgrade** command in the **ANALYZE** mode and it went fine this time. The following is the log summary from the latest run (For more details, please refer to the *Known issues* section at the end of this chapter.):

```
[oracle@virtual-19crac1 jose12pr]$ $ORACLE_HOME/jdk/bin/java -jar
$ORACLE_HOME/rdbms/admin/autoupgrade.jar -config jose12pr_upgrade_config.
cfg -mode ANALYZE

AutoUpgrade tool launched with default options

Processing config file ...
+------------------------------+
| Starting AutoUpgrade execution |
+------------------------------+
```

```
1 databases will be analyzed
Type 'help' to list console commands
upg> lsj
---+---------+---------+-------+-------------+--------+--------------+
|Job#|  DB_NAME|STAGE|OPERATION| STATUS|START_TIME| UPDATED|MESSAGE|
---+---------+---------+-------+-------------+--------+--------------+
| 103|jose12pr1|PRECHECKS|PREPARING|RUNNING|21/03/18
17:35|17:35:23|Remaining 1/87|
---+---------+---------+-------+-------------+--------+--------------+

Total jobs 1

upg> Job 103 completed
------------------ Final Summary --------------------
Number of databases         [1]
Jobs finished               [1]
Jobs failed                 [0]
Jobs pending                [0]
```

Please check the summary report at the following links:

```
/u01/software/upgrade/jose12pr/cfgtoollogs/upgrade/auto/status/status.
html
/u01/software/upgrade/jose12pr/cfgtoollogs/upgrade/auto/status/status.
log
[oracle@virtual-19crac1 jose12pr]$
```

AutoUpgrade log file location

As we saw earlier, the **AutoUpgrade** utility creates multiple sub directories in the log location defined in the **config** file. In this case, it creates the following directories:

```
[oracle@virtual-19crac1 103]$ cd /u01/software/upgrade/jose12pr/
[oracle@virtual-19crac1 jose12pr]$ ls -ltr
total 24
drwx------ 3 oracle oinstall   21 Mar 18 13:08 cfgtoollogs
-rwx------ 1 oracle oinstall 5874 Mar 18 13:15 sample_config.cfg
-rwx------ 1 oracle oinstall  683 Mar 18 20:32 preupgrade_invalid_
object_count.log
-rwx------ 1 oracle oinstall 1656 Mar 18 20:32 pre-upgrade_SYS_SYSTEM_
invalid_Objects.log
-rwx------ 1 oracle oinstall 2383 Mar 18 20:32 pre-upgrade_non-SYS_
invalid_objects.log
-rwx------ 1 oracle oinstall 1299 Mar 18 20:42 jose12pr_upgrade_config.
cfg
drwx------ 8 oracle oinstall   73 Mar 18 21:05 jose12pr1
[oracle@virtual-19crac1 jose12pr]$ cd jose12pr1/
```

```
[oracle@virtual-19crac1 jose12pr1]$ ls -ltr
total 8
drwx------   3 oracle oinstall   119 Mar 18 13:12 100
drwx------   3 oracle oinstall   119 Mar 18 13:30 101
drwx------   3 oracle oinstall   119 Mar 18 17:17 102
drwx------   3 oracle oinstall   119 Mar 18 17:35 103
drwx------   2 oracle oinstall  4096 Mar 18 21:38 temp

[oracle@virtual-19crac1 jose12pr1]$ cd 103
[oracle@virtual-19crac1 103]$ ls -ltr
total 156
-rwx------ 1 oracle oinstall      0 Mar 18 17:35 autoupgrade_err.log
-rwx------ 1 oracle oinstall    302 Mar 18 17:35 autoupgrade_20210318_
user.log
drwx------ 2 oracle oinstall   4096 Mar 18 17:35 prechecks
-rwx------ 1 oracle oinstall 148912 Mar 18 17:35 autoupgrade_20210318.
log

[oracle@virtual-19crac1 103]$ cd prechecks/
[oracle@virtual-19crac1 prechecks]$ ls -ltr
total 252
-rwx------ 1 oracle oinstall 187076 Mar 18 17:35 prechecks_jose12pr1.log
-rwx------ 1 oracle oinstall   8016 Mar 18 17:35 jose12pr_checklist.xml
-rwx------ 1 oracle oinstall    154 Mar 18 17:35 jose12pr_checklist.json
-rwx------ 1 oracle oinstall   2384 Mar 18 17:35 jose12pr_checklist.cfg
-rwx------ 1 oracle oinstall  25759 Mar 18 17:35 jose12pr_preupgrade.
html
-rwx------ 1 oracle oinstall  13278 Mar 18 17:35 upgrade.xml
-rwx------ 1 oracle oinstall   8141 Mar 18 17:35 jose12pr_preupgrade.log
```

You can check the various directories/logs in **/u01/software/upgrade/jose12pr** in our case.

The following is the summary **logfile** information from the preceding run:

```
[oracle@virtual-19crac1 prechecks]$ cat jose12pr_preupgrade.log
Report generated by AutoUpgrade 21.1.1 (#8ee6880) on 2021-03-18 17:35:36

Upgrade-To version: 19.0.0.0.0

=======================================
Status of the database prior to upgrade
=======================================
      Database Name:  jose12pr1
     Container Name:  jose12pr1
       Container ID:  0
            Version:  12.1.0.2.0
      DB Patch Level:  No Patch Bundle applied
         Compatible:  12.1.0.2.0
```

```
        Blocksize:  8192
         Platform:  Linux x86 64-bit
   Timezone File:   18
Database log mode:  ARCHIVELOG
         Readonly:  false
          Edition:  EE
```

```
Oracle Component                        Upgrade Action    Current Status
----------------                        --------------    --------------
Oracle Workspace Manager                [to be upgraded]  VALID
OLAP Analytic Workspace                 [to be upgraded]  VALID
Oracle Text                             [to be upgraded]  VALID
Oracle Database Vault                   [to be upgraded]  VALID
Oracle Server                           [to be upgraded]  VALID
Real Application Clusters               [to be upgraded]  VALID
Oracle Java Packages                    [to be upgraded]  VALID
Oracle XDK for Java                     [to be upgraded]  VALID
Oracle Label Security                   [to be upgraded]  VALID
Oracle XML Database                     [to be upgraded]  VALID
Oracle Multimedia                       [to be upgraded]  VALID
Oracle OLAP API                         [to be upgraded]  VALID
JServer JAVA Virtual Machine            [to be upgraded]  VALID
Oracle Spatial                          [to be upgraded]  VALID
```

```
==============
BEFORE UPGRADE
==============
```

```
  REQUIRED ACTIONS
  ================
```

  1. (AUTOFIXUP) Empty the RECYCLEBIN immediately before the database
     upgrade.

     The database contains one object in the recycle bin. The   recycle
     bin must be completely empty before the database upgrade.

  2. (AUTOFIXUP) Set   the   DB_RECOVERY_FILE_DEST_SIZE   initialization
     parameter to at least 6229 MB (6 GB). Check the alert log during
     the upgrade to ensure there is remaining free space available in
     the recovery area.

     DB_RECOVERY_FILE_DEST_SIZE is set at 4785 MB (5 GB).   There is
     currently 3174 MB (3 GB) of free space remaining, which may not be
     adequate for the upgrade.

```
      Currently:
          Fast recovery area :  +DATAC1
          Limit              :  4785 MB (5 GB)
          Used               :  1611 MB (2 GB)
```

```
        Available          :  3174 MB (3 GB)
```

The database has the archivelog and flashback enabled, and the upgrade process will need free space to generate the archived and flashback logs to the recovery area specified by the initialization parameter DB_RECOVERY_FILE_DEST.

The logs generated must not overflow the limit set by DB_RECOVERY_FILE_DEST_SIZE, as that can cause the upgrade to not proceed.

INFORMATION ONLY

================

3. (AUTOFIXUP) Mandatory changes are applied automatically in the during_upgrade_pfile_dbname.ora file. Some of these changes maybe present in the after_upgrade_pfile_dbname.ora file. The during_upgrade_pfile_dbname.ora is used to start the database in the upgrade mode. The after_upgrade_pfile_dbname.ora is used to start the database once the upgrade has completed successfully.

```
   Parameter
   ---------
   cluster_database='FALSE'
```

Mandatory changes are required to perform the upgrade. These changes are implemented in the during_ and after_upgrade_pfile_dbname.ora files.

4. Check the Oracle Backup and Recovery User's Guide for information on how to manage an RMAN recovery catalog schema.

If you are using a version of the recovery catalog schema that is older than that required by the RMAN client version, then you must upgrade the catalog schema.

It is a good practice to have the catalog schema as the same or higher version than the RMAN client version you are using.

5. To help you keep track of your tablespace allocations, the following AUTOEXTEND tablespaces are expected to successfully EXTEND during the upgrade process:

```
                                         Min Size
    Tablespace              Size     For Upgrade
    ----------              ----------  -----------
        SYSTEM              840 MB       1070 MB
        TEMP                 60 MB        240 MB
        UNDOTBS1            375 MB        401 MB
        SYSAUX              690 MB        704 MB
```

The minimum tablespace sizes for the upgrade are estimates.

6. Follow the instructions in the Oracle Multimedia README.txt file in <19 ORACLE_HOME>/ord/im/admin/README.txt, or MOS note 2555923.1 to determine if Oracle Multimedia is being used. If Oracle Multimedia is being used, refer to MOS note 2347372.1 for suggestions on replacing Oracle Multimedia.

The Oracle Multimedia component (ORDIM) is installed.

Starting with release 19c, Oracle Multimedia is desupported. The object types still exist, but the methods and procedures will raise an exception. Refer to the 19 Oracle Database Upgrade Guide, the Oracle Multimedia README.txt file in <19 ORACLE_HOME>/ord/im/admin/README.txt, or MOS note 2555923.1 for more information.

```
==============
AFTER UPGRADE
==============
REQUIRED ACTIONS
================
None
RECOMMENDED ACTIONS

===================
```

7. (AUTOFIXUP) Upgrade the database time zone file using the DBMS_DST package.

The database is using the time zone file version 18 and the target 19 release ships with t the ime zone file version 32.

Oracle recommends upgrading to the desired (latest) version of the time zone file. For more information, refer to "Upgrading the Time Zone File and Timestamp with Time Zone Data" in the 19 Oracle Database Globalization Support Guide.

8. (AUTOFIXUP) Recompile the objects with timestamp mismatch. Please refer to MOS note 781959.1 for more details.

There are objects whose timestamp are mismatched with its parent objects. Timestamp of the dependent objects must coincide with the timestamp of parent objects.

9. (AUTOFIXUP) Gather the dictionary statistics after the upgrade using the following command:

EXECUTE DBMS_STATS.GATHER_DICTIONARY_STATS;

Oracle recommends gathering the dictionary statistics after the upgrade.

The dictionary statistics provide essential information to the Oracle optimizer to help it find the efficient SQL execution plans. After a database upgrade, the statistics need to be re-gathered as there can now be tables that have significantly changed during the upgrade or new tables that do not have the statistics gathered yet.

10. Gather the statistics on fixed objects after the upgrade and when there is a representative workload on the system using the following command:

EXECUTE DBMS_STATS.GATHER_FIXED_OBJECTS_STATS;

Oracle recommends gathering the fixed object statistics after the upgrade. This recommendation is given for all the preupgrade runs.

The fixed object statistics provide essential information to the Oracle optimizer to help it find the efficient SQL execution plans. Those statistics are specific to the Oracle Database release that generates them, and can be stale upon the database upgrade.

For information on managing optimizer statistics, refer to the 12.1.0.2 Oracle Database SQL Tuning Guide.

11. (AUTOFIXUP) Run @?/rdbms/admin/utlrp.sql in order to recompile any invalid objects.

There are invalid objects in the database after the upgrade.

The invalid database objects need to be recompiled after the upgrade.

Since the upgrade summary **logfile** looks clean now, we can upgrade the source database by running **the** AutoUpgrade utility in **the DEPLOY** mode.

Running the AutoUpgrade command in 'DEPLOY' mode

We can now run the **AutoUpgrade** in **the deploy** mode to upgrade the database, and we need to run this from 19c home. So, lets export the Oracle home to point to **19c** first and then run the **AutoUpgrade** command as shown in the following section.

Since we have given **the target_cdb** database in the configuration file, it should upgrade the database first and then convert it as the **PDB** database, as follows:

```
[oracle@virtual-19crac1 jose12pr]$ export ORACLE_HOME=/u01/app/oracle/
product/19c/db_1

[oracle@virtual-19crac1 jose12pr]$ export PATH=$PATH:$ORACLE_HOME/
bin:$PATH
[oracle@virtual-19crac1 jose12pr]$ echo $ORACLE_HOME

/u01/app/oracle/product/19c/db_1

[oracle@virtual-19crac1 jose12pr]$ cd /u01/software/upgrade/jose12pr
```

Run the **AutoUpgrade** command in the **DEPLOY** mode to upgrade the database:

```
[oracle@virtual-19crac1 jose12pr]$ $ORACLE_HOME/jdk/bin/java -jar
$ORACLE_HOME/rdbms/admin/autoupgrade.jar -config jose12pr_upgrade_config.
cfg -mode DEPLOY
```

The following is part of the output when the preceding command is still running:

```
[oracle@virtual-19crac1 jose12pr]$ $ORACLE_HOME/jdk/bin/java -jar
$ORACLE_HOME/rdbms/admin/autoupgrade.jar -config jose12pr_upgrade_config.
cfg -mode DEPLOY
AutoUpgrade tool launched with default options
Processing config file ...
+------------------------------+
| Starting AutoUpgrade execution |
+------------------------------+
1 databases will be processed
Type 'help' to list console commands
upg> lsj
--------+-------+-------------+--------+--------------------------+
|Job#|  DB_NAME|STAGE|OPERATION| STATUS|START_TIME| UPDATED|MESSAGE|
--+---------+---------+-------+--------------+--------+--------------
| 104|jose12pr1|PREFIXUPS|EXECUTING|RUNNING|21/03/18
21:05|21:06:14|Loading database information|
----+---------+---------+-------+--------------+--------+-----------+
Total jobs 1
upg> lsj
-----+---------+---------+-------+--------------+--------+----------+
|Job#|DB_NAME|STAGE|OPERATION| STATUS|START_TIME| UPDATED|    MESSAGE|
------+---------+---------+-------+--------------+--------+-----------
| 104| jose12pr1|DBUPGRADE|EXECUTING|RUNNING|21/03/18
21:05|21:15:14|43%Upgraded |
----+---------+---------+-------+--------------+--------+----------+
Total jobs 1
upg> lsj
+----+-------+---------+---------+-------+--------------+--------+---
|Job#|DB_NAME|STAGE|OPERATION| STATUS|START_TIME| UPDATED|    MESSAGE|
+----+-------+---------+---------+-------+--------------+--------+---
| 104| jose12pr1|DBUPGRADE|EXECUTING|RUNNING|21/03/18
21:05|21:23:14|54%Upgraded |
```

This step will take around 50 minutes. While its running, we can open a new terminal and check the different directories that the **AutoUpgrade** tool creates for the various logs, including the prefix/postfix directories. Please see the following different log directories it created:

```
[oracle@virtual-19crac1 jose12pr1]$ pwd
```

```
/u01/software/upgrade/jose12pr/jose12pr1

[oracle@virtual-19crac1 jose12pr1]$ ls -ltr
total 4
drwx------ 3 oracle oinstall  119 Mar 18 13:12 100
drwx------ 3 oracle oinstall  119 Mar 18 13:30 101
drwx------ 3 oracle oinstall  119 Mar 18 17:17 102
drwx------ 3 oracle oinstall  119 Mar 18 17:35 103
drwx------ 2 oracle oinstall  131 Mar 18 21:05 temp
drwx------ 6 oracle oinstall 4096 Mar 18 21:06 104

[oracle@virtual-19crac1 104]$    cd 104
[oracle@virtual-19crac1 104]$ ls -ltr
total 456
-rwx------ 1 oracle oinstall      0 Mar 18 21:05 autoupgrade_20210318_
user.log.lck
-rwx------ 1 oracle oinstall      0 Mar 18 21:05 autoupgrade_20210318.
log.lck
-rwx------ 1 oracle oinstall      0 Mar 18 21:05 autoupgrade_err.log.lck
-rwx------ 1 oracle oinstall      0 Mar 18 21:05 autoupgrade_err.log
drwx------ 2 oracle oinstall     64 Mar 18 21:05 drain
drwx------ 2 oracle oinstall     28 Mar 18 21:05 preupgrade
drwx------ 2 oracle oinstall   4096 Mar 18 21:06 prechecks
drwx------ 2 oracle oinstall     89 Mar 18 21:06 prefixups
-rwx------ 1 oracle oinstall 291655 Mar 18 21:07 autoUpgrade_20210318.
log
-rwx------ 1 oracle oinstall   3427 Mar 18 21:07 autoUpgrade_20210318_
user.log
```

Check the **autoupgrade_20210318_user.log** for more information about the process, as follows:

```
[oracle@virtual-19crac1 104]$ tail -f autoupgrade_20210318_user.log


2021-03-18 21:06:13.786 INFO Updating parameter *.cluster_
database='true' to *.cluster_database='FALSE' in /u01/software/upgrade/
jose12pr/jose12pr1/temp/during_upgrade_pfile_jose12pr1.ora

2021-03-18 21:06:17.426 INFO Analyzing jose12pr1, 87 checks will run
using 2 threads
2021-03-18 21:07:41.131 INFO Defer redo log shipping to standby database

2021-03-18 21:08:47.595 INFO Password file /u01/app/oracle/product/12c/
db_1/dbs/orapwjose12pr1 is not found Post Upgrade is continuing

2021-03-18 21:08:47.857 INFO [virtual-19crac2] Password file /u01/app/
oracle/product/12c/db_1/dbs/orapwjose12pr2 is not found on remote host

2021-03-18 21:09:12.098 INFO Total Number of upgrade phases is 108
2021-03-18 21:09:12.102 INFO Begin Upgrade on Database [jose12pr]
```

```
2021-03-18 21:09:17.284 INFO 0%Upgraded
2021-03-18 21:12:17.659 INFO 14%Upgraded
2021-03-18 21:15:17.858 INFO 23%Upgraded
2021-03-18 21:18:18.139 INFO 44%Upgraded
2021-03-18 21:21:18.467 INFO 49%Upgraded
2021-03-18 21:24:18.816 INFO 61%Upgraded
2021-03-18 21:27:19.366 INFO 81%Upgraded
2021-03-18 21:30:20.038 INFO 91%Upgraded
2021-03-18 21:33:20.555 INFO 91%Upgraded
2021-03-18 21:36:11.102 INFO SUCCESSFULLY UPGRADED [jose12pr]
2021-03-18 21:36:11.102 INFO End Upgrade on Database [jose12pr]
2021-03-18 21:36:16.629 INFO SUCCESSFULLY UPGRADED [jose12pr]
2021-03-18 21:36:16.645 INFO jose12pr Return status is SUCCESS
2021-03-18 21:36:41.932 INFO Analyzing jose12pr1, 14 checks will run
using 2 threads
2021-03-18 21:36:42.870 INFO Using /u01/software/upgrade/jose12pr/
jose12pr1/104/prechecks/jose12pr_checklist.cfg to identify required
fixups
2021-03-18 21:36:42.871 INFO Content of the checklist /u01/software/
upgrade/jose12pr/jose12pr1/104/prechecks/jose12pr_checklist.cfg is:
```

We should also keep an eye on both the source and the target database alert logs, as we can see some valuable information regarding the upgrades and non-cdb to pdb conversion information. Check the following from the source database (**jose12pr**) alert log file:

```
[oracle@virtual-19crac1 ~]$ tail -f /u01/app/oracle/diag/rdbms/jose12pr/
jose12pr1/trace/alert_jose12pr1.log

Starting background process CJQ0
Completed: ALTER DATABASE OPEN MIGRATE
2021-03-18T21:34:46.499008-05:00
CJQ0 started with pid=60, OS id=12695
2021-03-18T21:34:48.520276-05:00
SERVER ACTION=UPGRADE id=: Upgraded from 12.1.0.2.0 to 19.9.0.0.0
2021-03-18T21:34:48.522949-05:00
ALTER SYSTEM SET _enable_cdb_upgrade_capture=TRUE SCOPE=MEMORY;
alter pluggable database application APP$CDB$CATALOG begin upgrade
'19.0.0.0.0.partial' to '19.0.0.0.0'
Completed: alter pluggable database application APP$CDB$CATALOG begin
upgrade '19.0.0.0.0.partial' to '19.0.0.0.0'
SERVER COMPONENT id=DBRESTART: timestamp=2021-03-18 21:34:48
SERVER COMPONENT id=POSTUP_BGN: timestamp=2021-03-18 21:34:48
SERVER COMPONENT id=CATREQ_BGN: timestamp=2021-03-18 21:34:48
2021-03-18T21:34:59.183856-05:00
Thread 1 advanced to log sequence 143 (LGWR switch),  current SCN:
3249860
```

```
  Current log# 1 seq# 143 mem# 0: +DATAC1/JOSE12PR/ONLINELOG/
group_1.947.1067461847
  Current log# 1 seq# 143 mem# 1: +DATAC1/JOSE12PR/ONLINELOG/
group_1.948.1067461847
2021-03-18T21:34:59.448988-05:00
ARC1 (PID:12687): Archived Log entry 146 added for T-1.S-142 ID
0x45bbce55 LAD:1
2021-03-18T21:35:06.508808-05:00
SERVER COMPONENT id=CATREQ_END: timestamp=2021-03-18 21:35:06
SERVER COMPONENT id=POSTUP_END: timestamp=2021-03-18 21:35:06
SERVER COMPONENT id=CATUPPST: timestamp=2021-03-18 21:35:06
alter pluggable database application APP$CDB$CATALOG end upgrade

Completed: alter pluggable database application APP$CDB$CATALOG end
upgrade
2021-03-18T21:35:07.491724-05:00
ALTER SYSTEM SET _enable_cdb_upgrade_capture=FALSE SCOPE=MEMORY;2021-03-
18T21:35:07.683855-05:00
```

The following is from the target database (**questpr**) alert log file where we can see the source database information while it was being converted as a **PDB** database:

```
[oracle@virtual-19crac1 ~]$ tail -f /u01/app/oracle/diag/rdbms/jose12pr/
jose12pr1/trace/alert_jose12pr1.log

2021-03-18T21:38:33.794536-05:00
create pluggable database «JOSE12PR»  using  '/u01/software/upgrade/
jose12pr/jose12pr1/104/noncdbtopdb/JOSE12PR.xml' NOCOPY tempfile reuse

2021-03-18T21:38:33.946893-05:00
NOTE: dependency between database questpr and diskgroup resource ora.
DATAC1.dg is established
2021-03-18T21:38:34.059181-05:00
JOSE12PR(4):Endian type of dictionary set to little
******************************************************************
Pluggable Database JOSE12PR with pdb id - 4 is created as UNUSABLE.
If any errors are encountered before the pdb is marked as NEW,then the
pdb must be dropped local undo-1, localundoscn-0x0000000000000007
******************************************************************
JOSE12PR(4):Autotune of undo retention is turned on.
JOSE12PR(4):This instance was first to open pluggable database JOSE12PR
(container=4)
2021-03-18T21:38:35.007097-05:00
JOSE12PR(4):queued attach DA request 0x996ea460 for pdb 4, ospid 15880
2021-03-18T21:38:35.011507-05:00
Increasing priority of 1 RS
Domain Action Reconfiguration started (domid 4, new da inc 1, cluster inc
4)
```

```
Instance 1 is attaching to domain 4
JOSE12PR(4):[15880] Successfully onlined Undo Tablespace 2.
JOSE12PR(4):Undo initialization online undo segments: err:0 start:
193789120 end: 193789281 diff: 61 ms (0.2 seconds)
JOSE12PR(4):Undo initialization finished serial:0 start:193789117
end:193789283 diff:166 ms (0.2 econds)
Increasing priority of 1 RS
Domain Action Reconfiguration started (domid 4, new da inc 2, cluster inc
4)
Instance 1 is detaching from domain 4 (lazy abort? 0)
 Global Resource Directory partially frozen for domain action
* domain detach - domain 4 valid ? 1Non-local Process blocks cleaned out
Set master node info
 Dwn-cvts replayed, VALBLKs dubious
 All grantable enqueues granted
freeing rdom 4
freeing the fusion rht of pdb 4
freeing the pdb enqueue rht
Domain Action Reconfiguration complete (total timc 0.0 secs)
Decreasing priority of 1 RS
Completed: create pluggable database "JOSE12PR"  using /u01/software/
upgrade/jose12pr/jose12pr1/104/noncdbtopdb/JOSE12PR.xml' NOCOPY tempfile
euse
2021-03-18T21:38:36.846602-05:00
JOSE12PR(4):ALTER PLUGGABLE DATABASE  OPEN UPGRADE
JOSE12PR(4):Autotune of undo retention is turned on.
2021-03-18T21:38:37.023986-05:00
JOSE12PR(4):This instance was first to open pluggable database JOSE12PR
(container=4)
```

From the target database alert log file, you can see that once the source database **jose12pr** (12.1) upgrades to 19.9, it will be converted as a pluggable database. It's marvelous how **AutoUpgrade** take cares of the upgrade and migration to **pdb** using one single command. Now, let us check back the output from the actual upgrade command, as follows:

```
upg> lsj
+----------+-------+-------------+--------+----------------------------+
Job#|  DB_NAME|STAGE|OPERATTON| STATUS|START_TIME| UPDATED|MESSAGE|
-+----------+---------+-------+-------------+--------+----------------
| 104|jose12pr1|POSTFIXUPS|EXECUTING|RUNNING|21/03/18
21:05|21:36:43|Loading database information|
----------+---------+-------+-------------+--------+----------------
Total jobs 1
upg> lsj
--------+----------+---------+-------+-------------+--------+--------
|Job#|  DB_NAME|STAGE|OPERATION| STATUS|START_TIME| UPDATED|MESSAGE|
```

```
--------+----------+---------+-------+--------------+--------+--------
| 104|jose12pr1|NONCDBTOPDB|EXECUTING|RUNNING|21/03/18
21:05|21:41:06|noncdb_to_pdb - 64%|
--------+----------+---------+-------+--------------+--------+-------

Total jobs 1
upg> lsj
+----+---------+-----------+---------+-------+--------------+-------+
|Job#|  DB_NAME|STAGE|OPERATION| STATUS|START_TIME| UPDATED|MESSAGE|
+----+---------+-----------+---------+-------+--------------+-------+
| 104|jose12pr1|NONCDBTOPDB|EXECUTING|RUNNING|21/03/18
21:05|21:41:06|noncdb_to_pdb - 64%|
+----+---------+-----------+---------+-------+--------------+-------+

Total jobs 1
upg> Job 104 completed
------------------ Final Summary -------------------
Number of databases          [1]
Jobs finished                [1]
Jobs failed                  [0]
Jobs pending                 [0]
Please check the summary report at the following link:

/u01/software/upgrade/jose12pr/cfgtoollogs/upgrade/auto/status/status.
html
/u01/software/upgrade/jose12pr/cfgtoollogs/upgrade/auto/status/status.
log
```

Once the upgrade and migration as **pdb** completes for the database **jose12pr**, let's check the **CDB** database to see its status, as follows:

```
SQL>@rac_database_info.sql

DATABASE_HOST      DB_NAME     DATABASE_ROLE    OPEN_MODE    STARTUP_TIME
---------------    --------    -------------    ----------   -----------
virtual-19crac1    questpr1    PRIMARY          READ WRITE   18-MAR-21
virtual-19crac2    questpr2    PRIMARY          READ WRITE   18-MAR-21

SQL> show pdbs

CON_ID    CON_NAME        OPEN MODE    RESTRICTED
--------- -----------     ---------    ----------
      2   PDB$SEED        READ ONLY    NO
      3   TEXAPR          READ WRITE   NO
      4   JOSE12PR        READ WRITE   NO

SQL> alter session set container=JOSE12PR;
Session altered.

SQL> SELECT BANNER FROM v$version WHERE banner LIKE 'Oracle%';

BANNER
--------------------------------------------------------------------------
```

```
Oracle Database 19c Enterprise Edition Release 19.0.0.0.0 - Production
```

We can also see that the test table is present in this **PDB**, as follows:

```
SQL> show con_name;
CON_NAME
-------------
JOSE12PR

SQL> select * from BEFORE_UPGRADE;
NAME
------------------------------
This Table is from 12.1
```

This is impressive right? Our 12.1 source database (**jose12pr**) has been upgraded to **19c** and has been converted from non-cdb to **PDB** and plugged in to a **CDB** database with just a single command.

Post upgrade checks

Once the upgrade completes, we can proceed with the following steps to check and complete the post upgrade checks:

1. Run the **utlrp** script in the pluggable database (**jose12pr**) to compile the invalid objects and then take the count of the invalid objects along with the count as follows:

    ```
    SQL>@$ORACLE_HOME/rdbms/admin/utlrp;

    spool /u01/software/upgrade/tee12cdb/preupgrade_invalid_object_
    count.log
    SQL> select count(*) from dba_objects where status='INVALID';
    spool off;


    spool /u01/software/upgrade/tee12cdb/pre-upgrade_SYS_SYSTEM_
    invalid_Objects.log
    SQL> SELECT i.HOST_NAME "DATABASE_HOST" ,
          i.INSTANCE_NAME "DB_NAME", d.DATABASE_ROLE " DATABASE_ROLE",
          d.OPEN_MODE " OPEN_MODE    ", STARTUP_TIME
          from GV$DATABASE d, gv$instance i
          where i.INST_ID=d.INST_ID;
    SQL> select owner,object_type,count(*)
          from dba_objects
          where status='INVALID' and owner in
          'SYS','SYSTEM') group by owner,object_type order by owner;
    ```

```
SQL> select owner,object_name,object_type,status
     from dba_objects
     where status='INVALID' and owner in ('SYS','SYSTEM')
     order  by owner;

spool off;
```

2. Now, check the registry to see if all the components are upgraded and are in the valid state, as follows:

```
SQL> show con_name;

CON_NAME
---------
JOSE12PR

SQL> select COMP_ID,COMP_NAME,VERSION,STATUS from dba_registry;
```

COMP_ID	COMP_NAME	VERSION	STATUS
CATALOG	Oracle Database Catalog Views	19.0.0.0.0	VALID
CATPROC	Oracle Database Packages and Types	19.0.0.0.0	VALID
JAVAVM	JServer JAVA Virtual Machine	19.0.0.0.0	VALID
XML	Oracle XDK	19.0.0.0.0	VALID
CATJAVA	Oracle Database Java Packages	19.0.0.0.0	VALID
APS	OLAP Analytic Workspace	19.0.0.0.0	VALID
RAC	Oracle Real Application Clusters	19.0.0.0.0	VALID
XDB	Oracle XML Database	19.0.0.0.0	VALID
OWM	Oracle Workspace Manager	19.0.0.0.0	VALID
CONTEXT	Oracle Text	19.0.0.0.0	VALID
ORDIM	Oracle Multimedia	19.0.0.0.0	VALID
SDO	Spatial	19.0.0.0.0	VALID
XOQ	Oracle OLAP API	19.0.0.0.0	VALID
OLS	Oracle Label Security	19.0.0.0.0	VALID
APEX	Oracle Application Express	20.2.0.00.20	VALID
DV	Oracle Database Vault	19.0.0.0.0	VALID

```
16 rows selected.
```

3. We can also check the timezone version to see if it has been upgraded to 32 (**19c** version), as follows:

```
SQL> show con_name;

CON_NAME
---------------
JOSE12PR

SQL> SELECT version FROM v$timezone_file;
   VERSION
----------
```

32

4. Check the logfiles to see if we have any invalid objects after the database upgrade. If we find any invalid objects, we need to fix them.

5. Also, please note that if we have any TDE enabled in the source database, we just need to export the keys before starting the upgrade and then import the keys back to the CDB database after the database upgrade/migration completes.

Fallback method

As mentioned earlier, for fallback, we just need to drop the 19.9 pluggable database and restore the non-cdb from 12.1 home using the **RMAN** backup that has been taken before staring the database upgrade activity. The following are the high-level steps for this:

1. Drop the pluggable database, **jose12pr**.

   We can connect to the container database, **questpr** and stop the **PDB** and then drop it as follows:

   ```
   SQL> alter pluggable database jose12pr close instances=all;
   Pluggable database altered.


   SQL> drop pluggable database jose12pr including datafiles;
   Pluggable database dropped.
   ```

2. Restore the database from the 12.1 home using the pre-upgrade **RMAN** backup.

   We can restore the backup that we took before starting the upgrade activity. In our case, we can use the following **RMAN** command from the 12.1 home; it will restore the database with the backup which we took before starting the upgrade (If you have any **RMAN** restore commands that you already tested in your environment, you can use those scripts.):

   ```
   RMAN >
   run
   {
   startup nomount;
   RESTORE CONTROLFILE FROM "/u01/app/software/19cupgrade/
   potter12_upgrade/backup_before_upgrade/DATA_CONTOL_
   JOSE12PR_20210314_27-1-1067193513";
   alter database mount;
   restore database;
   recover database;
   }
   ```

Below is the sample Output from one of the restore that we tried later for this database.

```
[oracle@virtual-19crac1 dbs]$ rman target /

Recovery Manager: Release 12.1.0.2.0 - Production on Sun May 2
17:38:10 2021
Copyright (c) 1982, 2014, Oracle and/or its affiliates.  All rights
reserved.
connected to target database (not started)

RMAN> run
{
startup nomount;
RESTORE CONTROLFILE FROM "/u01/19cupgrade/DATA_CONTROL_
JOSE12PR_20210502_10-1-1071507530";
alter database mount;
restore database;
set until time="to_date('02052021 16:56:00','ddmmyyyy
hh24:mi:ss')";
recover database;
}
Oracle instance started
Total System Global Area     3590324224 bytes

Fixed Size                      2930608 bytes
Variable Size                 889194576 bytes
Database Buffers             2684354560 bytes
Redo Buffers                   13844480 bytes

Starting restore at 02-MAY-21
using target database control file instead of recovery catalog
allocated channel: ORA_DISK_1
channel ORA_DISK_1: SID=36 instance=jose12pr1 device type=DISK

channel ORA_DISK_1: restoring control file
channel ORA_DISK_1: restore complete, elapsed time: 00:00:07
output file name=+DATA/JOSE12PR/CONTROLFILE/current.406.1071509937
output file name=+DATA/JOSE12PR/CONTROLFILE/current.529.1071509937
Finished restore at 02-MAY-21

Statement processed
released channel: ORA_DISK_1

Starting restore at 02-MAY-21
Starting implicit crosscheck backup at 02-MAY-21
allocated channel: ORA_DISK_1
Crosschecked 9 objects
Finished implicit crosscheck backup at 02-MAY-21
```

```
Starting implicit crosscheck copy at 02-MAY-21
using channel ORA_DISK_1
Finished implicit crosscheck copy at 02-MAY-21

searching for all files in the recovery area
cataloging files...
no files cataloged

using channel ORA_DISK_1

channel ORA_DISK_1: starting datafile backup set restore
channel ORA_DISK_1: specifying datafile(s) to restore from backup
set
channel ORA_DISK_1: restoring datafile 00001 to +DATAC1/JOSE12PR/
DATAFILE/system.993.1071506697
channel ORA_DISK_1: reading from backup piece /u01/19cupgrade/
DATA_L0_JOSE12PR_20210502_5-1-1071507519
channel ORA_DISK_1: piece handle=/u01/19cupgrade/DATA_L0_
JOSE12PR_20210502_5-1-1071507519 tag=TAG20210502T165838
channel ORA_DISK_1: restored backup piece 1
channel ORA_DISK_1: restore complete, elapsed time: 00:00:03
channel ORA_DISK_1: starting datafile backup set restore
channel ORA_DISK_1: specifying datafile(s) to restore from backup set
channel ORA_DISK_1: restoring datafile 00003 to +DATAC1/JOSE12PR/
DATAFILE/sysaux.998.1071506643
channel ORA_DISK_1: restoring datafile 00006 to +DATAC1/JOSE12PR/
DATAFILE/users.990.1071506763
channel ORA_DISK_1: reading from backup piece /u01/19cupgrade/
DATA_L0_JOSE12PR_20210502_6-1-1071507519
channel ORA_DISK_1: piece handle=/u01/19cupgrade/DATA_L0_
JOSE12PR_20210502_6-1-1071507519 tag=TAG20210502T165838

channel ORA_DISK_1: restored backup piece 1
channel ORA_DISK_1: restore complete, elapsed time: 00:00:03

channel ORA_DISK_1: starting datafile backup set restore
channel ORA_DISK_1: specifying datafile(s) to restore from backup
set
channel ORA_DISK_1: restoring datafile 00004 to +DATAC1/JOSE12PR/
DATAFILE/undotbs1.989.1071506765
channel ORA_DISK_1: restoring datafile 00005 to +DATAC1/JOSE12PR/
DATAFTLE/undotbs2.971.1071506845
channel ORA_DISK_1: reading from backup piece /u01/19cupgrade/
DATA_L0_JOSE12PR_20210502_7-1-1071507520
channel ORA_DISK_1: piece handle=/u01/19cupgrade/DATA_L0_
JOSE12PR_20210502_7-1-1071507520 tag=TAG20210502T165838
channel ORA_DISK_1: restored backup piece 1
channel ORA_DISK_1: restore complete, elapsed time: 00:00:01
Finished restore at 02-MAY-21
executing command: SET until clause
```

```
Starting recover at 02-MAY-21
using channel ORA_DISK_1
starting media recovery
unable to find archived log
archived log thread=2 sequence=3
RMAN-00571: ======================================================
RMAN-00569: ======== ERROR MESSAGE STACK FOLLOWS ==============
RMAN-00571: ======================================================
RMAN-03002: failure of recover command at 05/02/2021 17:39:14
RMAN-06054: media recovery requesting unknown archived log for
thread 2 with sequence 3 and starting SCN of 1620754

RMAN> alter database open resetlogs;
Statement processed


RMAN>exit
```

You can check the database now.

[oracle@virtual-19crac1 dbs]$ sqlplus / as sysdba

```
SQL*Plus: Release 12.1.0.2.0 Production on Sun May 2 17:40:34
2021
Copyright (c) 1982, 2014, Oracle.  All rights reserved.


Connected to:
Oracle Database 12c Enterprise Edition Release 12.1.0.2.0 - 64bit
Production With the Partitioning, Real Application Clusters,
Automatic Storage Management, OLAP,

Advanced Analytics and Real Application Testing options


SQL> SELECT i.HOST_NAME "DATABASE_HOST" ,
     i.INSTANCE_NAME "DB_NAME", d.DATABASE_ROLE " DATABASE_ROLE",
     d.OPEN_MODE " OPEN_MODE ", STARTUP_TIME
     from GV$DATABASE d, gv$instance i
     where i.INST_ID=d.INST_ID;

DATABASE_HOST    DB_NAME   DATABASE_ROLE   OPEN_MODE   STARTUP_TIME
---------------  --------- --------------- ----------- -----------
virtual-19crac1  jose12pr1 PRIMARY         READ WRITE  02-MAY-21
```

As shown earlier, we can restore the database back with the pre-upgrade backup that was taken before starting the database upgrade. For this reason, we should take an **RMAN** backup whenever we want to convert a non-cdb as a pluggable database.

Known issues

The following are a few known issues that we observed in few of the upgrades that we worked on:

Issue-1

The following is the violation reported when **AutoUpgrade** was run in the **ANALYZE** mode for one of the upgrades (12.1non-CDB to 19.9 PDB) that we worked on:

Our source and target databases information are as follows:

- **Source database**: **camary12** (12.1), Non-CDB

- **Target database**: **questpr** (19.9), Container database

"The following plugin violations were found:

CAMARY12 1 ERROR PENDING APEX mismatch: PDB installed version 4.2.5.00.08 CDB installed version 20.2.0.00.20

Before plugging in database camry121 as a PDB of CDB questpr1, there should not be any plugin violations that have an ERROR type"

Solution

To fix this issue, we have to install the latest version of the APEX into the source database. Once you install the latest version of APEX, this violation will go away.

Issue-2

The database upgrade fails with the space issue in the **SYSTEM** tablespaces as follows:

```
AutoUpgrade console log message

upg> lsj
+----+-------+---------+---------+-------+--------------+------
|Job#|DB_NAME|   STAGE|OPERATION| STATUS| START_TIME| UPDATED|MESSAGE|
+----+-------+---------+---------+-------+--------------+--------+-----
| 103| mono12pr|DBUPGRADE|EXECUTING|RUNNING|21/04/15
09:43|10:08:02|95%Upgraded |
+----+-------+---------+----- ----+-------+--------------+--------+-----

Total jobs 1
upg>
- - - - - - - - - - - - - - - - - - - - - - - - - - - - - - - - - - - -
Errors in database [mono12pr]
Stage      [DBUPGRADE]
Operation [STOPPED]
Status     [ERROR]
```

```
Info    [
Error: UPG-1400
UPGRADE FAILED [MONO12PR]
Cause: Database upgrade failed with errors
For further details, see the log file located at
/u01/app/software/mono12pr_upgrade/mono12pr/103/autoupgrade_20210415_
user.log]
```

The following error message from the **autoupgrade_log** log file appears:

```
2021-04-15 10:10:04.856 ERROR
DATABASE NAME: mono12pr
CAUSE: ERROR at Line 165730 in [/u01/app/software/mono12pr_upgrade/
mono12pr/103/dbupgrade/catupgrd20210515094338mono12pr2.log]
REASON: ORA-01654: unable to extend index SYS.I_PDBSYNC4 by 128 in
tablespace SYSTEM

ACTION: [MANUAL]

DETAILS: 01654, 00000, "unable to extend index %s.%s by %s in tablespace
%s"
// *Cause:  Failed to allocate an extent of the required number of
blocks for
//          an index segment in the tablespace indicated.
// *Action: Use ALTER TABLESPACE ADD DATAFILE statement to add one or
more
//          files to the tablespace indicated.
```

Cause

In this case, the **SYSTEM** tablespace was only 1GB with the **autoextend** off.

Solution

Once we increased the tablespace size and resumed the upgrade job, it completed successfully without any issues, as follows:

```
SQL> alter database datafile '+DATA/MONO12PR/DATAFILE/
system.259.926444909' autoextend on next 100M maxsize 10G
```

Resume the AutoUpgrade job as below and we can see that the upgrade job completes without any issues.

```
upg> resume -job 103              ← Resuming job with resume option.

Resuming job: [103][mono12pr]
upg> lsj
+----+-------+--------+---------+-------+------------+--------+----+
|Job#|DB_NAME|STAGE|OPERATION| STATUS|START_TIME| UPDATED| MESSAGE|
```

```
+----+-------+--------+----------+-------+--------------+--------+-----+
| 103| mono12pr|DBUPGRADE|EXECUTING|RUNNING|21/04/15
09:43|10:15:10|Running|
+----+-------+--------+----------+-------+--------------+------+-----+
Total jobs 1
upg> lsj
+----+-------+--------+----------+-------+-----------+--------+--------+
|Job#|DB_NAME|STAGE|OPERATION| STATUS|   START_TIME| UPDATED|MESSAGE|
+----+-------+--------+----------+-------+-----------+------+---------+
| 103| mono12pr|DBUPGRADE|EXECUTING|RUNNING|21/04/15
09:43|10:08:02|95%Upgraded |
+----+-------+--------+----------+-------+-----------+------+---------+
upg> lsj
+----+-------+--------+----------+-------+-----------+--------+----------+
|Job#|DB_NAME|STAGE|OPERATION| STATUS|   START_TIME| UPDATED|MESSAGE|
+----+-------+--------+----------+-------+-----------+--------+----------+
| 103| mono12pr|POSTFIXUPS|EXECUTING|RUNNING|21/04/15
9:43|10:28:38|Remaining 1/5|
+----+-------+--------+----------+-------+----- --------+------+--------+
Total jobs 1
upg> Job 103 completed
----------------- Final Summary -------------------
Number of databases          [1]

Jobs finished                [1]
Jobs failed                  [0]
Jobs pending                 [0]


---- Drop GRP at your convenience once you consider it is no longer
needed ----
Drop GRP from crwprd: drop restore point AUTOUPGRADE_9212_MONO12PR121020
```

Please check the summary report at the following link:

```
/u01/app/software/mono12pr_upgrade/cfgtoollogs/upgrade/auto/status/
status.html
/u01/app/software/mono12pr_upgrade/cfgtoollogs/upgrade/auto/status/
status.log

[oracle@virtual-19crac1 mono12pr]
```

Conclusion

In this chapter, we saw how impressive the AutoUpgrade tool is. We can upgrade and convert non-cdb from the lower version to 19c using one single command. It reduces a lot of manual steps that we have to perform if we don't use this tool.

Oracle strongly recommends using AutoUpgrade for all the future upgrades, and we strongly agree on this.

In the next chapter, we will see how we can use AutoUpgrade to upgrade multiple Oracle databases running from the different Oracle versions to **19c** using a single `AutoUpgrade` command.

Multiple choice questions

1. **What is the parameter in the configuration file that defines the target Container database to which the source non-cdb will be plugged into as a pluggable database?**

     a. target_container_database

     b. cdb_target

     c. target_cdb

2. **When we want to upgrade and convert non-cdb to the 19c pluggable, do we need to mention in the configuration file that the source database is a non-container database?**

     a. Yes

     b. No

Answers

1. c

2. b

Key terms

- Single AutoUpgrade command

- target_cdb

- drop pluggable database

References

For more details, please refer to the following link:

https://docs.oracle.com/en/database/oracle/oracle-database/19/upgrd/non-cdb-to-pdb-upgrade-guidelines-examples.html#GUID-F84E4B4D-8305-488C-B32E-CDCE1D9C95C4

CHAPTER 7

Upgrading Multiple Database Versions (11g/12c/18c) to 19c Using a Single AutoUpgrade Command

Introduction

In the previous chapters, we saw how strong a utility the AutoUpgrade tool is. It not only has the capability to upgrade the database, it can also upgrade and convert the database from the non-container to the container database in a single operation.

In this chapter, we will explore one more option of the AutoUpgrade tool. We will see how we can use the AutoUpgrade utility to upgrade multiple databases running from the different database homes to 19c in one single operation using one single **AutoUpgrade** command.

Structure

In this chapter, we will cover the following topics:

- The high-level steps required for upgrading 11g, 12c, and 18c databases to 19c using a single **AutoUpgrade** command

- The source and target setup environments used to demonstrate the database upgrade

- The pre-requisite steps required for the database upgrade

- How to download the AutoUpgrade utility

- The configuration file required by the AutoUpgrade tool

- Running AutoUpgrade in the '**Analyze**' mode to verify the database readiness and fixing any issues that can impact the database upgrade activity

- The AutoUpgrade log locations

- Running the AutoUpgrade in the '**Deploy**' mode to upgrade all the three Oracle databases which are running from 11g, 12c, and 18c to 19c

- The post-upgrade checks

- Validating the database upgrade

- The fallback methods that can be used to downgrade the Oracle database from the upgraded version back to the source version

- A few known issues that can occur during the database upgrade or database downgrade

Objective

After studying this chapter, you will get familiar with upgrading multiple databases running from the different Oracle versions to 19c using a single **AutoUpgrade** command. This is specifically helpful in case we have a large number of databases (same version or different Oracle versions) that need to be upgraded to 19c. We can upgrade multiple databases in groups and save some effort.

An overview of the database upgrade

Figure 7.1 is a pictorial representation of the multiple database upgrades that are performed using a single **AutoUpgrade** command. It also shows the Oracle version of the databases before and after the upgrade, as follows:

Figure 7.1: *Upgrading multiple versions of Oracle databases to Oracle 19c using a single command*

Setting up the source environment

Check the database versions and the patch set levels for the 11g / 12c and 18c database homes. The RAC cluster and the grid infrastructure information are given as follows:

```
RAC nodes           : virtual-19crac1
                      virtual-19crac2
OS version          : Oracle Enterprise Linux 7.1 64 bit
Oracle Home         : /u01/app/oracle/product/12c/db_1
Database Version    : 12.1.0.2 with July 2020 Database Patch Set Update
Grid Version        : 19.9.0 (Oct,2020 patch set)
```

The Oracle 11g database home and patch set details are as follows:

```
[oracle@virtual-19crac1 ~]$ echo $ORACLE_HOME
/u01/app/oracle/product/11.2.0.4/db_1
[oracle@virtual-19crac1 ~]$ cd /u01/app/oracle/product/11.2.0.4/db_1/
OPatch
[oracle@virtual-19crac1 OPatch]$ ./opatch lspatches
28125601;
30670774;Database Patch Set Update : 11.2.0.4.200414 (30670774)
OPatch succeeded.
[oracle@virtual-19crac1 OPatch]$
```

Oracle 12c database home and patch set details are as follows:

```
[oracle@virtual-19crac1 ~]$ echo $ORACLE_HOME
/u01/app/oracle/product/12c/db_1
[oracle@virtual-19crac1 OPatch]$ pwd
/u01/app/oracle/product/12c/db_1/OPatch

[oracle@virtual-19crac1 OPatch]$ ./opatch lspatches
27487279;
28125601;
31136382;OCW PATCH SET UPDATE 12.1.0.2.200714 (31136382)
31001106;Database Bundle Patch : 12.1.0.2.200714 (31001106)

OPatch succeeded.
[oracle@virtual-19crac1 OPatch]$
```

The Oracle 18c database home and patch set details are as follows:

```
[oracle@virtual-19crac1 ~]$ echo $ORACLE_HOME
/u01/app/oracle/product/18c
[oracle@virtual-19crac1 OPatch]$ cd /u01/app/oracle/product/18c/OPatch
[oracle@virtual-19crac1 ~]$ $ORACLE_HOME/OPatch/opatch lspatches
32552752;OJVM RELEASE UPDATE: 18.14.0.0.210420 (32552752)
32524155;Database Release Update : 18.14.0.0.210420 (32524155)
28090553;OCW RELEASE UPDATE 18.3.0.0.0 (28090553)

OPatch succeeded.
[oracle@virtual-19crac1 OPatch]$
```

> **We have created the following script which we can use to check the current database configuration of the RAC database; we will be using this script throughout this chapter.**

Script-1: The following script will pull the current database details like, name, mode, and role of the database:

```
[oracle@virtual-19crac1] cat /home/oracle/rac_database_info.sql

SQL> set lines 200
SQL> col DATABASE_HOST for a30;
SQL> col HOST_NAME for a15;
SQL> col DATABASE_ROLE for a10
SQL> col OPEN_MODE for a10
SQL> col STARTUP_TIME for a20
SQL> set lines 200
SQL> col DATABASE_HOST for a20;
SQL> col OPEN_MODE for a10
SQL> col STARTUP_TIME for a20
```

```
SQL> SELECT i.HOST_NAME "DATABASE_HOST" ,i.INSTANCE_NAME "DB_NAME",
d.OPEN_MODE " OPEN_MODE ", STARTUP_TIME
from GV$DATABASE d, gv$instance i
where i.INST_ID=d.INST_ID;
```

The source databases details are given in the following section. For this exercise, we will upgrade the following three databases which are running in 11g/12c and 18c versions to **19c**. All our source databases are the 2-node **RAC** databases.

The source database names and their versions are as follows:

```
Database      Oracle Version
---------     --------------
shft11g       11.2.0.4
global12      12.1.0.2
hope18c       18.3.0.0
```

The **11g** database information is given as follows:

```
SQL> @/home/oracle/rac_database_info.sql
DATABASE_HOST          DB_NAME           OPEN_MODE          STARTUP_TIME
-------------------    ---------------   ---------------    -------------
virtual-19crac1        shft11g1          READ WRITE         30-MAY-21
virtual-19crac2        shft11g2          READ WRITE         30-MAY-21
```

12c database information is given here:

```
SQL> @/home/oracle/rac_database_info.sql
DATABASE_HOST          DB_NAME           OPEN_MODE          STARTUP_TIME
-------------------    ---------------   ------------------  -------------
virtual-19crac1        global121         READ WRITE          30-MAY-21
virtual-19crac2        global122         READ WRITE          30-MAY-21
```

The **18c** database information is given as follows:

```
SQL> @/home/oracle/rac_database_info.sql
DATABASE_HOST          DB_NAME           OPEN_MODE           STARTUP_TIME
------------------     ---------------   --------------------  -------------
virtual-19crac1        hope18c1          READ WRITE          30-MAY-21
virtual-19crac2        hope18c2          READ WRITE          30-MAY-21
```

Setting up the target environment

For the target environment, we have the Oracle 19c (19.3.0) binaries installed and patched with the October 2020 **patch set update** (**PSU**), as follows:

```
RAC nodes           : virtual-19crac1
                      virtual-19crac2
OS version          : Oracle Enterprise Linux 7.1 64 bit
Oracle Home         : /u01/app/oracle/product/19c/db_1
Database Version    : 19.3.0.0 with October 2020 Database Bundle Patch
Grid Version        : 19.9.0
[oracle@virtual-19crac1 ~]$ $ORACLE_HOME/OPatch/opatch lspatches
31771877;Database Release Update : 19.9.0.0.201020 (31771877)
29585399;OCW RELEASE UPDATE 19.3.0.0.0 (29585399)
OPatch succeeded.
```

Pre-requisite checks required for the database upgrades

Check some of the pre-requisites and a few upfront tasks that we can perform before planning and starting the database upgrade.

Perform a full backup of the primary source database

It is always a good idea to take a FULL level 0 backup of the source database before we upgrade it to a newer version. The following is a sample script that we can use to take a Full level 0 backup of all the databases that we upgraded (You can use any script that works for your environment.):

```
RMAN >
run
{
 allocate channel ch1 device type disk format '/u01/19cupgrade/DATA_
L0_%d_%Y%M%D_%s-%p-%t';
 allocate channel ch2 device type disk format '/u01/19cupgrade/DATA_
L0_%d_%Y%M%D_%s-%p-%t';
 allocate channel ch3 device type disk format '/u01/19cupgrade/DATA_
L0_%d_%Y%M%D_%s-%p-%t';
 allocate channel ch4 device type disk format '/u01/19cupgrade/DATA_
L0_%d_%Y%M%D_%s-%p-%t';
 backup incremental level 0 database plus archivelog TAG='FULL_BACKUP_
B4_UPGRADE' format  '/u01/19cupgrade/DATA_L0_%d_%Y%M%D_%s-%p-%t';
 backup tag 'CONTROL_BACKUP_B4_UPGRADE' current controlfile format '/
u01/19cupgrade/DATA_CONTROL_%d_%Y%M%D_%s-%p-%t';
 release channel ch1;
 release channel ch2;
 release channel ch3;
 release channel ch4;
```

```
}
```

Enabling flashback in the source database

The AutoUpgrade utility creates a guaranteed restore point before starting the upgrade, and for this, we need to enable Flashback in the source database. The database upgrade will fail in the early stages if the flashback is not enabled.

Login to all the source databases and enable the flashback using the following SQL statement:

```
SQL> alter database flashback on;
Database altered.
```

Check to make sure that the flashback is enabled successfully for the **11g**, **12c**, and **18c** database, shown as follows:

11g database:

```
SQL> select name,db_unique_name,log_mode,force_logging,flashback_on from
gv$database;
NAME       DB_UNIQUE_ LOG_MODE     FORCE_LOGGING    FLASHBACK_ON
---------  ---------- ------------ ---------------- ----------------
SHFT11G    shft11g    ARCHIVELOG   NO               YES
SHFT11G    shft11g    ARCHIVELOG   NO               YES
```

12c database:

```
SQL> select name,db_unique_name,log_mode,force_logging,flashback_on from
gv$database;
NAME       DB_UNIQUE_ LOG_MODE     FORCE_LOGGING    FLASHBACK_ON
---------  ---------- ------------ ---------------- ----------------
GLOBAL12   global12   ARCHIVELOG   NO               YES
GLOBAL12   global12   ARCHIVELOG   NO               YES
```

18c database:

```
SQL> select name,db_unique_name,log_mode,force_logging,flashback_on from
gv$database;
NAME       DB_UNIQUE_ LOG_MODE     FORCE_LOGGING    FLASHBACK_ON
---------  ---------- ------------ ---------------- ----------------
HOPE18C    hope18c    ARCHIVELOG   NO               YES
HOPE18C    hope18c    ARCHIVELOG   NO               YES
```

The registry components' status for the source databases are as follows:

11g database:

```
SQL> col COMP_ID for a10
```

```
SQL> col COMP_NAME for a40
SQL> col VERSION for a15
SQL> set lines 180
SQL> set pages 999
SQL> select COMP_ID,COMP_NAME,VERSION,STATUS from dba_registry;

COMP_ID     COMP_NAME                                 VERSION         STATUS
----------- ----------------------------------------- --------------- -------
OWB         OWB                                       11.2.0.4.0      VALID
APEX        Oracle Application Express                3.2.1.00.12     VALID
EM          Oracle Enterprise Manager                 11.2.0.4.0      VALID
AMD         OLAP Catalog                              11.2.0.4.0      VALID
SDO         Spatial                                   11.2.0.4.0      VALID
ORDIM       Oracle Multimedia                         11.2.0.4.0      VALID
XDB         Oracle XML Database                       11.2.0.4.0      VALID
CONTEXT     Oracle Text                               11.2.0.4.0      VALID
EXF         Oracle Expression Filter                  11.2.0.4.0      VALID
RUL         Oracle Rules Manager                      11.2.0.4.0      VALID
OWM         Oracle Workspace Manager                  11.2.0.4.0      VALID
CATALOG     Oracle Database Catalog Views             11.2.0.4.0      VALID
CATPROC     Oracle Database Packages and Types        11.2.0.4.0      VALID
JAVAVM      JServer JAVA Virtual Machine              11.2.0.4.0      VALID
XML         Oracle XDK                                11.2.0.4.0      VALID
CATJAVA     Oracle Database Java Packages             11.2.0.4.0      VALID
APS         OLAP Analytic Workspace                   11.2.0.4.0      VALID
XOQ         Oracle OLAP API                           11.2.0.4.0      VALID
RAC         Oracle Real Application Clusters          11.2.0.4.0      VALID

19 rows selected.
```

12c database:

```
SQL> col COMP_ID for a10
SQL> col COMP_NAME for a40
SQL> col VERSION for a15
SQL> set lines 180
SQL> set pages 999
SQL> select COMP_ID,COMP_NAME,VERSION,STATUS from dba_registry;

COMP_ID     COMP_NAME                                 VERSION         STATUS
----------- ----------------------------------------- --------------- -----------
DV          Oracle Database Vault                     12.1.0.2.0      VALID
APEX        Oracle Application Express                4.2.5.00.08     VALID
OLS         Oracle Label Security                     12.1.0.2.0      VALID
SDO         Spatial                                   12.1.0.2.0      VALID
ORDIM       Oracle Multimedia                         12.1.0.2.0      VALID
CONTEXT     Oracle Text                               12.1.0.2.0      VALID
OWM         Oracle Workspace Manager                  12.1.0.2.0      VALID
```

```
XDB          Oracle XML Database                12.1.0.2.0     VALID
CATALOG      Oracle Database Catalog Views      12.1.0.2.0     VALID
CATPROC      Oracle Database Packages and Types 12.1.0.2.0     VALID
JAVAVM       JServer JAVA Virtual Machine       12.1.0.2.0     VALID
XML          Oracle XDK                         12.1.0.2.0     VALID
CATJAVA      Oracle Database Java Packages      12.1.0.2.0     VALID
APS          OLAP Analytic Workspace            12.1.0.2.0     VALID
XOQ          Oracle OLAP API                    12.1.0.2.0     VALID
RAC          Oracle Real Application Clusters   12.1.0.2.0     VALID

16 rows selected.
```

18c database:

```
SQL> col COMP_ID for a10
SQL> col COMP_NAME for a40
SQL> col VERSION for a15
SQL> set lines 180
SQL> set pages 999
SQL> select COMP_ID,COMP_NAME,VERSION,STATUS from dba_registry;
COMP_ID      COMP_NAME                          VERSION        STATUS
----------   --------------------------------   -----------    ------
CATALOG      Oracle Database Catalog Views      18.0.0.0.0     VALID
CATPROC      Oracle Database Packages and Types 18.0.0.0.0     VALID
RAC          Oracle Real Application Clusters   18.0.0.0.0     VALID
JAVAVM       JServer JAVA Virtual Machine       18.0.0.0.0     VALID
XML          Oracle XDK                         18.0.0.0.0     VALID
CATJAVA      Oracle Database Java Packages      18.0.0.0.0     VALID
APS          OLAP Analytic Workspace            18.0.0.0.0     VALID
XDB          Oracle XML Database                18.0.0.0.0     VALID
OWM          Oracle Workspace Manager           18.0.0.0.0     VALID
CONTEXT      Oracle Text                        18.0.0.0.0     VALID
ORDIM        Oracle Multimedia                  18.0.0.0.0     VALID
SDO          Spatial                            18.0.0.0.0     VALID
XOQ          Oracle OLAP API                    18.0.0.0.0     VALID
OLS          Oracle Label Security              18.0.0.0.0     VALID
DV           Oracle Database Vault              18.0.0.0.0     VALID

15 rows selected.
```

Check and make sure we have enough space in FRA

We must ensure that we have enough free space in the Fast recovery area (FRA) as the AutoUpgrade utility will create the restore point and save the recovery logs. So, please check and set **db_recovery_file_dest_size** to a higher value, and note that we have to perform this step in all the three source databases, as follows:

```
SQL> alter system set db_recovery_file_dest_size=20G scope=both sid='*';
System altered.
```

Purge recyclebin

Please check the **recyclebin** and purge it; in some cases, it might take more time if we have too many objects in the **recyclebin**. So, it's always a good idea to purge the recycle bin before starting the upgrade as this can significantly reduce the overall time taken for the database upgrade. It might be a good idea if we can check this well in advance and purge the **recyclebin**. If the **recyclebin** has too many objects, sometimes, it might even take at least a couple of hours to get them purged which will significantly increase the downtime required for the database upgrade. So, please check ahead and take care of this in all the databases that are being upgraded, as follows:

1. Check the object count in the **recyclebin**, as follows:

   ```
   SQL> select count(*)  from recyclebin;
   ```

2. Purge the recycle bin using the following SQL statement:

   ```
   SQL> purge dba_recyclebin;
   DBA Recyclebin purged.
   ```

3. Re-check the object count in the **recyclebin**, as follows:

   ```
   SQL> select count(*)  from recyclebin;
   ```

Gather dictionary statistics

It's always good to collect the dictionary stats before the database upgrade. Having good stats on the dictionary tables and fixed objects can help the database upgrade to run faster, and thus it can help in reducing the overall downtime required for the database upgrade. We have to perform this step in all the three source databases.

We can use the following SQL statement to check when the dictionary statistics were last collected:

```
SQL> SELECT OPERATION,to_char(MAX(END_TIME),'DD-MON-YY hh24:mi') LATEST
     FROM dba_optstat_operations
     where OPERATION in ('gather_fixed_objects_stats','gather_dictionary_
stats') group by operation;

OPERATION                         LATEST
--------------------------------- ---------------
gather_fixed_objects_stats        29-MAY-21 21:42
gather_dictionary_stats           29-MAY-21 21:41
```

We can gather the dictionary stats using the following statements:

```
SQL> EXECUTE DBMS_STATS.GATHER_DICTIONARY_STATS;
PL/SQL procedure successfully completed.

SQL> EXECUTE DBMS_STATS.GATHER_FIXED_OBJECTS_STATS;
PL/SQL procedure successfully completed.
```

Working directories

Please create a staging directory with the primary database name. We will use this directory as the working directory to save all the required log files. Since we are upgrading multiple databases in one single operation, let's create a generic directory which we can use for the upgrade, as follows:

```
[oracle@virtual-19crac1 ~] mkdir -p /u01/software/upgrade/MULTI-VERSION-DBs-UPGRADE
```

Copy the required files from the all the source database homes to **19c** database home, as follows:

- **Network files**: For the network related files, add the source database TNS entry in the **tnsnames.ora** file of **19c** home, shown as follows:

```
[oracle@virtual-19crac1 ~] cd /u01/app/oracle/product/19c/db_1/network/admin
[oracle@virtual-19crac1 admin ~]$. cp tnsnames.ora tnsnames.ora.May30

[oracle@virtual-19crac1 admin ~]$. vi tnsnames.ora

SHFT11G =
  (DESCRIPTION =
   (ADDRESS = (PROTOCOL = TCP)(HOST = virtual-19crac-scan)(PORT = 1521))
    (CONNECT_DATA =
      (SERVER = DEDICATED)
      (SERVICE_NAME = shft11g)
    )
  )
GLOBAL12 =
  (DESCRIPTION =
   (ADDRESS = (PROTOCOL = TCP)(HOST = virtual-19crac-scan)(PORT = 1521))
    (CONNECT_DATA =
      (SERVER = DEDICATED)
      (SERVICE_NAME = global12)
    )
```

```
        )
     HOPE18C =
       (DESCRIPTION =
         (ADDRESS = (PROTOCOL = TCP)(HOST = virtual-19crac-scan)(PORT
= 1521))
         (CONNECT_DATA =
           (SERVER = DEDICATED)
           (SERVICE_NAME = hope18c)
         )
       )
```

- **Primary database initialization parameter (pfiles/spfile) files**: Copy the primary database **pfile** and **spfile** files from 11g/12c and 18c to 19c DB home.

- **Password files**: Copy the password files for all the three databases from their respective homes to the 19c home.

Check the INVALID objects' count in the primary database

It's always a good idea to take a snapshot of the invalid objects' count before starting the database upgrade. For each source database, run **utlrp** to compile any **INVALID** objects and then take a count of the invalid objects, so that we can compare the count after the database upgrade, as follows:

```
SQL> @$ORACLE_HOME/rdbms/admin/utlrp
```

```
SQL> select count(*) from dba_objects where status='INVALID';
```

Take the count of the invalid objects in the **SYS** and **SYSTEM** schemas, and we will have to run the following script in each source database:

```
SQL> /u01/software/upgrade/MULTI-VERSION-DBs-UPGRADE/database_name_pre-
upgrade_SYS_SYSTEM_invalid_Objects.log
```

```
SQL> SELECT i.HOST_NAME "DATABASE_HOST" ,
     i.INSTANCE_NAME "DB_NAME", d.DATABASE_ROLE " DATABASE_ROLE",
     d.OPEN_MODE " OPEN_MODE ", STARTUP_TIME
     from GV$DATABASE d, gv$instance i
     where i.INST_ID=d.INST_ID;
```

```
SQL> select owner,object_name,object_type,status
     from dba_objects
     where status='INVALID' and owner in ('SYS','SYSTEM')
     order by owner ;
spool off;
```

Next, take the invalid object count for the non-sys and non-system schemas, as follows:

```
SQL> spool /u01/software/upgrade/MULTI-VERSION-DBs-UPGRADE/database_
name_pre-upgrade_non-SYS_invalid_objects.log

SQL> SELECT i.HOST_NAME "DATABASE_HOST" ,
     i.INSTANCE_NAME "DB_NAME", d.DATABASE_ROLE " DATABASE_ROLE",
     d.OPEN_MODE " OPEN_MODE ", STARTUP_TIME
     from GV$DATABASE d, gv$instance i
     where i.INST_ID=d.INST_ID;
SQL> select count(*)
     from dba_objects
     where status='INVALID' and owner not in ('SYS','SYSTEM');
SQL> select owner,object_type,count(*)
     from dba_objects
     where status='INVALID' and owner not in ('SYS','SYSTEM')
     group by owner,object_type order by owner ;
SQL> select owner,object_name,object_type,status
     from dba_objects
     where status='INVALID' and owner not in ('SYS','SYSTEM')
     order by owner ;
spool off;s
```

Download the latest AutoUpgrade tool

As mentioned earlier, Oracle strongly recommends downloading the latest version and using it instead of the default one. We can download the latest AutoUpgrade tool from the MOS Doc ID 2485457.1:

Download the latest version and copy it to the **19c** home, as follows:

```
[oracle@virtual-19crac1 jose12pr]$ cd /u01/software/upgrade/jose12pr/

[oracle@virtual-19crac1 jose12pr]$ ls -ltr AutoUpgrade*
-rwxr-x--- 1 oracle oinstall 2868558 Mar 18 20:37 AutoUpgrade.jar

[oracle@virtual-19crac1 jose12pr]$  cp /u01/software/upgrade/jose12pr/
AutoUpgrade.jar /u01/app/oracle/product/19c/db_1/rdbms/admin/

[oracle@virtual-19crac1 jose12pr]$ ls -ltr  /u01/app/oracle/product/19c/
db_1/rdbms/admin/AutoUpgrade.jar

-rwxr-x--- 1 oracle oinstall 2868558 Mar 18 20:37 /u01/app/oracle/
product/19c/db_1/rdbms/admin/AutoUpgrade.jar
```

AutoUpgrade version

For this exercise, we will use AutoUpgrade version 21.1.1. We can check the AutoUpgrade tool version using the following command:

```
[oracle@virtual-19crac1 ~]$ $ORACLE_HOME/jdk/bin/java -jar $ORACLE_HOME/
rdbms/admin/AutoUpgrade.jar -version
build.hash 8ee6880
build.version 21.1.1
build.date 2020/12/14 14:41:34
build.max_target_version 21
build.supported_target_versions 12.2,18,19,21
build.type production
```

Configuration file

For this chapter, we will use the following configuration file (Please refer to the earlier chapters if you want to see how to create a sample configuration file.):

```
############### 11G Database Parameters ############################
global.autoupg_log_dir=/u01/software/upgrade/MULTI-VERSION-DBs-
UPGRADEupg1.log_dir=/u01/software/upgrade/MULTI-VERSION-DBs-UPGRADE
upg1.sid=shft11g1
upg1.source_home=/u01/app/oracle/product/11.2.0.4/db_1
upg1.target_home=/u01/app/oracle/product/19c/db_1
upg1.tee12cd_time=NOW
upg1.upgrade_node=virtual-19crac1
upg1.run_utlrp=yes
upg1.timezone_upg=yes
upg1.target_version=19
############### END OF 11G DATABASE PARAMETERS ######################

############### 12C DATABASE Parameters ############################
upg2.log_dir=/u01/software/upgrade/MULTI-VERSION-DBs-UPGRADE
upg2.sid=global121
upg2.source_home=/u01/app/oracle/product/12c/db_1
upg2.target_home=/u01/app/oracle/product/19c/db_1
upg2.start_time=NOW
upg2.upgrade_node=virtual-19crac1
upg2.run_utlrp=yes
upg2.timezone_upg=yes
upg2.target_version=19

############### END OF 12C DATABASE PARAMETERS ######################

############### 18C DATABASE Parameters ############################
upg3.log_dir=/u01/software/upgrade/MULTI-VERSION-DBs-UPGRADE
upg3.sid=hope18c1
```

```
upg3.source_home=/u01/app/oracle/product/18c
upg3.target_home=/u01/app/oracle/product/19c/db_1
upg3.start_time=NOW
upg3.upgrade_node=virtual-19crac1
upg3.run_utlrp=yes
upg3.timezone_upg=yes
upg3.target_version=19
################ END OF 18C DATABASE PARAMETERS #######################
```

As you can see, we have included the parameters for all the three databases which are running from three different database homes.

Upgrading Oracle 11g (11.2.0.4)/12c (12.1.0.2) and 18c (18.3.0.0) databases to Oracle 19c (19.9.0)

We can first run the AutoUpgrade in the **analyze** mode to analyze all the three databases and then upgrade the databases.

Running AutoUpgrade in Analyze mode

As you know the modes by now, let's run the AutoUpgrade in the **Analyze** mode for our upgrade. As mentioned earlier, this mode will only read the source database and check if the database is ready for the upgrade. Please note that this mode will not make any changes to the source database. We need to run this from **19c** home, so we have to export **ORACLE_HOME** to a new home (**19c** in this case) and then run the command as follows:

```
[oracle@virtual-19crac1 MULTI-VERSION-DBs-UPGRADE]$
export ORACLE_HOME=/u01/app/oracle/product/19c/db_1

[oracle@virtual-19crac1 MULTI-VERSION-DBs-UPGRADE]$
export PATH=$ORACLE_HOME/bin:$PATH

[oracle@virtual-19crac1 MULTI-VERSION-DBs-UPGRADE]$ ls -ltr
total 4
-rwx------ 1 oracle oinstall 1677 May 29 21:38 multi_db_upgrades.cfg

[oracle@virtual-19crac1 MULTI-VERSION-DBs-UPGRADE]$ $ORACLE_HOME/jdk/
bin/java -jar $ORACLE_HOME/rdbms/admin/AutoUpgrade.jar -config multi_db_
upgrades.cfg -mode ANALYZE
```

Since we are upgrading multiple databases using the same configuration file, the AutoUpgrade tool processes one database at a time. It will pick any database from the configuration file randomly and start performing the prechecks, and once it finishes with the prechecks for this database, it will move to the next database in the list and so on. For the upgrade phase, it will follow the same pattern. You can observe this behavior from the output of the **analyze** command, shown as follows:

```
[oracle@virtual-19crac1 MULTI-VERSION-DBs-UPGRADE]$ $ORACLE_HOME/jdk/
bin/java -jar $ORACLE_HOME/rdbms/admin/AutoUpgrade.jar -config multi_db_
upgrades.cfg -mode ANALYZE
AutoUpgrade tool launched with default options
Processing config file ...
+------------------------------+
| Starting AutoUpgrade execution |
+------------------------------+
3 databases will be analyzed
Type 'help' to list console commands
upg> lsj
+----+---------+---------+---------+--------+--------------+------+---
|Job#|  DB_NAME|STAGE|OPERATION|  STATUS|START_TIME| UPDATED|MESSAGE|
----+---------+---------+---------+--------+--------------+------+---
| 100|global121|PRECHECKS|PREPARING| RUNNING|21/05/30
8:03|08:03:39|Loading database information|
| 101| hope18c1|    SETUP|PREPARING|FINISHED|21/05/30 08:03|08:03:38
               Scheduling|
| 102| shft11g1|    SETUP|PREPARING|FINISHED|21/05/30 08:03|08:03:38
               Scheduling|
+----+---------+---------+---------+--------+--------------+------+---
Total jobs 3upg> lsj
+----+---------+---------+---------+--------+--------------+------+---
|Job#|  DB_NAME|STAGE|OPERATION|  STATUS|START_TIME| UPDATED|MESSAGE|
+----+---------+---------+---------+--------+--------------+--------
100|global121|PRECHECKS|PREPARING| RUNNING|21/05/30
08:03|08:03:39|Loading database information|
| 101| hope18c1|    SETUP|PREPARING|FINISHED|21/05/30 08:03|08:03:38
               Scheduling|
| 102| shft11g1|    SETUP|PREPARING|FINISHED|21/05/30 08:03|08:03:38
               Scheduling|
+----+---------+---------+---------+--------+--------------+----+---
Total jobs 3upg> lsj
+---------+---------+--------+--------------+--------+-------------+
|Job#|  DB_NAME|STAGE|OPERATION|  STATUS|START_TIME| UPDATED|MESSAGE|
+----+---------+---------+---------+--------+--------------+------+--
| 100|global121|PRECHECKS|PREPARING| RUNNING|21/05/30
08:03|08:03:47|Remaining 77/87|
| 101| hope18c1|    SETUP|PREPARING|FINISHED|21/05/30 08:03|08:03:38|
Scheduling|
| 102| shft11g1|    SETUP|PREPARING|FINISHED|21/05/30 08:03|08:03:38|
Scheduling|
--------+---------+--------+--------------+--------+-------------+
```

```
Total jobs 3upg> lsj

+----+---------+---------+---------+---------+-------------+-----+---
|Job#|  DB_NAME|    STAGE|OPERATION|  STATUS|   START_TIME| UPDATED|
MESSAGE|
+----+---------+---------+---------+---------+-------------+------+--
| 100|global121|PRECHECKS|PREPARING| RUNNING|21/05/30
08:03|08:03:50|Remaining 65/87|
| 101| hope18c1|    SETUP|PREPARING|FINISHED|21/05/30 08:03|08:03:38|
Scheduling|
| 102| shft11g1|    SETUP|PREPARING|FINISHED|21/05/30 08:03|08:03:38|
Scheduling|
-+---------+---------+--------+-------------+--------+-------------+

Total jobs 3
upg> Job 100 completed
lsj
+----+---------+---------+---------+-------+-------------+-------+-
|Job#|  DB_NAME|STAGE|OPERATION|STATUS|START_TIME| UPDATED|MESSAGE|
---------+---------+--------+-------------+--------+--------------
| 100|global121|PRECHECKS|  STOPPED|FINISHED|21/05/30 08:03|08:03:57|
Ended database checks|
| 101| hope18c1|PRECHECKS|PREPARING| RUNNING|21/05/30
08:03|08:03:57|Loading database information|
| 102| shft11g1|    SETUP|PREPARING|FINISHED|21/05/30 08:03|08:03:38
|              Scheduling|
+----+---------+---------+---------+--------+-------------+--------+

Total jobs 3
upg> Job 101 completed
lsj

+----+---------+---------+---------+---------+-------------+-----+---
|Job#|  DB_NAME|STAGE|OPERATION|  STATUS|START_TIME| UPDATED|MESSAGE|
+----+---------+---------+---------+---------+-------------+-----+---
| 100|global121|PRECHECKS|  STOPPED|FINISHED|21/05/30
08:03|08:03:57|Ended database checks|
| 101| hope18c1|PRECHECKS|  STOPPED|FINISHED|21/05/30
08:03|08:04:32|Ended database checks|
| 102| shft11g1|PRECHECKS|PREPARING| RUNNING|21/05/30 08:03|08:04:32
|                    |
---------+---------+--------+-------------+--------+--------------
Total jobs 3

upg> lsj
+----+---------+---------+---------+---------+-------------+-------+---
|Job#|  DB_NAME|STAGE|OPERATION|  STATUS|START_TIME| UPDATED|MESSAGE|
+---------+---------+--------+-------------+--------+---------------
| 100|global121|PRECHECKS|  STOPPED|FINISHED|21/05/30 08:03|08:03:57|
Ended database checks|
```

```
| 101| hope18c1|PRECHECKS|  STOPPED|FINISHED|21/05/30 08:03|08:04:32|
Ended database checks|
| 102| shft11g1|PRECHECKS|PREPARING| RUNNING|21/05/30
08:03|08:04:36|Loading database information|
---------+---------+--------+-------------+--------+---------------
Total jobs 3
upg> lsj
----+---------+--------+-------------+--------+-------------------+
|Job#|   DB_NAME|STAGE|OPERATION|  STATUS|START_TIME| UPDATED|MESSAGE|
+---------+---------+--------+-------------+--------+---------------
| 100|global121|PRECHECKS|  STOPPED|FINISHED|21/05/30
08:03|08:03:57|Ended database checks|
| 101| hope18c1|PRECHECKS|  STOPPED|FINISHED|21/05/30
08:03|08:04:32|Ended database checks|
| 102| shft11g1|PRECHECKS|PREPARING| RUNNING|21/05/30 08:03|08:04:51|
Remaining 88/88|
---+---------+--------+-------------+--------+-------------------+

Total jobs 3
upg> Job 102 completed
------------------ Final Summary -------------------
Number of databases          [3]
Jobs finished                [3]
Jobs failed                  [0]
Jobs pending                 [0]
```

Please check the summary report at the following link:

```
/u01/software/upgrade/MULTI-VERSION-DBs-UPGRADE/cfgtoollogs/upgrade/
auto/status/status.html
/u01/software/upgrade/MULTI-VERSION-DBs-UPGRADE/cfgtoollogs/upgrade/
auto/status/status.log
[oracle@virtual-19crac1 MULTI-VERSION-DBs-UPGRADE]$
```

As you can see, the AutoUpgrade tool, at any moment of time, will be working only on one database.

AutoUpgrade log file location

As we saw in the earlier chapters, the AutoUpgrade utility creates multiple sub directories in the log location defined in the config file. In this case, it created separate log directories for each database that was being upgraded, shown as follows:

```
[oracle@virtual-19crac1 MULTI-VERSION-DBs-UPGRADE]$ ls -ltr
total 4
-rwx------ 1 oracle oinstall 1677 May 29 21:38 multi_db_upgrades.cfg
drwx------ 3 oracle oinstall   21 May 30 08:03 cfgtoollogs
drwx------ 4 oracle oinstall   29 May 30 08:03 global121
drwx------ 4 oracle oinstall   29 May 30 08:03 hope18c1
```

```
drwx------ 4 oracle oinstall   29 May 30 08:03 shft11g1
[oracle@virtual-19crac1 MULTI-VERSION-DBs-UPGRADE]$
```

As you can see, AutoUpgrade has created three directories for the three databases.

Preupgrade summary

Check the preupgrade summary log for each of these databases. Let's start with the **11g** database first, as follows:

```
[oracle@virtual-19crac1 MULTI-VERSION-DBs-UPGRADE]$ cd shft11g1/

[oracle@virtual-19crac1 shft11g1]$ ls -ltr
total 0
drwx------ 2 oracle oinstall 128 May 30 08:04 temp
drwx------ 3 oracle oinstall 119 May 30 08:05 102
[oracle@virtual-19crac1 shft11g1]$ cd 102
[oracle@virtual-19crac1 102]$ ls -ltr
total 176
-rwx------ 1 oracle oinstall      0 May 30 08:03 AutoUpgrade_err.log
-rwx--    1 oracle oinstall    301 May 30 08:04 AutoUpgrade_20210530_
user.log
drwx------ 2 oracle oinstall   4096 May 30 08:05 prechecks
-rwx------ 1 oracle oinstall 170563 May 30 08:05 AutoUpgrade_20210530.
log

[oracle@virtual-19crac1 102]$ cd prechecks/
[oracle@virtual-19crac1 prechecks]$ ls -ltr
total 260
-rwx------ 1 oracle oinstall 181954 May 30 08:05 prechecks_shft11g1.log
-rwx------ 1 oracle oinstall  11664 May 30 08:05 shft11g_checklist.xml
-rwx------ 1 oracle oinstall    152 May 30 08:05 shft11g_checklist.json
-rwx------ 1 oracle oinstall   3181 May 30 08:05 shft11g_checklist.cfg
-rwx------ 1 oracle oinstall  30593 May 30 08:05 shft11g_preupgrade.html
-rwx------ 1 oracle oinstall  15578 May 30 08:05 upgrade.xml
-rwx------ 1 oracle oinstall  11473 May 30 08:05 shft11g_preupgrade.log
```

Preupgrade summary log file for the 11g database, shft11g

```
[oracle@virtual-19crac1 prechecks]$ cat shft11g_preupgrade.log

Report generated by AutoUpgrade 21.1.1 (#8ee6880) on 2021-05-30 08:05:07
Upgrade-To version: 19.0.0.0.0

==========================================
Status of the database prior to upgrade
==========================================
      Database Name:  shft11g1
     Container Name:  Not Applicable in Pre-12.1 database
       Container ID:  Not Applicable in Pre-12.1 database
```

```
              Version:  11.2.0.4.0
       DB Patch Level:  PSU 11.2.0.4.200414
           Compatible:  11.2.0.4.0
            Blocksize:  8192
             Platform:  Linux x86 64-bit
        Timezone File:  14
   Database log mode:  ARCHIVELOG
             Readonly:  false
              Edition:  EE

Oracle Component                           Upgrade Action       Current Status
----------------                           --------------       -------------
OLAP Analytic Workspace                    [to be upgraded]     VALID
Oracle Workspace Manager                   [to be upgraded]     VALID
Rule Manager                               [to be upgraded]     VALID
Oracle Enterprise Manager Repository       [to be upgraded]     VALID
Oracle Text                                [to be upgraded]     VALID
Expression Filter                          [to be upgraded]     VALID
Oracle Server                              [to be upgraded]     VALID
Real Application Clusters                  [to be upgraded]     VALID
Oracle XDK for Java                        [to be upgraded]     VALID
Oracle Java Packages                       [to be upgraded]     VALID
Oracle XML Database                        [to be upgraded]     VALID
Oracle Multimedia                          [to be upgraded]     VALID
JServer JAVA Virtual Machine               [to be upgraded]     VALID
Oracle OLAP API                            [to be upgraded]     VALID
Oracle Spatial                             [to be upgraded]     VALID
==============
BEFORE UPGRADE
==============

  REQUIRED ACTIONS
  ================
  None

  RECOMMENDED ACTIONS
  ===================
```

1.   (AUTOFIXUP) Remove the OLAP Catalog by running the 11.2.0.4.0 SQL script $ORACLE_HOME/olap/admin/catnoamd.sql.
     The OLAP Catalog component, AMD, exists in the database.

     Starting with Oracle Database 12c, the OLAP Catalog (OLAP AMD) is desupported and will be automatically marked as OPTION OFF during the database upgrade, if present. Oracle recommends removing OLAP Catalog (OLAP AMD) before the database upgrade. This step can be manually performed before the upgrade to reduce downtime.

  2. (AUTOFIXUP) Remove the EM repository.

     - Copy the $ORACLE_HOME/rdbms/admin/emremove.sql script from the target 19 ORACLE_HOME into the source 11.2.0.4.0 ORACLE_HOME.

Step 1: If the database control is configured, stop EM Database Control, using the following command:
```
$> emctl stop dbconsole
```

Step 2: Connect to the database using the SYS account AS SYSDBA, as follows:
```
SET ECHO ON;
SET SERVEROUTPUT ON;
@emremove.sql
```

Without the set echo and server-output commands, you will not be able to follow the progress of the script.

The database has an Enterprise Manager Database Control repository.

Starting with Oracle Database 12c, the local Enterprise Manager Database Control does not exist anymore. The repository will be removed from your database during the upgrade. This step can be manually performed before the upgrade to reduce downtime.

3. (AUTOFIXUP) Update NUMERIC INITIALIZATION PARAMETERS to meet the estimated minimums. This action may be done now or when starting the database in the upgrade mode using the 19 ORACLE HOME, as follows:

Parameter	Currently	19 minimum
processes	150	300

The database upgrade process requires certain initialization parameters to meet the minimum values. The Oracle upgrade process itself has minimum values which may be higher and are marked with an asterisk. After upgrading, those asterisked parameter values may be reset if needed.

4. Upgrade the Oracle Application Express (APEX) manually before or after the database upgrade.

The database contains APEX version 3.2.1.00.12, which is not supported on the target version 19.0.0.0.0. APEX must be upgraded to at least version 18.2.0.00.12 either before or after the database is upgraded.

Starting with Oracle Database Release 18, APEX is not upgraded automatically as part of the database upgrade. Refer to My Oracle Support Note 1088970.1 for information about the APEX installation and upgrades. Refer to MOS Note 1344948.1 for the minimum APEX version supported for your target database release. The unsupported versions of APEX will be in an INVALID state when its database dependencies are not in sync with the upgraded database.

5. (AUTOFIXUP) Directly grant the ADMINISTER DATABASE TRIGGER privilege to the owner of the trigger or drop and re-create the trigger with a user that was granted directly with such. You can list those triggers using SELECT OWNER, TRIGGER_NAME FROM DBA_TRIGGERS, where TRIM(BASE_OBJECT_TYPE)='DATABASE' AND OWNER NOT IN (SELECT GRANTEE FROM DBA_SYS_PRIVS WHERE PRIVILEGE='ADMINISTER DATABASE TRIGGER').

There is one or more database triggers whose owner does not have the right privilege on the database.

The creation of the database triggers must be done by users granted with the ADMINISTER DATABASE TRIGGER privilege. Privilege must have been granted directly.

    INFORMATION ONLY

    =================

6. (AUTOFIXUP) Run $ORACLE_HOME/rdbms/admin/catnoexf.sql located in the new Oracle Database Oracle home to remove both EXF and RUL.

The Expression Filter (EXF) or Rules Manager (RUL) exist in the database.

Starting with Oracle Database release 12.1, the Expression Filter (EXF) and Database Rules Manager (RUL) features are desupported, and are removed during the upgrade process. This step can be manually performed before the upgrade to reduce downtime.

7. (AUTOFIXUP) Mandatory changes are applied automatically in the during_upgrade_pfile_dbname.ora file. Some of these changes maybe present in the after_upgrade_pfile_dbname.ora file. The during_upgrade_pfile_dbname.ora is used to start the database in the upgrade mode. The after_upgrade_pfile_dbname.ora is used to start the database once the upgrade is completed successfully.

    Parameter

    ----

    cluster_database='FALSE'

Mandatory changes are required to perform the upgrade. These changes are implemented in the during_ and after_upgrade_pfile_dbname.ora files.

8. Check the Oracle Backup and Recovery User's Guide for information on how to manage an RMAN recovery catalog schema.

If you are using a version of the recovery catalog schema that is older than that required by the RMAN client version, then you must upgrade the catalog schema.

It is a good practice to have the catalog schema as the same or higher version than the RMAN client version you are using.

9. To help you keep track of your tablespace allocations, the following AUTOEXTEND tablespaces are expected to successfully EXTEND during the upgrade process:

| | | Min Size |
Tablespace	Size	For Upgrade
SYSTEM	750 MB	987 MB
UNDOTBS2	25 MB	401 MB
TEMP	20 MB	240 MB
SYSAUX	510 MB	724 MB

The minimum tablespace sizes for the upgrade are estimates.

10. Follow the instructions in the Oracle Multimedia README.txt file n <19 ORACLE_HOME>/ord/im/admin/README.txt, or MOS note 2555923.1 to determine if Oracle Multimedia is being used. If Oracle Multimedia is being used, refer to MOS note 2347372.1 for suggestions on replacing Oracle Multimedia.

The Oracle Multimedia component (ORDIM) is installed.

Starting with release 19c, Oracle Multimedia is desupported. The object types still exist, but the methods and procedures will raise an exception. Refer to the 19 Oracle Database Upgrade Guide, the Oracle Multimedia README.txt file in <19 ORACLE_HOME>/ord/im/admin/ README.txt, or MOS note 2555923.1 for more information.

```
=============
AFTER UPGRADE
=============
REQUIRED ACTIONS
================
None
RECOMMENDED ACTIONS

====================
```

11. (AUTOFIXUP) Upgrade the database time zone file using the DBMS_DST package.

The database is using the time zone file version 14 and the target 19 release ships with the time zone file version 32.

Oracle recommends upgrading to the desired (latest) version of the time zone file. For more information, refer to "Upgrading the Time Zone File and Timestamp with Time Zone Data" in the 19 Oracle Database Globalization Support Guide.

12. (AUTOFIXUP) Recompile the objects with timestamp mismatch. Please refer to MOS note 781959.1 for more details. There are objects whose timestamp are mismatched with its parent objects. Timestamp of the dependent objects must coincide with the timestamp of parent objects.

13. (AUTOFIXUP) Gather the dictionary statistics after the upgrade using the following command:
EXECUTE DBMS_STATS.GATHER_DICTIONARY_STATS;
Oracle recommends gathering the dictionary statistics after the upgrade.

The dictionary statistics provide essential information to the Oracle optimizer to help it find the efficient SQL execution plans. After a database upgrade, the statistics need to be re-gathered as there can now be tables that have significantly changed during the upgrade or new tables that do not have the statistics gathered yet.

14. Gather the statistics on fixed objects after the upgrade and when there is a representative workload on the system using the following command:

EXECUTE DBMS_STATS.GATHER_FIXED_OBJECTS_STATS;

Oracle recommends gathering the fixed object statistics after the upgrade. This recommendation is given for all the preupgrade runs.

The fixed object statistics provide essential information to the Oracle optimizer to help it find the efficient SQL execution plans. Those statistics are specific to the Oracle Database release that generates them, and can be stale upon the database upgrade.

For information on managing optimizer statistics, refer to the 11.2.0.4 Oracle Database Performance Tuning Guide.

15. (AUTOFIXUP) Run @?/rdbms/admin/utlrp.sql in order to recompile any invalid objects.

There are invalid objects in the database after the upgrade.

The invalid database objects need to be recompiled after the upgrade.

[oracle@virtual-19crac1 prechecks]$

The 11G preupgrade summary looks good. Next, let's check the preupgrade summary for the 12c database, as follows:

```
[oracle@virtual-19crac1 MULTI-VERSION-DBs-UPGRADE]$ cd global121

[oracle@virtual-19crac1 global121]$ ls -ltr
total 0
drwx------ 2 oracle oinstall 131 May 30 08:03 temp
```

```
drwx------ 3 oracle oinstall 119 May 30 08:03 100
[oracle@virtual-19crac1 global121]$ cd 100
[oracle@virtual-19crac1 100]$ ls -ltr
total 168
-rwx------ 1 oracle oinstall      0 May 30 08:03 AutoUpgrade_err.log-
rwx------ 1 oracle oinstall    302 May 30 08:03 AutoUpgrade_20210530_
user.log
drwx------ 2 oracle oinstall   4096 May 30 08:03 prechecks
-rwx------ 1 oracle oinstall 162424 May 30 08:03 AutoUpgrade_20210530.
log
[oracle@virtual-19crac1 100]$ cd prechecks/
[oracle@virtual-19crac1 prechecks]$ ls -ltr
total 244

-rwx------ 1 oracle oinstall 169820 May 30 08:03 prechecks_global121.log
-rwx------ 1 oracle oinstall   9038 May 30 08:03 global12_checklist.xml
-rwx------ 1 oracle oinstall    154 May 30 08:03 global12_checklist.json
-rwx------ 1 oracle oinstall   2588 May 30 08:03 global12_checklist.cfg
-rwx------ 1 oracle oinstall  26994 May 30 08:03 global12_preupgrade.
tml
-rwx------ 1 oracle oinstall  14416 May 30 08:03 upgrade.xml
-rwx------ 1 oracle oinstall   9012 May 30 08:03 global12_preupgrade.log
```

Below is the preupgrade summary for the 12c database, global121.

```
[oracle@virtual-19crac1 prechecks]$ cat global12_preupgrade.log
```

```
Report generated by AutoUpgrade 21.1.1 (#8ee6880) on 2021-05-30 08:03:56
```

```
Upgrade-To version: 19.0.0.0.0
=======================================
Status of the database prior to upgrade
=======================================
        Database Name:  global121
       Container Name:  global121
         Container ID:  0
              Version:  12.1.0.2.0
       DB Patch Level:  No Patch Bundle applied
           Compatible:  12.1.0.2.0
            Blocksize:  8192
             Platform:  Linux x86 64-bit
        Timezone File:  18

    Database log mode:  ARCHIVELOG
             Readonly:  false
              Edition:  EE
Oracle Component                          Upgrade Action    Current Status
---- -----------                          --------------    --------------
Oracle Workspace Manager                  [to be upgraded]  VALID
```

```
OLAP Analytic Workspace              [to be upgraded]   VALID
Oracle Text                          [to be upgraded]   VALID
Oracle Database Vault                [to be upgraded]   VALID
Oracle Server                        [to be upgraded]   VALID
Real Application Clusters            [to be upgraded]   VALID
Oracle Java Packages                 [to be upgraded]   VALID
Oracle XDK for Java                  [to be upgraded]   VALID
Oracle Label Security                [to be upgraded]   VALID
Oracle XML Database                  [to be upgraded]   VALID
Oracle Multimedia                    [to be upgraded]   VALID
Oracle OLAP API                      [to be upgraded]   VALID
JServer JAVA Virtual Machine         [to be upgraded]   VALID
Oracle Spatial                       [to be upgraded]   VALID
==============
BEFORE UPGRADE
==============
  REQUIRED ACTIONS
  ================
```

1. (AUTOFIXUP) Empty the RECYCLEBIN immediately before the database upgrade.

   The database contains one object in the recycle bin.

   The recycle bin must be completely empty before the database upgrade.

   ```
   RECOMMENDED ACTIONS

   ====================
   ```

3. Upgrade the Oracle Application Express (APEX) manually before or after the database upgrade.

   The database contains APEX version 4.2.5.00.08, which is not supported on the target version 19.0.0.0.0. APEX must be upgraded to at least version 18.2.0.00.12 either before or after the database is upgraded.

   Starting with Oracle Database Release 18, APEX is not upgraded automatically as part of the database upgrade. Refer to My Oracle Support Note 1088970.1 for information about the APEX installation and upgrades. Refer to MOS Note 1344948.1 for the minimum APEX version supported for your target database release. The unsupported versions of APEX will be in an INVALID state when its database dependencies are not in sync with the upgraded database.

   ```
   INFORMATION ONLY
   ================
   ```

4. (AUTOFIXUP) Mandatory changes are applied automatically in the during_upgrade_pfile_dbname.ora file. Some of these changes maybe present in the after_upgrade_pfile_dbname.ora file.   The during_

upgrade_pfile_dbname.ora is used to start the database in the upgrade mode. The after_upgrade_pfile_dbname.ora is used to start the database once the upgrade is completed successfully.

```
Parameter
---------
cluster_database='FALSE'
```

Mandatory changes are required to perform the upgrade. These changes are implemented in the during_ and after_upgrade_pfile_ dbname.ora files.

5. Check the Oracle Backup and Recovery User's Guide for information on how to manage an RMAN recovery catalog schema.

   If you are using a version of the recovery catalog schema that is older than that required by the RMAN client version, then you must upgrade the catalog schema.

   It is a good practice to have the catalog schema as the same or higher version than the RMAN client version you are using.

6. To help you keep track of your tablespace allocations, the following AUTOEXTEND tablespaces are expected to successfully EXTEND during theupgrade process:

```
                                     Min Size
   Tablespace              Size    For Upgrade
   ----------           ----------  -----------
   SYSTEM                  780 MB      1009 MB
   TEMP                     60 MB       240 MB
   UNDOTBS1                280 MB       401 MB
   SYSAUX                  630 MB       838 MB
```

   The minimum tablespace sizes for the upgrade are estimates.

7. Follow the instructions in the Oracle Multimedia README.txt file in <19 ORACLE_HOME>/ord/im/admin/README.txt, or MOS note 2555923.1 to determine if Oracle Multimedia is being used. If Oracle Multimedia is being used, refer to MOS note 2347372.1 for suggestions on replacing Oracle Multimedia.

   The Oracle Multimedia component (ORDIM) is installed.

   Starting with release 19c, Oracle Multimedia is desupported. The object types still exist, but the methods and procedures will raise an exception. Refer to the 19 Oracle Database Upgrade Guide, the Oracle Multimedia README.txt file in <19 ORACLE_HOME>/ord/im/admin/ README.txt, or MOS note 2555923.1 for more information.

```
   ==============
   AFTER UPGRADE
```

```
==============
REQUIRED ACTIONS
=================
None
RECOMMENDED ACTIONS
====================
```

8. (AUTOFIXUP) Upgrade the database time zone file using the DBMS_DST package.

   The database is using the time zone file version 18 and the target 19 release ships with the time zone file version 32.

   Oracle recommends upgrading to the desired (latest) version of the time zone file. For more information, refer to "Upgrading the Time Zone File and Timestamp with Time Zone Data" in the 19 Oracle Database Globalization Support Guide.

9. (AUTOFIXUP) Recompile the objects with timestamp mismatch. Please refer to MOS note 781959.1 for more details.

   There are objects whose timestamp are mismatched with its parent objects. Timestamp of the dependent objects must coincide with the timestamp of parent objects.

10. (AUTOFIXUP) Gather the dictionary statistics after the upgrade using the following command:

    EXECUTE DBMS_STATS.GATHER_DICTIONARY_STATS;

    Oracle recommends gathering the dictionary statistics after the upgrade.

    The dictionary statistics provide essential information to the Oracle optimizer to help it find the efficient SQL execution plans. After a database upgrade, the statistics need to be re-gathered as there can now be tables that have significantly changed during the upgrade or new tables that do not have the statistics gathered yet.

11. Gather the statistics on fixed objects after the upgrade and when there is a representative workload on the system using the following command:

    EXECUTE DBMS_STATS.GATHER_FIXED_OBJECTS_STATS;

    Oracle recommends gathering the fixed object statistics after the upgrade. This recommendation is given for all the preupgrade runs. The fixed object statistics provide essential information to the Oracle optimizer to help it find the efficient SQL execution plans. Those statistics are specific to the Oracle Database release that generates them, and can be stale upon the database upgrade.

For information on managing optimizer statistics, refer to the 12.1.0.2 Oracle Database SQL Tuning Guide.

12. (AUTOFIXUP) Run @?/rdbms/admin/utlrp.sql in order to recompile any invalid objects.

There are invalid objects in the database after the upgrade.

The invalid database objects need to be recompiled after the upgrade.

[oracle@virtual-19crac1 prechecks]$

The **12c** database preupgrade summary also looks good. Now, let's check the preupgrade summary for the **18c** database, as follows:

```
[oracle@virtual-19crac1 shft11g1]$ cd ..
[oracle@virtual-19crac1 MULTI-VERSION-DBs-UPGRADE]$ ls -ltr
total 4
-rwx------ 1 oracle oinstall 1677 May 29 21:38 multi_db_upgrades.cfg
drwx------ 3 oracle oinstall   21 May 30 08:03 cfgtoollogs
drwx------ 4 oracle oinstall   29 May 30 08:03 global121
drwx------ 4 oracle oinstall   29 May 30 08:03 hope18c1
drwx------ 4 oracle oinstall   29 May 30 08:03 shft11g1
[oracle@virtual-19crac1 MULTI-VERSION-DBs-UPGRADE]$ cd hope18c1/
[oracle@virtual-19crac1 hope18c1]$ ls -ltr
total 0
drwx------ 2 oracle oinstall 128 May 30 08:03 temp
drwx------ 3 oracle oinstall 119 May 30 08:04 101
[oracle@virtual-19crac1 hope18c1]$ cd 101
[oracle@virtual-19crac1 101]$ ls -ltr
total 160
-rwx------ 1 oracle oinstall      0 May 30 08:03 AutoUpgrade_err.log
-rwx------ 1 oracle oinstall    301 May 30 08:04 AutoUpgrade_20210530_
user.log
drwx------ 2 oracle oinstall   4096 May 30 08:04 prechecks
-rwx------ 1 oracle oinstall 151939 May 30 08:04 AutoUpgrade_20210530.
log
[oracle@virtual-19crac1 101]$ cd prechecks/
[oracle@virtual-19crac1 prechecks]$ ls -ltr
total 220
-rwx------ 1 oracle oinstall 159785 May 30 08:04 prechecks_hope18c1.log
-rwx------ 1 oracle oinstall   6417 May 30 08:04 hope18c_checklist.xml
-rwx------ 1 oracle oinstall    152 May 30 08:04 hope18c_checklist.json
-rwx------ 1 oracle oinstall   1976 May 30 08:04 hope18c_checklist.cfg
-rwx------ 1 oracle oinstall  23753 May 30 08:04 hope18c_preupgrade.html
-rwx------ 1 oracle oinstall  11268 May 30 08:04 upgrade.xml
-rwx------ 1 oracle oinstall   7000 May 30 08:04 hope18c_preupgrade.log
```

Below is the preupgrade summary for the **18c** database, hope18c.

```
[oracle@virtual-19crac1 prechecks]$ cat hope18c_preupgrade.log
Report generated by AutoUpgrade 21.1.1 (#8ee6880) on 2021-05-30 08:04:31
Upgrade-To version: 19.0.0.0.0
=======================================
Status of the database prior to upgrade
=======================================
        Database Name:  hope18c1
       Container Name:  hope18c1
         Container ID:  0
              Version:  18.3.0.0.0
       DB Patch Level:  Database Release Update : 18.3.0.0.180717
28090523)
           Compatible:  18.0.0
            Blocksize:  8192
             Platform:  Linux x86 64-bit
        Timezone File:  31
    Database log mode:  ARCHIVELOG
             Readonly:  false
              Edition:  EE
Oracle Component                      Upgrade Action       Current Status
----------------                      --------------       --------------
Oracle Workspace Manager              [to be upgraded]     VALID
OLAP Analytic Workspace               [to be upgraded]     VALID
Oracle Text                           [to be upgraded]     VALID
Oracle Database Vault                 [to be upgraded]     VALID
Oracle Server                         [to be upgraded]     VALID
Real Application Clusters             [to be upgraded]     VALID
Oracle Java Packages                  [to be upgraded]     VALID
Oracle XDK for Java                   [to be upgraded]     VALID
Oracle Label Security                 [to be upgraded]     VALID
Oracle XML Database                   [to be upgraded]     VALID
Oracle Multimedia                     [to be upgraded]     VALID
JServer JAVA Virtual Machine          [to be upgraded]     VALID
Oracle OLAP API                       [to be upgraded]     VALID
Oracle Spatial                        [to be upgraded]     VALID
==============
BEFORE UPGRADE
==============
  REQUIRED ACTIONS
  ================
  None
  INFORMATION ONLY
  ================
    1. (AUTOFIXUP) Mandatory changes are applied automatically in the
       during_upgrade_pfile_dbname.ora file. Some of these changes maybe
```

present in the after_upgrade_pfile_dbname.ora file. The during_
upgrade_pfile_dbname.ora is used to start the database in the upgrade

mode. The after_upgrade_pfile_dbname.ora is used to start the
database once the upgrade is completed successfully.

```
Parameter
---------
local_listener='remove'
cluster_database='FALSE'
```

Mandatory changes are required to perform the upgrade. These
changes are implemented in the during_ and after_upgrade_pfile_
dbname.ora files.

2. Check the Oracle Backup and Recovery User's Guide for information
   on how to manage an RMAN recovery catalog schema.

   If you are using a version of the recovery catalog schema that is
   older than that required by the RMAN client version, then you must
   upgrade the catalog schema.

   It is a good practice to have the catalog schema as the same or
   higher version than the RMAN client version you are using.

3. To help you keep track of your tablespace allocations, the following
   AUTOEXTEND tablespaces are expected to successfully EXTEND during
   theupgrade process:

   ```
                                            Min Size
   Tablespace                     Size      For Upgrade
   ----------                     ----      ----------
   SYSTEM                         850 MB     1084 MB
   TEMP                            37 MB      240 MB
   UNDOTBS1                       310 MB      400 MB
   SYSAUX                         560 MB      765 MB
   ```
   The minimum tablespace sizes for the upgrade are estimates.

4. Follow the instructions in the Oracle Multimedia README.txt file in
   <19 ORACLE_HOME>/ord/im/admin/README.txt, or MOS note 2555923.1 to
   determine if Oracle Multimedia is being used. If Oracle Multimedia
   is being used, refer to MOS note 2347372.1 for suggestions on
   replacing Oracle Multimedia.

   The Oracle Multimedia component (ORDIM) is installed.

   Starting with release 19c, Oracle Multimedia is desupported. The
   object types still exist, but the methods and procedures will raise
   an exception. Refer to the 19 Oracle Database Upgrade Guide, the
   Oracle Multimedia README.txt file in <19 ORACLE_HOME>/ord/im/admin/
   README.txt, or MOS note 2555923.1 for more information.

```
=============
AFTER UPGRADE
=============
REQUIRED ACTIONS
================
None
RECOMMENDED ACTIONS
===================
```

5. (AUTOFIXUP) Upgrade the database time zone file using the DBMS_DST package.

   The database is using the time zone file version 31 and the target 19 release ships with the time zone file version 32.

   Oracle recommends upgrading to the desired (latest) version of the time zone file. For more information, refer to "Upgrading the Time Zone File and Timestamp with Time Zone Data" in the 19 Oracle Database Globalization Support Guide.

6. (AUTOFIXUP) Recompile the objects with timestamp mismatch. Please refer to MOS note 781959.1 for more details.

   There are objects whose timestamp are mismatched with its parent objects.

   Timestamp of the dependent objects must coincide with the timestamp of parent objects.

7. (AUTOFIXUP) Gather the dictionary statistics after the upgrade using the following command:

   EXECUTE DBMS_STATS.GATHER_DICTIONARY_STATS;

   Oracle recommends gathering the dictionary statistics after the upgrade.

   The dictionary statistics provide essential information to the Oracle optimizer to help it find the efficient SQL execution plans. After a database upgrade, the statistics need to be re-gathered as there can now be tables that have significantly changed during the upgrade or new tables that do not have the statistics gathered yet.

8. Gather the statistics on fixed objects after the upgrade and when there is a representative workload on the system using the following command:

   EXECUTE DBMS_STATS.GATHER_FIXED_OBJECTS_STATS;

   Oracle recommends gathering the fixed object statistics after the upgrade. This recommendation is given for all the preupgrade runs.

The fixed object statistics provide essential information to the Oracle optimizer to help it find the efficient SQL execution plans. Those statistics are specific to the Oracle Database release that generates them, and can be stale upon the database upgrade.

For information on managing optimizer statistics, refer to the 18.0.0.0 Oracle Database Upgrade Guide.

9. (AUTOFIXUP) Run @?/rdbms/admin/utlrp.sql in order to recompile any invalid objects.

There are invalid objects in the database after the upgrade.

The invalid database objects need to be recompiled after the upgrade.

The **18c** database preupgrade summary log also looks good. We are good to proceed with the upgrade step.

Run the AutoUpgrade command in the DEPLOY mode

Since the pre-upgrade summary logfile looks clean for all the three databases, we can now upgrade all the three databases which are running from three different versions to **19c** by running one single **AutoUpgrade** command in the **DEPLOY** mode.

Export the Oracle home to point to **19c** first and then run the **AutoUpgrade** command as follows:

```
[oracle@virtual-19crac1 MULTI-VERSION-DBs-UPGRADE]$ export ORACLE_HOME=/
u01/app/oracle/product/19c/db_1
[oracle@virtual-19crac1 MULTI-VERSION-DBs-UPGRADE]$ export
PATH=$PATH:$ORACLE_HOME/bin:$PATH
[oracle@virtual-19crac1 MULTI-VERSION-DBs-UPGRADE]$ echo $ORACLE_HOME/
u01/app/oracle/product/19c/db_1
```

Run the **AutoUpgrade** command in the **DEPLOY** mode to upgrade the database, as follows:

```
[oracle@virtual-19crac1 MULTI-VERSION-DBs-UPGRADE]$ $ORACLE_HOME/jdk/
bin/java -jar $ORACLE_HOME/rdbms/admin/AutoUpgrade.jar -config multi_db_
upgrades.cfg -mode DEPLOY
```

As mentioned earlier, the AutoUpgrade tool will pick one database in the list and start upgrading it to **19c**; please see the following as the first part of the output of the **AutoUpgrade** command:

```
[oracle@virtual-19crac1 MULTI-VERSION-DBs-UPGRADE]$ $ORACLE_HOME/jdk/
bin/java -jar $ORACLE_HOME/rdbms/admin/AutoUpgrade.jar -config multi_db_
upgrades.cfg -mode DEPLOY
```

```
AutoUpgrade tool launched with default options
Processing config file ...
+-------------------------------+
| Starting AutoUpgrade execution |
+-------------------------------+
3 databases will be processed
Type 'help' to list console commands
upg> lsj
+----+---------+---------+---------+--------+-------------+--------+-
|Job#|DB_NAME|STAGE|OPERATION|STATUS|START_TIME| UPDATED| MESSAGE|
+--------+---------+---------+--------+-------------+----------------
| 103|global121|PREFIXUPS|EXECUTING| RUNNING|21/05/30
08:13|08:14:02|Loading database information|
| 104| hope18c1|    SETUP|PREPARING|FINISHED|21/05/30 08:14|08:13:32
|               Scheduling|
| 105|  shft11g1|    SETUP|PREPARING|FINISHED|21/05/30 08:16|08:13:32
|               Scheduling|
--+---------+---------+--------+-------------+--------+--------------
Total jobs 3
upg> lsj
+----+---------+-----+---------+--------+-------------+--------+------
|Job#|DB_NAME|STAGE|OPERATION|STATUS| START_TIME| UPDATED|    MESSAGE|
+---------+-----+---------+--------+-------------+--------+----------+
| 103|global121|DRAIN|PREPARING| RUNNING|21/05/30 08:13|08:14:24|
|
| 104| hope18c1|SETUP|PREPARING|FINISHED|21/05/30
08:14|08:13:32|Scheduling|
| 105|  shft11g1|SETUP|PREPARING|FINISHED|21/05/30
08:16|08:13:32|Scheduling|
--------+-----+---------+--------+-------------+--------+----------+
Total jobs 3
upg> lsj
-+-----+---------+--------+-------------+--------+------------------
|Job#|DB_NAME|STAGE|OPERATION|  STATUS|START_TIME| UPDATED| MESSAGE|
----+---------+--------+-------------+--------+------------------
| 103|global121|DRAIN|EXECUTING| RUNNING|21/05/30 08:13|08:15:26|
Shutting down database|
| 104| hope18c1|SETUP|PREPARING|FINISHED|21/05/30 08:14|08:13:32|
Scheduling|
| 105|  shft11g1|SETUP|PREPARING|FINISHED|21/05/30
08:16|08:13:32|Scheduled, starts in 0 min|
-+-----+---------+--------+-------------+--------+-----------------
Total jobs 3
upg> lsj
--+-----+---------+--------+-------------+--------+------------------
|Job#|DB_NAME|STAGE|OPERATION|STATUS| START_TIME| UPDATED|MESSAGE|
```

```
+----+---------+-----+---------+--------+-------------+--------+------
| 103|global121|DRAIN|EXECUTING| RUNNING|21/05/30 08:13|08:15:26|
Shutting down database|
| 104| hope18c1|SETUP|PREPARING|FINISHED|21/05/30 08:14|08:13:32|
Scheduling|
| 105| shft11g1|SETUP|PREPARING|FINISHED|21/05/30
08:16|08:13:32|Scheduled, starts in 0 min|
+----+---------+-----+---------+--------+-------------+--------+------
Total jobs 3
upg> lsj
-+---------+---------+--------+-------------+--------+---------------
|Job#|  DB_NAME|STAGE|OPERATION|  STATUS|START_TIME| UPDATED|MESSAGE|
+---------+--------+-------------+--------+-------------------------+
| 103|global121|DBUPGRADE|EXECUTING| RUNNING|21/05/30 08:13|08:17:06
|                Running|
| 104| hope18c1|     SETUP|PREPARING|FINISHED|21/05/30 08:14|08:13:32|
Scheduling|
| 105| shft11g1|     SETUP|PREPARING|FINISHED|21/05/30
08:16|08:13:32|Scheduled, starts in 0 min|
-+---------+---------+--------+-------------+--------+---------------
Total jobs 3
upg> lsj
-+---------+---------+--------+-------------+--------+---------------
|Job#|  DB_NAME|    STAGE|OPERATION|  STATUS|    START_TIME| UPDATED|
MESSAGE|
-+---------+---------+--------+-------------+--------+---------------
| 103|global121|DBUPGRADE|EXECUTING| RUNNING|21/05/30 08:13|08:17:12|
0%Upgraded |
| 104| hope18c1|SETUP|PREPARING|FINISHED|21/05/30 08:14|08:13:32|
Scheduling|
| 105| shft11g1|     SETUP|PREPARING|FINISHED|21/05/30
08:16|08:13:32|Scheduled, starts in 0 min|
+----+------+---------+--------+-------------+--------+---------------
```

Total jobs 3

As you can see in the preceding output, **AutoUpgrade** has picked **global12** as the first database to upgrade. Once the upgrade process reaches 100% competition status, it will pick up the remaining databases randomly from the configuration **file/Job#'s** list.

We can open a new terminal and tail the upgrade log file for the first database (**global12**) that's being upgraded, as follows:

```
[oracle@virtual-19crac1 ~]$ cd /u01/software/upgrade/MULTI-VERSION-DBs-
UPGRADE/global121/
[oracle@virtual-19crac1 global121]$ ls -ltr
total 8
```

```
drwx------  3 oracle oinstall  119 May 30 08:03 100
drwx------  2 oracle oinstall 4096 May 30 09:01 temp
drwx------ 10 oracle oinstall 4096 May 30 09:03 103
[oracle@virtual-19crac1 global121]$ cd 103
[oracle@virtual-19crac1 103]$ pwd
/u01/software/upgrade/MULTI-VERSION-DBs-UPGRADE/global121/103
[oracle@virtual-19crac1 103]$ ls -ltr
total 728
drwx------ 2 oracle oinstall     28 May 30 08:13 preupgrade
drwx------ 2 oracle oinstall   4096 May 30 08:13 prechecks
drwx------ 2 oracle oinstall     89 May 30 08:14 prefixups
drwx------ 2 oracle oinstall     33 May 30 08:16 drain
drwx------ 2 oracle oinstall   4096 May 30 09:00 dbupgrade
drwx------ 2 oracle oinstall   4096 May 30 09:01 postchecks
-rwx------ 1 oracle oinstall   1412 May 30 09:01 AutoUpgrade_err.log
drwx------ 2 oracle oinstall     92 May 30 09:01 postfixups
drwx------ 2 oracle oinstall     29 May 30 09:01 postupgrade
-rwx------ 1 oracle oinstall  24782 May 30 09:01 AutoUpgrade_20210530_
ser.log
-rwx------ 1 oracle oinstall 697049 May 30 09:03 AutoUpgrade_20210530.
og
[oracle@virtual-19crac1 103]$
```

Tail the upgrade log file as shown below

```
[oracle@virtual-19crac1 103]$ tail -f AutoUpgrade_20210530_user.log
2021-05-30 08:20:12.942 INFO 8%Upgraded

2021-05-30 08:23:13.361 INFO 21%Upgraded
2021-05-30 08:26:13.736 INFO 21%Upgraded
2021-05-30 08:29:14.011 INFO 23%Upgraded
2021-05-30 08:32:14.293 INFO 39%Upgraded
2021-05-30 08:32:14.293 INFO 39%Upgraded
2021-05-30 08:35:14.612 INFO 49%Upgraded
2021-05-30 08:38:15.548 INFO 49%Upgraded
2021-05-30 08:41:15.873 INFO 49%Upgraded
2021-05-30 08:44:16.150 INFO 52%Upgraded
2021-05-30 08:47:16.375 INFO 71%Upgraded
2021-05-30 08:50:16.779 INFO 81%Upgraded
2021-05-30 08:53:17.082 INFO 91%Upgraded
2021-05-30 08:56:17.587 INFO 91%Upgraded
2021-05-30 08:59:17.774 INFO 95%Upgraded
2021-05-30 09:00:28.842 INFO SUCCESSFULLY UPGRADED [global12]
2021-05-30 09:00:28.842 INFO End Upgrade on Database [global12]
2021-05-30 09:00:33.937 INFO SUCCESSFULLY UPGRADED [global12]
2021-05-30 09:00:33.993 INFO global12 Return status is SUCCESS
2021-05-30 09:01:01.857 INFO Analyzing global121, 14 checks will run
using 2 threads
```

```
2021-05-30 09:01:04.239 INFO Using /u01/software/upgrade/MULTI-VERSION-
DBs-UPGRADE/global121/103/prechecks/global12_checklist.cfg to identify
required fixups
2021-05-30 09:01:04.242 INFO Content of the checklist /u01/software/
upgrade/MULTI-VERSION-DBs-UPGRADE/global121/103/prechecks/global12_
checklist.cfg is:
```

As you can see from above output, upgrade of the database, **global12** is completed successfully.

Now switch back the original session where the **AutoUpgrade** command is still running and continue to monitor the output of the AutoUpgrade command. Please see the following output of the still running **AutoUpgrade** command in the **deploy** mode:

```
Total jobs 3
upg> lsj
-+----------+---------+--------+--------------+--------+----------------
|Job#|  DB_NAME|STAGE|OPERATION|STATUS|START_TIME| UPDATED|    MESSAGE|
+---------+---------+--------+--------------+--------+----------------
| 103|global121|DBUPGRADE|EXECUTING|  RUNNING|21/05/30 08:13|08:41:15|
49%Upgraded |
| 104| hope18c1|    SETUP|PREPARING|FINISHED|21/05/30 08:14|08:13:32|
Scheduling|
| 105| shft11g1|    SETUP|PREPARING|FINISHED|21/05/30
08:16|08:13:32|Scheduled, starts in 0 min|
+----+---------+---------+---------+--------+----------+--------+---
Total jobs 3
pg> Job 103 completed
lsj
-+----------+---------+--------+--------------+--------+--------------
|Job#|  DB_NAME| STAGE|OPERATION|STATUS| START_TIME| UPDATED|   MESSAGE|
+---------+---------+--------+--------------+--------+--------------
| 103|global121|POSTUPGRADE|  STOPPED|FINISHED|21/05/30 08:13|09:03:24|
Completed job 103|
| 104| hope18c1|  DBUPGRADE|EXECUTING|  RUNNING|21/05/30 08:14|09:16:27|
49%Upgraded |
| 105| shft11g1|      SETUP|PREPARING|FINISHED|21/05/30
08:16|08:13:32|Scheduled, starts in 0 min|
+----+---------+----------+---------+--------+----------+--------+---------
Total jobs 3
upg> lsj
-+----------+---------+--------+--------------+--------+--------------
|Job#|  DB_NAME| STAGE|OPERATION| STATUS| START_TIME| UPDATED MESSAGE|
-+---------+---------+--------+--------------+--------+--------------
| 103|global121|POSTUPGRADE|  STOPPED|FINISHED|21/05/30 08:13|09:03:24|
Completed job 103|
```

```
| 104| hope18c1|  DBUPGRADE|EXECUTING| RUNNING|21/05/30 08:14|09:25:28|
91%Upgraded |
| 105| shft11g1| SETUP|PREPARING|FINISHED|21/05/30
08:16|08:13:32|Scheduled, starts in 0 min|
--------+---------+--------+--------------+--------+--------------
Total jobs 3
```

As you can see from the above output, once the **AutoUpgrade** process completed the upgrade of the **global121** database, it picked the **18c** database (**hope18c**) and started upgrading it.

In a separate terminal, tail the upgrade log for this database (**hope18c**) that is being upgraded, as follows:

```
[oracle@virtual-19crac1 MULTI-VERSION-DBs-UPGRADE]$ cd hope18c1/
[oracle@virtual-19crac1 hope18c1]$ ls -lr
total 8
drwx------ 2 oracle oinstall 4096 May 30 09:10 temp
drwx------ 7 oracle oinstall 4096 May 30 09:06 104
drwx------ 3 oracle oinstall  119 May 30 08:04 101
[oracle@virtual-19crac1 hope18c1]$ cd 104

[oracle@virtual-19crac1 104]$ ls -ltr
total 464
-rwx------ 1 oracle oinstall      0 May 30 08:13 AutoUpgrade_err.log.lck
-rwx------ 1 oracle oinstall      0 May 30 08:13 AutoUpgrade_err.log
-rwx------ 1 oracle oinstall      0 May 30 08:13 AutoUpgrade_20210530_
user.log.lck
-rwx------ 1 oracle oinstall      0 May 30 08:13 AutoUpgrade_20210530.
log.lck
drwx------ 2 oracle oinstall     28 May 30 09:03 preupgrade
drwx------ 2 oracle oinstall   4096 May 30 09:04 prechecks
drwx------ 2 oracle oinstall     87 May 30 09:04 prefixups
drwx------ 2 oracle oinstall     32 May 30 09:06 drain
drwx------ 2 oracle oinstall   4096 May 30 09:23 dbupgrade
-rwx------ 1 oracle oinstall   4622 May 30 09:25 AutoUpgrade_20210530_
user.log
-rwx------ 1 oracle oinstall 415550 May 30 09:25 AutoUpgrade_20210530.
log
```

Tail the upgrade log file as shown below

```
[oracle@virtual-19crac1 104]$ tail -f AutoUpgrade_20210530_user.log

2021-05-30 09:06:58.832 INFO [virtual-19crac2] Password file /u01/app/
oracle/product/18c/dbs/orapwhope18c2 is not found on remote host
2021-05-30 09:07:21.751 INFO Total Number of upgrade phases is 108
2021-05-30 09:07:21.752 INFO Begin Upgrade on Database [hope18c]
```

```
2021-05-30 09:07:26.975 INFO 0%Upgraded
2021-05-30 09:10:27.112 INFO 18%Upgraded
2021-05-30 09:13:27.311 INFO 23%Upgraded
2021-05-30 09:16:27.487 INFO 49%Upgraded
2021-05-30 09:19:27.701 INFO 61%Upgraded
2021-05-30 09:22:28.042 INFO 81%Upgraded
2021-05-30 09:28:28.552 INFO 91%Upgraded
2021-05-30 09:30:33.986 INFO SUCCESSFULLY UPGRADED [hope18c]
2021-05-30 09:30:33.986 INFO End Upgrade on Database [hope18c]
2021-05-30 09:30:39.608 INFO SUCCESSFULLY UPGRADED [hope18c]
2021-05-30 09:30:39.626 INFO hope18c Return status is SUCCESS
2021-05-30 09:31:03.385 INFO Analyzing hope18c1, 14 checks will run
using 2 threads
2021-05-30 09:31:04.368 INFO Using /u01/software/upgrade/MULTI-VERSION-
DBs-UPGRADE/hope18c1/104/prechecks/hope18c_checklist.cfg to identify
required fixups
2021-05-30 09:31:04.370 INFO Content of the checklist /u01/software/
upgrade/MULTI-VERSION-DBs-UPGRADE/hope18c1/104/prechecks/hope18c_
checklist.cfg is:
```

As you can see from above output, upgrade of the database, **hope18c** is completed successfully.

Once the AutoUpgrade utility finishes upgrading this database, it moves to the final database in the list and starts upgrading it. Please see the following output of the still running **AutoUpgrade** command in the **deploy** mode:

```
upg> lsj
+----+---------+-----------+---------+--------+--------------+--------+-
|Job#|  DB_NAME| STAGE|OPERATION|  STATUS|  START_TIME| UPDATED|MESSAGE|
+----+---------+-----------+---------+--------+--------------+--------+-
| 103|global121|POSTUPGRADE|  STOPPED|FINISHED|21/05/30 08:13|09:03:24|
Completed job 103|
| 104| hope18c1|  DBUPGRADE|EXECUTING| RUNNING|21/05/30 08:14|09:25:28|
91%Upgraded |
| 105| shft11g1|      SETUP|PREPARING|FINISHED|21/05/30
08:16|08:13:32|Scheduled, starts in 0 min|
+----+---------+-----------+---------+--------+--------------+--------+
Total jobs 3
upg> Job 104 completed
upg>lsj
+----------+---------+--------+--------------+--------+-------------
|Job#|  DB_NAME|  STAGE|OPERATION| STATUS| START_TIME| UPDATED| MESSAGE|
+----+---------+-----------+---------+--------+--------------+--------+-
| 103|global121|POSTUPGRADE|  STOPPED|FINISHED|21/05/30
08:13|09:03:24|Completed job 103|
| 104| hope18c1|POSTUPGRADE|  STOPPED|FINISHED|21/05/30
```

```
08:14|09:32:41|Completed job 104|
| 105| shft11g1|  PREFIXUPS|EXECUTING| RUNNING|21/05/30 08:16|09:33:32|
Remaining 6/7|
+----+---------+-----------+---------+--------+--------------+------+
Total jobs 3
upg> lsj
+----+---------+-----------+---------+--------+--------------+-------+
|Job#|  DB_NAME|  STAGE|OPERATION|  STATUS|START_TIME| UPDATED| MESSAGE|
+----+---------+-----------+---------+--------+--------------+------+-

| 103|global121|POSTUPGRADE|  STOPPED|FINISHED|21/05/30
08:13|09:03:24|Completed job 103|
| 104| hope18c1|POSTUPGRADE|  STOPPED|FINISHED|21/05/30
08:14|09:32:41|Completed job 104|
| 105| shft11g1|  PREFIXUPS|EXECUTING| RUNNING|21/05/30 08:16|09:33:32|
Remaining 6/7|
+----+---------+-----------+---------+--------+--------------+------+-
Total jobs 3
upg> lsj
+----+---------+-----------+---------+--------+--------------+------+-
|Job#|  DB_NAME|STAGE|OPERATION|  STATUS|START_TIME|  UPDATED|   MESSAGE|
+----+---------+-----------+---------+--------+--------------+-------+-
| 103|global121|POSTUPGRADE|  STOPPED|FINISHED|21/05/30 08:13|09:03:24|
Completed job 103|
| 104| hope18c1|POSTUPGRADE|  STOPPED|FINISHED|21/05/30 08:14|09:32:41|
Completed job 104|
| 105| shft11g1|       DRAIN|EXECUTING| RUNNING|21/05/30
08:16|09:36:21|Shutting
down database|
+----+---------+-----------+---------+--------+--------------+------+-
Total jobs 3
```

As you can see, it started working on the final database, **shft11g**. We can monitor
the **logfile** for this database (**shift11g**) that is being upgraded now, as follows:

```
[oracle@virtual-19crac1 MULTI-VERSION-DBs-UPGRADE]$ ls -ltr
total 4
-rwx------ 1 oracle oinstall 1677 May 29 21:38 multi_db_upgrades.cfg
drwx------ 3 oracle oinstall   21 May 30 08:03 cfgtoollogs
drwx------ 5 oracle oinstall   40 May 30 08:13 global121
drwx------ 5 oracle oinstall   40 May 30 08:13 hope18c1
drwx------ 5 oracle oinstall   40 May 30 08:13 shft11g1
[oracle@virtual-19crac1 MULTI-VERSION-DBs-UPGRADE]$ cd shft11g1/
[oracle@virtual-19crac1 shft11g1]$ ls -ltr
total 4
drwx------ 2 oracle oinstall  128 May 30 08:04 temp
drwx------ 3 oracle oinstall  119 May 30 08:05 102
```

```
drwx------ 7 oracle oinstall 4096 May 30 09:37 105
[oracle@virtual-19crac1 shft11g1]$ cd 105
[oracle@virtual-19crac1 105]$ ls -ltr
total 528
-rwx------ 1 oracle oinstall        0 May 30 08:13 AutoUpgrade_err.log.lck

-rwx------ 1 oracle oinstall        0 May 30 08:13 AutoUpgrade_err.log
-rwx------ 1 oracle oinstall        0 May 30 08:13 AutoUpgrade_20210530_
user.log.lck
-rwx------ 1 oracle oinstall        0 May 30 08:13 AutoUpgrade_20210530.
log.lck
drwx------ 2 oracle oinstall       28 May 30 09:32 preupgrade
drwx------ 2 oracle oinstall     4096 May 30 09:33 prechecks
drwx------ 2 oracle oinstall       87 May 30 09:35 prefixups
drwx------ 2 oracle oinstall       32 May 30 09:37 drain
drwx------ 2 oracle oinstall     4096 May 30 09:37 dbupgrade

-rwx------ 1 oracle oinstall     5808 May 30 09:37 AutoUpgrade_20210530_
user.log
-rwx------ 1 oracle oinstall 375675 May 30 09:37 AutoUpgrade_20210530.
log
```

Tail the upgrade logfile for the last database, shft11g.

```
[oracle@virtual-19crac1 105]$ tail -f AutoUpgrade_20210530_user.log


2021-05-30 09:35:27.875 INFO Updating parameter *.cluster_
database='true' to *.cluster_database='FALSE' in /u01/software/upgrade/
MULTI-VERSION-DBs-UPGRADE/shft11g1/temp/during_upgrade_pfile_shft11g1.ora
2021-05-30 09:35:39.195 INFO Analyzing shft11g1, 88 checks will run
using 2 threads
2021-05-30 09:36:20.812 INFO Defer redo log shipping to standby database
2021-05-30 09:37:01.657 INFO Copying password file from /u01/app/oracle/
product/11.2.0.4/db_1/dbs/orapwshft11g1 to /u01/app/oracle/product/19c/
db_1/dbs/orapwshft11g1
2021-05-30 09:37:01.794 INFO Copying password file completed with success
2021-05-30 09:37:01.794 INFO Copying password file from /u01/app/oracle/
product/11.2.0.4/db_1/dbs/orapwshft11g1 to /u01/app/oracle/product/19c/
db_1/dbs/orapwshft11g1
2021-05-30 09:37:01.796 INFO Copying password file completed with success
2021-05-30 09:37:31.992 INFO Total Number of upgrade phases is 108
2021-05-30 09:37:31.994 INFO Begin Upgrade on Database [shft11g]
2021-05-30 09:37:37.535 INFO 0%Upgraded
2021-05-30 09:40:37.748 INFO 10%Upgraded
2021-05-30 09:43:37.943 INFO 21%Upgraded
2021-05-30 09:46:38.139 INFO 39%Upgraded
2021-05-30 09:49:38.420 INFO 49%Upgraded
```

```
2021-05-30 09:52:38.668 INFO 61%Upgraded
2021-05-30 09:55:39.088 INFO 81%Upgraded
2021-05-30 09:58:39.347 INFO 91%Upgraded
2021-05-30 10:01:40.403 INFO 91%Upgraded
2021-05-30 10:04:40.754 INFO 95%Upgraded
2021-05-30 10:05:57.516 INFO SUCCESSFULLY UPGRADED [shft11g]
2021-05-30 10:05:57.517 INFO End Upgrade on Database [shft11g]
2021-05-30 10:06:01.918 INFO SUCCESSFULLY UPGRADED [shft11g]
2021-05-30 10:06:01.943 INFO shft11g Return status is SUCCESS
2021-05-30 10:06:25.901 INFO Analyzing shft11g1, 14 checks will run
sing 2 threads
2021-05-30 10:06:27.233 INFO Using /u01/software/upgrade/MULTI-VERSION-
DBs-UPGRADE/shft11g1/105/prechecks/shft11g_checklist.cfg to identify
required fixups
2021-05-30 10:06:27.236 INFO Content of the checklist /u01/software/
upgrade/MULTI-VERSION-DBs-UPGRADE/shft11g1/105/prechecks/shft11g_
checklist.cfg is:
```

As we can see, the upgrade of the third database is now completed. We can come back to the first screen where we started the **AutoUpgrade** in the **deploy** mode and we can see that **AutoUpgrade** has upgraded all the three databases successfully. The following is the final part of the output from this command:

```
upg> lsj
+----+---------+-----------+---------+--------+--------------+--------+
|Job#|  DB_NAME|  STAGE|OPERATION| STATUS| START_TIME| UPDATED| MESSAGE|
+----+---------+-----------+---------+--------+--------------+--------+-
| 103|global121|POSTUPGRADE|  STOPPED|FINISHED|21/05/30
08:13|09:03:24|Completed job 103|
| 104| hope18c1|POSTUPGRADE|  STOPPED|FINISHED|21/05/30
08:14|09:32:41|Completed job 104|
| 105| shft11g1|POSTUPGRADE|EXECUTING|FINISHED|21/05/30 08:16|10:07:35|
+----+---------+-----------+---------+--------+--------------+--------+
Total jobs 3
upg> Job 105 completed
------------------ Final Summary ------------------
Number of databases         [3]
Jobs finished               [3]
Jobs failed                 [0]
Jobs pending                [0]
---- Drop GRP at your convenience once you consider it is no longer
needed ----
Drop GRP from hope18c1:
drop restore point AUTOUPGRADE_9212_HOPE18C1183000
Drop GRP from global121:
drop restore point AUTOUPGRADE_9212_GLOBAL121121020
```

```
Drop GRP from shft11g1:
drop restore point AUTOUPGRADE_9212_SHFT11G1112040
```

Please check the summary report at the following links:

```
/u01/software/upgrade/MULTI-VERSION-DBs-UPGRADE/cfgtoollogs/upgrade/
auto/status/status.html
/u01/software/upgrade/MULTI-VERSION-DBs-UPGRADE/cfgtoollogs/upgrade/
auto/status/status.log
[oracle@virtual-19crac1 MULTI-VERSION-DBs-UPGRADE]$
```

Post upgrade checks

Once the upgrade of all the three databases is completed, we can perform a few post-upgrade checks to ensure that the upgrade was successful.

Oratab entries

Check the oratab to see if AutoUpgrade has updated the database homes for the three databases, as follows:

```
[oracle@virtual-19crac1 ~]$ cat /etc/oratab | grep 19c
+ASM1:/u01/app/19c/grid:N
shft11g1:/u01/app/oracle/product/19c/db_1:N      # line added by Agent
hope18c1:/u01/app/oracle/product/19c/db_1:N
global121:/u01/app/oracle/product/19c/db_1:N     # line added by Agent
[oracle@virtual-19crac1 ~]$
```

Check the cluster configuration of the database to see if AutoUpgrade has upgraded the information. The following is the **srvctl config** information for the database, **shft11g** (this was our **11g** database):

```
[oracle@virtual-19crac1 ~]$ srvctl config database -d shft11g
Database unique name: shft11g
Database name: shft11g
Oracle home: /u01/app/oracle/product/19c/db_1
Oracle user: oracle
Spfile: +DATAC1/shft11g/spfileshft11g.ora
Password file:
Domain:
Start options: open
Stop options: immediate
Database role: PRIMARY
Management policy: AUTOMATIC
Server pools:
Disk Groups: DATAC1
Mount point paths:
Services:
```

```
Type: RAC
Start concurrency:
Stop concurrency:
OSDBA group: oinstall
OSOPER group: oinstall
Database instances: shft11g1,shft11g2
Configured nodes: virtual-19crac1,virtual-19crac2
CSS critical: no
CPU count: 0
Memory target: 0
Maximum memory: 0
Default network number for database services:
Database is administrator managed
```

The following is the **srvctl config** information for the database, **global12** (this was our **12c** database):

```
[oracle@virtual-19crac1 ~]$ . oraenv
ORACLE_SID = [global121] ?
The Oracle base remains unchanged with value /u01/app/oracle

[oracle@virtual-19crac1 ~]$ srvctl config database -d global12
Database unique name: global12
Database name: global12
Oracle home: /u01/app/oracle/product/19c/db_1
Oracle user: oracle
Spfile: +DATAC1/GLOBAL12/PARAMETERFILE/spfileglobal12.ora
Password file: +DATAC1/GLOBAL12/PASSWORD/pwdglobal12.1386.1073857535
Domain:
Start options: open
Stop options: immediate
Database role: PRIMARY
Management policy: AUTOMATIC
Server pools:
Disk Groups: DATAC1
Mount point paths:
Services:
Type: RAC
Start concurrency:
Stop concurrency:
OSDBA group: oinstall
OSOPER group: oinstall
Database instances: global121,global122
Configured nodes: virtual-19crac1,virtual-19crac2
CSS critical: no
CPU count: 0
```

```
Memory target: 0
Maximum memory: 0
Default network number for database services:
Database is administrator managed
[oracle@virtual-19crac1 ~]$
```

The following is the **srvctl config** for the database, **hope18c** (this was our **18c** database):

```
oracle@virtual-19crac1 ~]$ srvctl config database -d hope18c
Database unique name: hope18c
Database name: hope18c
Oracle home: /u01/app/oracle/product/19c/db_1
Oracle user: oracle
Spfile: +DATAC1/HOPE18C/PARAMETERFILE/spfilehope18c.ora
Password file: +DATAC1/HOPE18C/PASSWORD/pwdhope18c.1839.1073855351
Domain:
Start options: open
Stop options: immediate
Database role: PRIMARY
Management policy: AUTOMATIC
Server pools:
Disk Groups: DATAC1
Mount point paths:
Services:
Type: RAC
Start concurrency:
Stop concurrency:
OSDBA group: oinstall
OSOPER group: oinstall
Database instances: hope18c1,hope18c2
Configured nodes: virtual-19crac1,virtual-19crac2
CSS critical: no
CPU count: 0
Memory target: 0
Maximum memory: 0
Default network number for database services:
Database is administrator managed
[oracle@virtual-19crac1 ~]$
```

Check the GRP information for each database

Check if the AutoUpgrade utility has created the guaranteed restore point in the primary database, as follows:

- The following is the GRP in the database, **shft11g**:

```
SQL> set lines 200
SQL> col name for a40
SQL> col GUARANTEE_FLASHBACK_DATABASE for a20
SQL> col TIME for a60
SQL> set lines 190
SQL> select NAME,GUARANTEE_FLASHBACK_DATABASE,TIME from
V$restore_point;

NAME                               GUARANTEE_F  TIME
--------------------------------   -----------  ----------------------
AUTOUPGRADE_9212_SHFT11G1112040    YES          30-MAY-21
                                                09.32.42.000000000 AM
```

- The following is the GRP in the database, **global12c**:

SQL> set lines 200

```
SQL> col name for a40
SQL> col GUARANTEE_FLASHBACK_DATABASE for a20
SQL> col TIME for a60
SQL> set lines 190
SQL> select NAME,GUARANTEE_FLASHBACK_DATABASE,TIME from
V$restore_point

NAME                               GUARANTEE_F  TIME
--------------------------------   -----------  ----------------------
AUTOUPGRADE_9212_HOPE18C1183000    YES          30-MAY-21
                                                09.03.25.000000000 AM
```

- The following is the GRP in the database, **hope18c**:

```
SQL> set lines 200
SQL> col name for a40
SQL> col GUARANTEE_FLASHBACK_DATABASE for a20
SQL> col TIME for a60
SQL> set lines 190
SQL> select NAME,GUARANTEE_FLASHBACK_DATABASE,TIME from
V$restore_point

NAME                               GUARANTEE_F  TIME
--------------------------------   -----------  ----------------------
AUTOUPGRADE_9212_HOPE18C1183000    YES          30-MAY-21
                                                09.03.25.000000000 AM
```

Run the **utlrp** script and check the registry components and the timezone version in all the three databases. The following information is from **shft11g** (this was our **11g**) database. Run the **utlrp** script to compile the invalid objects, as follows:

```
SQL>@$ORACLE_HOME/rdbms/admin/utlrp;
```

We can also check the **timezone** version to see if it has been upgraded to 32 (**19c** version), as follows:

```
SQL> SELECT version FROM v$timezone_file;

   VERSION
----------
        32

SQL> @/home/oracle/rac_database_info.sql


DATABASE_HOST           DB_NAME           OPEN_MODE            STARTUP_TIME
--------------------    ---------------   -------------------  ------------
virtual-19crac1         shft11g1          READ WRITE           30-MAY-21
virtual-19crac2         shft11g2          READ WRITE           30-MAY-21

SQL> col COMP_ID for a10
SQL> col COMP_NAME for a40
SQL> col VERSION for a15
SQL> set lines 180
SQL> set pages 999
SQL> select COMP_ID,COMP_NAME,VERSION,STATUS from dba_registry;


COMP_ID     COMP_NAME                                 VERSION     STATUS
----------  ----------------------------------------  ----------  ------
CATALOG     Oracle Database Catalog Views             19.0.0.0.0  VALID
CATPROC     Oracle Database Packages and Types        19.0.0.0.0  VALID
JAVAVM      JServer JAVA Virtual Machine              19.0.0.0.0  VALID
XML         Oracle XDK                                19.0.0.0.0  VALID
CATJAVA     Oracle Database Java Packages             19.0.0.0.0  VALID
APS         OLAP Analytic Workspace                   19.0.0.0.0  VALID
RAC         Oracle Real Application Clusters          19.0.0.0.0  VALID
OWM         Oracle Workspace Manager                  19.0.0.0.0  VALID
CONTEXT     Oracle Text                               19.0.0.0.0  VALID
XDB         Oracle XML Database                       19.0.0.0.0  VALID
ORDIM       Oracle Multimedia                         19.0.0.0.0  VALID
SDO         Spatial                                   19.0.0.0.0  VALID
XOQ         Oracle OLAP API                           19.0.0.0.0  VALID
APEX        Oracle Application Express                3.2.1.00.12 VALID

14 rows selected.
```

The following information is from **global12** (this was our **12c**) database. Run the **utlrp** script to compile the invalid objects, as follows:

```
SQL>@$ORACLE_HOME/rdbms/admin/utlrp;

SQL> @/home/oracle/rac_database_info.sql
DATABASE_HOST           DB_NAME           OPEN_MODE            STARTUP_TIME
--------------------    ---------------   -------------------  ------------
```

```
virtual-19crac1      global121      READ WRITE         30-MAY-21
virtual-19crac2      global122      READ WRITE         30-MAY-21

SQL> col COMP_ID for a10
SQL> col COMP_NAME for a40
SQL> col VERSION for a15
SQL> set lines 180
SQL> set pages 999
SQL> select COMP_ID,COMP_NAME,VERSION,STATUS from dba_registry;

COMP_ID     COMP_NAME                                VERSION         STATUS
----------  ---------------------------------------  --------------  ------
CATALOG     Oracle Database Catalog Views            19.0.0.0.0      VALID
CATPROC     Oracle Database Packages and Types       19.0.0.0.0      VALID
JAVAVM      JServer JAVA Virtual Machine              19.0.0.0.0      VALID
XML         Oracle XDK                               19.0.0.0.0      VALID
CATJAVA     Oracle Database Java Packages            19.0.0.0.0      VALID
APS         OLAP Analytic Workspace                  19.0.0.0.0      VALID
RAC         Oracle Real Application Clusters         19.0.0.0.0      VALID
XDB         Oracle XML Database                      19.0.0.0.0      VALID
OWM         Oracle Workspace Manager                 19.0.0.0.0      VALID
CONTEXT     Oracle Text                              19.0.0.0.0      VALID
ORDIM       Oracle Multimedia                        19.0.0.0.0      VALID
SDO         Spatial                                  19.0.0.0.0      VALID
XOQ         Oracle OLAP API                          19.0.0.0.0      VALID
OLS         Oracle Label Security                    19.0.0.0.0      VALID
APEX        Oracle Application Express               4.2.5.00.08     VALID
DV          Oracle Database Vault                    19.0.0.0.0      VALID

16 rows selected.
```

Check the **timezone** version to see if it has been upgraded to 32 (**19c** version), as follows:

```
SQL> SELECT version FROM v$timezone_file;

   VERSION
----------
        32
```

The following information is from **hope18c** (this was our **18c**) database. Run the **utlrp** script to compile the invalid objects, as follows:

```
SQL>@$ORACLE_HOME/rdbms/admin/utlrp;

SQL> @/home/oracle/rac_database_info.sql
DATABASE_HOST        DB_NAME           OPEN_MODE          STARTUP_TIME
```

```
----------------------    -----------------    -----------------    ------------
virtual-19crac1           hope18c1             READ WRITE           30-MAY-21
virtual-19crac2           hope18c2             READ WRITE           30-MAY-21

SQL> col COMP_NAME for a40
SQL> col VERSION for a15
SQL> set lines 180
SQL> set pages 999
SQL> select COMP_ID,COMP_NAME,VERSION,STATUS from dba_registry;

COMP_ID        COMP_NAME                                      VERSION          STATUS
----------     ---------------------------------------------  ---------------  ---
CATALOG        Oracle Database Catalog Views                  19.0.0.0.0       VALID
CATPROC        Oracle Database Packages and Types             19.0.0.0.0       VALID
RAC            Oracle Real Application Clusters               19.0.0.0.0       VALID
JAVAVM         JServer JAVA Virtual Machine                   19.0.0.0.0       VALID
XML            Oracle XDK                                     19.0.0.0.0       VALID
CATJAVA        Oracle Database Java Packages                  19.0.0.0.0       VALID
APS            OLAP Analytic Workspace                        19.0.0.0.0       VALID
XDB            Oracle XML Database                            19.0.0.0.0       VALID
OWM            Oracle Workspace Manager                       19.0.0.0.0       VALID
CONTEXT        Oracle Text                                    19.0.0.0.0       VALID
ORDIM          Oracle Multimedia                              19.0.0.0.0       VALID
SDO            Spatial                                        19.0.0.0.0       VALID
XOQ            Oracle OLAP API                                19.0.0.0.0       VALID
OLS            Oracle Label Security                          19.0.0.0.0       VALID
DV             Oracle Database Vault                          19.0.0.0.0       VALID

15 rows selected.
```

Check the **timezone** version to see if it has been upgraded to 32 (**19c** version), as follows:

```
SQL> SELECT version FROM v$timezone_file;
   VERSION
----------
        32
```

As we can see, the upgrade went fine and all the components in all the three databases are valid and looking good. Pretty impressive right? Well, that's how powerful the **AutoUpgrade** tool is and how it was able to upgrade multiple databases which were running from the different database versions to **19c** using one configuration file and one single operation.

Multiple instances of the AutoUpgrade process

Another way to upgrade multiple databases is to use multiple configuration files and start multiple **AutoUpgrade** instances. In this method, we can create a separate configuration file for each database and each configuration file should have a different log directory defined. We can start multiple **AutoUpgrade** instances with different configuration files. In the following section, please see the configuration file and the **analyze** command that has been run at the same time.

We have to make sure that each configuration file has a different log directory, configuration file name, and database name (that's being upgraded).

The first configuration file is as follows:

```
[oracle@virtual-19crac1 disk11g]$ cat disk11g_config.cfg
upg1.log_dir=/u01/software/upgrade/disk11g
upg1.source_home=/u01/app/oracle/product/11.2.0.4/db_1
upg1.target_home=/u01/app/oracle/product/19c/db_1
upg1.sid=disk11g1
upg1.upgrade_node=virtual-19crac1
```

The first instance of AutoUpgrade is as follows:

```
[oracle@virtual-19crac1 pop18c]$ export ORACLE_HOME=/u01/app/oracle/
product/19c/db_1

[oracle@virtual-19crac1 pop18c]$ $ORACLE_HOME/jdk/bin/java -jar $ORACLE_
HOME/rdbms/admin/autoupgrade.jar -config pop18c_config.cfg -mode ANALYZE

AutoUpgrade tool launched with default options
Processing config file ...
+------------------------------+
| Starting AutoUpgrade execution |
+------------------------------+
1 databases will be analyzed
Type 'help' to list console commands
upg> lsj
------+---------+-------+--------------+--------+-----------------+
|Job#|DB_NAME| STAGE|OPERATION| STATUS|  START_TIME| UPDATED| MESSAGE|
--------+---------+-------+--------------+--------+-----------------+
| 100|pop18c1|PRECHECKS|PREPARING|RUNNING|21/07/11
15:58|15:58:05|Loading database information|
--+---------+---------+-------+--------------+--------+-------------+
|Job#|DB_NAME| STAGE|OPERATION| STATUS|   START_TIME| UPDATED|MESSAGE|
+----+-------+---------+---------+-------+---------------+------+----+
| 100|pop18c1|PRECHECKS|PREPARING|RUNNING|21/07/11
15:58|15:58:28|Remaining 69/85|
--+---------+---------+-------+--------------+--------+-------------+
Total jobs 1
upg> lsj
```

The second configuration file is as follows:

```
[oracle@virtual-19crac1 pop18c]$ cat pop18c_config.cfg
global.autoupg_log_dir=/u01/software/upgrade/pop18c
upg2.log_dir=/u01/software/upgrade/pop18c                    # Path of the
log directory for the upgrade job
upg2.source_home=/u01/app/oracle/product/18c
upg2.target_home=/u01/app/oracle/product/19c/db_1            # Path of
the target ORACLE_HOME
upg2.sid=pop18c1
upg2.upgrade_node=virtual-19crac1
```

The second instance of the **AutoUpgrade** command run from the same node as the first one but for a different database is as follows:

```
[oracle@virtual-19crac1 disk11g]$ $ORACLE_HOME/jdk/bin/java -jar
$ORACLE_HOME/rdbms/admin/autoupgrade.jar -config disk11g_config.cfg -mode
ANALYZE

AutoUpgrade tool launched with default options
Processing config file ...
+-------------------------------+
| Starting AutoUpgrade execution |
+-------------------------------+
1 databases will be analyzed
Type 'help' to list console commands
upg> lsj
+----+------+-------+---------+-------+--------------+--------+------+
|Job#| DB_NAME| STAGE|OPERATION| STATUS|   START_TIME|UPDATED|MESSAGE|
+----+------+-------+---------+-------+--------------+--------+------+
| 100|disk11g1|PRECHECKS|PREPARING|RUNNING|21/07/11 15:58|15:58:06|
+----+------+-------+---------+-------+--------------+--------+------+
Total jobs 1
upg> lsj
---+---------+---------+-------+--------------+--------+-------------+
|Job#| DB_NAME| STAGE|OPERATION| STATUS| START_TIME| UPDATED| MESSAGE|
--+---------+---------+-------+--------------+--------+-------------+
| 100|disk11g1|PRECHECKS|PREPARING|RUNNING|21/07/11
15:58|15:58:24|Remaining 33/88|
--+---------+---------+-------+--------------+--------+-------------+
Total jobs 1
upg>
```

We can invoke multiple **AutoUpgrade** to run in the **DEPLOY** mode as well.

Fallback method

Since the AutoUpgrade utility has created GRP, we can always Flashback the database to these restore points to downgrade the database back to their source versions.

Conclusion

In this chapter, we saw how to use **AutoUpgrade** to upgrade multiple databases with different Oracle versions to 19c using a single **AutoUpgrade** command. This will be very useful if we have hundreds of databases that we have to upgrade, or we can simply upgrade tens of databases in one shot, saving us a lot of time.

Multiple choice questions

1. **Can we specify multiple databases of the same version in one configuration file and upgrade all of them in one single operation using one AutoUpgrade command?**

   a. No, each database should have its own configuration file.

   b. Yes, we can upgrade multiple databases of the same version to 19c using one configuration file and in one operation.

2. **Is it possible to upgrade multiple databases with different versions to 19c in one single operation?**

   a. Yes, we can do this.

   b. No, it is not possible to upgrade multiple databases with different versions to 19c in one single operation.

Answers

1. **b**
2. **a**

Key terms

- Doc ID 2485457.1
- global.autoupg_log_dir
- dba_optstat_operations
- upg1, upg2, upg3

Index

Made in the USA
Middletown, DE
12 December 2021

55423476R00250